Ronald Moody

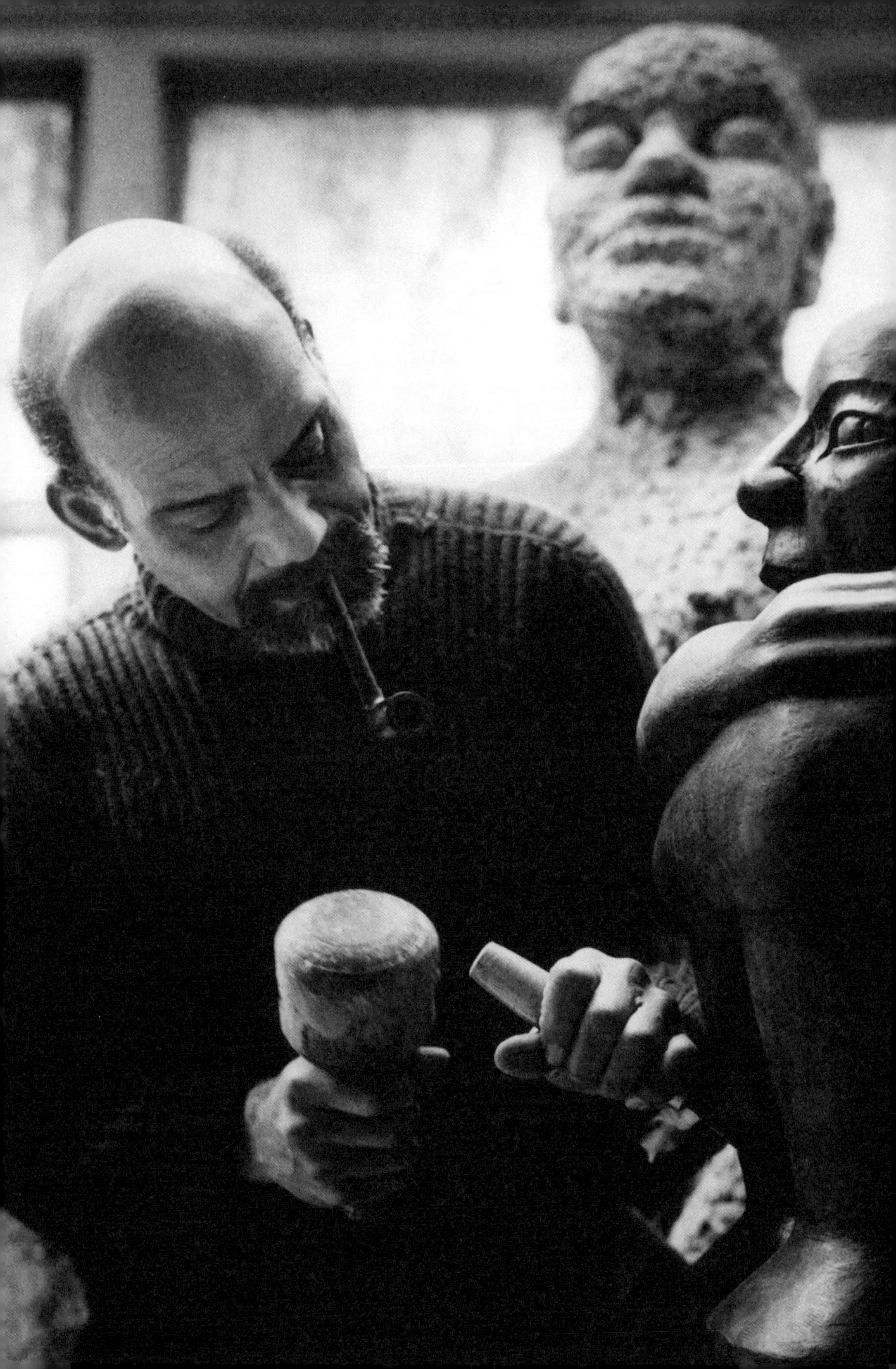

Ego Ahaiwe Sowinski

Ronald Moody
Sculpting Life

Edited by **Eleanor Clayton**
Foreword by **Paul Dash**

With contributions from **David A. Bailey, Errol Lloyd, Cynthia Moody** and **Val Wilmer**

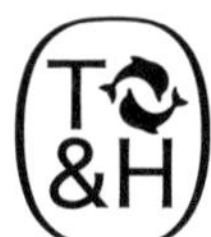

Dedicated to Cynthia Moody

Frontispiece: Ronald Moody with *The Onlooker* at Fleming Close Studios, Fulham, in 1963. Photograph by Val Wilmer

First published in the United Kingdom in 2024 by
Thames & Hudson Ltd, 181A High Holborn, London WC1V 7QZ

First published in the United States of America in 2024 by
Thames & Hudson Inc., 500 Fifth Avenue, New York, New York 10110

Published on the occasion of the exhibition 'Ronald Moody: Sculpting Life' at The Hepworth Wakefield, 22 June–3 November 2024

Edited by Ego Ahaiwe Sowinski and Eleanor Clayton
With assistance from Farah Dailami
Interior designed by Anna Perotti

British Library Cataloguing-in-Publication Data
A catalogue record for this book is available from the British Library

Library of Congress Control Number 2023946089

ISBN 978-0-500-02703-5

Printed and bound in Italy by Printer Trento SrL

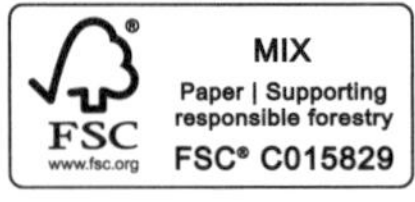

Contents

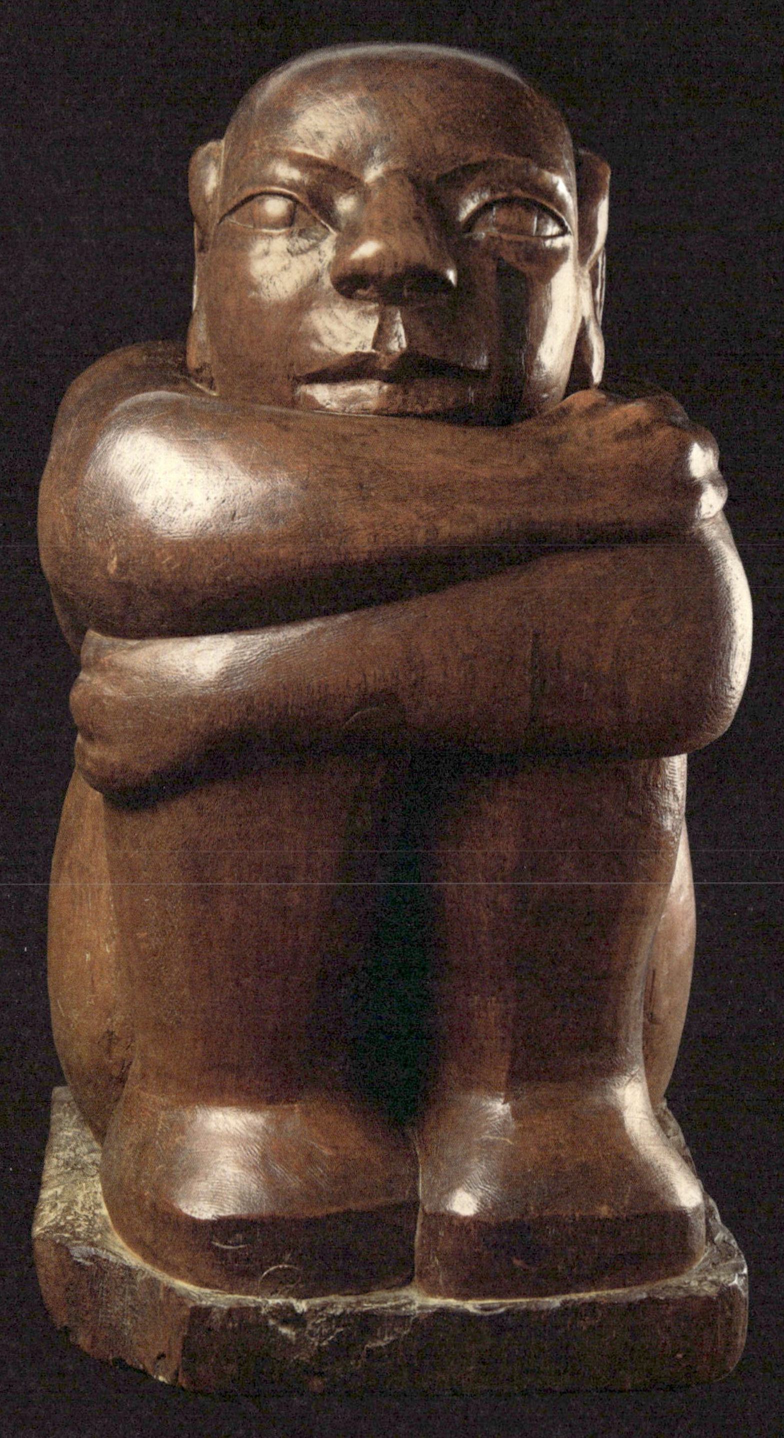

Ronald Moody, *The Onlooker*, 1958–62, teak, 62.2 × 34.3 × 39 cm (24 ½ × 13 ⅝ × 15 ⅜ in.)

FOREWORD

Paul Dash

I met Ronald Moody in London during a Caribbean Artists Movement (CAM) exhibition in the 1960s and was immediately struck by his sartorial elegance, dignified presence and penetrating gaze. Opposite me was a confident and well-educated man, clearly intent – in that brief engagement – on making an in-depth assessment of my abilities and presence. It was an overwhelming and almost uneasy experience. This first encounter was set against the backdrop of work by Caribbean artists including that of Moody himself. Yet further knowledge of Moody and his art was left to a later time through my acquaintance with his niece, Cynthia Moody. My friendship with Cynthia flourished in the 1990s until her death in 2013. Jean, my wife, and I regularly attended parties and functions at her home in Clifton, Bristol. Visits for such events were marked by the presence of Ronald's sculptures everywhere. Seeing his work in that context was uplifting. I particularly cherish the memory of a typically generous gesture after the sale of a sculpture, in which Cynthia symbolically bound my practice to her uncle's by the gift of £100, which was presented to me with the words, 'From Ronald's art to your art, Paul.'

Three carvings stood out in that apartment for their charismatic beauty and the quality of workmanship. The first was *Johanaan* (1936), which was permanently positioned at Cynthia's large bay window as if to greet each visitor. Indeed, she informed me of neighbours and passers-by calling at her apartment to share their delight at catching a glimpse of the piece as they went about their lives. It had become a feature of the street, if not the district. On gaining entry to her apartment, the similarly charismatic though smaller and less imposing *Onlooker* (1958–60) charmed the eye. Here was a work that, to my mind, drew comparison with Constantin Brancusi's *The Kiss* (1916), if only by the similarity of scale and the feeling of warmth that I think they both elicit.

Midonz (1937), thoughtfully positioned on a piece of antique furniture just inside the living room space, further enchanted Cynthia's guests. I couldn't resist the urge to stroke it each time I visited and would marvel at the way the markings of a great knot in the timber seem to explode in streaks from the carved lips, as if blowing a puckered kiss to the world. Then there was *Orchid Bird* (1968), a low-slung, fragile and tantalizingly mysterious piece in plaster, that occupied the corner of the bay alongside *Johanaan*.

Caribbean artists of Moody's generation such as Aubrey Williams (1926–1990), the young Frank Bowling (b. 1934), Althea McNish (1924–2020) and of course Ronald himself were active during the rise of Black Resistance campaigns in the 1960s, before the advent of the Black Art era of the 1980s. As such, they weren't members of a galvanizing artistic movement that partly honed modes of making work. Instead, each devised their own aesthetic around undergirding exposure to fine art practices culled from different Caribbean social and cultural experiences, formal art education, often in British art colleges, associations with people of like mind in the UK and of course their wider self-education.

In that regard, Althea McNish was influenced at least initially by her association with fellow Trinidadian artists. Later, on migration to the UK, she found visits to Kew Gardens an important resource for her making. Aubrey Williams, on the other hand, was often inspired

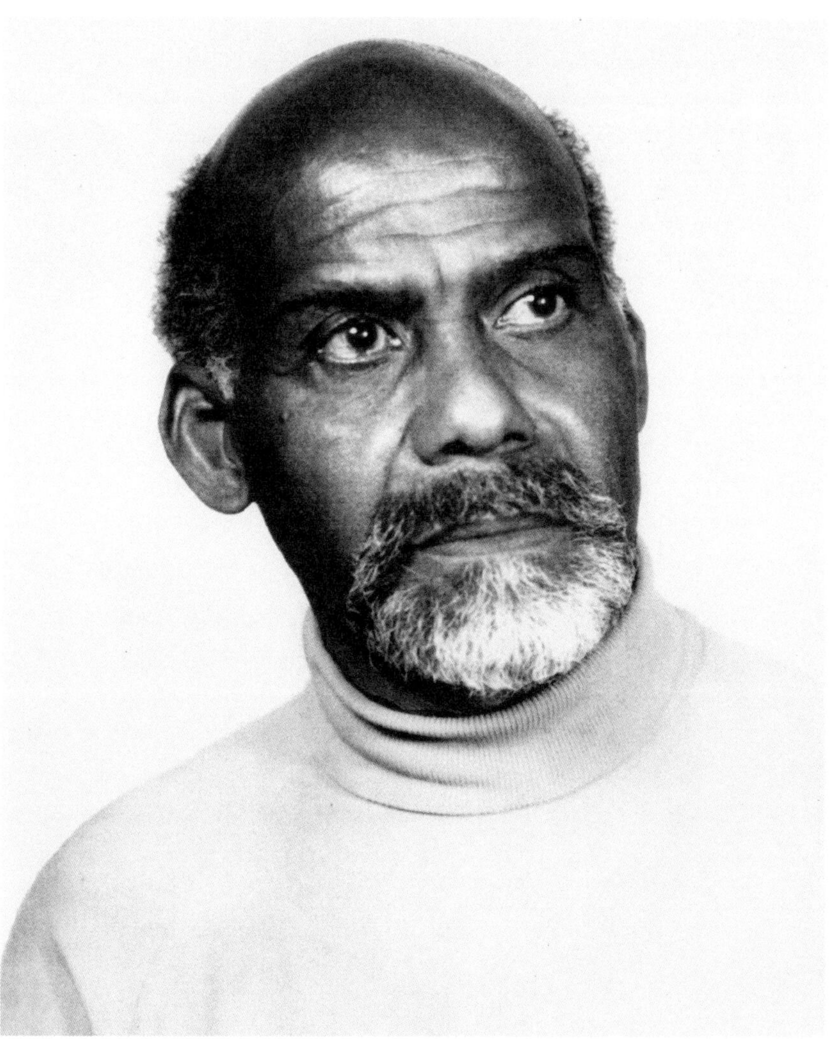

Portrait of Ronald Moody, 1966.
Photograph by David Sharkey

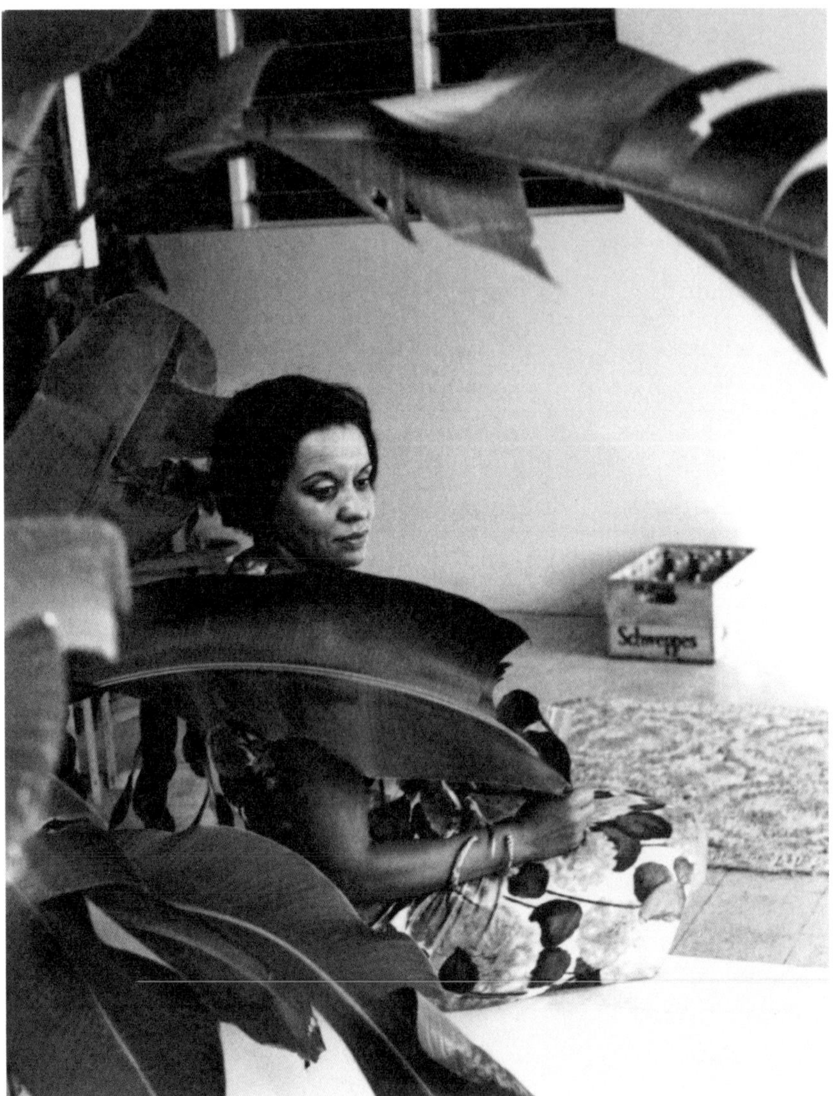

Portrait of Cynthia Moody at home, n.d.

by the art and mythology of pre-Colombian cultures and the music of Dmitri Shostakovich (1906–1975). Ronald Moody, however, looked to the Orient, India and ancient Egyptian art for inspiration. As he said in the BBC Radio broadcast 'Anything to Declare' in 1950, 'I have a very Eastern point of view in art – there is something in the calm inscrutability of Eastern art which appeals to me.'

In Ronald's work, there is a contemplative dimension that reminds one of thinkers and religious practitioners who draw on the spirit world for clarification of ideas and guidance. Indeed, his art has a depth and gravitas that conjures thoughts of Eastern mysticism, while *Johanaan* and *Midonz*, to my mind, exude a calming peace – nay, an inscrutability – that engenders thoughts of spiritual devotion.

I cannot end this tribute to Ronald without reflecting, if only briefly, on other aspects of his life that contribute enormously to our appreciation of him and indeed other people of Caribbean origin who chose to make Britain their home in those pre- and post-war years. Apart from being a standout sculptor and a trained dentist, Ronald Moody was a painter, scholar, poet, essayist and BBC Radio broadcaster. In other words, he was a well-educated and highly qualified man whose presence and activity in Britain debunks notions of twentieth-century Caribbean migrants to the UK as a social and educative homogeneity – a lowly, ill-educated labour force, fit generally for menial work.

As such, *Ronald Moody: Sculpting Life* should not only shine a light on Ronald's extraordinary contributions to British life, but serve as a reminder of the potentialities of many others who may not have been given the opportunity to speak their Truth.

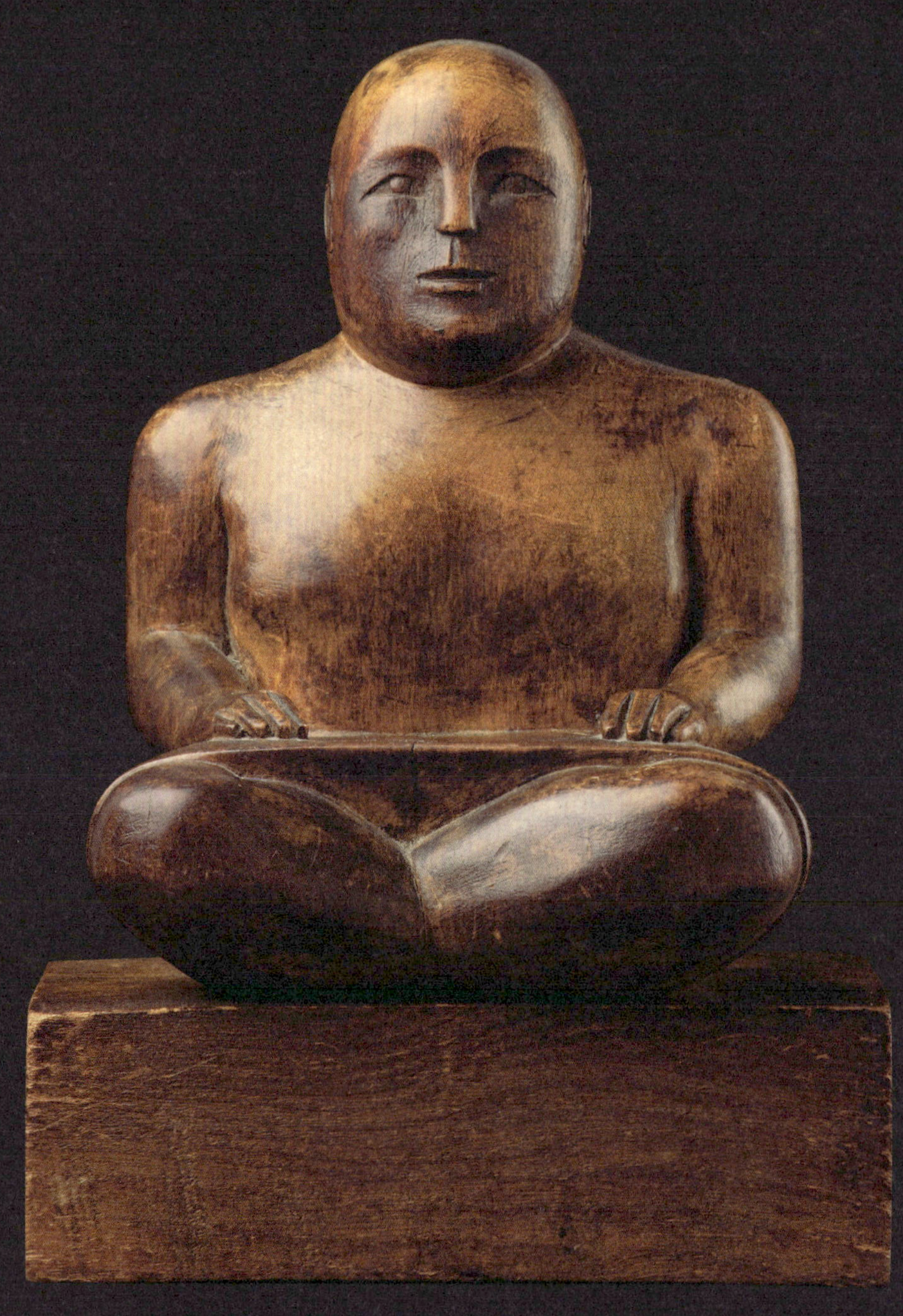

Ronald Moody, *Seated Sarong Figure*, 1938,
beech (tinted), 27 × 18 × 14 cm (10 ¾ × 7 ⅛ × 5 ⅝ in.)

INTRODUCTION

Ronald Moody: His Universe Then and Now

Eleanor Clayton

In 1989, artist Rasheed Araeen (b. 1935) curated the seminal exhibition 'The Other Story: Afro-Asian Artists in Post-War Britain' at the Hayward Gallery, London. The opening text for the show declared,

> The end of World War II represents a historical watershed: with decolonisation, the wall which separated the peoples of the metropolis and the colonies began to come down. The subsequent movement of people from the impoverished part of the world to the metropolis changed the demographic and cultural map of Europe.
>
> The arrival here of artists from Asia, Africa or the Caribbean in the post-war period was part of this movement. But, in many cases, it was also the result of the individual artist's desire to realise their artistic ambitions internationally. Inspired by the modern art movements of the twentieth century and wishing to participate in their development, it was necessary for these artists to be in the metropolis.
>
> 'The Other Story' is the story of their engagement with Modernism, their problematic relationship with its philosophical assumption, and their exclusion from official histories on the basis that the place of Afro-Asian

> artists was somewhere else, outside the evolutionary paradigm of Modernism. It is the story of their struggles and their achievements, their successes and their failures. It is not a story of so-called 'black art' or 'ethnic minority arts'. The Other Story is a recognition of Afro-Asian contributions to post-war British Art.[1]

Moody's presence in this exhibition was perhaps somewhat unexpected, given that he had arrived in the United Kingdom from Jamaica in 1923, decades prior to the period outlined in this statement by Araeen. Nonetheless, he was represented by a large group of works in the exhibition, from major early carvings from the 1930s through to later, experimental work such as *Man... His Universe*, made in 1969 in glass resin, showcasing his considerable sculptural talents and undeniable importance to the story of Modernism in Britain.

1923 was also the year that the Wakefield Permanent Art Collection was established in the north of England, aiming to nurture in the public an understanding of contemporary art and how it might relate to modern life. As the birthplace of Barbara Hepworth (1903–1975) and Henry Moore (1898–1986), two famous British sculptors, who, like Moody, became known for their carvings in the 1930s, the city of Wakefield was home to one of the first public collections to acquire and exhibit their work. In the early decades of the collection, it acquired works by many of Moody's peers whom he exhibited alongside and lived among – artists who were part of the canon of British Modernism such as Jacob Epstein (1880–1959), Elisabeth Frink (1930–1993), Eileen Agar (1899–1991), Barbara Hepworth and Henry Moore. Wakefield's collection, now cared for by The Hepworth Wakefield, has continued to grow and tell the story of British Modernism, but until recently, Moody's work was conspicuously absent, affirming Araeen's damning statement of exclusion.

In 2021, Moody's work entered Wakefield's collection nearly a century after its foundation, through the donation of three significant sculptures by the Ronald Moody Trust: *Seated Sarong Figure* (1938), *Harpy* (1960) and *Savacou* (1964). This began a dialogue with the Trust that would lead to this publication and the retrospective exhibition 'Ronald Moody: Sculpting Life', held at The Hepworth Wakefield (22 June–3 November 2024). Through these conversations, it became clear that although important examples of Moody's work were held in public collections across the country, often donated by the Ronald Moody Trust or given by his niece Cynthia Moody (1924–2013), who had initiated the Trust's subsequent activities, there had been no major retrospective exhibition of his work. The most significant show was an in-focus room within Tate Liverpool's 'International Modern Art' collection displays in 2004, and there have been no monographic

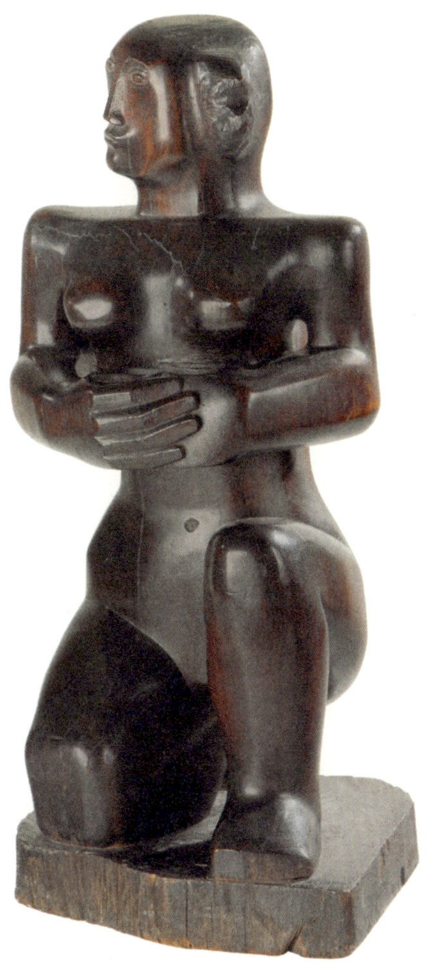

Barbara Hepworth, *Kneeling Figure*, 1932, rosewood, 67.5 × 28.8 × 32 cm (26 5/8 × 11 3/8 × 12 5/8 in.)

publications produced to make his work accessible to a broader public. Although many public institutions exhibit the sculptures they own by Moody within collection displays, the lack of a comprehensive survey limits knowledge of the breadth of Moody's career, the range of his creative outputs and his far-reaching influence.

There is no doubt that Moody's long and celebrated career has been made more visible through the tireless work of Cynthia Moody. She inherited Moody's personal archive on his death in 1984 and began to compile a catalogue raisonné, but it was never realised and is still held in note form by the Ronald Moody Trust. Cynthia presented Moody's archive to the Tate in 1995 and although part of it is still uncatalogued, it became part of the source material studied by Ego Ahaiwe Sowinski for her PhD with the Tate and Chelsea College, University of the Arts London, which was partially funded by the Ronald Moody Trust. Ahaiwe Sowinski's research, in her words, aims 'to contextualise Moody as a complex, networked figure and...examine the interconnectedness of key artistic relationships.... to move beyond the dominant, accepted narrative that grounds Moody as forgotten, invisible and marginalised, and instead to recast Moody through a lens that explores his art practice, contributions, impact and value to the landscape of British and diasporic art.' Ahaiwe Sowinski is a trained archivist, and her projects more broadly explore archives as a way to tell the stories of Black histories and experiences in Britain and throughout the diaspora. Her work in co-curating the exhibition at The Hepworth Wakefield and compiling this publication draws on her years of research into Moody's personal papers. It also acknowledges the depth of archival work done by Cynthia Moody in her lifetime through quotations sourced from the unrealised Moody catalogue raisonné. Alongside two published essays written by Cynthia Moody, Ahaiwe Sowinski has brought together a range of contributors in this publication, who go some way to articulate the interconnectedness of Moody within British art and the diaspora.

The book opens with a series of chapters by Ahaiwe Sowinski offering a biographical outline of Ronald Moody's early life and career, and includes some of his previously unpublished poetry and excerpts from his BBC broadcasts of the 1940s and '50s. Cynthia Moody's essay on the lost carving *Midonz* (1937) follows this biography. Her account of the search for and retrieval of the artwork also indicates the ease with which art, history and legacy are lost without an active and determined champion. In Chapter 5, Ahaiwe Sowinski focuses on Ronald Moody's portraiture to reveal his extensive networks and evolution of material processes. Experimentation with materials is a theme expanded on in Chapter 6 in a short text by Cynthia (prepared for her unrealised catalogue raisonné) on Moody's important post-war sculptural group, *Concrete Family* (1958–62). The later chapters examine Moody's post-war work and include contributions from Val Wilmer (b. 1941), who interviewed and photographed Ronald Moody in his studio for *Flamingo* magazine in 1964, and artist David A. Bailey (b. 1961), as well a focus on Moody's major public sculpture *Savacou* (1964), and his involvement with both the Caribbean Artists Movement (1966–72) and the Second Festival of Arts & Culture 1977 (FESTAC '77). The book concludes with a personal tribute to Moody by fellow artist and CAM member Errol Lloyd (b. 1943).

CHAPTER I

The Early Years, from Kingston to London

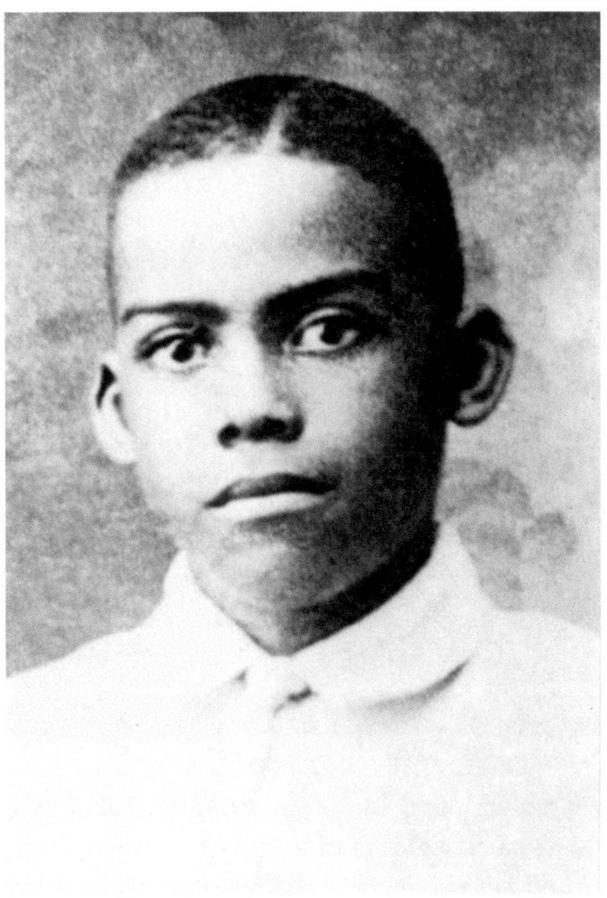

Pioneering Modernist sculptor and philosopher Ronald Clive Moody was born at the turn of the twentieth century in Jamaica, on 12 August 1900. Son of Christina Emmeline Ellis[1] and pharmicist Charles Ernest Moody,[2] he was brought up among medical and legal professionals that included his brother Locksley, a Supreme Court judge, his sister Elise, a well-respected nurse, and Charles, a dentist.[3] His older brother Harold arrived in Britain in 1904 to study medicine at King's College London, graduating at the top of his class in 1910. Unable to find work as a doctor because of the colour of his skin, Harold set up his own practice at his home in Peckham, London. A civil rights activist and a leading advocate for abolishing the colour bar in

Childhood photograph of Ronald Moody, n.d.

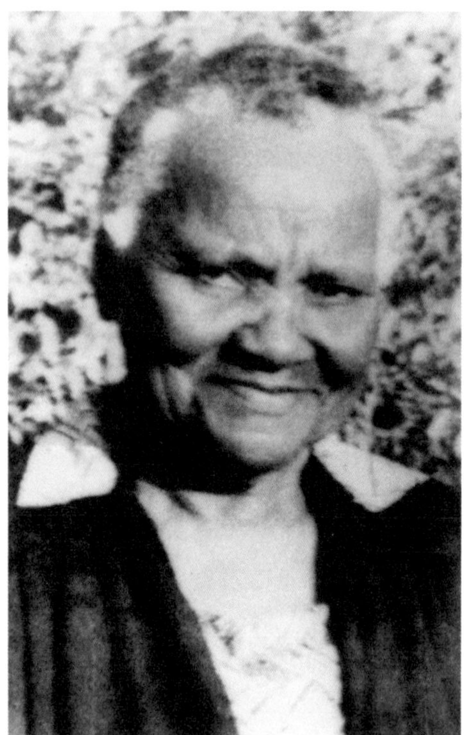

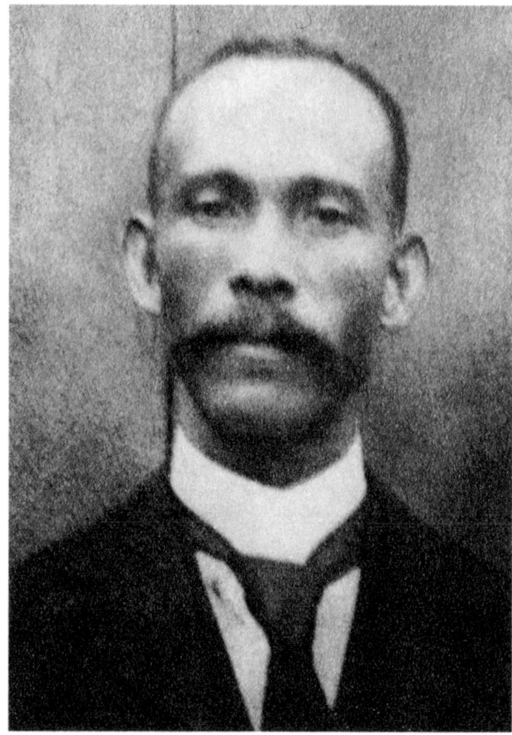

Britain, in 1931 he founded the League of Coloured Peoples (LCP) in London. As president he worked tirelessly, lobbying politicians, the civil service and trade unions and seeking to build and strengthen race relations and challenge injustices.[4] Prominent members of the LCP included Jamaican activist Una Marson; Trinidadian historian C. L. R. James; Jomo Kenyatta, the first prime minister of Kenya; noted Pan-Africanist George Padmore; and renowned American singer, actor and civil rights campaigner Paul Robeson, whom Ronald Moody would eventually depict in a 1968 portrait.[5] In 1946, Ronald Moody created a portrait of his brother Harold, a year before his death.[6]

Moody grew up near Knutsford, just outside of Kingston, and from his bedroom window he was able to see the glorious Blue Mountains of Jamaica, which ran 'the length of the island like the backbone of some prehistoric animal'.[7] Moody received a sound classical secondary education at Calabar College, a prominent all-boys school. He

Christina Emmeline Moody, *née* Ellis, 'Mater', Ronald Moody's mother, n.d.

Charles Ernest Moody, 'Pater', Ronald Moody's father, n.d.

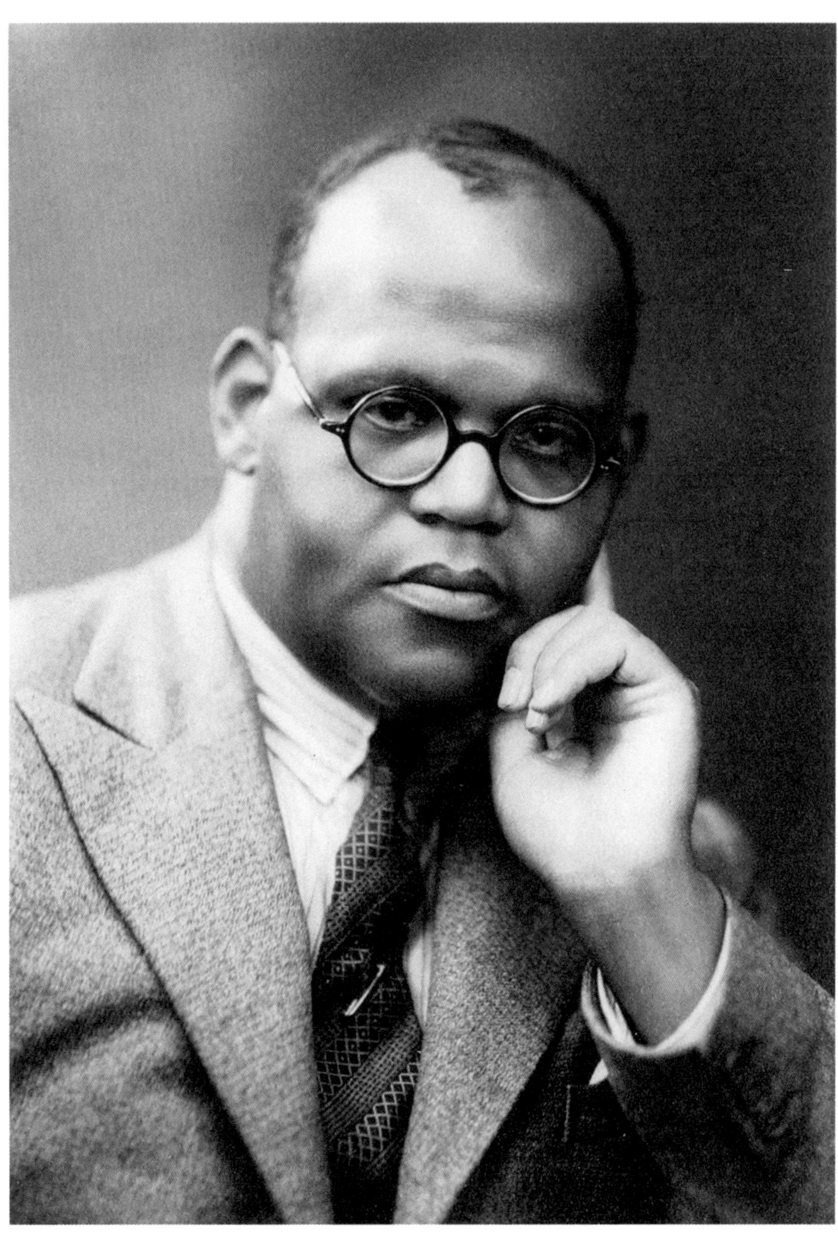

Harold Arundel Moody, physician, lay preacher and founder of the League of Coloured Peoples, Ronald Moody's eldest brother, n.d.

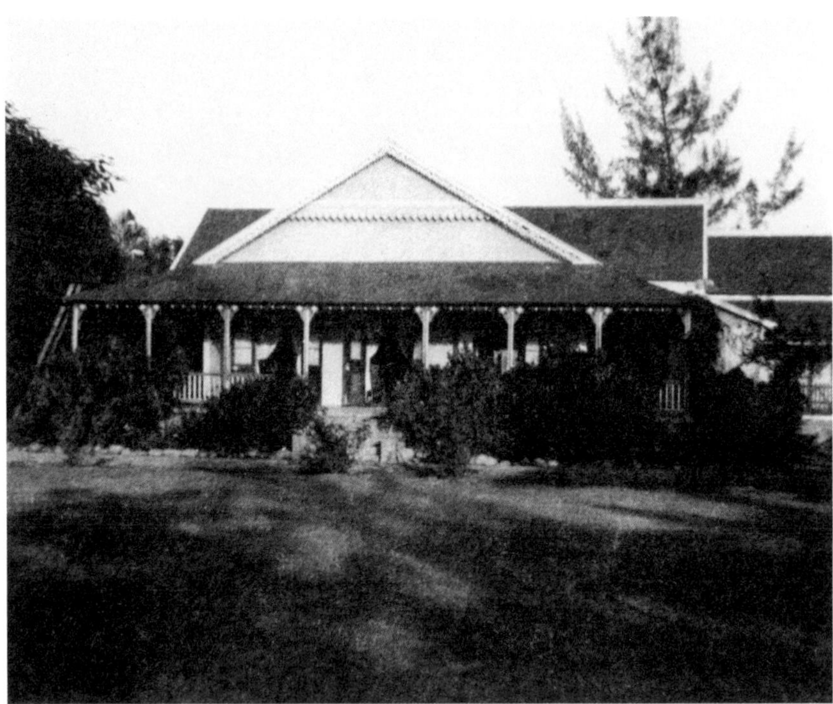

was keen on English, Music, Art and Latin, while also participating in inter-school football matches, winning a medal from the Jamaica Football Association in 1921–22. He grew up spending time surfing on the Palisadoes, camping and hiking. Moody recalls his experience of leaving Jamaica and relocating to the Britain in 1923:

> I left home on a beautiful, sunny day, on a ship called R. M. S. P. Oriana, a name I shall never, never forget. You know, I was prepared to love the sea, as I had spent much of my time at home in open boats, but it was fated to remain unrequited. We got into the wake of a hurricane. I never knew until then how much a ship could be pitched about in every direction at the same time, or so it seemed, with no regard for the comfort of the passengers. Most of the journey I was sea-sick, and at times death would have been welcomed as a happy release.

'Brightside', the Moody family home, Half-Way-Tree, St Andrews, near Knutsford, Kingston, Jamaica, n.d.

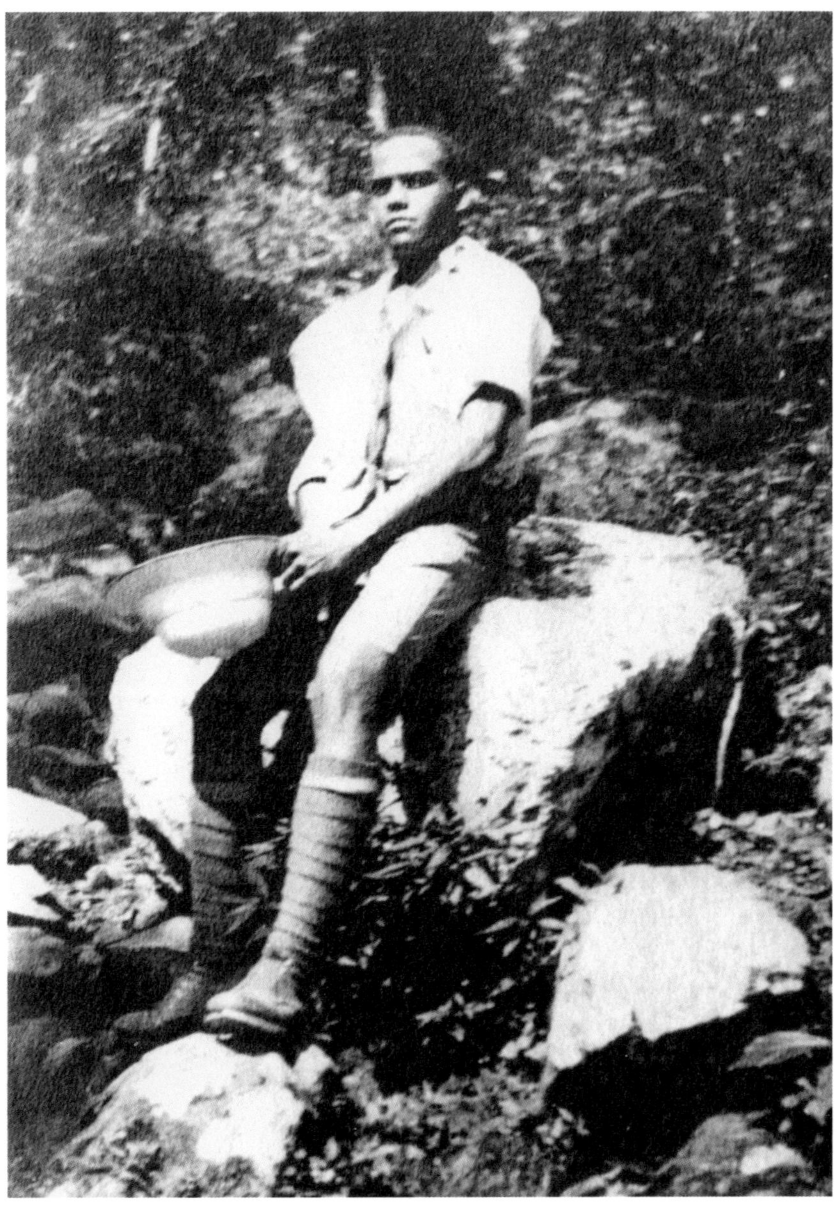

Ronald Moody camping in the Blue Mountains, Jamaica

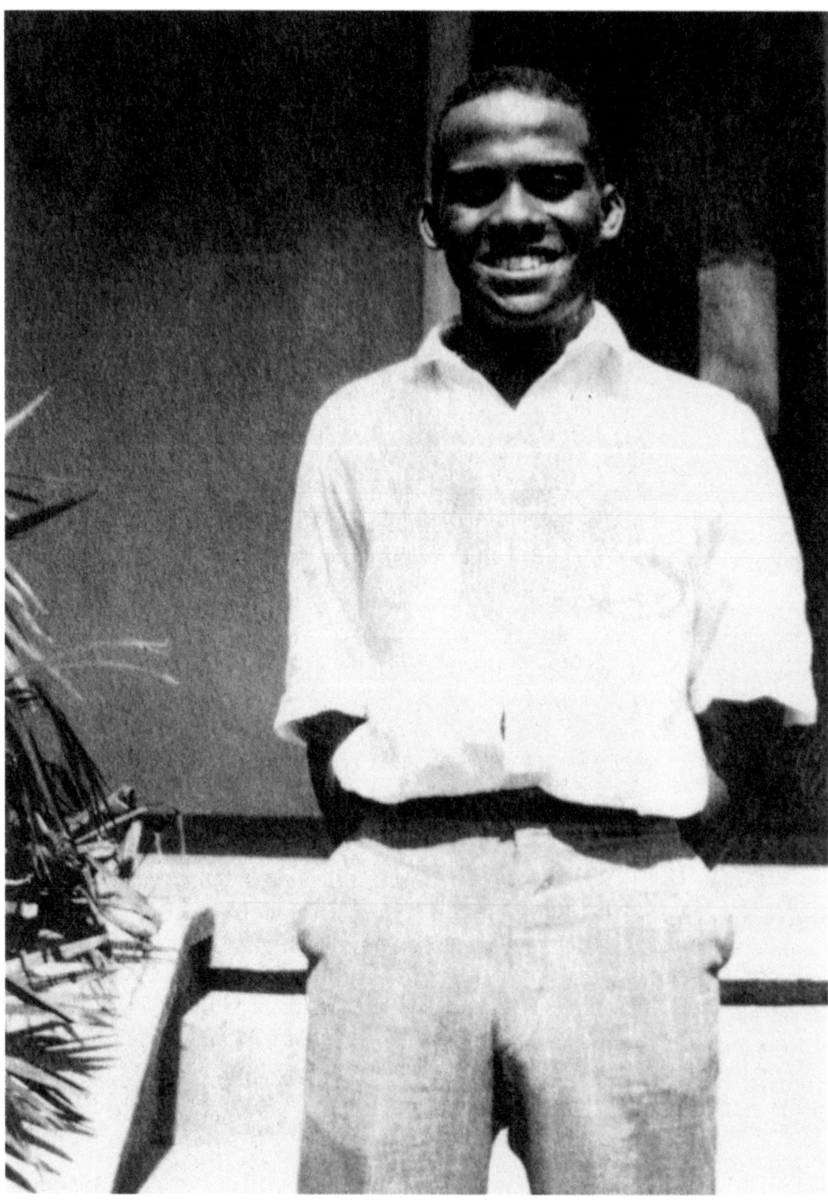

Ronald Moody outside the Moody family home 'Brightside', Jamaica, *c.* 1920

> Eventually, more or less whole, I arrived at Avonmouth on a typically dull English day, only I did not know then, it was typical. The movement of the sea was still in my legs. To say that I was depressed would have been a gross understatement. Very little of the journey to London remains in my memory. I was probably too sorry for myself to notice anything. At Paddington, I was met by my brother, whisked off to 'digs' and then taken to have a meal at his home. The noise of the traffic was deafening and the streets, all looking exactly the same, with houses joined to each other for miles on end, gave me a feeling of claustrophobia.[8]

When the time came to choose a career, Moody toyed with the idea of pursuing an art degree, much to the dismay of his family.[9] Jamaica, up to the turn of the twentieth century, had been considered first and foremost in economic terms by its British colonial rulers, who retained the island for its profitability. As a result, the pursuit of the fine arts up until the 1930s was tolerated as a hobby and scorned as a profession; it was considered primarily a leisure-time pursuit enjoyed by a privileged few.[10] Moody chose a career in dentistry and began studies at the Royal Dental Hospital at King's College London in 1923. It was one of the professions his family considered appropriate to their standing and, in part, it enabled him to think things out for himself, away from the claustrophobia of home-grown pressures, while conforming to his family's high expectations.[11] Moody would also have been among the very few, and very likely one of the first, Jamaicans to choose the difficult path of becoming an artist. He soon got used to the hustle and bustle of London, living among other students studying Medicine, Law, Engineering and Economics, and recalls:

> During my college days, I never met a West Indian or African who thought any of the Arts worth studying. The cause of this may have been partly economic. The other professions would quickly gain a living;

> but I also think this attitude was one of the results of Colonial status. In Africa, the African tended to look down on his rich sculptural past as the fruits of superstition. In the West Indies, the cultural heritage had been destroyed during successive occupations, and the slave trade and indentured labour brought new races to live on the islands. When I really began to get interested in sculpture, I found this attitude of indifference made me feel a little isolated. Though everyone, including myself, worked hard and many passed with distinctions, I knew it was useless to suggest a visit to a museum or contemporary exhibition.[12]

As Moody continued his medical studies, he became increasingly interested in all forms of art, and philosophy – from Plato to the metaphysics of China and India – had a long-lasting impact on his life. Moody spent more and more time visiting galleries and museums, and on one afternoon in 1928 he made a fateful trip to the British Museum, where he strayed into the Egyptian Room and, transfixed by what he saw and felt, resolved to become a sculptor.[13] The British Museum had been a significant social and educational space for many people of African and Asian heritage in London in the early twentieth century, particularly the reading rooms, which were used by activists that include Marcus Garvey (1887–1940) and Claude McKay (1890–1948).[14] In his 1950 BBC radio broadcast on Egyptian art for the overseas service, 'Calling the West Indies', he reflects on being particularly 'struck by the perfect craftmanship shown in a wooden comb' from the Coptic period, on view at the British Museum.[15] With no formal art training, Moody instead sought the guidance of friends, many of whom were sculptors, and by dint of trial and error, and perseverance, gained confidence through experiments in plaster. Moody qualified as a dentist in 1930 and initially worked in his brother Harold's practice. During this time, he met Helene Coppel-Cowan (1902–1978), who less than a decade later would become his lifetime partner and a sitter for many of his portraits.

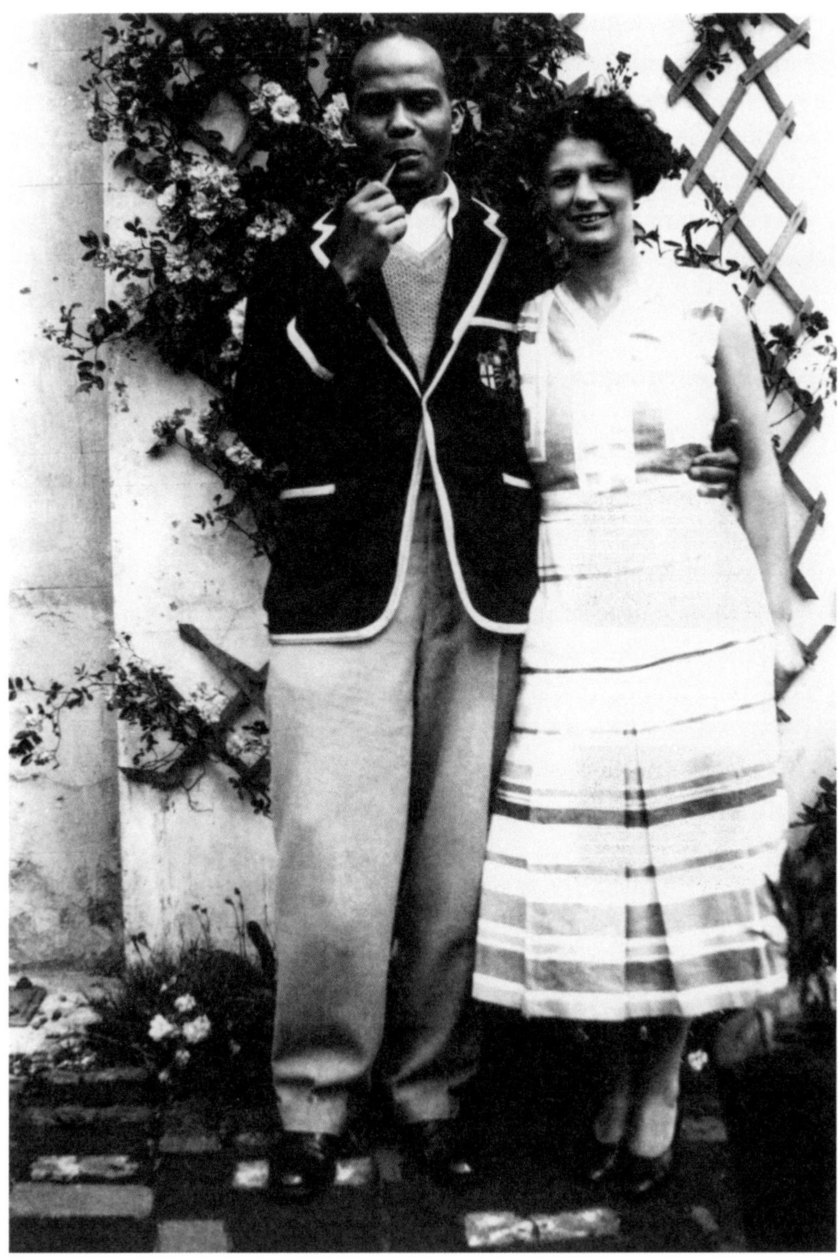

Ronald and Helene 'Lulu' Coppel-Cowan, *c.* 1928

Between 1928 and 1929, Moody wrote a series of parodic poems relating to his and fellow students' experiences during dentistry training, which were published in the *Royal Dental Hospital Magazine*. In addition to showing his wit, and occasional frustrations with his field of study, they also reveal both his broad knowledge of literature and a keen mind with an ability to adapt and expand on existing form that would become evident in his artistic career.

On Learning to Give Gas, with Apologies to Milton

When I consider how my time is spent
From two to five in this square room and high,
Learning under the wary Hilliard's eye
The whims on N_2O. My mind much bent
With help of feet and hands once more to thwart
Asphyxiation and the agile prop
From jumping down or out the mouth; and mop
My dripping brows in sore distress. Though thought
I to see the signs of stertor and thus
Coo one, two, three and deftly face-piece move
Without so much as eyelash agitate.
I must agree sans any further fuss
That Milton's saying was quite right, by Jove!
'They also serve who only stand and wait'.

November 1928

On Reading Mr Packham's Article in the Last Magazine, with Apologies to Wordsworth

There was a time when cricket, bridge and 'Punch',
Lyons and morning coffee
With usual 'Bunch'

Was all that life did mean to me;
With one addition, that was 'draughts' at lunch.
Alas, 'tis not so now I do deplore, – Try whatso'er I may,
By night or day
The things which once I did I now can do no more.

A student now I am,
Henceforth I drop all sham,
My days are all too short,
Hither and thither do I dash
Without even a thought
To sausages and mash.
All 'scales' and 'polishes' I do,
E'en as I swab, some other job
Appears for me – oh, 'DAY', why are your hours so few!

With classes, lectures, dresserships enow
At 'Charing Cross' or here,
With exams...always near
And 'Collier' my constant friend at eve.
Why should I now still fret and grieve
Or wrinkle my smooth brow?
Yet am I thrown into a state of gloom
When I in retrospective mood review
My eighteen months of work and all I knew
As 'dresser' in the 'Conservation Room'.
The swelling that I saw
'Circum' tooth
I swabbed with iodine to soothe.
Fool, unlearned and raw!
I should have stopped; on memory draw;
Compare likeness
To phagocytic battle in frogs web; else why G. S.?

January 1929

Confessions of a Dresser in the Conservation Room, with the Usual Apologies

I come from out of my room at nine,
And for a train I sally,
Just saunter in ’bout ten o’clock,
And round my chair I dally.

Of course I should be there at nine,
But what’s a fleeting hour?
They should be glad I came at all
Instead of looking sour.
Still Jackson scowls and H. S. swears,
But should I start to worry,
With other dressers on the job,
I ask you, should I hurry?
Then deftly drawers I pull out,
And make a show and bustle;
Put in a zinc oxide or two
To show how I can hustle!

From day to day I work away
In mouths of all description,
Thank Heaven, I’ll keep sane after all,
This day ends my affliction.

May 1929

Advice to a Student Beginning His First Tooth, with Apologies to Hood

Just chisel it gently
Bur it with care,
Excavate warily
Exposure's near.

Arsenic's not a nice thing
Stringy and red,
And such great work placing
Where pulp has bled.

So out with zinc oxide
Mix it with clove,
Stick it right inside,
And pray to Jove.

May 1929[16]

CHAPTER 2

An Artistic Pioneer: The 1930s and the Interwar Period in Europe and the United States

> I began by doing little figures in plasticine and gradually becoming more audacious, I tried modelling in clay. Then, I finally got a piece of a tree trunk, and set about carving a man's head for the first time.[1]
>
> *Ronald Moody*

Between 1935 and 1941, Moody exhibited sculptures in London, Paris, Amsterdam and the United States, producing a body of some forty known sculptures in bronze and wood. This period in Moody's development as an artist saw him find his voice and evolve a style of carving that would eventually become his distinctive way of working. His ability to combine a sense of movement and stillness in a single figure, alongside his talent for reading woodgrain and employing it to great expressive effect, created works that are at once abstract and modern but also redolent with what curator Guy Brett called 'symbolic or allegorical overtones'.[2]

Following his revelatory moment in the British Museum in 1928, Moody began to sculpt in earnest, using leftover plaster of Paris from his dental work. Perhaps inevitably, he found that as his interest in sculpture grew, his interest in dentistry decreased. In 1934, Moody relocated his dental practice to 6 Cavendish Place, London, moving into a garden flat close to Regents Park. He converted the greenhouse into an art studio and designed his own furniture, commissioning Alperton Woodworks, the furniture manufacturing firm owned by Helene Coppel-Cowan and her sister, to make it. The firm would go on to supply him with the wood from which some of his most significant sculptures were carved. An aspiring painter, Helene Coppel-Cowan came from a wealthy Jewish family. Moody soon became part of her extensive artistic circle, and many of them becoming his own lifelong friends. Among these were Wyn Henderson, who managed the Guggenheim Jeune gallery, writer Antonia White (1899–1980), diplomat Eric Earnshaw-Smith (1893–1972), entrepreneur Elsie Cohen (1895–1972), Brazilian film director Alberto Cavalcanti (1897–1982) and artist Leon Underwood (1890–1975), who would become one of Moody's most valued mentors.

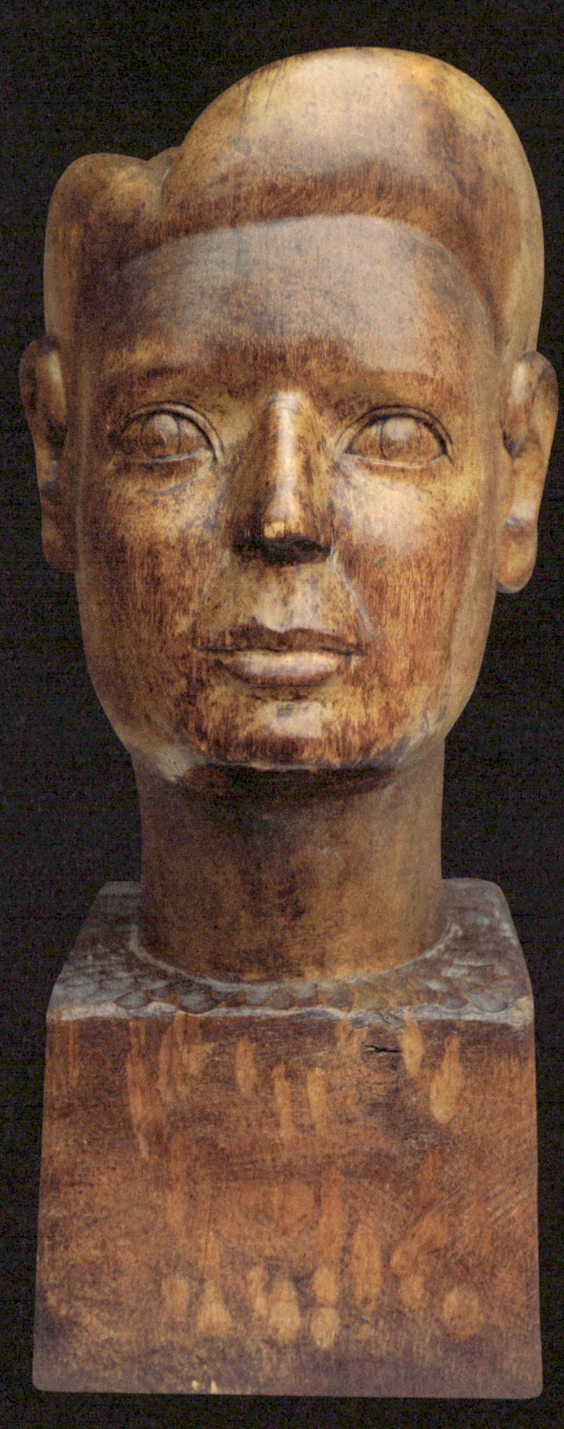

Ronald Moody, *Helene 2*, 1938, oak,
52 × 20 × 24 cm (20 ½ × 7 ⅞ × 9 ½ in.)

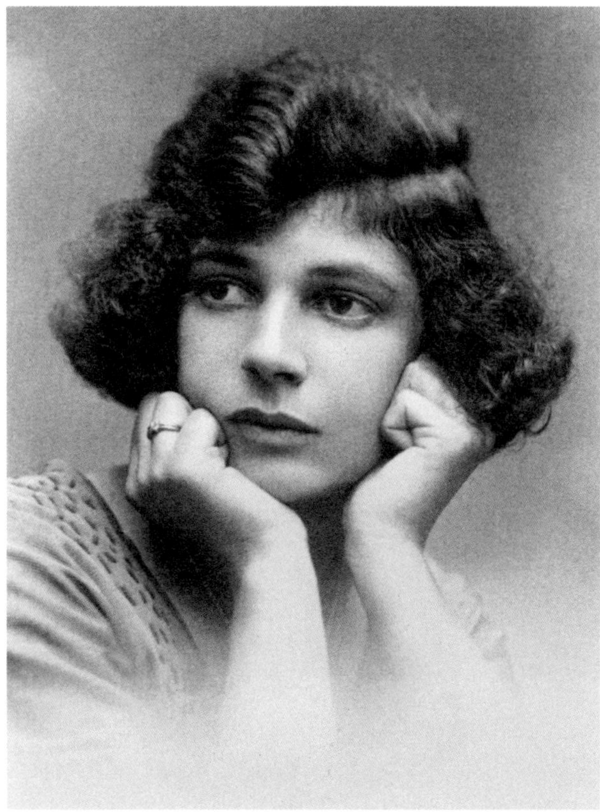

In 1934, with some trepidation, Moody embarked on his first work in wood, *Wohin* (1935), which he completed the following year. Standing 46 centimetres (18 in.) tall and carved from oak, the sculpture was inspired by the Franz Schubert song 'Wohin?', and its intention was to personify mankind's questioning as to its spiritual destiny.[3] The completion of the sculpture left Moody filled with wonder. He had made a tremendous leap forward, and the artwork astounded his friends. 1935 was a significant year for Moody for other reasons too, as his work was shown publicly for the first time in the exhibition 'Negro Art' at the Adams Gallery in Pall Mall Place, London. The exhibition was partly sponsored by the League of Coloured Peoples (LCP).[4] Other exhibitors included Jacob Epstein (1880–1959), Eileen Agar (1899–1991), Hilda Spencer (1889–1950), John Banting (1902–1972) and Kalifala

Helene Coppel-Cowan, n.d.

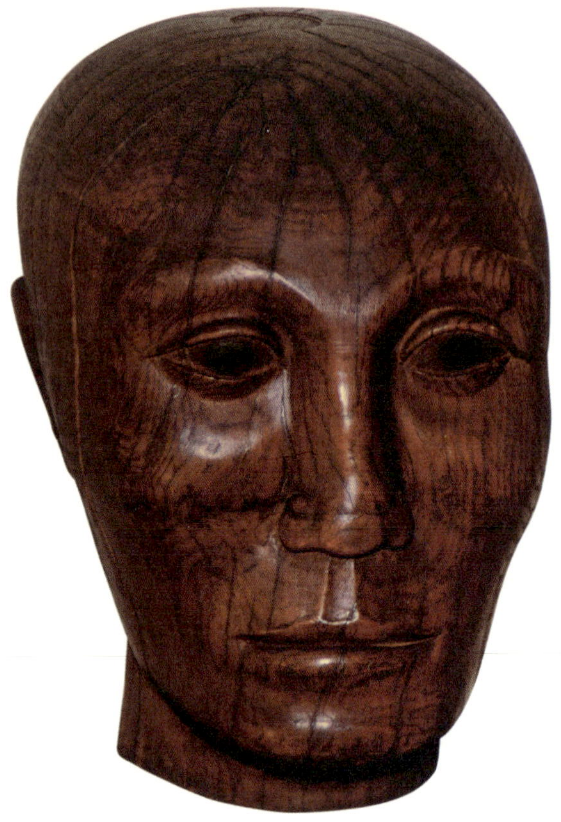

Sidibé (1900–1930). 'Negro Art' showcased Modern art made in Britain alongside sculpture from West Africa, including bronze plaques from *c.* 1600, collected during the Punitive Expedition of 1897. The so-called 'punitive expedition' marked a stark turning point in the history of the Benin Kingdom (modern-day Nigeria). The palace in Benin City was burned and looted in February 1897, and the oba (king) was exiled. To break the power of the monarchy, the British confiscated all of the royal treasures, giving some to individual officers but taking most to auction in London to pay for the cost of the expedition. The looted objects eventually made their way into museum and private collections around the world. The objects remain contested today, with some Nigerian scholars and museum professionals, and the royal court of Benin, advocating for their return.[5] The exhibition took place in conjunction

Ronald Moody, *Wohin*, 1935, oak, 46 cm (18 1/8 in.) high

with the publication *Arts of West Africa* by Oxford University Press at the suggestion of the Education Committee at the Colonial Office.[6]

In a review of the opening cocktail reception in the LCP's official quarterly journal *The Keys*, it was noted that included among the press, poets, musicians and critics were the artists Henry Moore (1898–1986) and Frank Dobson (1940–2019).[7] Both Moody's and Moore's Modernism was informed by the ancient, and inspired by visits to the British Museum in the 1920s and the sculptures of ancient Egypt, Africa and Mexico that they saw there.[8] Moody, like Moore, and alongside other artists such as Edna Manley (1900–1987), Barbara Hepworth (1903–1975) and John Skeaping (1901–1980), was part of a younger generation of Modernists in 1930s Britain who helped to change the perception and status of carving in wood. This period saw such artists adopt wood as a sculptural material, which distinguished them from the older generation of Modernists such as Epstein,

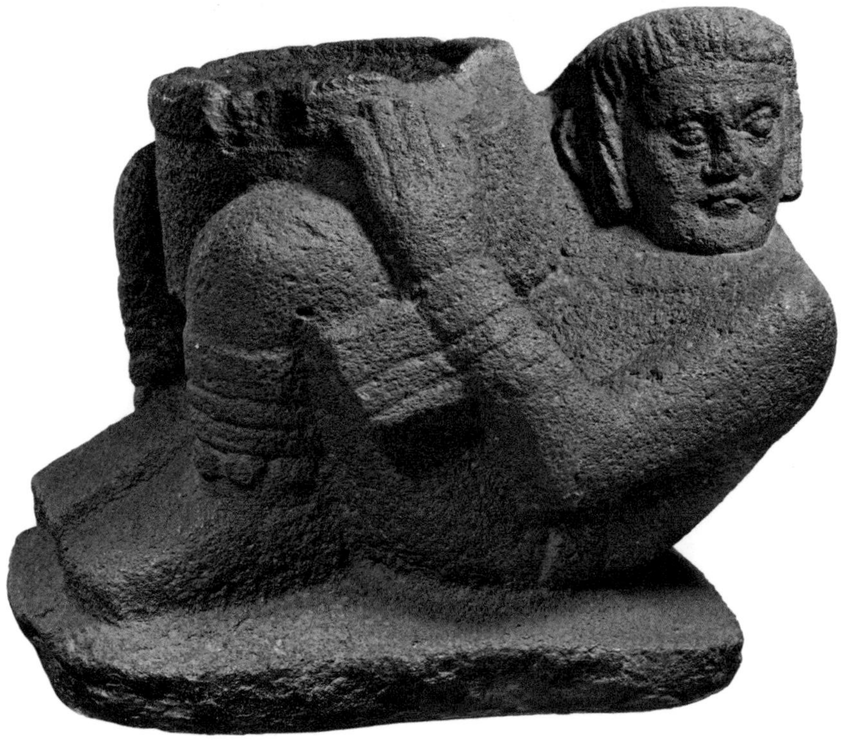

Seated human figure (supposed to have served as an incense burner), Mexico, Aztec, basalt, 37 × 42 × 33 cm (14 5/8 × 16 5/8 × 13 in.)

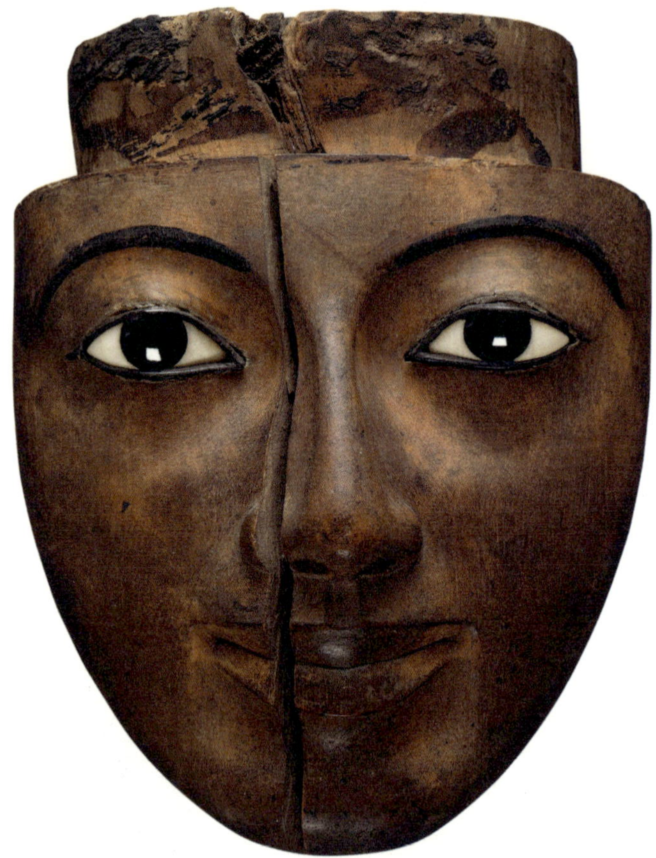

who predominately worked in stone and bronze. This moment saw a significant shift from wood being considered a utilitarian material, only suited to making architectural embellishments and small-scale functional or decorative objects, to it being employed to create the highest forms of art.[9] Moody's work was noticed by Marie Seton, a British actress and critic and the biographer of Paul Robeson who would become a lifelong friend of Moody, and soon after the exhibition she purchased *Wohin*.

This heralded a period of international recognition for Moody's burgeoning practice. Alberto Cavalcanti was so impressed and intrigued by Moody's art that he invited him to Paris for a solo show. In May 1937, Moody exhibited fifteen works at Galerie Billiet-Vorms, including

Coffin, 18th Dynasty, Egypt, *c.* 1400 BC, wood, obsidian, ivory and bronze, 18 × 14 cm (7 1/8 × 5 5/8 in.)

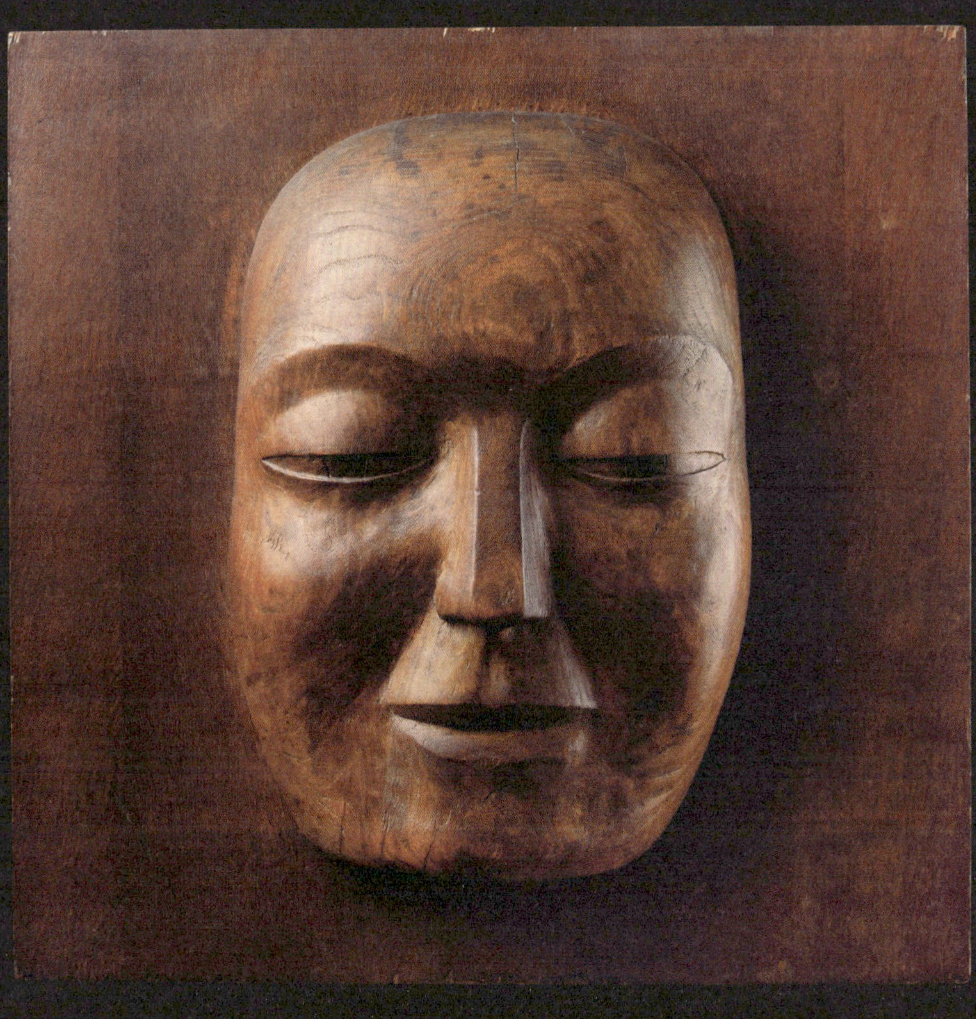

Ronald Moody, *L'Homme*, 1937–38,
oak, 48 × 35 × 14 cm (19 × 13⅞ × 5⅝ in.)

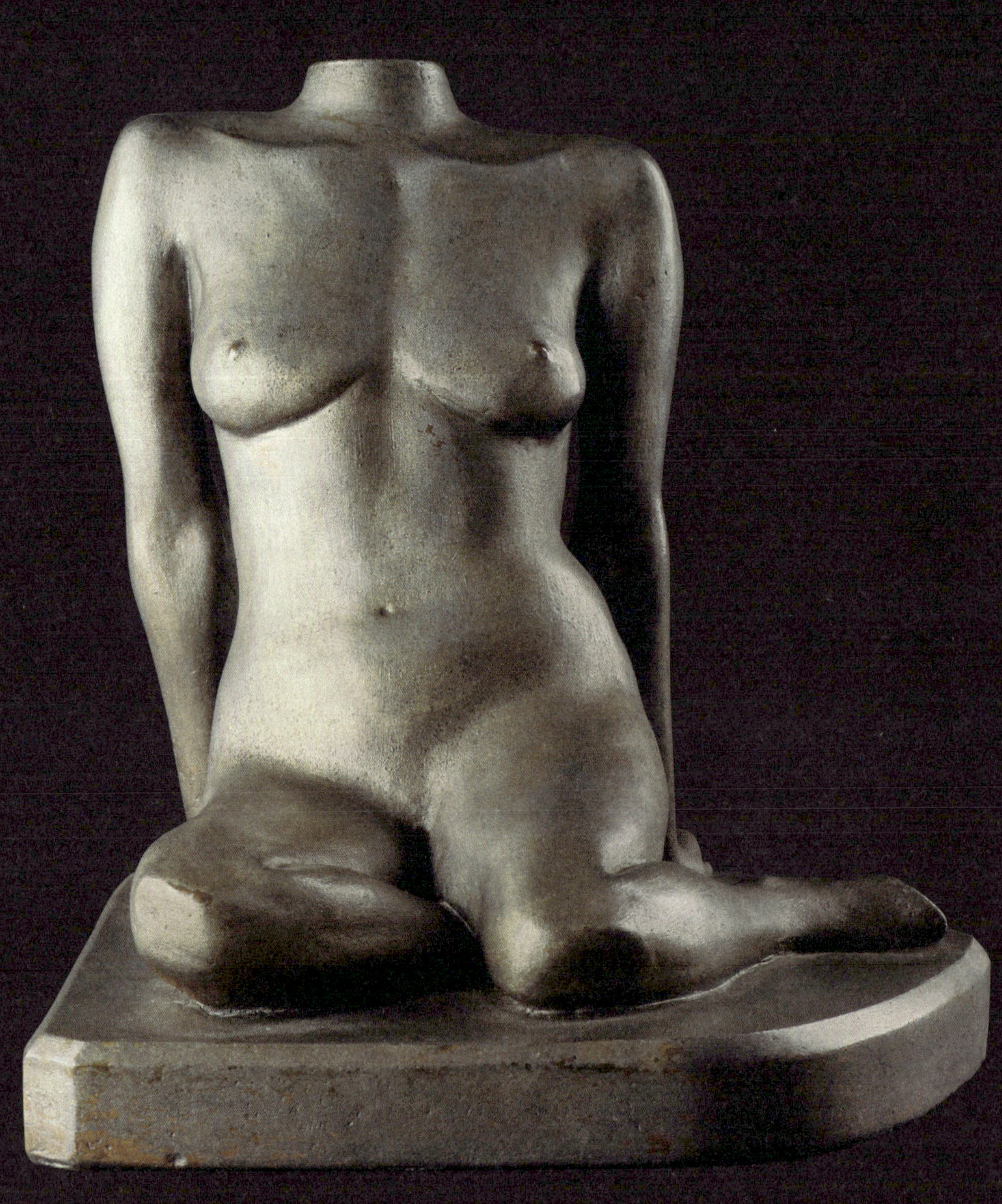

Ronald Moody, *Naissante*, 1937, bronze with a silver patina, 30 × 28 × 30 cm (11 7/8 × 11 1/8 × 11 7/8 in.)

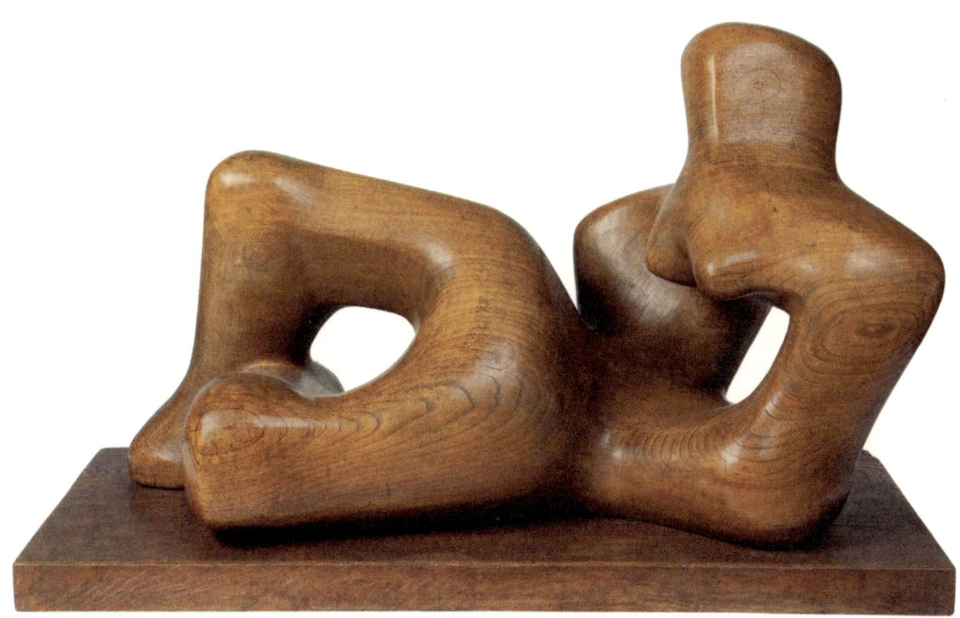

Johanaan (1936),[10] *Midonz*,[11] *Naissante*,[12] *Self-Portrait 2*, *Self-Portrait 3*, *Lilith* (all 1937)[13] and *L'Homme* (1937–38),[14] attracting a positive reception. Moody states:

> With the amazing faith and optimism of a young artist, I launched out and went to Paris in the summer of 1937 to give an exhibition...I exhibited altogether fifteen pieces, of which nine were carvings, two bronzes and four portraits. The French on the whole preferred my carvings to my portraits at this exhibition, at least, the critics, I should say. This was exactly the opposite of [*sic*] the London critics.

Johanaan was Moody's most significant sculpture at that point, a monumental carving in elm, the trunk of which he had been given by Helene Coppel-Cowan. It was displayed at Galerie Billiet-Vorms as *Johanaan, L'Évangélis*te (St John the Evangelist), giving the figure a spiritual aspect. A very well-received show in Amsterdam followed at the Kunstzaal van Lier, owned by Carek van Lier, a friend of Marie

Henry Moore, *Reclining Figure*, 1936, elm, 64 × 115 × 525 cm (25 1/4 × 45 3/8 × 206 3/4 in.)

Seton's, in January 1938.[15] *Johanaan* caught the attention of the press there: one review particularly noted 'the mighty *Johanaan* out of which leaps heroism as though it were tangible'.[16]

Between his travels in Europe organising his exhibitions, Moody carved *L'Homme*, a mask made from and mounted on a square oak plaque. He also returned to his work *Lilith*, created in 1935 and exhibited that same year in the London Group exhibition at the Burlington Galleries, and reworked it, making modifications to the hair and the drapery, which were filed down to refine and streamline the black, stained oak form into a column-like form.[17] The sculpture became very sleek, inspired by his elm *Female Torso 2* (1937). Moody's work began to flourish, and over the next four years he completed eight more carvings and produced several bronze portraits.

Moody fell in love with Paris and decided to live there, despite concerns expressed by his friends Marie Seton and Antonia White, who had grave misgivings about the impending war. The warm reception and positive reviews in Europe resulted in Moody settling with Helene Coppel-Cowan in 1938 in La Petite Maison Jaune at 134 rue de la Tombe Issoire, Montparnasse. He had the support of Pierre Vorms, the gallerist who had established Galerie Billiet-Vorms alongside international art critic Joseph Billiet, with a commitment to creating an incubator to support artists.[18] Moody and Coppel-Cowan were married on the 22 July 1938 at the British Consulate,[19] with Seton and Vorms as their witnesses.[20] In June that year, Moody exhibited his newest work, *Tacet* (1938), with *Midonz* at the XVième Salon des Tuileries. *Tacet* and *Midonz* are each other's counterparts. The features of the two works are similar, as are their dimensions and their shared colours and textures, suggesting that they were carved from the same piece of elm. In both cases, it is cut vertically against the grain, highlighting the contours of the features in a distinct yet subtle manner.[21] Another group exhibition took place at Galerie l'Équipe a month later, in July; and in October of that same year, Moody exhibited once again at Galerie Billiet-Vorms in the group show 'Tropiques', which included Henri Matisse (1869–1954). Here, he exhibited *Tacet* and

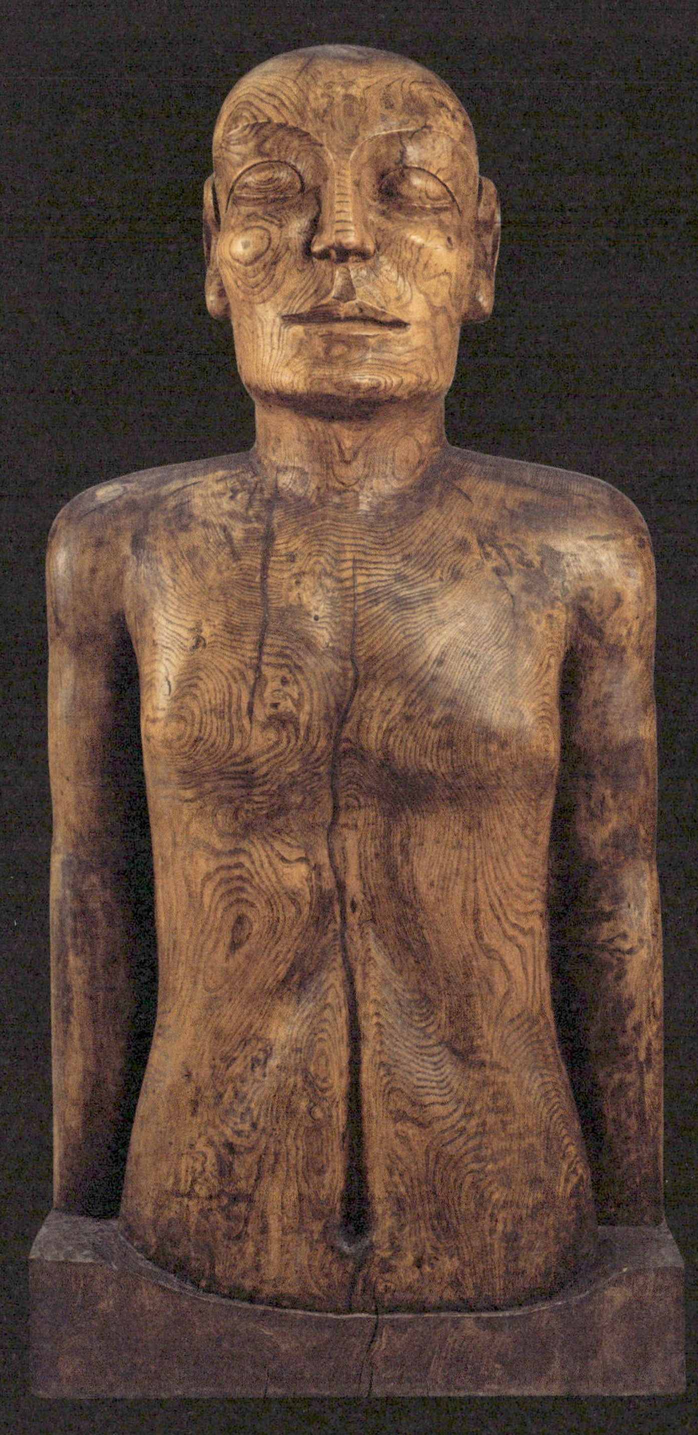

Ronald Moody, *Johanaan*, 1936, elm,
157 × 74 × 40 cm (61 7/8 × 29 1/4 × 15 3/4 in.)

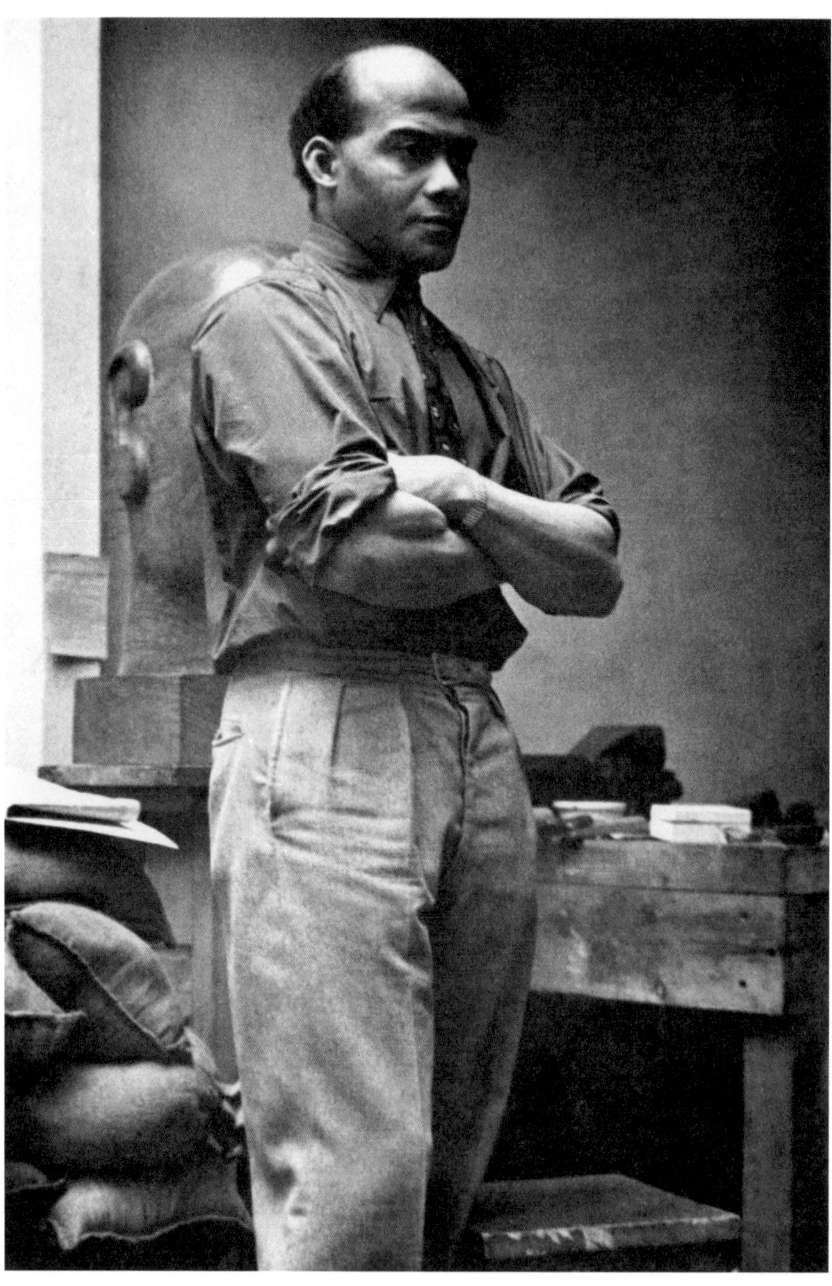

Ronald Moody in his Montparnasse studio
at 134 rue de la Tombe-Issoire, Paris, 1938

Helene 2 (1938), and his *Seated Sarong Figure* (1938) was also produced around this time. Reflecting on his experiences in Paris, Moody said:

> Settling down in Paris had its difficulties.... My knowledge of colloquial French increased perforce enormously, even though heard through the booming and staccato voice of the decorator. I settled down in this house not far from Montparnasse and began to live the life of an artist of the Left Bank. Perhaps I should explain what is meant by the phrase 'left bank'. The left bank of the Seine is, broadly speaking, where most of the artists live. The 'right bank' is populated by the wealthy.
>
> It is estimated that about forty thousand artists lived in Paris. And certainly, art was, and still is, I understand, a real force in the life of the people. It was quite a common sight to see workmen spending the Sunday painting by the river. My charwoman had very definite ideas as to what she liked and did not like of my work. And what's more, gave sound reason for her likes and dislikes. The artists were a truly international crowd, coming from almost every country in the world. Consequently, the clash of minds from so many countries was most stimulating and helpful.[22]

In 1939, Moody was invited to participate in a large survey exhibition at the Baltimore Museum of Art (BMA), titled 'Contemporary Negro Art', which took place in February 1939.[23] Moody was one of twenty-nine artists exhibiting, alongside African American artists Aaron Douglas (1899–1979),[24] Richmond Barthé (1901–1988),[25] Sargent Claude Johnson (1888–1967)[26] and Lois M. Jones (1905–1988).[27] Moody included twelve of his works in the show, a mixture of wood and bronze pieces counting the life-size bronze mask of Moroccan aristocrat *Madame de Muns* (1936), *Wohin*, *L'Homme*, *Midonz*, the tinted beech figure *Seated Sarong Figure* and the Dutch oak artwork *Annie* (1938) in their number.[28] The raw material for both *Seated Sarong Figure* and *Annie* came from the estate of Annie van Beuningen-Eschauzier, the sister-in-law of the internationally known art collector Daniël George van Beuningen. They had met at the opening of Moody's solo exhibition in Amsterdam at Kunztzaal van Lier on 8 January 1938 and became immediate friends. Beuningen-Eschauzier became a faithful patron and devoted friend, and remained so until her death in 1968.[29] 'Contemporary Negro Art' was one of the first major exhibitions in the US to feature African American artists, and the BMA saw it as a way to refocus the priorities of a traditional American museum from one serving the constituents of a private patron class to one serving the interests of its broader public. The exhibition was conceived by American writer, philosopher, educator, cultural leader and patron of the arts Alain Locke and funded by the Harmon Foundation,[30] which was founded in 1922 to promote the creative production of African Americans in the visual arts. The Harmon Foundation dominated in the promotion and production of exhibitions of Black art at the beginning of the 1930s and was a major resource of financial support for Black artists from 1926 to 1933.[31] In the foreword of the *Contemporary Negro Art* exhibition catalogue, Locke states the exhibition to be a 'declaration of principles as to what art should be in a democracy'.[32]

In 1938, the director of the Harmon Foundation, Mary Beattie Brady, expressed interest in Moody, asking if he had 'something unusual to bring to the attention of the people in this country' in a memorandum to Evelyn S. Brown, and suggesting that Elmer Carter might be able to provide context.[33] At the time, Carter was the editor for the National Urban League's publication *Opportunity: Journal of Negro Life*, the organ of the organisation.[34] Carter pointed the Harmon Foundation in the direction of James S. Watson,[35] a fellow countryman of Jamaica and in 1930, the first African American judge elected to the New York City Municipal Court, in 1930.[36] Through a serendipitous encounter with Watson at the English Speaking Union in London, Moody's friend Marie Seton learnt of the Harmon Foundation's enquiry. Seton contacted the Harmon Foundation to advocate on Moody's behalf, describing his positive reception and the impact of his artworks, and his exhibitions in Paris and Amsterdam. Seton also

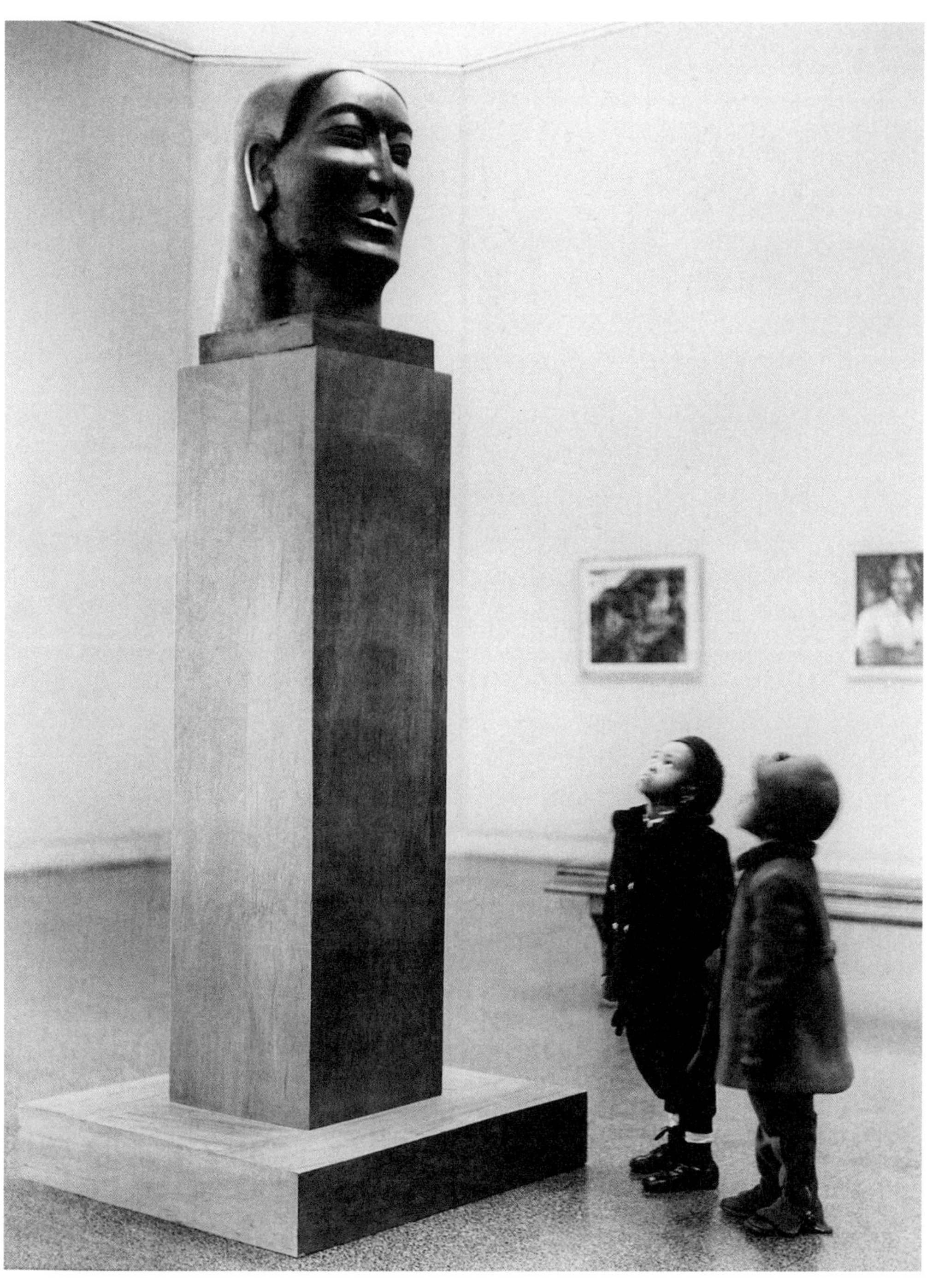

Midonz in the 'Contemporary Negro Art' exhibition at the Baltimore Museum of Art, 1939

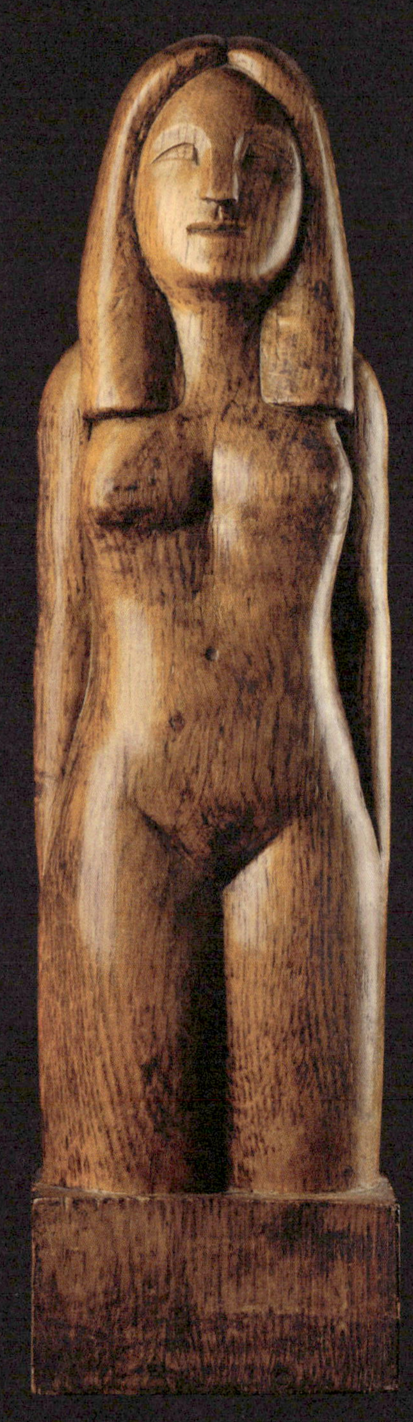

Ronald Moody, *Annie*, 1938, Dutch oak,
46 × 12 × 10 cm (18 ⅛ × 4 ¾ × 4 in.)

referred to a forthcoming solo show of Moody's work at Guggenheim Jeune, London.[37] The renowned art collector Peggy Guggenheim had opened the Guggenheim Jeune gallery in January 1938 on Cork Street in London's Mayfair.[38] The gallery, in its eighteen-month history, produced twenty exhibitions of contemporary sculpture, abstract and Surrealist art, and showed artists including Wassily Kandinsky, Henry Moore, Constantin Brancusi and Alexander Calder. The gallery was credited as a catalyst for the growing appreciation of Modern art in England.[39] Moody sent *Johanaan* back to London for the proposed exhibition.[40]

In Jeffrey C. Stewart's biography *The New Negro: The Life of Alain Locke*, he states that the enduring iconic image of the two young children looking up at Moody's large, mask-like sculpture *Midonz* on a plinth, towering above them, is demonstrative of what Locke achieved with 'Contemporary Negro Art': the children display hope, optimism and wonder at the huge possibilities before them.[41] Art historian Kobena Mercer attributes these hybridized mythological, monumental figures to Ronald Moody's lived experience of the intercultural history of the Caribbean and suggests that artworks such as *Wohin* and *Midonz* are indicative of the gravitational pull for cultural producers such as Aaron Douglas, Katherine Dunham and Zora Neale Hurston to visit the Caribbean in the 1930s and '40s.[42]

Moody's works continued to be exhibited in the US during the interwar period. In 1940, his bronze *Ripple* and elm *Self-Portrait 3* (both 1937) were shown at Howard University Art Gallery in Washington and again back in Paris at Galerie René Breteau in a group show. Later that year, *Ripple* was exhibited in Chicago's World Fair 'American Negro Exposition', held at Chicago Coliseum, a two-month event that took five years to plan. The Exposition featured over 120 exhibits that highlighted the artistic, cultural, industrial and scientific achievements of the Black people throughout history.[43] Moody's artworks were also exhibited at Columbia University and Wellesley College at the end of 1940, and, although the works that were exhibited there are unknown, it is likely that the Exposition would have featured his wood carvings *Wohin*,

Une Tête (1937), *L'Homme*, *Annie*, *Midonz* and *Seated Sarong Figure*, which he had exhibited at Wellesley College in Massachusetts.[44] The Second World War soon began, and Moody's artworks remained in the custody of the Harmon Foundation until 1952. *L'Homme* was returned to Moody that year, having been purchased by Helene Moody in 1937, and was hung in the living room in their home until her death.[45] His other sculptures were returned to England over an extended period with the support of Marie Seton, except for *Midonz*. In 1966, the Harmon Foundation was dismantled. Moody made one last attempt to have *Midonz* returned, but never received a response to his letter.

CHAPTER 3

Midonz... La Déesse de la Transmutation

Cynthia Moody

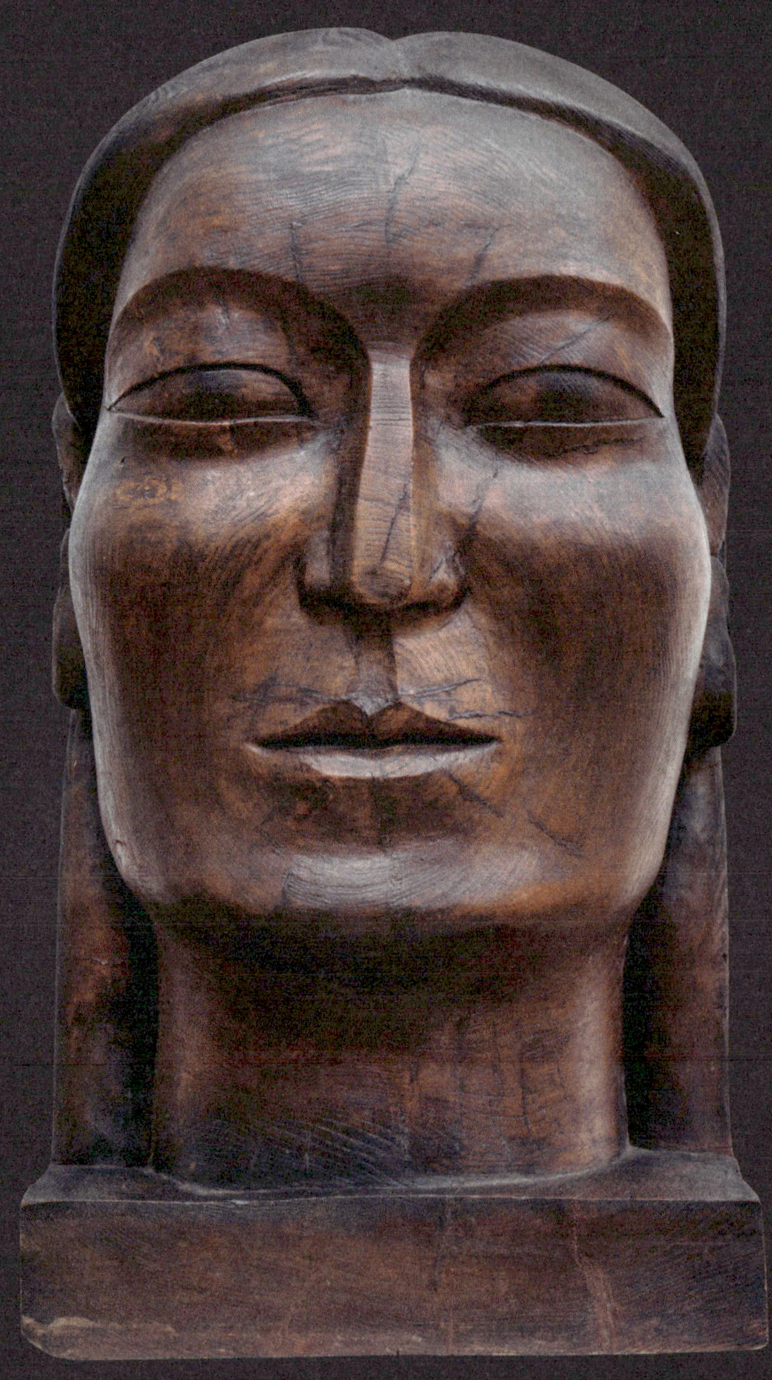

Ronald Moody, *Midonz*, 1937, elm,
69 × 28 × 39.5 cm (27 ¼ × 11 ⅛ × 15 ⅝ in.)

'Midonz-elm head.' When I first discovered these bald words on a scrap of paper among the effects of sculptor Ronald Moody, I had no inkling of how involved I would become with this very special work, nor of the impact it would have on me when I saw it for the first time, almost ten years later.

Ronald Moody, my uncle, died in 1984. The Moody family disapproved of Ronald's lifestyle and the 'dissolute' career he had chosen. They waxed long and loud about this, and when I began to display the same disreputable leaning toward 'the arts', the reaction was instantaneous: 'You'll end up like your Uncle Ronald.' I could think of nothing better, and resolved to get to know my 'idol' at the earliest opportunity. We met some years later in wartime London and cemented a lifelong friendship – an alliance of the 'black sheep' against the Philistines. Our alliance stood the test of time, and it was left to me, at my uncle's death nearly forty years later, to deal with his estate.

I soon discovered the enormity of my task. There were the sculptures and the personal effects, of course, but there was also the paper, decades worth. Ronald's flat and his studio were both jam-packed. There was paper stuffed into desk drawers, boxes and a hitherto unsuspected attic; scattered like confetti on every conceivable surface. I didn't know where to begin, so I dumped everything into black dustbin liners and had it shipped to my own home in Bristol.

It was many months before I could make a rough assortment of things. I had, of course, become familiar with a fair number of Ronald's sculptures over the years, but there were many that I knew little or nothing about. Ronald had kept no records of his work, not even in his diaries; what I had to work with were a few lists from exhibitions, as well as names jotted down on the odd slip of paper. It was on one of these that I first found reference to *Midonz*. I was immediately compelled by the name, by its exoticism; clearly its origin was mythological or cabalistic. Mesopotamia, Byzantium, Persia or Egypt came to mind. None of Ronald's surviving friends and associates were able to tell me anything about the work, for not one of them had seen it.

I had found a collection of photographs tucked behind a bookcase in Ronald's flat. When I eventually got round to going over them, I was struck by two photographs of a sculpture unknown to me, showing a female face with riveting features. Unfortunately, no name was noted on the back. Shortly thereafter, while sifting through forty-nine years of press clippings, I struck gold: a 1938 item from the *New York Amsterdam News*, with two photographs – one of Ronald and another of the now familiar face, captioned 'Midonz'.

I was then able to piece together a fragmentary history. The sculpture had appeared in a solo show at the Galerie Billiet-Vorms in Paris in November 1937, and three months later in Amsterdam at the Kunstzaal van Lier. *Midonz* had been returned to Paris and shown at the Salon des Tuileries in June 1938, before being shipped, together with eleven other works, to the Harmon Foundation in New York for inclusion in a 1939 exhibition at the Baltimore Museum of Art entitled 'Contemporary Negro Art'. Then the war came. The artworks remained in the custody of the Harmon Foundation until 1952, despite protracted efforts to have them returned. It was only the intervention of Ronald's close friend, Marie Seton, that resulted in the recovery of the works from the Foundation; she brought them back to England by hand over three different trips – everything except *Midonz*, which was too unwieldy for her to manage. In 1966, on hearing that the Harmon Foundation was about to be dismantled and its collections dispersed, Ronald made one last attempt to find out what had happened to the piece. But his letter remained unanswered, and he had to resign himself to the idea that he would never see *Midonz* again.

Over the course of my research, I came to realise how much *Midonz* had meant to Ronald, and that he had never really reconciled himself to its loss. I became convinced that this feeling of deprivation had induced him to undertake his *Large Female Head* (1974–76), an evocation of *Midonz*, to which it bears a striking likeness in conception and form. The fact that he should even consider tackling so massive a work, in so hard and unyielding a wood as teak, when he was in his mid-seventies and already in very frail health, would seem to substantiate this. I find it very poignant that *Large Female Head* took over two years to complete, whereas *Midonz* was only the first of twelve works he created during 1937. These twelve works included major pieces, such as the serene, oversized mask *L'Homme* and the dark, column-like *Lilith*. According to the Talmud, Lilith was Eve's precursor, a formidable woman who refused to submit to Adam and deserted Paradise for the ethereal regions – a prefiguration, perhaps, of *Midonz*.

Ironically, *Large Female Head* is reminiscent of *Midonz* in another way, one their creator never envisaged: it, too, seems to have disappeared. Just before Ronald's death, *Large Female Head* and two other major pieces, *Anima* and *Vision*, were acquired by the Centre for Black and African Arts and Civilization in Lagos, Nigeria; since then, every attempt to divine their fate has failed. This second loss made me all the more determined to find *Midonz* and restore it to the artist's collection.

The grandson of the man who established the Harmon Foundation was unable to help; the records were 'no longer in existence', he assured me. In January 1993, however, I learned from painter Uzo Egonu (1931–1996) that the Harmon Foundation's records – and the Foundation's art collection – had been dispersed among several American institutions, including the Smithsonian, the National Archives and the Library of Congress. This encouraged me to renew my efforts.

Still, eight months and twenty institutions later, I had again nearly given up hope of finding *Midonz*. Then, out of the blue, I was directed toward the Hampton University Museum in Virginia – which, I discovered, had received *Midonz* as a loan from the Harmon Foundation in 1958 and had kept the work in storage, unseen, for two decades. The Hampton showed tremendous goodwill toward me, and readily agreed to part with the sculpture. Thus, finally, did *Midonz* return to England after fifty-seven years. On 24 June 1994, I saw it for the first time.

Nothing had prepared me for it. I had long known its dimensions, but I was not prepared for the work's sheer massiveness, nor for the immensity of its presence. The photographs had given no inkling of the colour of the wood, which seems to glow, or of the way the grain enhances and animates the planes of the features, so that the face's expression seems to change, subtly, even as one looks at it. Least of all was I prepared for the timeless serenity that *Midonz* exudes. During the following weeks, I heard from many visitors normally far from inarticulate one constant refrain: 'Wow!'

Midonz, together with *Wohin* (1935) and *Tacet* (1938), is part of a trinity of heroic sculptures created by Ronald in the 1930s, at the very beginning of his career. They are closely interconnected. Marie Seton described *Midonz* as 'the female counterpart to *Wohin*', but *Tacet* is, in turn, clearly the male counterpart of *Midonz*. Manifest in each of the works is Ronald's passionate concern with the exploration of the inner life of man and the possibility of evolution through self-awareness. In each, he has captured an extraordinary sense of spiritual unity.

Wohin was not only the first of these formidable heads, but also the first sculpture Ronald attempted in wood. This haunting work was inspired by the Schubert song 'Whither, o brooklet, tell me whither?' and symbolizes man questioning his spiritual destiny. It was described by critic Max Osborn as 'an unforgettable head of a man, of strange enigmatical expression, lips parted, full of thirst, eyes wide open, fixed on space.' *Wohin* and the response it elicited led to Ronald's first solo show in Paris in 1937; it is the seminal piece from which his other work in this period of intense creativity stems. It is carved from oak, and the use of the grain of the wood is quite remarkable: the lines highlight the rounded planes of the head, forming a kind of contour map of the features. Black-filled fissure lines in the wood fringe across the forehead and converge at the top of the head in a scooped-out circle, the significance of which I have yet to discover.

Here I must mention *Johanaan*, completed exactly one year after *Wohin*, for this figure is an integral part of the progression toward *Midonz* and *Tacet* and, like them, is carved in elm. Again, the intuitive use of the grain underlines the contours of the figure, giving it a living quality. *Johanaan* is a full torso, but Ronald began carving the figure from the head; despite the beauty and the presence of the whole, it is the head that is the all-compelling feature. Author Antonia White wrote in her diary: 'Only the head is finished, yet [it] is really beautiful. I was

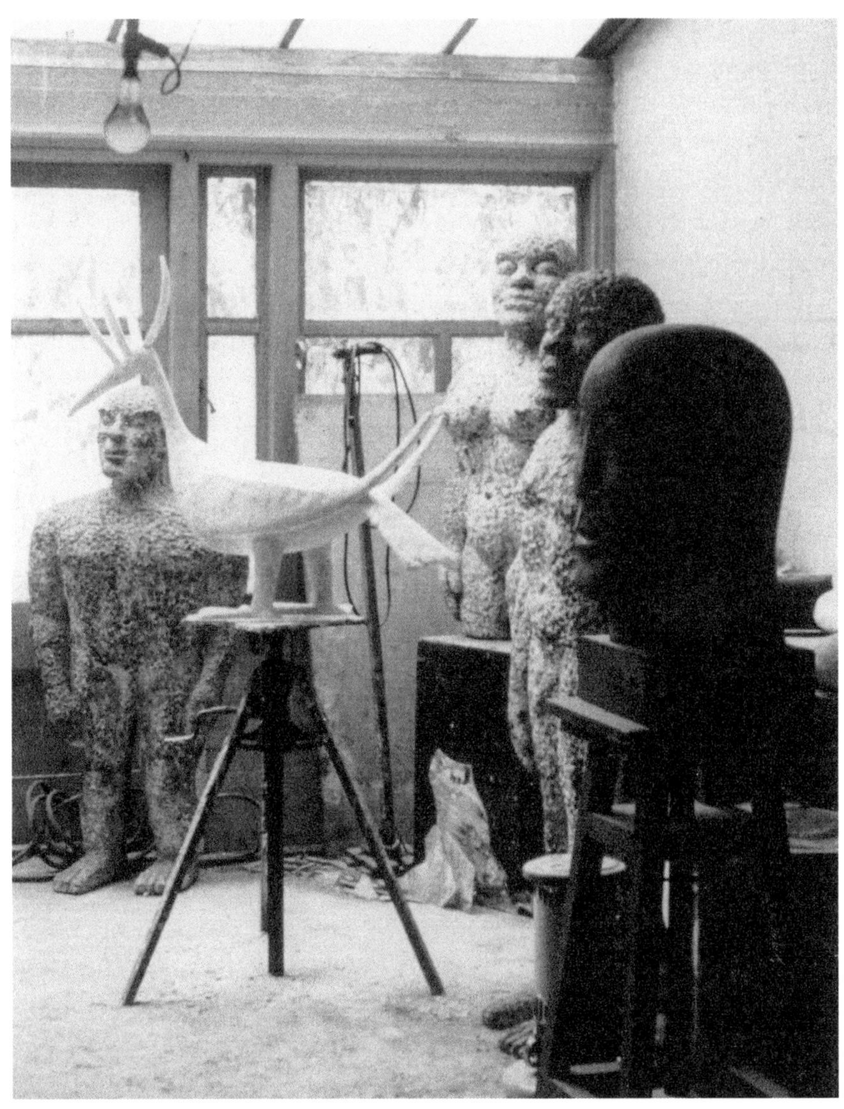

Orchid Bird (plaster model) with *Concrete Family* and *Tacet*, Fleming Close Studios, Fulham, 1968

moved, could hardly speak, and felt tears come to my eyes when I saw it the other day. It is so far beyond anything that R. has done yet, much more projected out of himself.... It really has a life of its own, complete.'

Midonz and *Tacet* followed *Johanaan* at yearly intervals. Their features are similar, their dimensions nearly identical and the colour and texture of the wood suggests that they may have been carved from the same piece of elm, which in both cases is cut vertically, against the grain, revealing the interior life of the work. In *Tacet*, the accentuation of the grain is far stronger, and the convergence of the rings at the barely parted lips is emphasised by the black fissure lines, radiating from the centre, creating a dramatic and exotic effect reminiscent of tribal markings. The radiation of lines, centring on the closed lips, underscores our attention on what Ronald was later to describe as 'a place within, which I call the place of silence, neither intellectual nor emotional...which helps us to see more clearly and achieve some sort of inner balance and outward action.' Hence the name *Tacet*: it is silent.

One gradually becomes aware of pre-Columbian overtones. This may have been subconscious, for when *Tacet* was created, Ronald's knowledge of the pre-Columbian cultures of the Arawaks and Caribs in the West Indies was skimpy, to say the least, having been gleaned from 'a very thin, soft-covered green book', to which he had given only cursory attention while in school. Max Osborn was convinced that Ronald's work displayed 'unconscious and profoundly racial memories, which come from his birthplace', and that memories of the pre-Columbian culture that once existed there, which even his ancestors did not know, lived on in the artist, under whose 'creative hands the visions of a mysterious tropical atmosphere of strange and astonishing faces, of a type more Indian than Negro, suddenly appeared'.

Although *Midonz*'s broad face, with its wide, shallow cheekbones and flattened nose, is more overtly Amerindian, the strongest influence is undeniably Egyptian, especially in the stylization of the hair. The overall effect is of a harmonious blending of the two cultures: pre-Columbian and ancient Egyptian. Above all, *Midonz* epitomises 'the tremendous inner force, the irresistible movement in stillness'

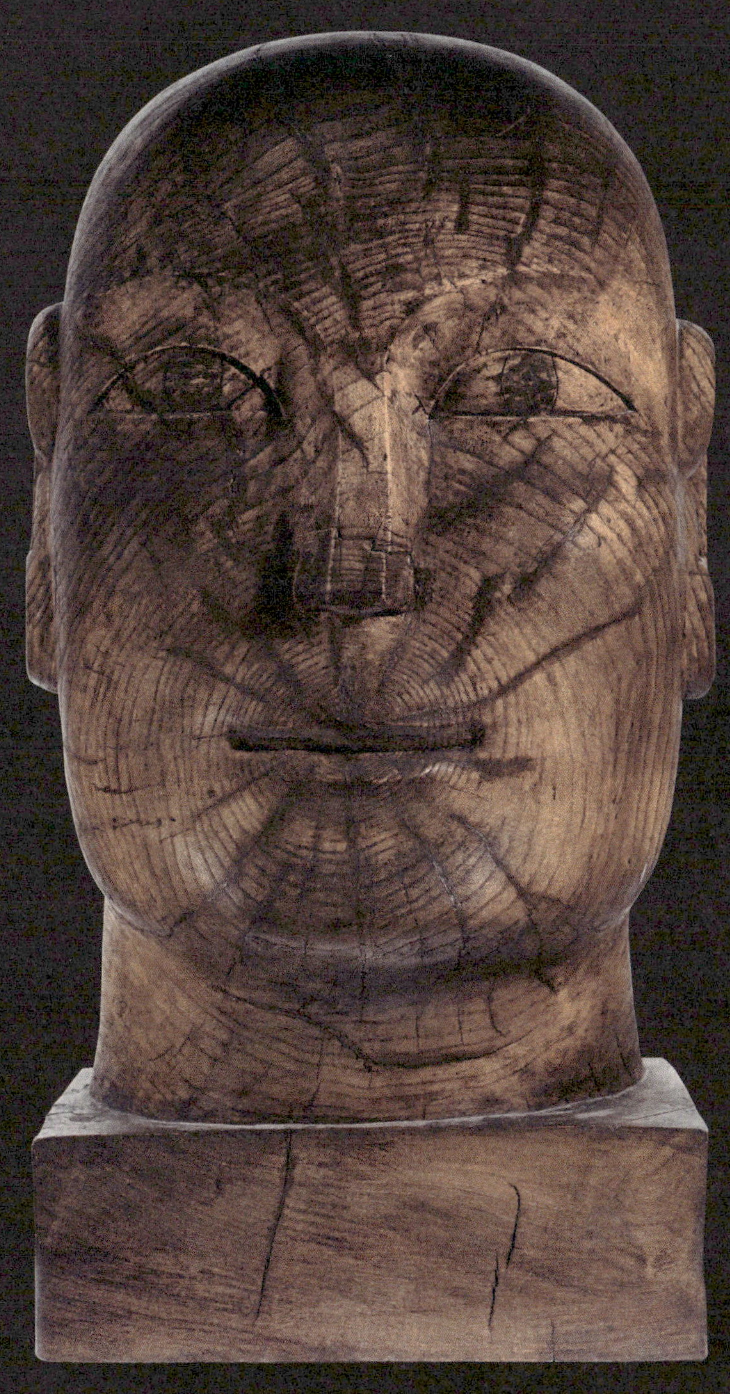

Ronald Moody, *Tacet*, 1938, elm, 76.2 cm (30 in.) high

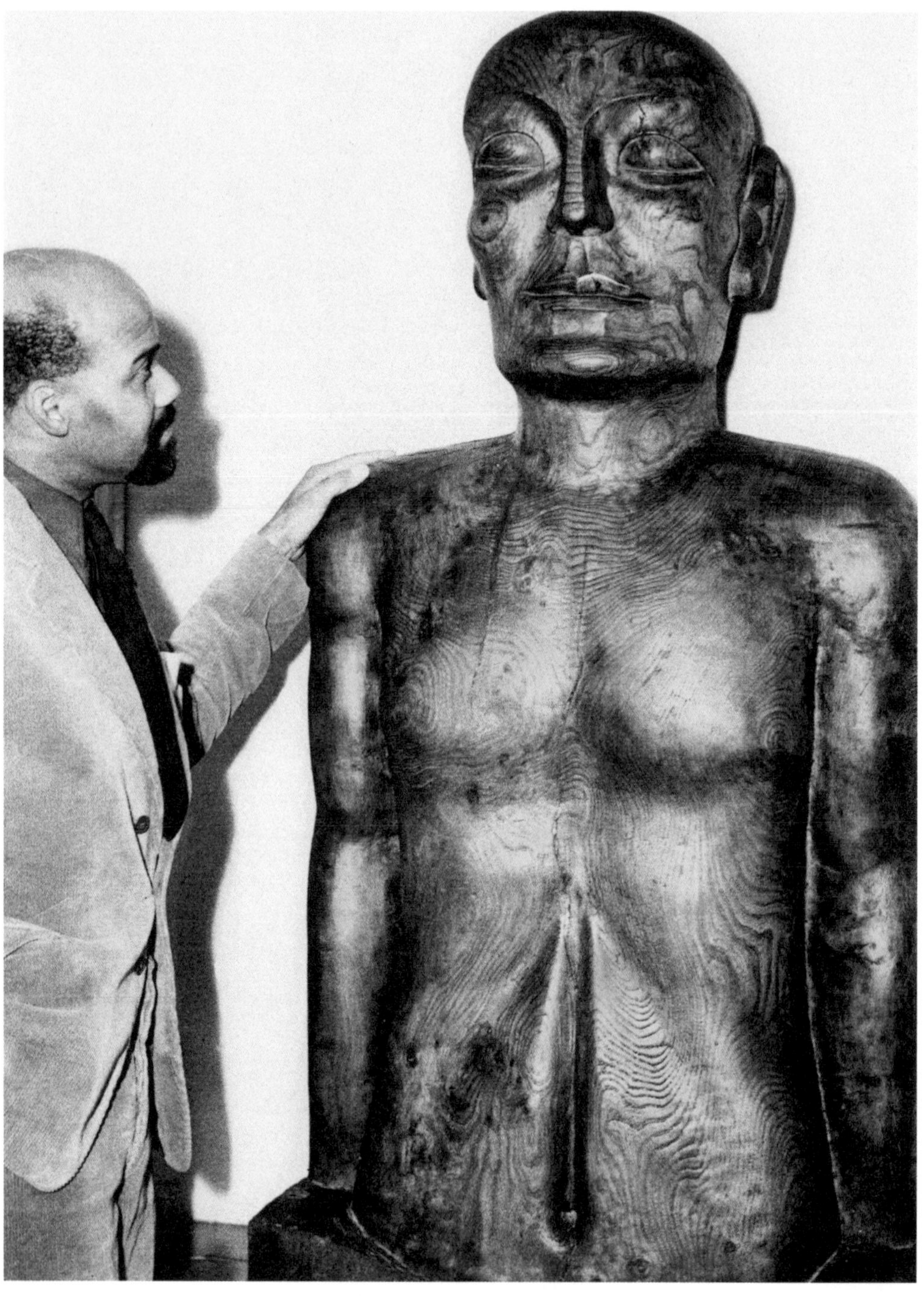

Ronald Moody with *Johanaan* at the exhibition 'The Works of Ronald Moody', Galerie Apollinaire, London, 1950

that transfixed Ronald when he first encountered Egyptian art at the British Museum in 1928, and which aroused in him the compulsion to create, to become a sculptor.

But who is *Midonz*? Marie Seton described the head as Ronald's 'own vision of woman, primordial and awakening...woman searching and striving to become a conscious human being'. Primordial, certainly. But Ronald also called her 'La Déesse de la Transmutation [the goddess of transmutation]', far beyond human limitations. Transmutation is an alchemical process, a passing into a new form, nature or substance; Ronald Moody, steeped in gnosticism, may have intended her to personify the redemption of the spirit from matter by spiritual knowledge. Whoever she may be, when I look at *Midonz*, I feel myself to be in the presence of one of the Great Mothers of antiquity who dominate the world of myth and legend.

This text was originally published in *Transition*, no. 77 (1998), pp. 10–18.

CHAPTER 4

The 1940s and Moody as Broadcaster

The idea of France falling felt unimaginable to Ronald and Helene Moody, and they continued to live, work and exhibit in Paris until the outbreak of war in 1939. When war was declared, the British Consulate General in Paris advised British citizens who were resident there to stay put. On 1 November 1939, the Moodys moved to a small flat in rue Saint Jacques in the Latin Quarter.[1] By this time, they were fully integrated into the Montparnasse scene. Among those they called their friends were Lo Hakansson, a Swedish journalist, Czechoslovakian Robert Liebknecht (1903–1994), Lee Hersch (1896–1953), an American, and Charlotte von Schweinitz, an Austrian baroness, photographer Man Ray (1890–1976)[2] and Dutch artist Kobus Hooykaas (1903–1969). Despite these difficult times, Moody managed to produce some of his most serene works: *Petit Torse* (1938), *Anita*, *Petite Tête* and *Bob* (all 1939), a portrait mask of Robert Liebknecht and *The Priest* (1939). Few galleries remained open. Moody had one last show with three painters, one being Hooykaas, titled 'Matières et Formes' (Materials and Forms) at the Galerie René Breteau, which opened on 11 April 1940. Moody and Hooykaas had shared a studio at 66 avenue de Châtillion, where they both abandoned their artworks and tools when they had to flee.[3] On 11 June, the Moodys closed the door of their flat, taking only the possessions they were able to carry, and fled Paris with a small group of nine friends, which included Wifredo Lam, Lo Hakansson and Elis Eriksson, a Swedish sculptor, only two days before the Germans entered. They stayed in Charnizay on a farm, and after a few days, their friends began to head on foot to Bordeaux, where they thought it might be easier to get back to England. The Moodys continued south on their own, arriving at Bordeaux the morning after the fall of France, to find that they had missed the last boat back to England two days before.[4] A fortnight later, they eventually arrived in Marseilles, where they were able to send correspondence to England through the American Consulate General. They combined their efforts, contacting agencies and individuals such as the Foreign Office, the Colonial Office, the Governor of Jamaica, the American Embassy in London, the Red Cross in Geneva and the Friends Service Committee in Philadelphia

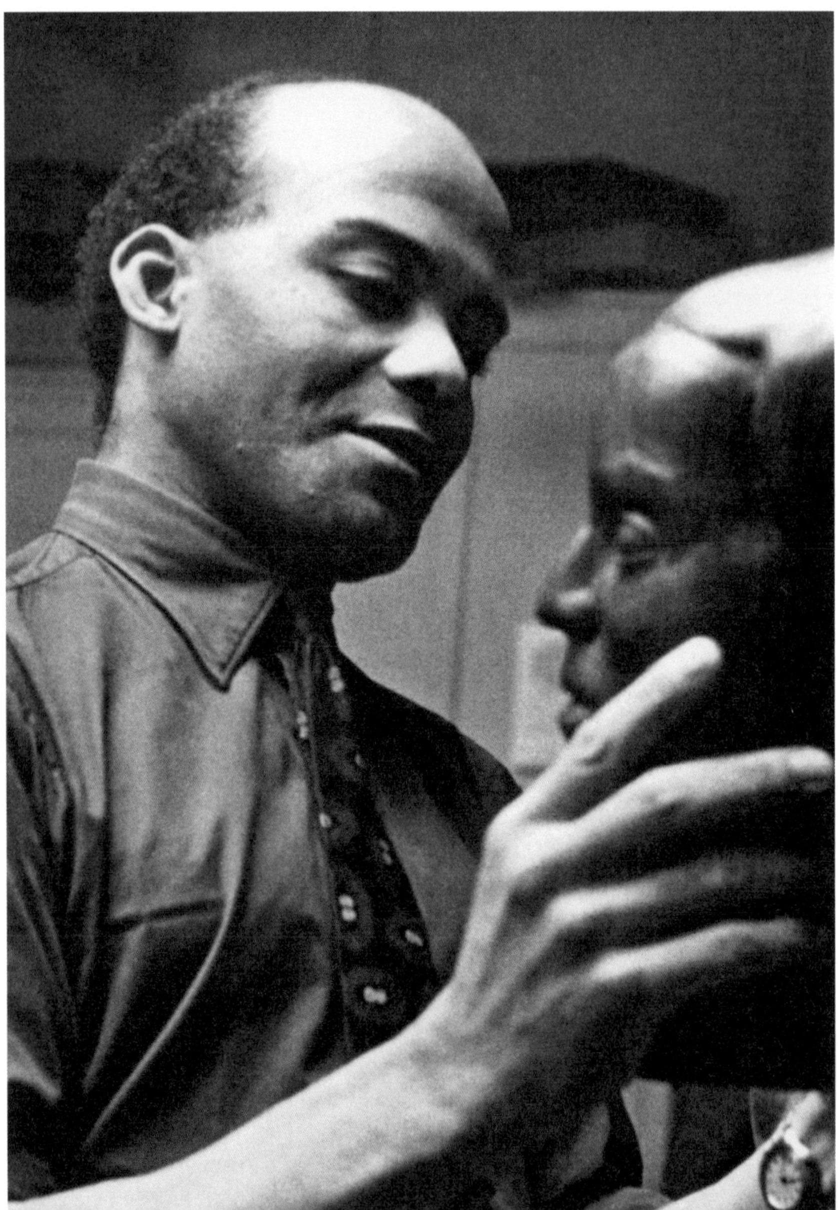

Ronald Moody with *Anita* in his
Montparnasse studio, Paris, 1938

for help with repatriation. All to no avail. Moody told Una Marson of these trials in an interview in 1943:

> For days we walked miles and miles, sleeping under hedges. My feet felt like Shredded Wheat, and my wife's feet were bleeding profusely, not only underneath, but on top too. Still, we trudged on, and eventually arrived at Toulouse. There we were fortunate enough to get a train to take us to Marseilles. We arrived, thinking we would stay a week, as we were rather tired, but it was fifteen months later that I finally got away...
>
> For the first few months, my carte d'identité was all in order and I could go about with a bold face, and even look at a policeman without dodging down the first street. But when my papers became out of date, I was unable to register at any known hotel or boarding house because the police would have been notified of my presence. As I had made up my mind to remain in Marseilles at all costs because this was one point from which it was possible to make an escape, I began to live my life like a hunted criminal – changing abode on average every fortnight. I [was] met with very many unexpected kindnesses in the shape of rooms and attics and became very, very expert in dodging the police. Eventually, after three attempts, with a great deal of luck I got away.[5]

This nomadic existence led Moody to contract pleurisy, which had a long-lasting and devastating impact on his health. Moody's extensive archive, now held at the Tate,[6] documents this trying time in France, his escape following the invasion by Germany and his eventual return to England, including letters and telegrams from his brother Harold and wife Helene regarding efforts to secure his return to England.[7] In a letter dated 6 October 1941, Harold wrote to Helene on the League of Coloured Peoples headed paper, informing her that he had received news from the Colonial Office in regard to

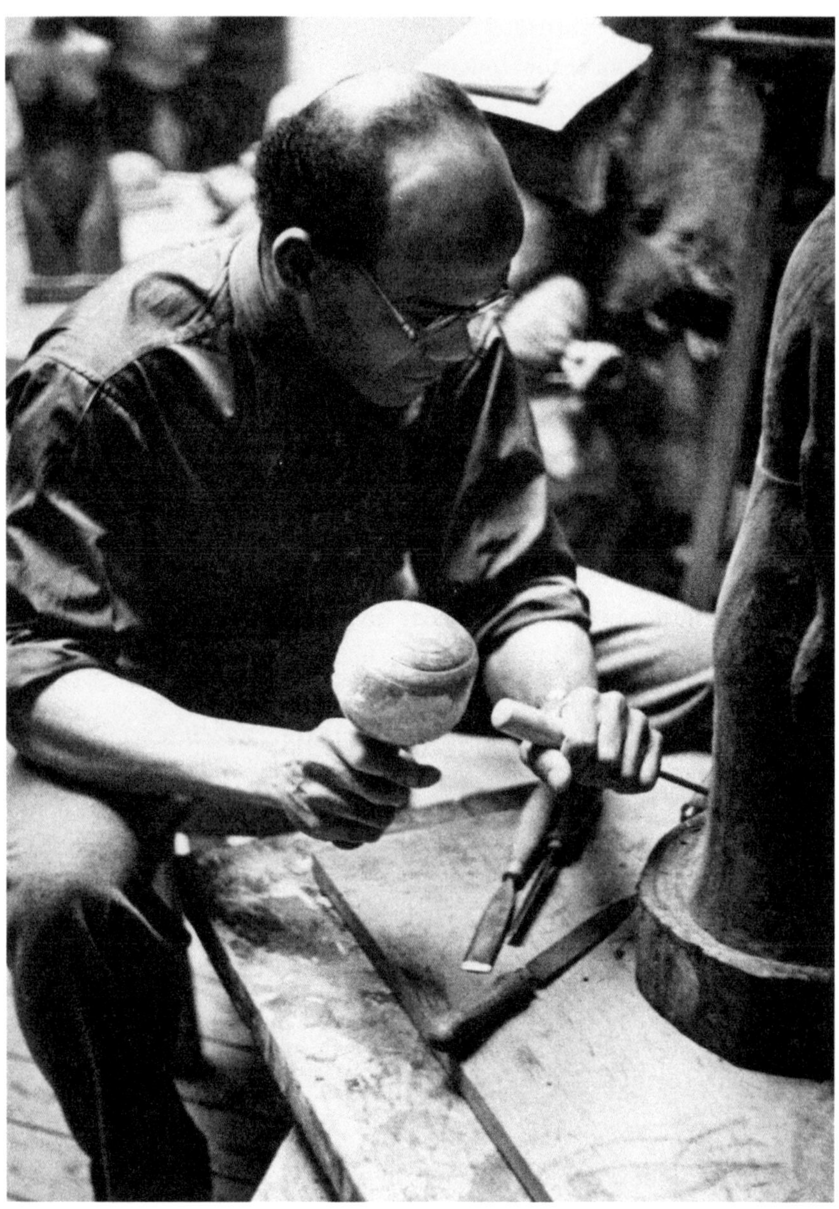

Moody carving *The Priest* in his Montparnasse studio, Paris, 1938

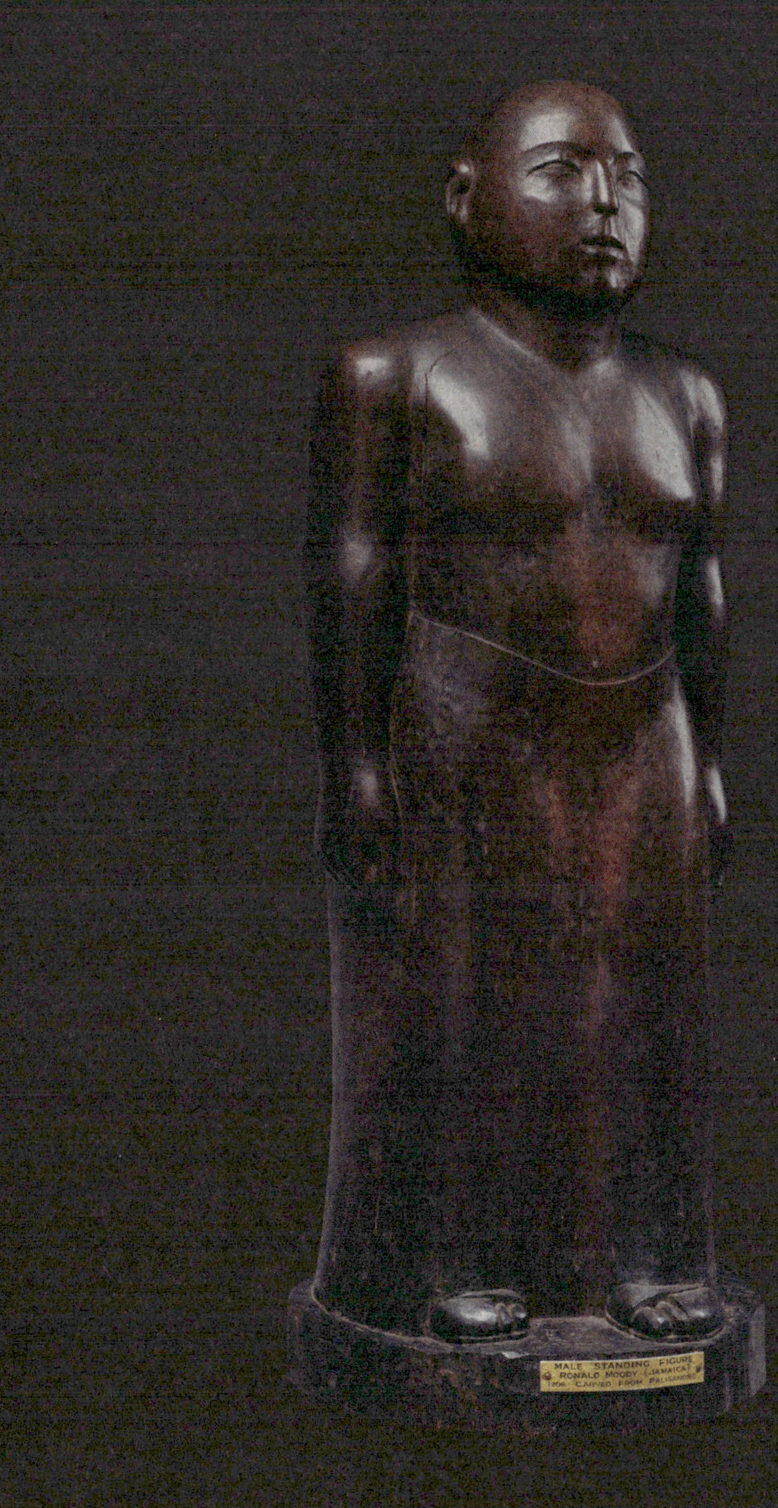

Ronald Moody, *The Priest*, 1939,
palisandre, 75 × 27 cm (29 ⅝ × 10 ¾ in.)

Ronald's welfare and location. The letter confirms that Ronald had successfully made it to Gibraltar and was to continue on to Lisbon, where it was hoped that safe air passage back to England could be arranged. Harold also relayed that he had received news in the form of a letter, directly from his brother, stating that his health was better 'but he has no passport and nothing to certify to the fact that he is a Dental Surgeon'. In his letter to his brother, Ronald expresses a desire to join the Army Dental Corps and requests that Harold support this endeavour. The letter ends with Harold stating, 'I am glad he is so well after all he has experienced.'[8]

On 10 February 1941, the Moodys made an unsuccessful and risky bid to escape over the Pyrenees into Spain. Helene, not wanting to leave Ronald, reluctantly accepted repatriation in May, after three months on the run. Moody's second attempt to escape ended with him imprisoned and interrogated. He was released after a week and immediately made his third and attempt, which would prove to be successful. After spending time in a 'safe house' in Barcelona, he was repatriated via Gibraltar and returned by ship to Liverpool on 1 October 1941. Ronald and Helene were reunited and moved to 30 Campden Hill Gardens, London, at which point he immediately applied to join the Army Dental Corps but was turned down by the War Office because of health reasons. He successfully applied to be a dental surgeon for the Public Health Department and took on duties as part of the Civil Defence fire watch.[9]

After Moody returned to England, he had little time for sculpture; he had no studio, no tools and usable wood was scarce.[10] However, his wartime experiences had a tangible legacy – in the midst of all this, he carved the tiny *Marseille Figure* (1940). Standing just 11 centimetres (4 in.) tall, it was made from a scrap of mahogany ceremoniously given to Moody as a Christmas present by his fellow refugees, purchased from the Marseille Fire Department for, as they described, 'a shameful pittance of eighteen sous'.[11] According to Cynthia Moody, Ronald carried it with him 'in his pocket, as a kind of talisman'.

The need to create was irresistible, and within six months he had written twenty-three poems.[12] In 1942, a final poem was added to complete the series.

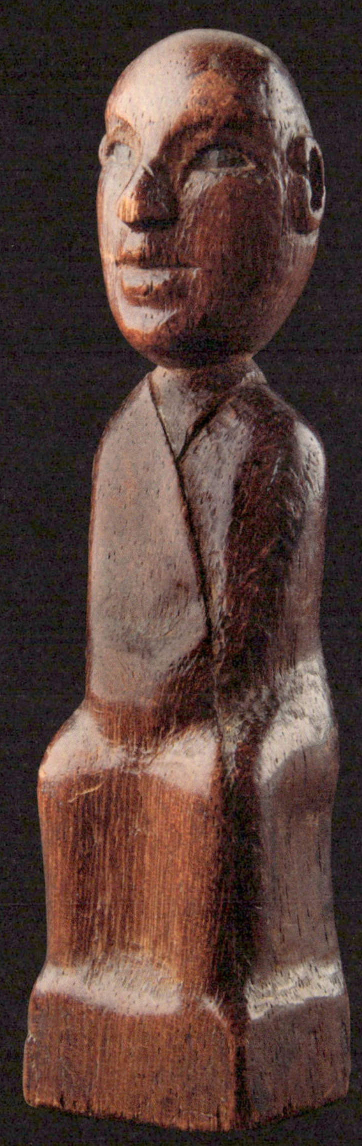

Ronald Moody, *Marseille Figure*, 1940, mahogany, 11 × 2.5 × 2 cm (4 3/8 × 1 × 7/8 in.)

Marseilles 1940

In burning sun
And sudden rain
The trams of this provincial town
Pursue their course
Of noise and jars
Immoderate
'Le Secours'
On thin and piping note
Scatters
Voluptuous women
And gaping men.
The Old Town sits
And through its doors
Breathes
Death and putrefaction,
And narrow winkled paths
Torture the eye
On the edge of nothing:
And always
The unrelenting sun.

In Cafes.
On the streets.
In many boats at anchor,
A restless crowd
Ambles.
Sits.
Some seek escape
From the God of Destruction:
How?
The face betrays
Unconscious death.
'To think is to be full of trouble?'...

And beyond thought
Perhaps a Path
Seen at times
Endless but enduring.

23 July 1940

Les Bains de Mer

Today,
I saw a hundred dazzling bodies
Wait the doom of pleasure and despair.
They laughed and dived
Proud in their strength and grace.
Food for war
Now prey for Life;
Life whose prodigality demands
The sacrifice of millions
For some great and secret task.
The sea,
In splintering fury,
Broke itself vainly against the rocks.
And when I plunged
Tugged hungrily
This time I fought and won.

24 July 1940

Husks of ideas.
Sown for many years
On willing soil.
Bear their harvest.
War and destruction,
Hate and betrayal
Of Father by Son
Are cherished and upheld.
A strange madness rules,
Its tempo quickens:
A civilization rushes
To its unthinking goal....
And I attempt to live,
To snatch from this chaos
Moments of calm
As a protection
From this New Death
So many eyes betray!

25 July 1940

Be Still!
Tho' every effort
Seems a wreck
Of broken sequences,
Where misdirection
But begets
Grosser complications.
Be Still!
The standards shattered.
The standards new,
The blood shed,
Grief and sorrow
Are shadows of a Shadow.

Turn inwards,
Suffer many deaths,
And, more awakened, know
One can be still
In body, action, thought.

26 July 1940

Love
Is
The unifying force
Which keeps
This World
Alive
Despite the
Cruelty and
Bloodshed
Now
Unloosened.
And should
It die.
Perhaps
This sphere,
Like a
Falling Star,
Will dive
To nothingness

27 July 1940

Knowledge, always so secretive,
In times of great upheaval
Is freer and less reserved
To those who become detached
From the miasma that is Self;
Which closes the eyes and ears,
Causes the mind to chatter.
The body to shrink with horror;
But for him who dares there lies
The merciless path to freedom.

6 August 1940

Weighted by a past
Half-faced and unresolved.
I seek in this disorder
To find some simple way
Of keeping the direction
Which, in more tranquil days.
I strove at my convenience
Not to completely lose.

7 August 1940

After the Armistice

'Il faut attendre.'
So many lips repeat
Where daily move the dispossessed.
Some, driven by fear of persecution,
Dream of a Land
Where what they call their freedom still exists.
Others seek only rest from war

And all its horror and uncertainty.
Many make this the reason for unthinking flight
Which accident of circumstance
Had hitherto denied.
All wish to escape some Ogre
This upheaval drives pitilessly
To the surface of their torpid minds.
A certain attitude or turn of phrase
Reveals its form of yesterday.
When with fearful and half-averted face
They slyly glanced and soon forgot.

11 August 1940

Excess of joy and grief
Leads to confusion,
For there are few
With soul so still
That all which enters
Turns to sustenance.
Yet this excess,
To the unwary
So indigestible,
Perhaps becomes
On other planes
A much-prized food;
In this Hierarchy
So pliant ye unbending.

22 August 1940[13]

The 1940s saw Moody continuing to produce smaller artworks. In part, this was due to having no studio for a time, so he was forced to work on a more domestic scale. He was using borrowed tools until a complete stranger who had heard of his predicament gave him a set of chisels and gauges. In 1942, he moved again with Helene to a maisonette at 29 Thurloe Street, London, which they shared with their writer friend Antonia White. During this period, he became a member of the International Art Centre, Bayswater, founded by Swiss-born painter Margaret Torrie (1912–1999). Moody gave a talk titled 'Art at the Crossroads' and exhibited at the Centre, where he also met Jacob Epstein, which led to visits to his studio for cups of tea. He also participated in the Artists International Association (AIA) conference in 1944, held at the Czech Institute, London. Wood was still scarce and was sourced for Moody by friends from boatyards, as well as wherever he could access it himself. Nonetheless, he managed to produce several wood carvings such as *Sleeper Mask* from a railway sleeper, *Helene 3* from a piece of elm and *Small Male Head* from oak (all 1943), *Walking Female Figure* (1944) from a piece of mahogany, and *Vision* (1943) and *Anima* (1944) from a dark oak beam that had been part of a cider press. This wood was part of a hoard discovered by his friend Ted Lacey.[14] Moody expressed his life-long affinity to wood as a material:

> My first love was, and still, is wood. The harder the better. I love its warmth and the fact that it is living, even after being cut from the tree. I have always felt that it has a very close connection with the thoughts and feelings that have informed my work. Large, simple sculptural forms live well within. However small, sculpture should be massive. It should never fly except in [the] thoughts it evokes. I have worked in most materials, including such modern mediums as concrete and fibreglass, which after much experimenting, I have found a way of using to my satisfaction.[15]

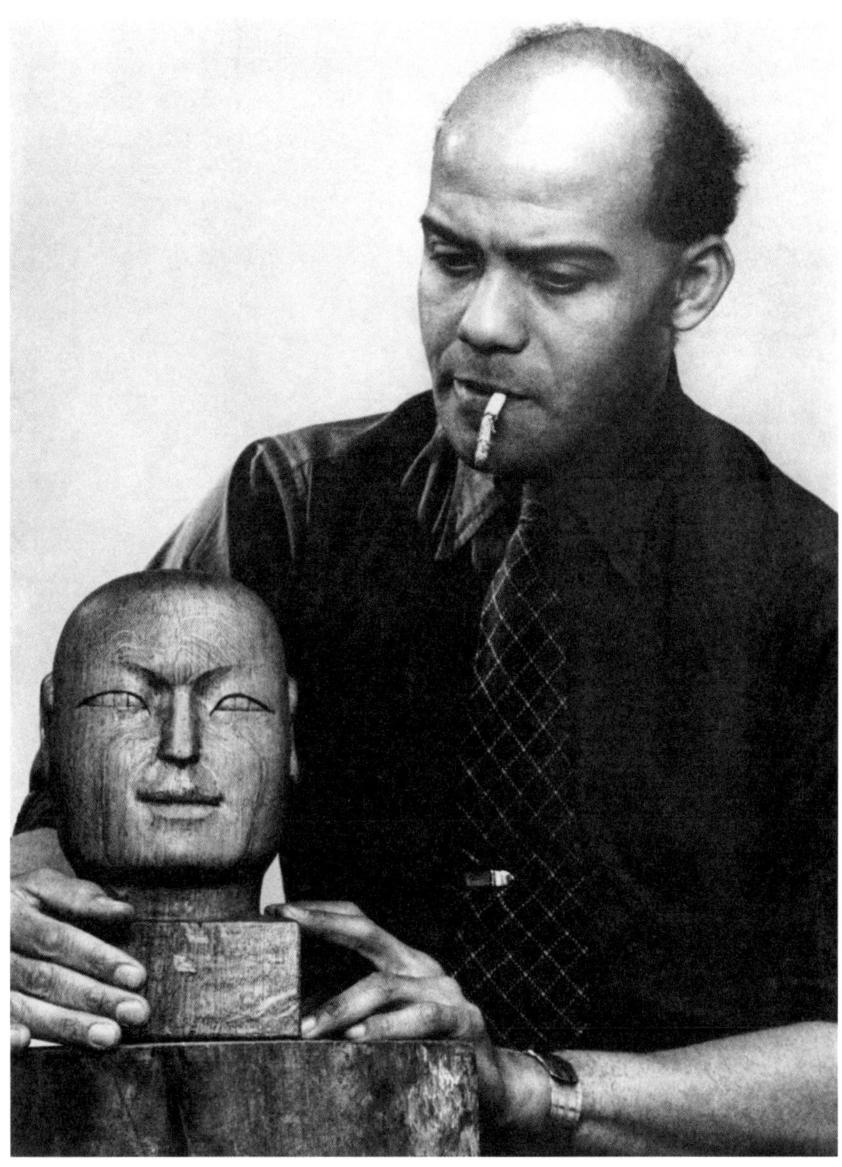

Moody with *Small Male Head* in Tregor Studio, Cathcart Road, Fulham, *c.* 1943

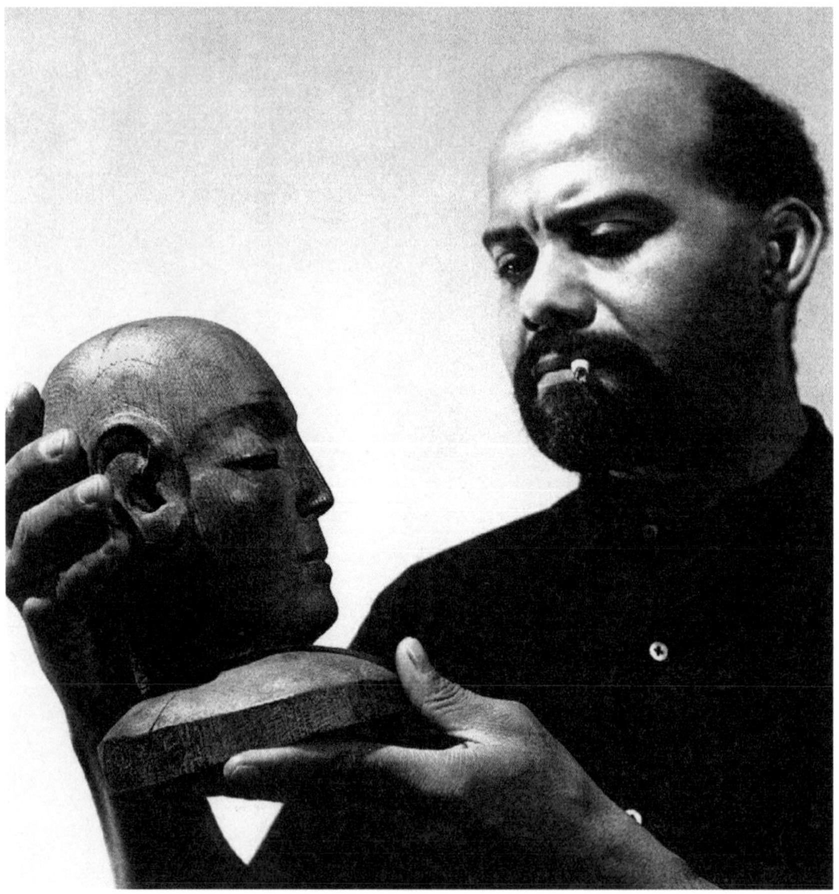

There was much upheaval for the Moodys during these years, moving to new accommodations, including a new studio space at the back of a friend's garden, which he named Tregor Studio. He continued to be profoundly affected by wartime experiences and the dropping of the atom bombs on Hiroshima and Nagasaki in 1945, remaining plagued by humankind's potential for self-annihilation.[16] It is at this point that Moody embarked on a series of symbolic sculptures, completing the sculptures *Three Heads* and *Tranquillity*. *Three Heads* (1946) was Moody's first overtly symbolic work and employed ideograms to visualize the stages of humankind's spiritual development. The head

Moody with *Tranquillity* in Tregor Studio, Fulham, 1950. Photograph by Ronnie Ziar

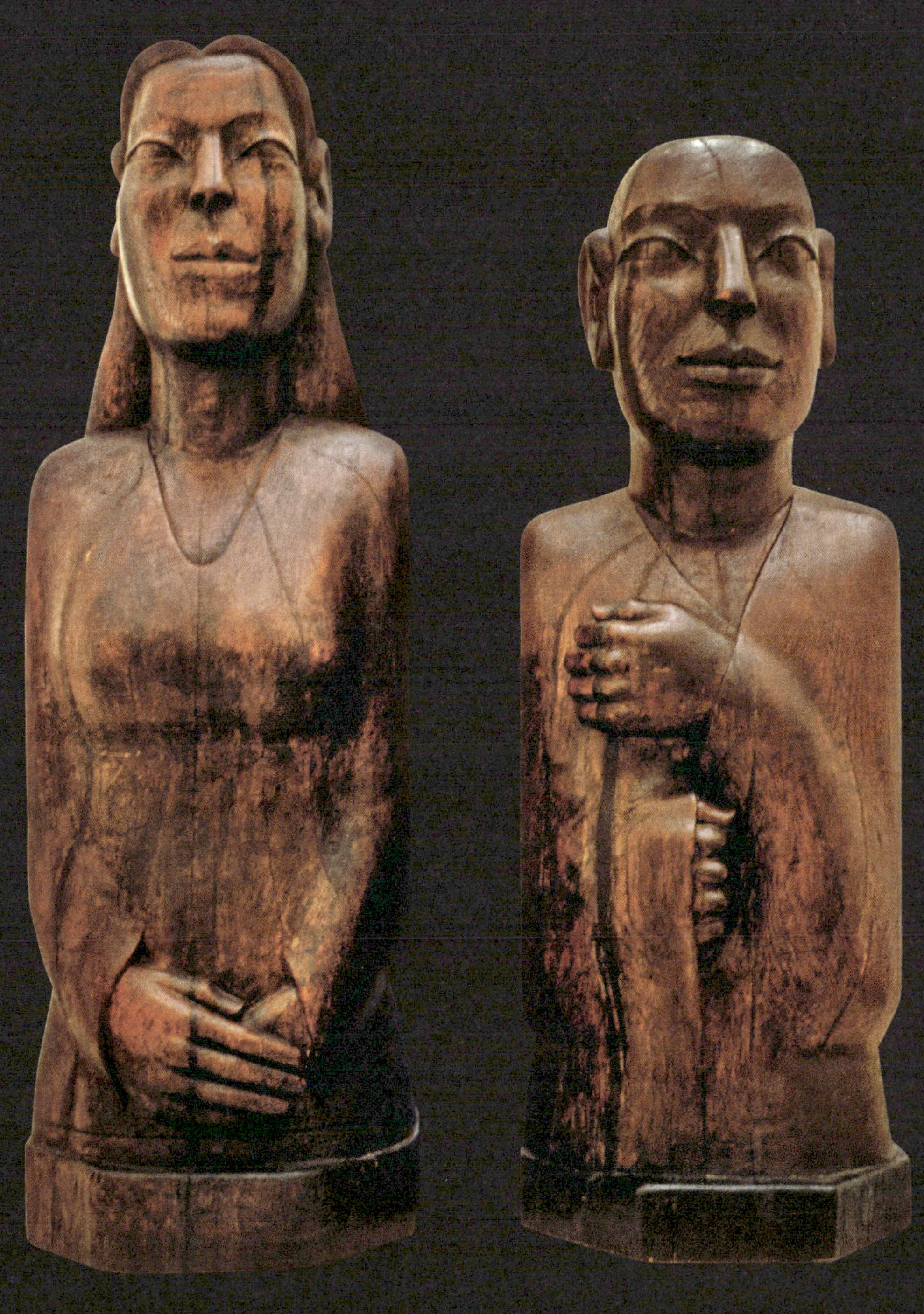

Vision and *Anima*, *c*. 1943–44, cider press, 102 × 33 cm (40 ¼ × 13 in.) and 99 × 33 cm (39 × 13 in.), respectively

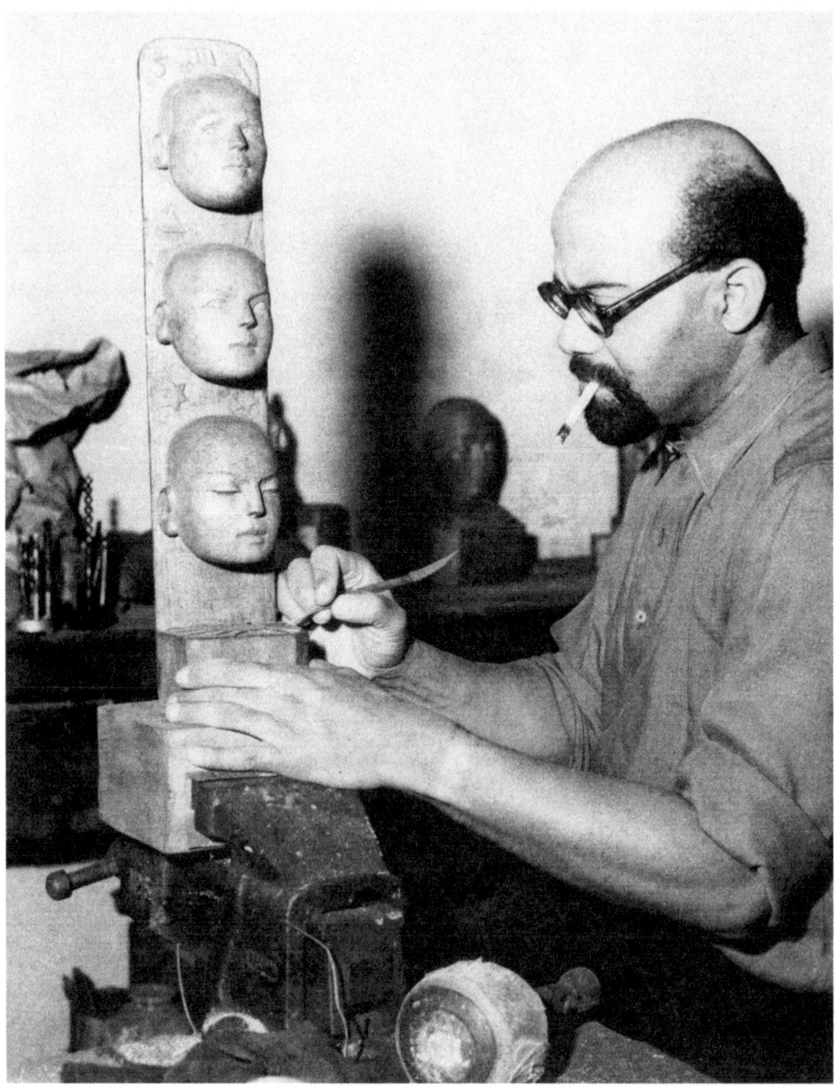

Moody carving *Three Heads* at Tregor Studio, Fulham, 1946

on top signifies science, knowledge and destruction with a book and a bomb; the second head has two triangles, indicating inner unity, which are interlocked above the third head underneath a radiating sun. In 1956, the work was purchased by Moody's friend Marie Seton to give to the Nehru Memorial Museum in New Delhi and soon-to-be prime minister of India, Indira Ghandi. At the time, *Three Heads* was the only modern piece in Jawaharal Nehru's collection of classical Buddhist figures.[17] The other small contemplative head carved in elm, *Tranquillity*, was one of the works shown in Moody's solo exhibition at Galerie Apollinaire, London, in 1950. The head was later bought by Meredith and Margaret Thring, friends of the Moody's through their shared connection and interest in J. G. Bennett's Institute for the Comparative Study of History, Philosophy and the Sciences. The Moodys were deeply involved with the teachings of the Institute for many decades. Professor Meredith Thring was a futurist engineer who focused on sustainable and responsible design for humanity's well-being. Moody's artwork *Tranquillity* inspired Professor Thring to begin to develop his own woodcarving practice.[18] While still a student, Moody had embraced the philosophy of J. G. Bennett (1897–1974), who had set up an institute dedicated to the mystic and spiritual teachings of philosopher George Gurdjieff (1866–1949) and produced an oak portrait of him 1946. Unfortunately, the location of the artwork is still unknown.[19]

The BBC began broadcasting the radio series 'Calling the West Indies' in 1939, as the Second World War took hold. For audiences in the Caribbean, it provided reassuring updates for the West Indian service men and women who had joined the armed forces and arrived in Britain to work in factories to support the Allied forces.[20] The show featured inspirational stories, music, Caribbean poetry and messages from loved ones. In 1941, pioneering Jamaican feminist, activist, poet and journalist Una Marson became its programme producer. She was the first Black female broadcaster at the BBC. In 1943, Moody was interviewed by Marson and opened up about his experience fleeing Paris and his pursuit of an art career. Their familiarity and friendship brought an intimacy to their conversation.[21] It is likely that Moody would have known Marson through his older brother Harold, given her time as secretary for the League of Coloured Peoples.[22] Not long after, in 1946, Moody began his first series of talks for the BBC Overseas Service, 'Calling the West Indies'. The broadcasts were part of a three-part series titled 'Discovering Art' and explored themes of being an artist – *A Sculptor*, *The Artist's Environment* and *The Artist's Education* – where Moody explored his own art practice and journey. Moody contributed to the BBC's Overseas Service throughout the 1940s, '50s and into the '60s on the main historical themes of art, exploring Primitive, Egyptian, Greek, Indian, Chinese, Gothic, Renaissance and Modern art. By the 1950s, Moody's broadcasts had become a combination of critique, discussion and interviews, including a two-part programme on the role of the artist: *The Artist in the Community* (1951), *A Visit to Epstein's Exhibition* (1952) and *The Role of the Artist in a New Society* (1962).

BBC OVERSEAS SERVICE BROADCASTS
'CALLING THE WEST INDIES'
'Discovering Art'
'A Sculptor' by Ronald Moody of Jamaica

Good evening. Of course, as you know, every self-respecting family has a black sheep, and I have a sneaking feeling that it is from this pool of black sheep that artists are drawn. Now, how does one reach the rank and status of a black sheep? By daring to revolt against the rules which society accepts as calculated to make you a worthy member of it. Your family acts as an agent of that society and tries to impress its rules upon you so that you will become a success - another feather in the family cap. Well now, the budding artist does not become a 'black sheep' all at once.

There is a 'grey' period when thoughts inside begin to suggest that the accepted rules and your ideas are at a variance. But as yet you dare not come into open revolt.

Nevertheless, you begin to look for a way of escape. If this state persists, one eventually declares oneself a rebel.

During my 'grey' period I remember thinking that soon I would have to make up my mind as to what profession I was going to embrace and was feeling very little enthusiasm about it. At that time I did not know what I wanted to do. I thought vaguely of an Arts Degree, but very, very vaguely. But gradually an overwhelming desire to get away and think out things for myself took hold of me. The way I could see of doing this was to take a Profession. I thought of Medicine - no, it would take too long. Law - I would have to return very soon and practise. Engineering! Heaven preserve me! Dentistry - at least not so difficult as Medicine and I would be able to earn a living whilst finding out what I wanted to do. Well, I suppose it's the least of all evils. So dentistry it became.

Eventually I came to England and started to study. Soon I became what I thought - all scientific - and felt wildly enthusiastic about the philosophical implications of the Darwinian theory, read all I could lay my hands on about it and talked and talked. How I blabbed: I had quite a following at College who used to listen daily to the pearls of wisdom that fell from my lips.

There was no problem that I couldn't solve! I did do some work at dentistry as well.

At the height of my philosophical wisdom I met one or two people who dared to say that my theories did not explain many things. First I just pitied their ignorance, then decided that the best way to refute their arguments completely was to read their warped literature. From Plato I found myself immersed in Indian and Chinese philosophy. Of course, I still talked 'science', perhaps with less assuredness. Then came the day I began to denounce my erstwhile wisdom with just as much enthusiasm. This was too much for my audience and one by one they disappeared.

Vowed as I was to search for truth whatever the consequences might be, I continued my way and found that I was taking an interest in Art. I often went to the British Museum, National Gallery and other Art Galleries, coming away, I am afraid, more puzzled than pleased, until one day I discovered Egyptian sculpture all for myself. It was an amazing experience and I haunted that room for a long time after. The use of the material, the massive forms treated with such amazing skill, sensitiveness, delicacy and daring, and lastly, the spirit behind it was strangely sympathetic. From that moment I felt I wanted to do sculpture. But how? I knew nothing about it and until now hardly thought of myself as an artist.

All of a sudden one day I crept out and bought some plasticine and dashed to my rooms full of excitement. Soon queer forms appeared to my utter astonishment as I tried to mould male heads, bodies or whatever I fancied. This went on for months until one day a friend saw my collection of 'masterpieces' and encouraged me all he could. Those days were most thrilling. I could not leave college quick enough to dash home to my beloved clay (for I had now spurned plasticine) to see what new discovery I would make. There comes to my mind the day I produced a recognizable portrait of someone by just thinking about her. Pure magic! I was amazed!

Just as I was amazed about so many things at that time. Yes, those were the days: for I set to work in earnest. What a hard taskmaster Sculpture is: I spent many, many months being encouraged on the one hand and being completely torn to bits on the other. You see, I could not find time to go to an art school for I had just got my diploma, so I got criticisms from other sculptors. For instance, I would proudly present what I thought was, well, not a flawless piece of work, but one at least worthy of very high praise. I had corrected all previous faults mentioned and had spent a great deal of time looking for new ones. How my heart

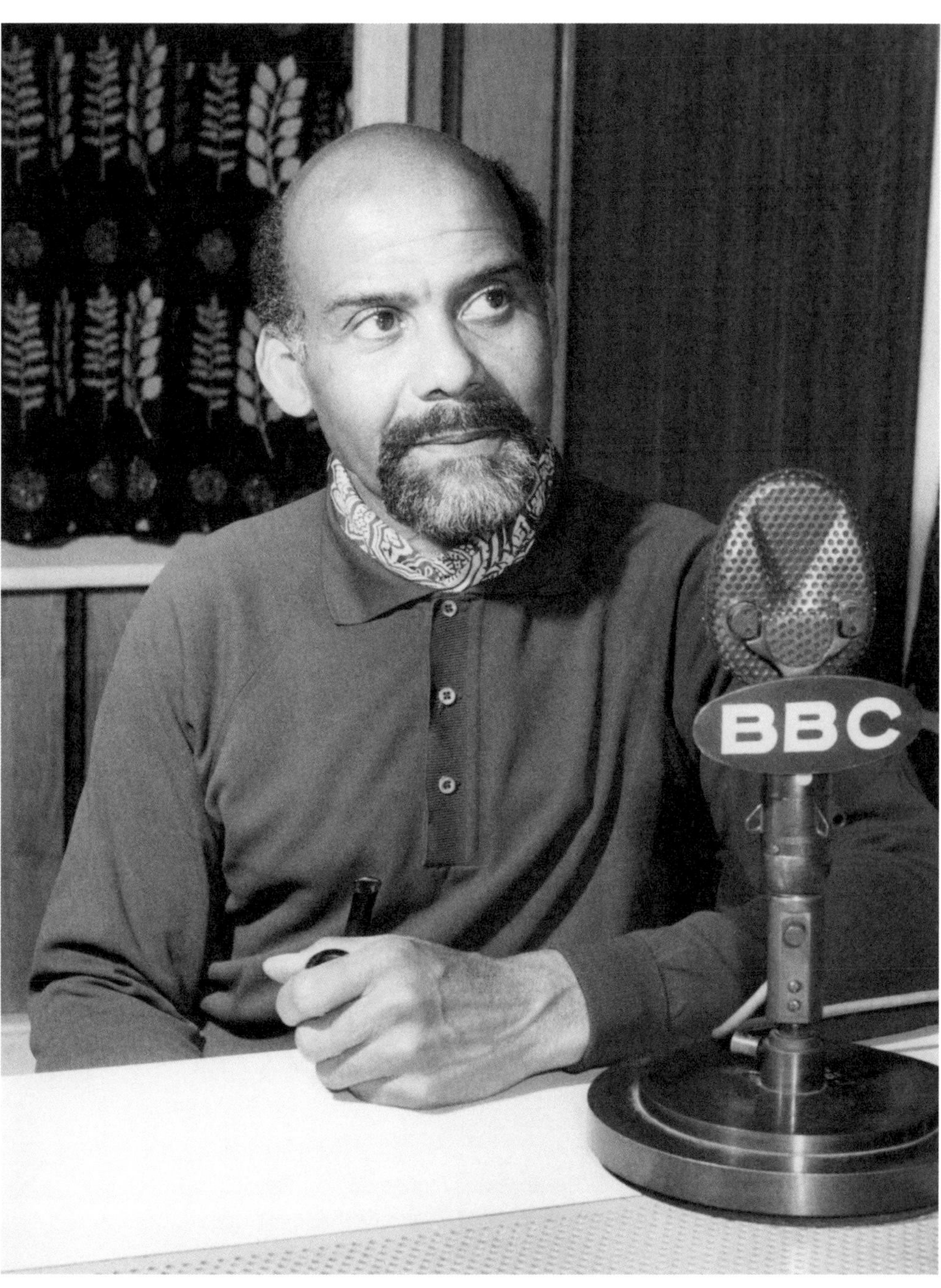

Ronald Moody during the BBC Caribbean Service
broadcast 'The Role of the Artist in the New Society', 1962

warmed when I heard, 'A very great improvement, Ronald.' Then there was a pause, followed by an ominous 'but'; and the number of 'buts' which followed made me wonder what I had done correctly. After I recovered from wondering if anyone existed who was as blind as I, once more I began all over again. This continued until I began to see my faults for myself. Then every few months I would have a 'field day', smashing up all I had done to date.

Well, things went on more or less like this until I found a one-room flat let with a greenhouse. Here I was my own cook, housemaid and general factotum. There was a pleasant garden and by now I knew in the very depths of my being that sculpture was the only thing I really wanted to do, and that simply nothing would prevent me from doing it whatever the sacrifices and difficulties might be. In short, I had become an out and out 'black sheep'. I settled in and decided that the time had come to carve in wood. Now wood is a difficult material. You can't dispose of it as easily as a plaster cast or a clay model. Any mistakes stare accusingly at you forever, and it requires a great deal of physical energy and concentration to give it form, apart from any other consideration. Perhaps I should say, as well, that by this time the influence of Eastern philosophical thought and the magical way they expressed it in their art, particularly in their sculpture, had become a reality and standard for me. With such a goal and all the other difficulties you can well imagine that I hesitated before beginning. In fact, I was four months planning the head which later became *Wohin*.

Wohin was born in the greenhouse which leaked from every conceivable place. No sooner I stopped one leak than at least another six appeared. Well, I dodged what leaks I could and often till one or two in the morning, knowing that I had to get to work the next day, I battled away.

Some days I was in despair. 'Was I treating the forms as broadly and fully as I had hoped?' 'Were the planes melting as gently and imperceptibly into each other as I wanted?' And oh! - the aches and pains everywhere! But somehow I would start to work and after a few hours, my pessimism would give way to a sort of cautious pleasure. There were the mornings when to my surprise I would be fully awake at six (I am not by nature an early riser), would sneak out to have a look at my previous night's efforts and, of course, begin to work. Fortunately these days were few for I was seldom punctual on such occasions. So I went on resisting all the time any temptation to change my original design as I knew it would be fatal, and fighting a hundred and one fears.

At the end of four months Wohin was receiving his final polish. With many misgivings I was getting up enough courage to have him criticized. On the day, however, the 'buts' for once were almost non-existent. I wouldn't believe it and suspected a sudden access of politeness or kindliness - but no. I was eventually persuaded that it was not so. Now Wohin is sold and his owner has gone to America.

After this work followed work born in an atmosphere of agony, doubt and that indescribable pleasure which is like an inner glow, brightening the faculties and bringing peace when things go fairly well.

I sent one or two pieces to exhibitions. The portraits and modelled works were accepted but the carvings returned. However, I was convinced that the carvings were more important. So on the advice of a friend, I decided to see what Paris thought about them. I went over and arranged an exhibition and the results proved that I was right. The following year I went to live in Paris.

Good night, West Indies.

'Discovering Art'
'The Artist's Environment' by Ronald Moody of Jamaica

Good evening, West Indies. The last time I spoke to you, I ended with saying that I gave an exhibition in Paris. That took place in November 1937 at the Galerie Billiet, rue La Boétie.

On the morning of the private view as I was busy putting the final 'spit and polish' on the various pieces, I gradually became aware of a man who had appeared from nowhere, trailing around the room and generally getting in my way. I am just about to ask the owner of the gallery whether the man knew that the private view didn't start until the afternoon, when he would be free to tramp about the place to his heart's content, then he turned to me and said, 'Would you like to have a prize?' 'Of course; how many can you spare?' I replied. 'Oh, but I am serious, would you like a prize? The gentlemen here is on the committee judging the sculpture at the world exhibition, but all the prizes to the British section have already been awarded. You can't change your nationality for a day or two I suppose, he so likes your work he would award you a prize.' Well, nationalities aren't easily changed but you can see how useful it would be to have a handful of passports put by for such occasions as these!

Although I didn't get my prize, the exhibition was on the whole successful. The critics appreciated my carvings and said some very nice things about them. That year the autumn was marvellous, as any of you who came over would remember; the World Exhibition offered us, among other things, the food and wine of many different countries which I tasted and enjoyed.

Settling down in Paris had its difficulties. I knew little French when I went over, and what I know was more than strained when I tried to get the delightful little two-floor studio and home combined that I had found, decorated. The man I got to do it up talked incessantly in an accent of the Midi, which is as different from Parisian French as that of a Londoner from a broad Yorkshireman. You who have met these differences will appreciate my difficulties. My knowledge of colloquial French increased perforce enormously even though heard through the booming and staccato voice of the decorator.... The artists were a truly international crowd, coming from almost every country in the world. Consequently, the clash of minds from so many countries was most stimulating and helpful.

Surrealism was on the wane. I personally think that it may be of great therapeutic value for the artist, but seldom rises to what I consider a work of art. When it does, it ceases to be Surrealism. The works of Hieronymus Bosch, a fifteenth-century Dutch painter whom the Surrealists claim as one of their ancestors, is an example. His reason for doing such work was entirely different from the Surrealists of today. He was a monk getting his sins out of his system. Surrealists claim their way is a mode of life as well as an art expression.

For me, broadly speaking, there are two kinds of art. Art concerned with the looking-glass reflection of Nature and art concerned with 'the imitation of nature in her manner of operation'.

The last phrase comes from a definition of art by St Thomas Aquinas, 'Art is an imitation of nature, in her manner of operation.' Unfortunately I haven't time to enlarge on these thoughts, but will do so on another occasion soon, I hope.... Surrealism, I am inclined to think, is both a symptom of decadence and a blind attempt to fight it. By decadence I mean the state where the vision of stable and unchanging truths has become obscured.

But to resume, one discussed to all hours of the night one's ideas on art in the cafes over an inexpensive cup of coffee or wine. All this contributed to that indefinable something in the atmosphere which is particular to Paris and which makes hard work a pleasure. It is very difficult to convey this atmosphere so much like champagne and yet where the artist can find peace and time for contemplation. One must live there to find this Paris. The tourist may do it accidentally, but this is rare; it is more through hard and serious work that it reveals itself....

Nor will I ever forget the magic of Spring in Paris. Faces seem to open and eyes shine. One detected a lightly concealed note of joy in the voices of people, breathing again after the long, cold winter. The cafes come out in their new dress of paint. On the Seine the barges, newly painted, seem to dance on the water and the trees on the 'grande Boulevards' appear to be infected with the same mood. One finds oneself walking with a more jaunty air and would not be at all surprised if the person in front suddenly did a little dance.

I had worked hard during the winter in preparation for the coming exhibition and felt that the spring was a just reward. Well, my work was shown in some of the current exhibitions and I used to have a few pieces in the yearly exhibition called the 'Salon des Tuileries'. I must confess that I felt rather pleased that my pieces were included in the handful of works picked out from among something like twelve thousand odd pictures, sculptures, etc., for praise. In 1939, I was invited to send over thirteen pieces to America. They were exhibited in the Baltimore Museum, Boston.

Then Hitler decided to end my career, and my wife and I found ourselves keeping a steady thirty kilometres in front of his armies on our walk to the South until they caught us up. We got away again and continued our walk until we got to Marseilles. There I caught Pleurisy.

When I was sufficiently better to move about, my wife was repatriated, but being of military age I was interned. About six months later, on my third attempt, I succeeded in escaping over the Pyrenees and started another walking tour, this time through Spain, finally reaching Gibraltar and arriving in England at the end of 1941.

That one passport was most useful in the end.

Goodnight, West Indies.

'Egyptian Art' by Ronald Moody of Jamaica

> 'Why do we tacitly assume that the artist and craftsman today are better than those in any other age?'
>
> 'Yes,' I replied, 'It has all been done before.'

This was the opening of a conversation I had with an Englishman as we were looking at a glass case in the British Museum. From it shone some exquisite rings in gold and lapis lazuli, necklaces and other ornaments made during the reign of the Pharaohs or Kings of Egypt over three thousand years ago. I was particularly struck by the perfect craftsmanship shown in a wooden comb. The fine and coarse teeth were beautifully made - bear in mind that in those days there were no machines to do this work. If you ever get to the British Museum do have a look at it. Its number is exhibit 51071.

As I take great delight in Egyptian art, it is with added pleasure that I speak to you about it this evening.

A story runs that Napoleon, in a fit of temper, fired at the Sphinx. Certainly it was a Napoleonic expedition which led to the investigation of the country and its monuments. Another cause was the search of modern art for simplicity. This they found in the bold, massive forms and daring simplifications of its sculpture.

In my previous talk I emphasised the important part religion played as the chief source of inspiration in Primitive art. This is also true of Egyptian art. Ra, the sun god, was supposed to be the physical father of the Pharaoh, who was the earthly embodiment of the god and so was a beneficent and divine ruler, divinely appointed. This rendered him free from mortal failing and, theoretically at least, infallible in all his actions.

The King, as the son of Ra, was naturally the high priest of this all-powerful god, his father, and was supposed to perform the temple services all over the land. In practice they were taken by high priests and priests of the god.

When the King died, he returned to the sun from which he had come forth. There he enjoyed eternal bliss in the company of Ra and his divine following.

A strong desire for immortality was indirectly responsible for much of the art of Egypt. The welfare of the person's soul in the next world was in some way closely bound up with the preservation of his earthly body from corruption as it lay in the tomb. Hence the custom of mummification. This is a process by which the dead body was preserved from the ordinary process of decay. The nearest thing to it today is embalming.

In order to make his Journey in the next world, called 'The Field of Reeds', it was necessary that he should be surrounded by reminders of his earthly life. It was believed that the dead continued to live their earthly life forever in a state of bliss in the next world.

Hence, if he was rich enough, on the walls of his tomb and on his coffin were painted and carved scenes from his life on earth. In the bandaged body were inserted jeweled amulets for its protection, and food was offered by his relations to help sustain him on his Journey.

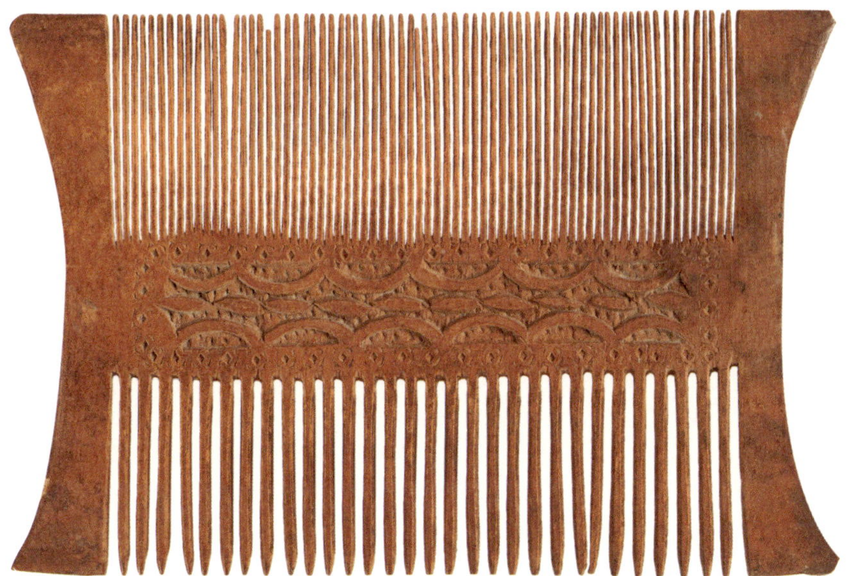

The part of the dead person which could enjoy this afterlife was called Ka. It is the eternal replica of the person which comes into being with his birth but exists in the spirit world. When a person died he went and joined his Ka in the next world, which from then on looked after him. For instance, a Ka could inhabit the dead man's portrait statues and enjoy the food left by his relations.

This brings me to another point worth remembering when considering Egyptian art. It was functional, in the sense that it was used for a definite purpose. But first let me tell you of another belief of the Egyptians which will underline this statement. It was in what they called 'Life force'; that is, that which makes a creature live. This force not only animated plants, fish, reptiles, animals and the human race, but could be communicated to works created by man. For instance, a model of a snake in clay, a relief of a person carved on a tomb. These could become as real as their living counterparts. But this could only happen if the objects were subjected to the

Comb, Coptic Egypt, wood,
11.3 × 0.8 × 7.8 cm (4 ½ × ⅜ × 3 ⅛ in.)

influence of the hike - we would call this magic. This hike was a supernatural force accessible to both gods and men. If, by some mischance, the food offerings of the living relation should cease, with the help of the hike the artist's work would become real in a sense no present day artist could believe his work to be, however useful this might prove in these days of rationed food!

I have dwelt on the religious background of Egypt at such length because it is inextricably bound with its art. No doubt you are already seeing this. The support and comfort of the dead by the living gave employment to the painter, sculptor and all branches of craft.

From its earliest time, which in Egypt is before history, works of art show a perfection in technique and real creative instinct. So far, what has been dug up of this period is small statues. The greatest attention was paid to detail but not at the expense of the general design or form. They have been described as 'miracles of form'. Glazed bronze figures were made, probably with coloured clay, which was later fired in a kiln. A great deal of jewelry was also made, and engravings on slate and other materials give a history of the time. This kind of work continued during the first historic period, called the Old Kingdom. Animals, as well as human figures, were done with equal perfection and the sculptures were felt in the open without the need of a wall or some background for support in order to bring out the full effect. You could walk round them and find interest in looking from all sides.

Architecture and sculpture developed. Statues of a colossal scale were built during this period which covered over eight hundred years. Many statues of the various gods were made.

I have spoken of Ra, the sun god and father of the Pharaoh. Perhaps it would be interesting to describe him to you. In his statues he has the body of a man and the head of a hawk. On his head is a disc representing the sun, surrounded by a serpent. He is clad in a short kilt from which an animal's tail hangs down. His form and name changed from time to time. In very early times he had an entirely human form, wore the double crown of Egypt representing the union of the North and South and was called 'Atum'. Towards the end of this period and during the next, called the Middle Kingdom, he becomes 'Amun-Ra'.

I have seen bronzes and carvings of this god that have all the majestic calm and greatness one associates with the portrait of a god, despite the incongruous mixture of animal and human. Often they were only a few inches high.

The portraits made at this period were not personal in the sense we adopt the term today. The sitter, especially if he was a king, was shown 'in the image of God' rather than marred by the impact of life. Noble traits were emphasised, showing the incorruptible essence of man. How could the son of Ra be anything but divine and noble....

After this period there was chaos. Egypt was invaded by a Semitic race called the Hyksos, the shepherd kings. It took a hundred years for her to throw off this yoke. Then followed an era called the New Kingdom. The Arts were restored to their brilliance. It was during this period that the well-known portrait of Queen Nefertiti was made. She is in the Berlin Museum. Hitler considered her so beautiful that he refused to part with her, though she certainly ought to have been included in what the Nazis at that time called degenerate art.

As the New Kingdom was coming to a close, there appeared a series of dynasties foreign in origin; the Libyan, Ethiopian, Setian and late times. Art tended to get more and more decorative and personal until we come to the time Rome conquered Egypt and the Greeks began to pour in, anxious to learn all that they could. Herodotus gives a glowing account of what he saw in his second book. Egyptian civilization virtually ended.

It is a pity that I have not been able to tell you about the pyramids, the purest form of architecture projected into space. Nor can I touch on the splendours of the tomb of Tutankhamun discovered in 1915; nor speak of the time of Akhenaten. He introduced something akin to Christianity into Egypt, and for a time influenced the Egyptian tradition in sculpture. But if I have stimulated you to continue the study of the culture and art of Egypt, I shall be content.

Goodnight.

Transcripts of broadcasts by Ronald Moody for the BBC Overseas Service: *A Sculptor* (1946), *The Artist's Environment* (1946), *Egyptian Art* (1950), published with permission from the Ronald Moody Trust and the BBC.

CHAPTER 5

Ronald Moody's (Self) Portraits

In 1947, the Moodys moved to a flat at 78 Redcliffe Square, London, where they would live together for the rest of their lives. That same year, Moody was diagnosed with tuberculosis, confined to bed for over five months and forced to postpone forthcoming exhibitions. With heavy work out of the question, he limited himself to modelling portraits.[23]

Moody began sculpting imaginative heads, masks and portraits of friends in plaster and plastercine during the 1920s, when still training to be a dentist. During the early years of his artistic career, he not only produced some of his most remarkable and imaginative sculptures as busts in wood, but also positioned himself as a society portraitist.[1] Through the decades, Moody's portraits could be considered the most consistent part of his practice and can be a way of exploring his approach to raw materials. A survey of some of these portraits made in the inter- and post-war period, and information gleaned from the biographies of some of the Moody's sitters – both key transnational figures and close family – provide essential cultural and historical background; they weave their stories and connections into the narrative of Moody's artistic life.

Between 1934 and 1936, Moody produced a portrait of his lifelong friend, the journalist and founding director of the Academy Cinema in London, Elsie Cohen.[2] In 1928, Cohen had hired a run-down cinema in the centre of London for a year and successfully showed many newly released Russian and German films. She then persuaded the owner of another cinema in a more prominent position on Oxford Street to let her relaunch it as the Academy Cinema, with a similar programme. It became the first and most prestigious British arthouse cinema. The Institute of Contemporary Arts (ICA) and the Marquee Club both originated in the basement of the Academy Cinema during its fifty-five-year history. The Academy Cinema closed its doors in 1986.[3] The bronze bust of Cohen is one of three portraits by Moody that are now part of the National Portrait Gallery's permanent collection, gifted by the Ronald Moody Trust in 2018.

The same year that he produced the bust of Cohen, Moody also produced bronze masks of two doyennes of Moroccan society, Madame Shoura de Muns and Vicomtesse de Almocade, which gave an indication

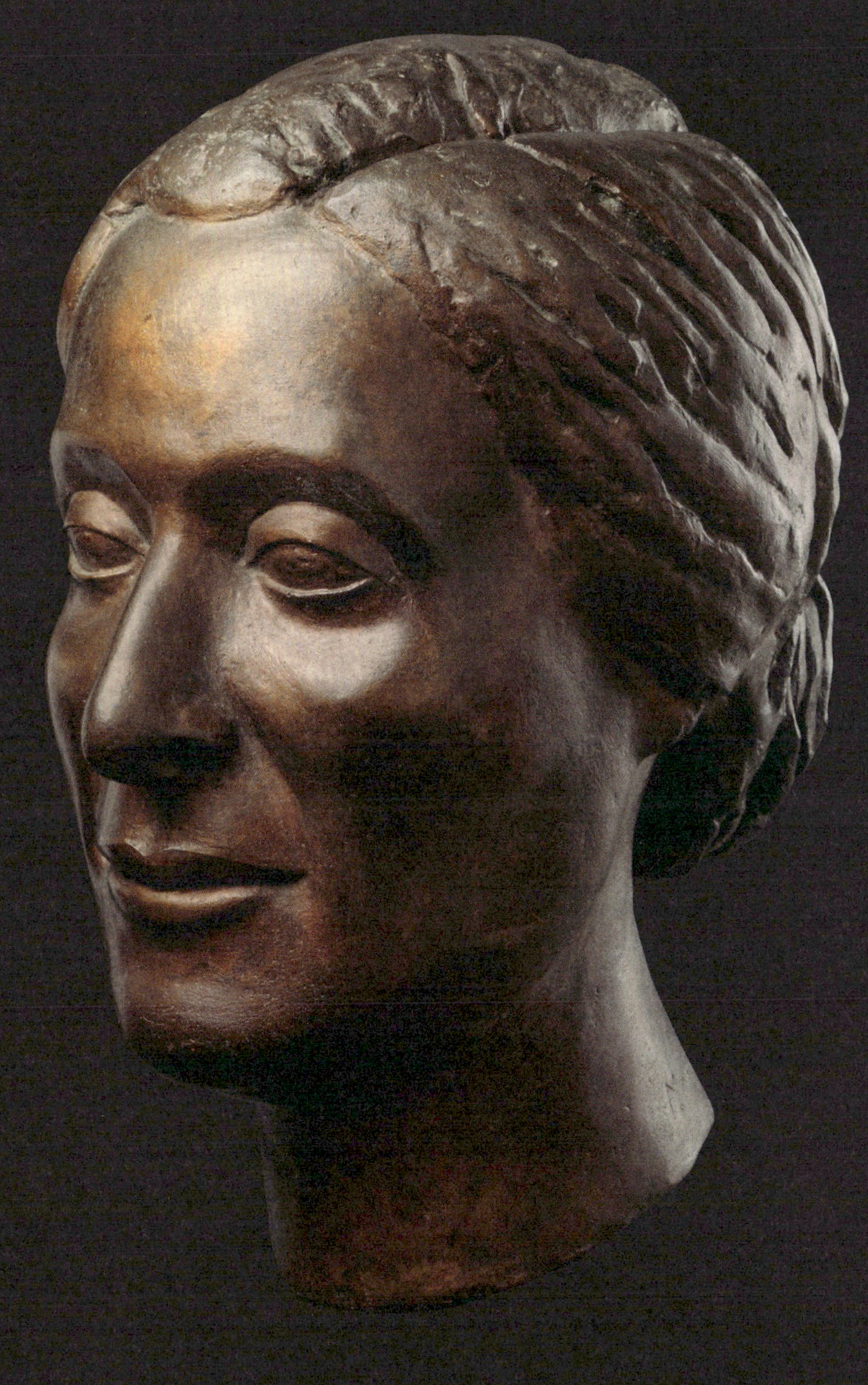

Ronald Moody, *Elsie Cohen*, 1934–36,
bronze, 35 × 21 cm (13 ⁷⁄₈ × 8 ³⁄₈ in.)

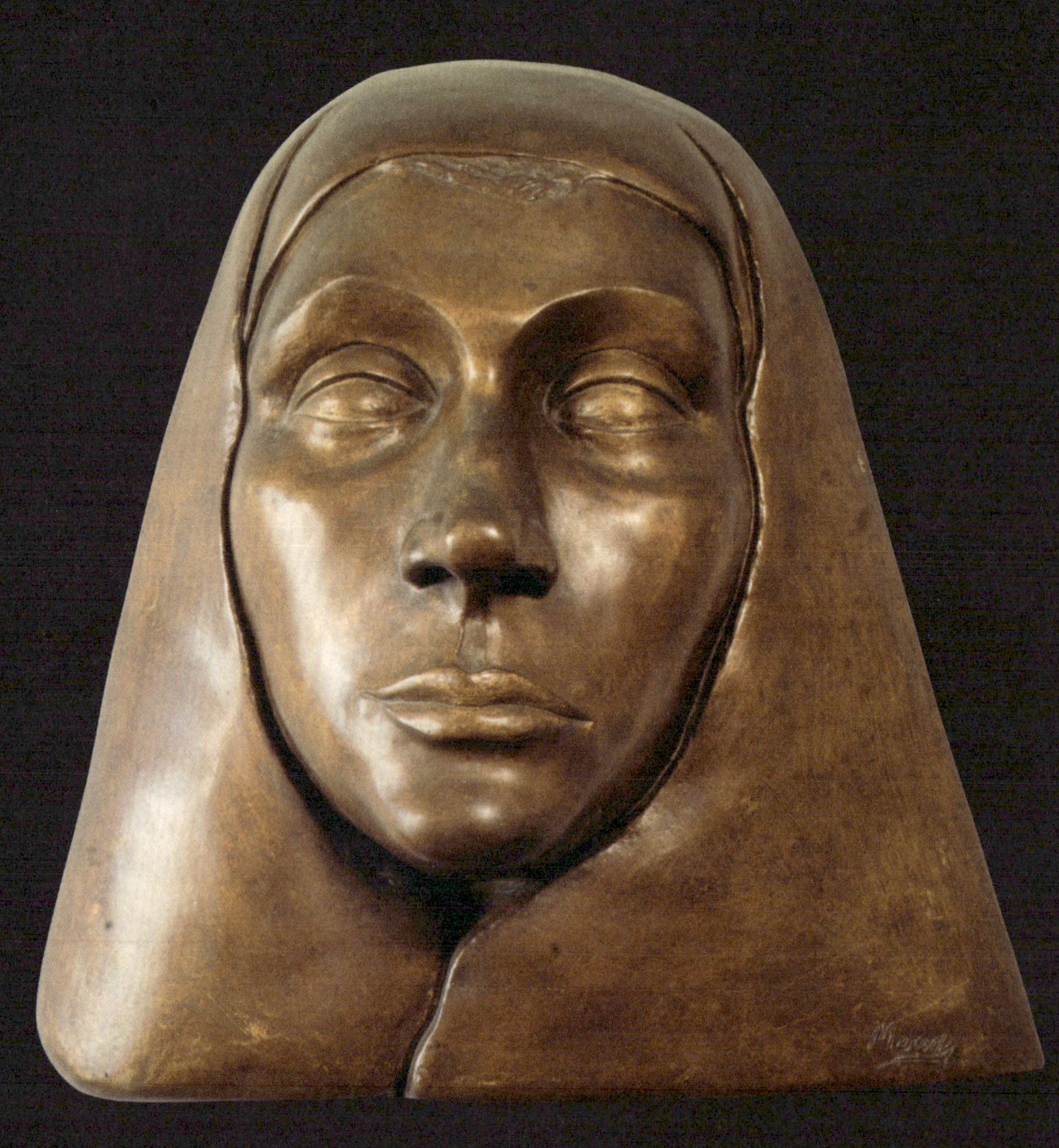

Ronald Moody, *Madame de Muns*, 1936, bronze, 32 × 32 × 13 cm (12 ⅝ × 12 ⅝ × 5 ⅛ in.)

of his potential. Madame de Muns, an aristocrat who had lived in Tangiers, is depicted wearing her hijab. The artwork was Moody's first use of the mask in portraiture: he was attracted to the ability of masks to express duality and the different layers of a personality.[4]

Moody later embarked on a series of self-portraits in bronze, but found his first attempt so dissatisfactory that he destroyed it. He preferred his second attempt, *Self-Portrait 2* (1937). His third, *Self-Portrait 3* (1937), is a version in elm. The three artworks are almost identical in form, but the bronze version presents a demure sombreness, while the stained woodgrain of the elm in the third version provides an expansive element to the contours of the face, adding animation and character.[5]

The more intimate portraits of Helene Coppel-Cowan bring his lifelong partner to the fore. He created six portraits of her through the decades, the last of which was poignantly created after her death in 1979.[6] The first was made in bronze in 1936, *Helene 1*; Moody then produced *Helene 2* in 1938 in highly patinated oak. *Helene 3* was made from elm; little is known about it apart from that it was exhibited at the Arcade Gallery exhibition, London, in 1946. Moody's terracotta head of 1950, *Helene 4*, depicts a weary, war-impacted and alert Helene. Another head of 1957 is now lost, its location unknown apart from a reference in a catalogue entry of the Society of Portrait Sculptors.[7]

In 1949, Moody is quoted in an article in the *Evening News* when discussing the long-awaited return of six of his sculptures that had been hastily abandoned at the outbreak of the Second World War. After months of negotiation and bureaucracy, the works were eventually brought back via London Airport by Dr M. Joseph Mitchell, who was at that time the general secretary of the League of Coloured Peoples. In the newspaper article, Moody disclosed that his favourite piece was the portrait of his wife, and that this was the first thing he looked for.[8]

Helene's correspondence with Moody held in his archive begins in 1932 and comprises 248 documents. Most of the letters exchanged are of a personal nature: sharing updates and news, or providing a window into his domestic life, and the majority cover their period apart when Moody was hospitalized and receiving treatment for tuberculosis. Her correspondence illustrates and expresses her dedication to and

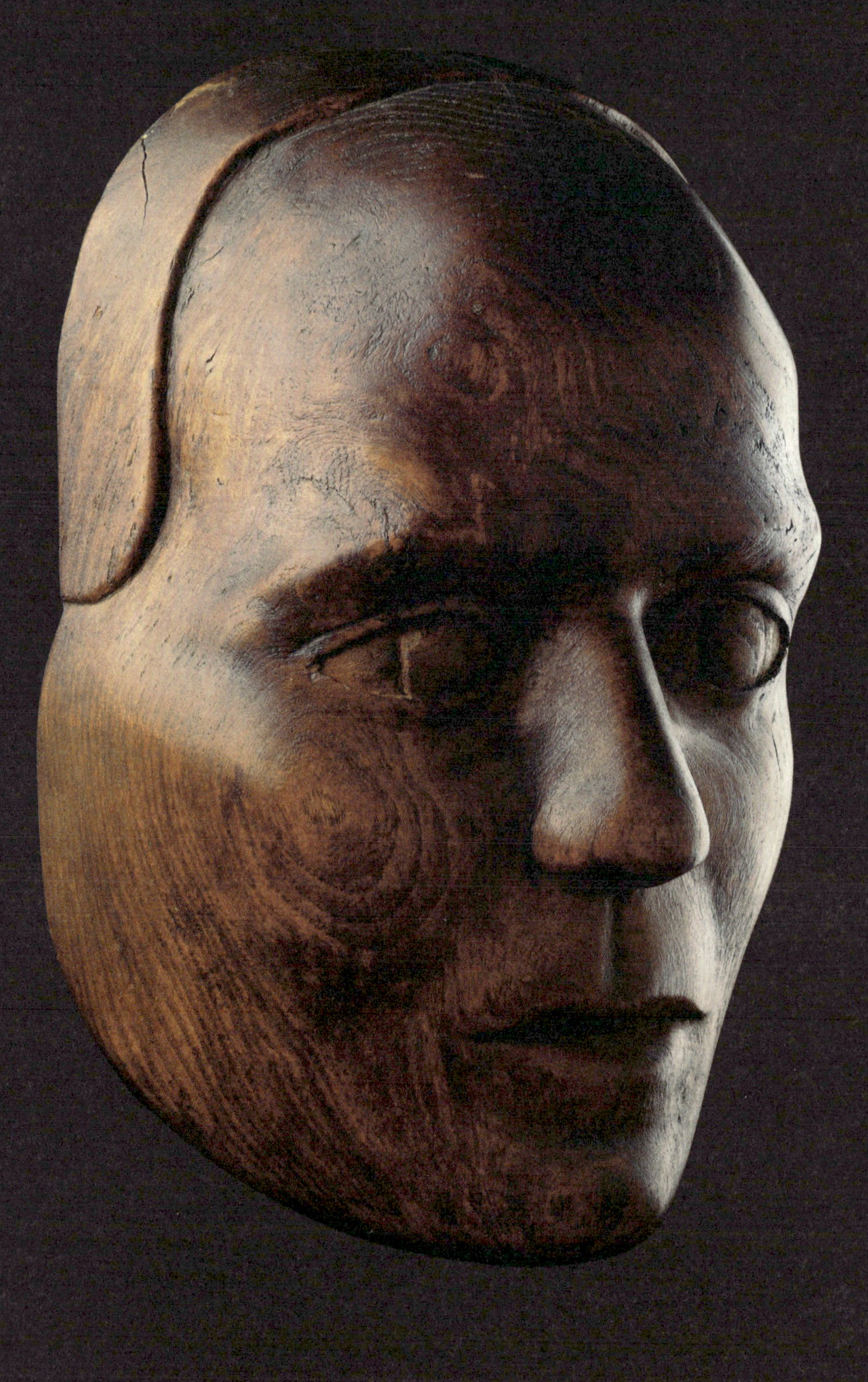

Ronald Moody, *Self-Portrait 3*, 1937, stained elm, 30 × 17 × 15 cm (11 7/8 × 6 3/4 × 6 in.)

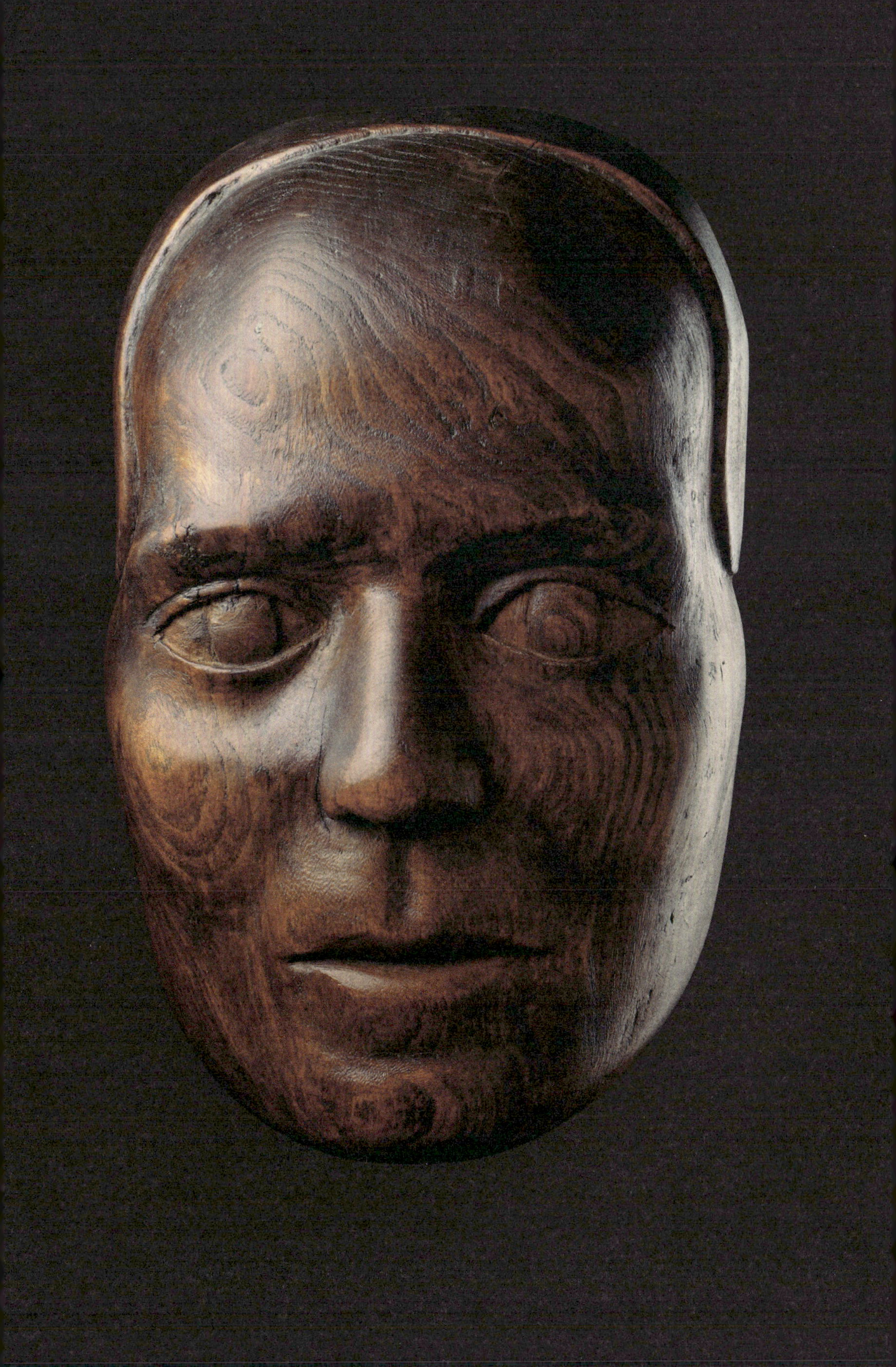

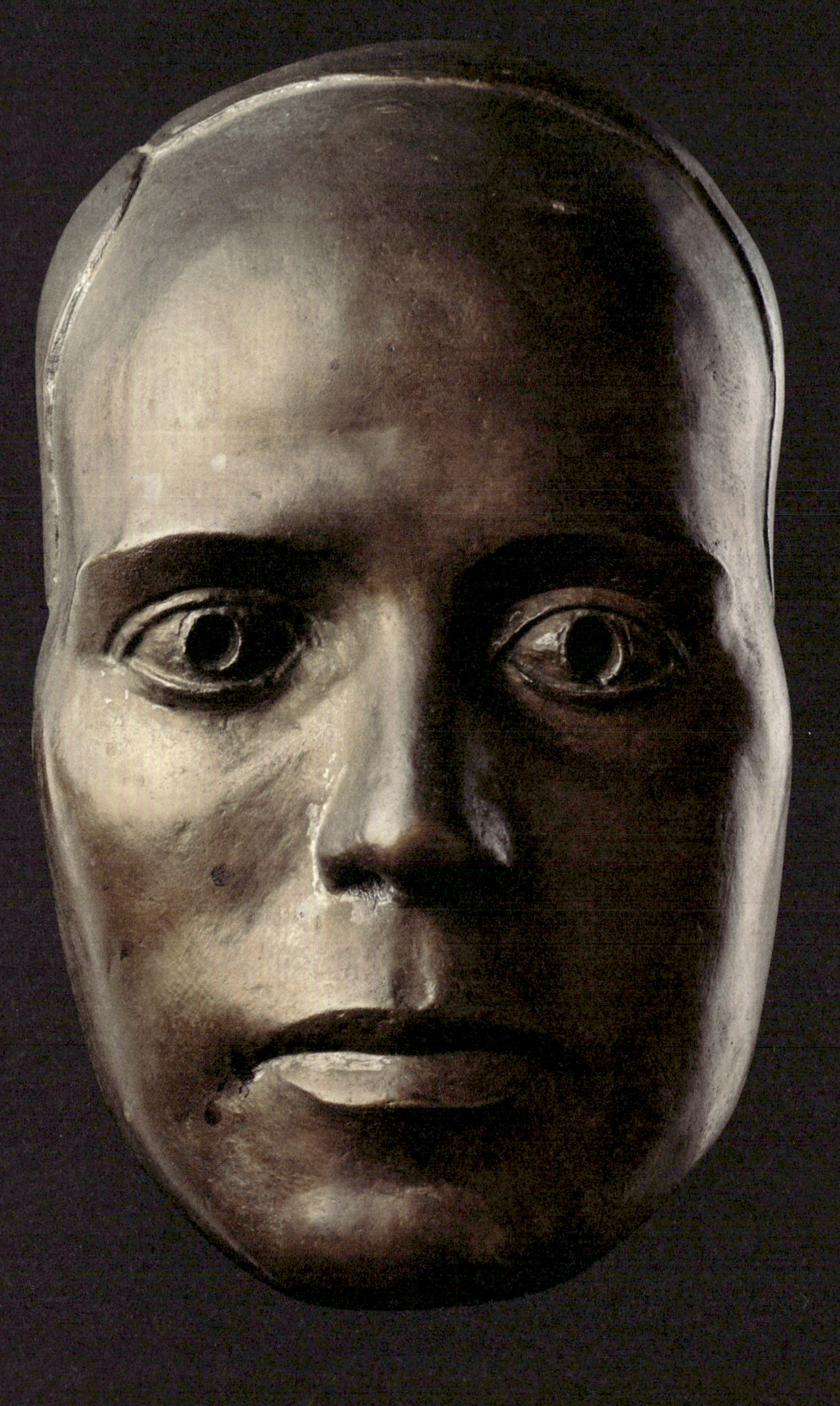

Ronald Moody, *Self-Portrait 2*, 1937,
bronze, 24 × 17 × 12 cm (9 ½ × 6 ¾ × 4 ¾ in.)

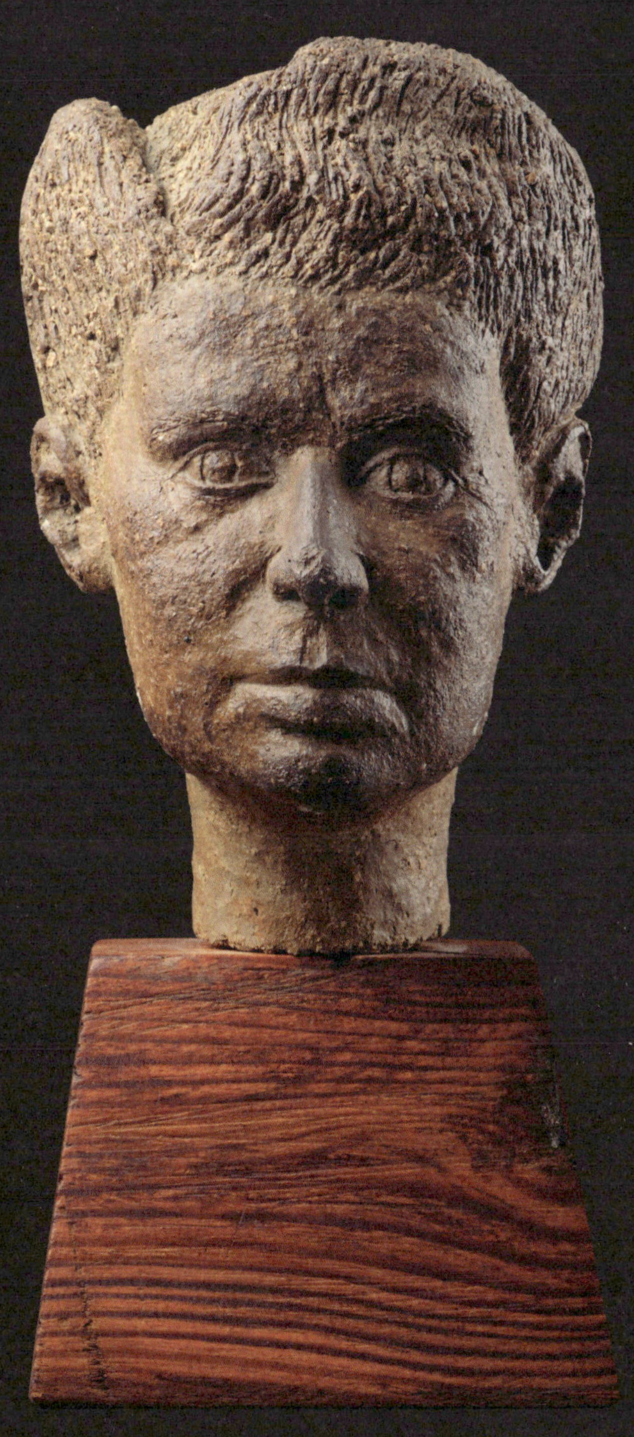

Ronald Moody, *Helene 4*, *c.* 1950, terracotta, height: 15 cm (6 in.)

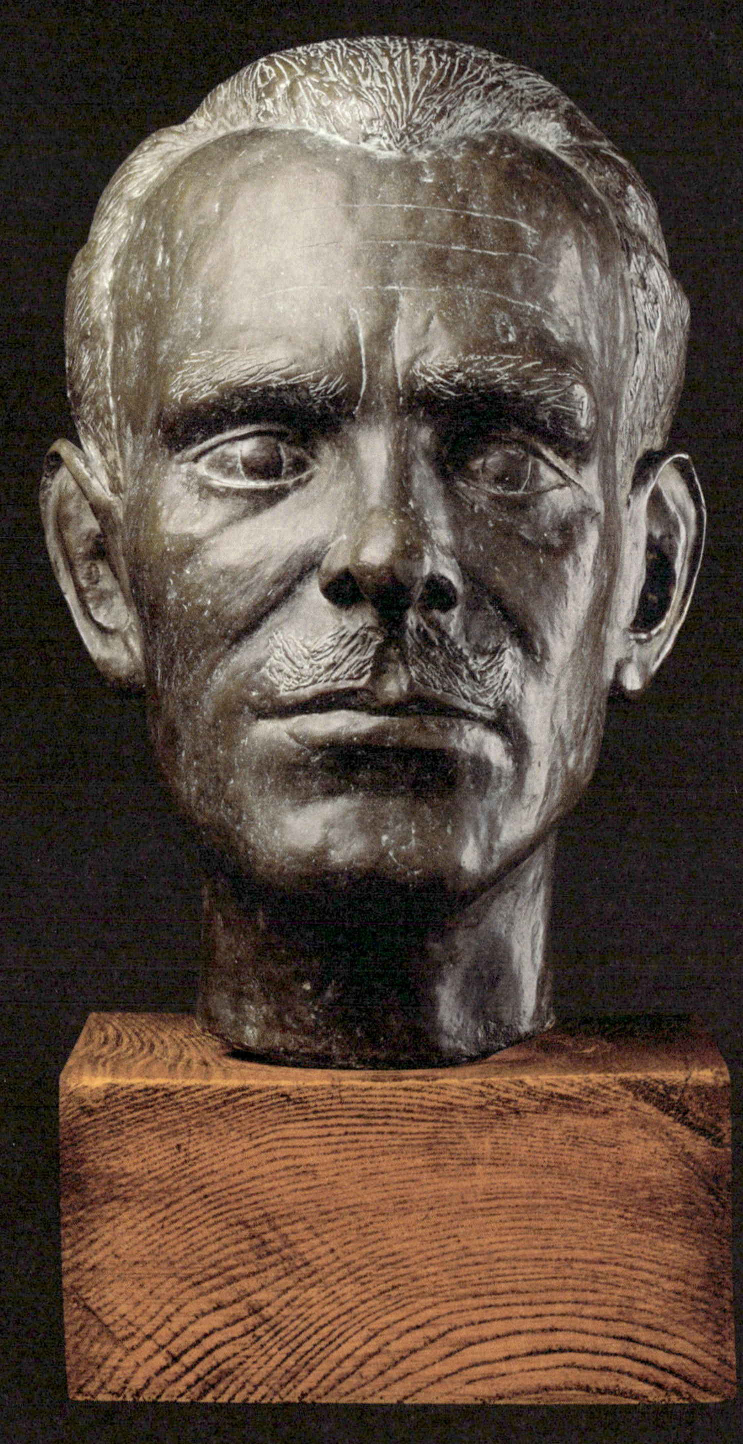

Ronald Moody, *Terry-Thomas*, 1953,
bronze, 33 × 18 × 24 cm (13 × 7 ⅛ × 9 ½ in.)

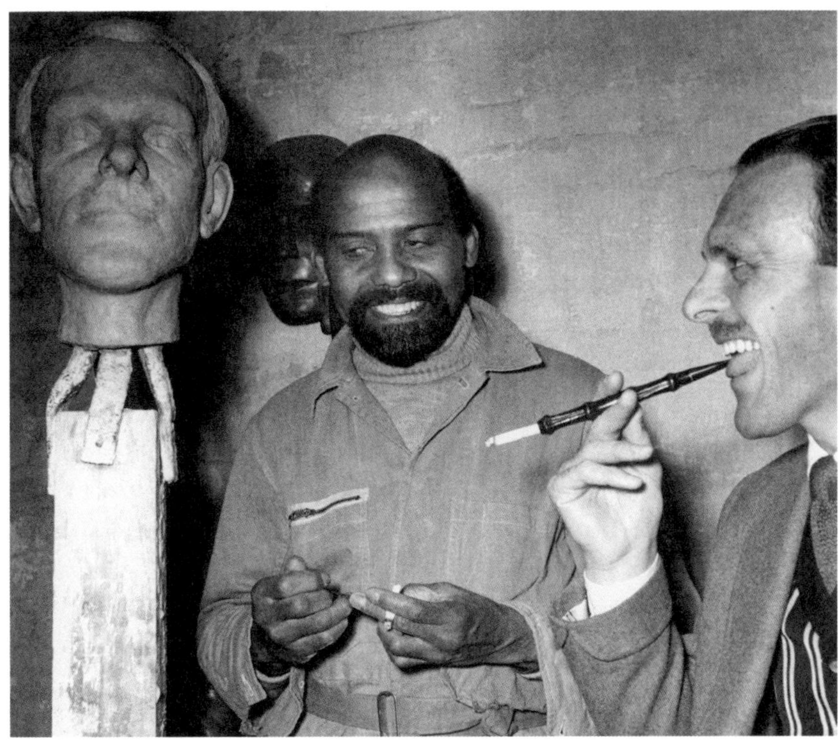

pride in Moody's work, practice and talent. During Moody's time in hospital, Helene describes going to see his exhibition in his absence, held at the Artists International Association (AIA) Gallery. She refers to his carved oak sculpture *Anima* (1944), the companion piece to *Vision* (1943). In a letter dated 23 June 1949, she wrote, '[Your] sculpture looks very fine on a revolving stand turning very slowly, all the time. There were crowds inside and a long queue waiting to go in. Your work is right in the middle of the room and had quite a crowd around it. Your name is in quite large letters.'[9]

In the late 1940s and '50s, Helene worked for actor and comedian Terry-Thomas (1911–1990).[10] In Graham McGann's aptly named biography *Bounder!* (2009), Helene is described as Thomas's 'long-standing' secretary, having worked for him for fifteen years. She was part of the team that ensured his morning newspaper was ironed and that he was always immaculate. Thomas was known for being quite meticulous,

Ronald Moody with Terry-Thomas and the clay model of his portrait at Tregor Studio, Fulham, 1953

and Helene kept an eye on his busy schedule.[11] The Moodys considered Thomas a friend, and evidence of their friendship is illustrated through a collection of handwritten greeting cards. This exchange between Thomas and the Moodys dates from the 1950s, when he was with his first wife, Pat Palanski (of whom Ronald also produced a portrait in 1950, his first work in concrete), to the 1970s, when Thomas was living in Ibiza with his then wife Belinda and their son. He addresses the Moodys in a familiar tone: 'Happy New Year Chaps, and of course bottoms up.'[12] Moody produced a bronze bust of Terry-Thomas in 1953, now considered a rare and more sombre portrayal of the actor – his signature gap-toothed grin is absent. Thomas passed away in 1990 after a lengthy battle with Parkinson's disease, in comparative obscurity, aged 78. Upon his death, Cynthia Moody donated the bust for auction to raise funds for the Parkinson's Disease Society in Bristol, where she lived. Cynthia had known the actor through her aunt and uncle, and described Thomas as 'great fun', and the bronze as 'a portrait of a friend.'[13]

In 1946, Moody created a portrait of his brother Harold Moody. By this time, Harold was distinguished among prominent figures such as C. L. R. James, George Padmore and Marcus Garvey as a progressive intellectual.[14] Harold Moody's portrait could arguably be the most significant portrait that the artist made in bronze. Cynthia Moody described it as 'outstanding' and that it did him 'full justice'. In 1953, a bronze copy was bought by public subscription and presented to the London Missionary Society for which Harold had been Chair. The portrait was placed in the London Missionary Society's library at Livingstone House and remained there until at least 1968. It was exhibited at the Society of Portrait Sculptors exhibition 'Portrait Tributes' in 1968, in honour of people of all nationalities who fought for human rights. When the portrait was requested for Rasheed Araeen's seminal exhibition 'The Other Story' at the Hayward Gallery in 1989, it was discovered missing. A copy of the bronze was later secured with the support of Cynthia and the encouragement of Stephen Bourne, a historian and Harold Moody expert. Bourne persuaded Southwark Council arts department to bid for it at auction, which led to the bronze portrait being placed

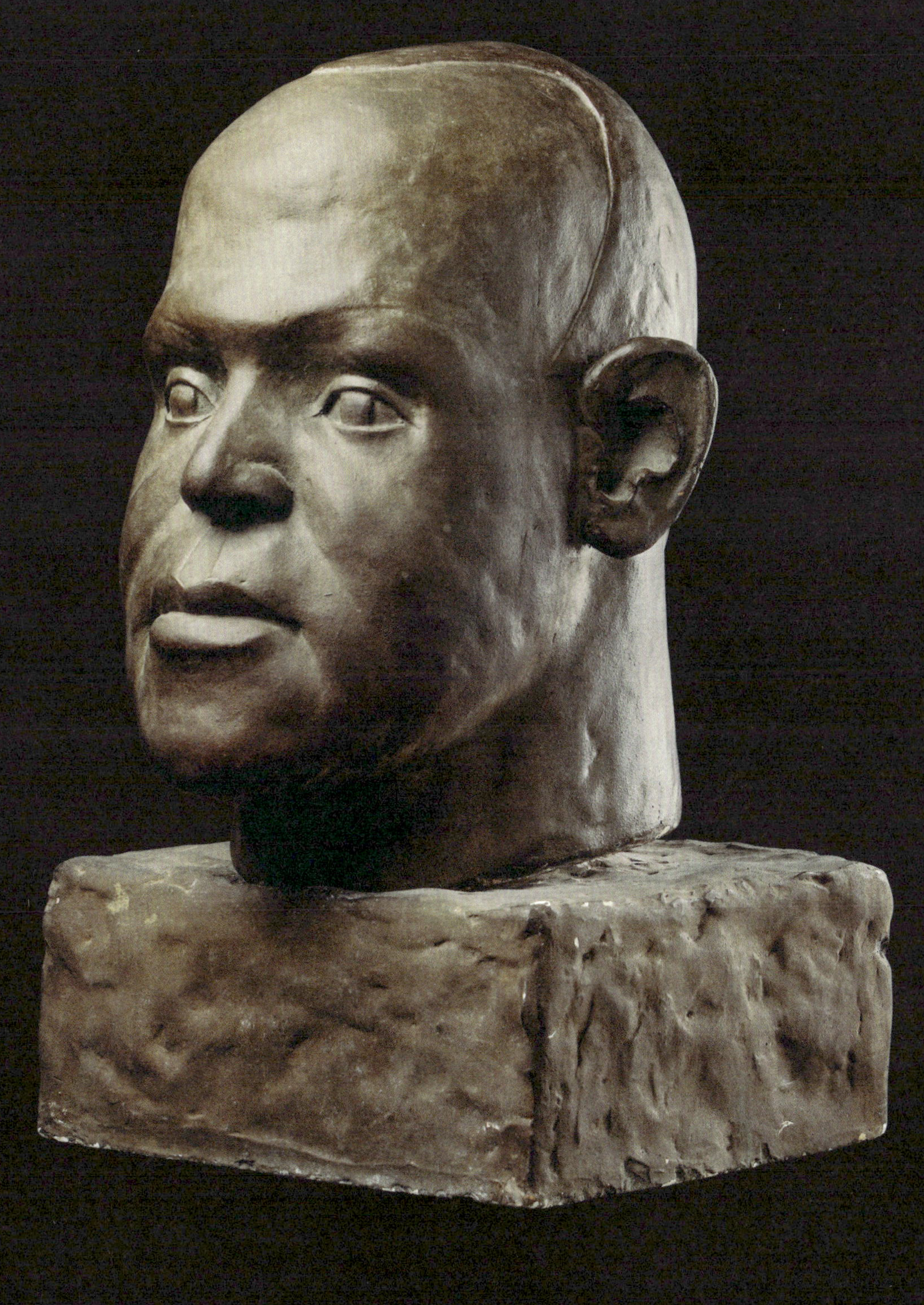

Ronald Moody, *Portrait Bust of Harold Moody*, 1946, painted plaster, height: 33 cm (13 in.)

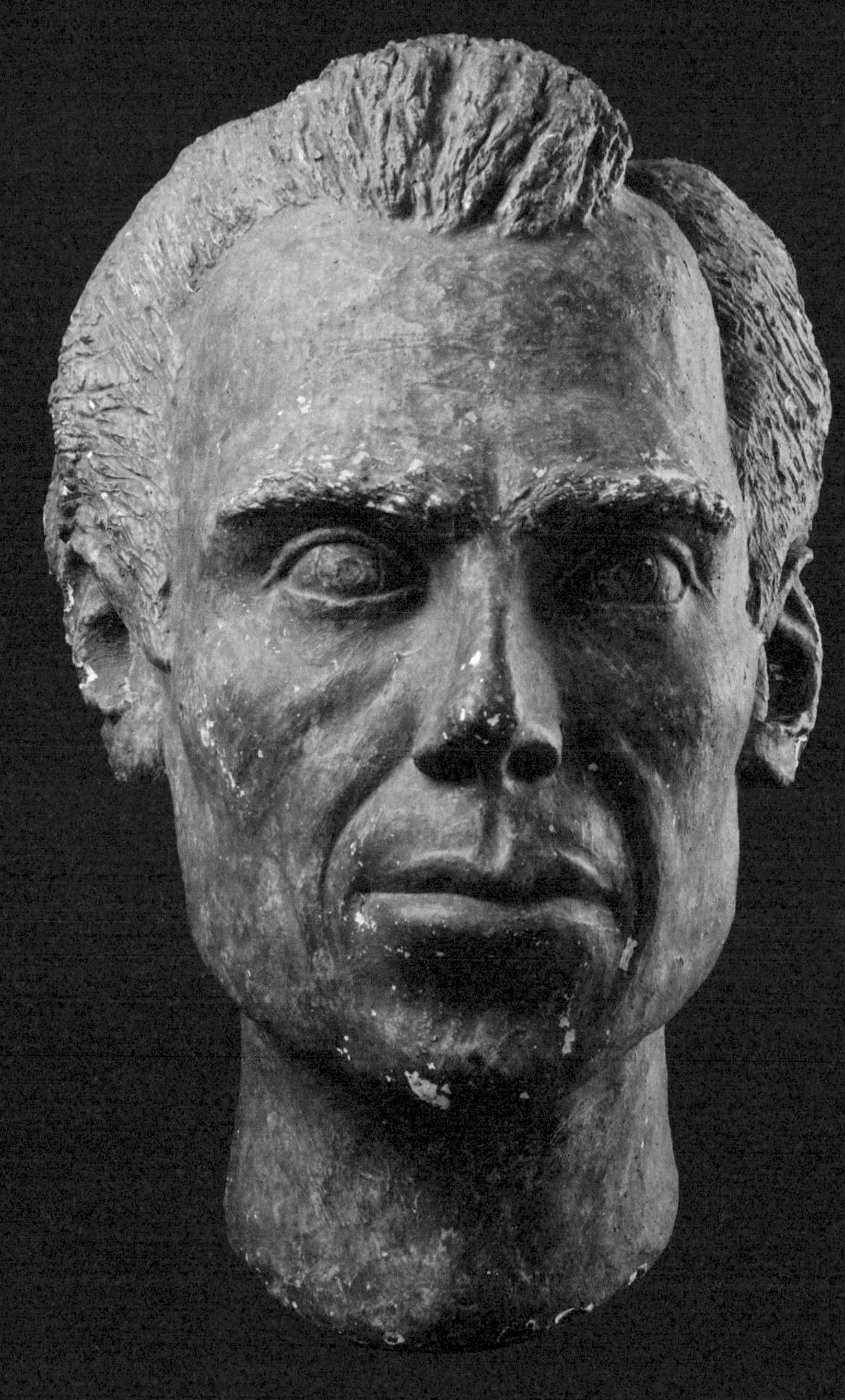

Ronald Moody, *Christopher Logue*, 1959,
ciment fondu, 38 × 23 × 33 cm (15 × 9 1/8 × 13 in.)

on permanent public display in Peckham Library, the London borough in which Dr Harold Moody had lived.[15]

Throughout the 1950s, Moody continued his exploration in portraiture; between 1950 and 1957, he made approximately fifteen portrait heads. He was constantly evolving his techniques during this period, creating several portraits in ciment fondu and terracotta. Moody joined the Society of Portrait Sculptors[16] – the representative body of professional sculptors committed to making portrait and figurative sculpture accessible to a wider public – just three years after it was founded in 1953. From 1954 to 1971 he was a regular exhibitor at their annual exhibitions, which showcased a community of contemporary British portrait sculptors. He was also a regular exhibitor at the Kensington Artists Exhibition (1953–59).[17] He showed work with distinguished groups such as Kensington Artists, Chelsea Artists, the London Group and the Royal Academy, and in 1959, the year that Jacob Epstein died, he was elected to the Council of the Society of Portrait Sculptors. Epstein was an honorary member of the Society of Portrait Sculptors and had exhibited with them regularly.[18]

Notably, that year, Moody produced a portrait in concrete of poet, playwright and political activist Christopher Logue (1926–2011). At the time it was being sculpted, in a letter addressed to Louis Wulff,[19] Moody noted that Logue had written the lyrics for *The Lily-White Boys*, which would be playing in the Court Theatre the following year. He also noted that Logue had recently recorded *Red Bird: Jazz and Poetry* with the musician and composer Tony Kinsey (b. 1927): a combination of jazz and Logue's versions of poems by Pablo Neruda (1904–1973).[20] Logue was responsible for some of the first poster poems and was a life-long advocate of performance verse, having published numerous collections of politically engaged and jazz-influenced poetry. He is known for his epic poem 'War Music', a modern rendition of *The Iliad*, Homer's ancient Greek account of the siege of Troy; he retains the original storyline, creating a bold hybrid of translation, adaption and invention. Logue reinvigorates the piece through his lived experience of war and the ability to implant his dramatic storytelling voice in the ancient work.[21] Moody's sculpture of Logue was included in the 1959 Annual Portrait Sculptors exhibition, alongside his portrait of biologist, botanist and environmental activist Richard St Barbe Baker (1889–1982), made in 1955. Moody had been working confidently with the medium of concrete for a while by this point; he was in his 'concrete period', which lasted for about twelve years.[22] During this productive time, Moody produced *The Mother* (1958–59) and *Man* (1959), *The Youth* (1960) and *Little Man* (1962), collectively described as the *Concrete Family*. In his artwork *Reclining Figure* of 1959–60, Moody continued his exploration of contrasting textures with his use of concrete and fibreglass. The final nodulous surface of the figure is enhanced by the coarse knobbles of the base and is reminiscent of the composition and interplay between textures of an earlier carving, the 1938 oak sculpture *Le Repos*.[23] In July of 1959, Moody leased a purpose-built artist's studio at Fleming Close Studios, Limerston Street, London, where he worked until his death. Sculptor Elisabeth Frink (1930–1993) occupied a studio adjacent to his, and they frequently chatted as neighbours.[24]

Many of Moody's portraits of significant figures are now lost, a situation sometimes symbolically but unknowingly mirroring the erasure of their sitters from the dominant histories of their own fields. An example is Moody's 1960 portrait of Rudolph Dunbar (1899–1988) – the whereabouts of this work is unknown. Dunbar was a conductor, clarinettist, composer and journalist. Cynthia Moody refers to a reproduction of the work in an article written by Dunbar in the *Jamaican Daily Gleaner* on Ronald Moody, titled 'Sculptor of Distinction', as the only visual record of the portrait.[25] The article is referred to in a letter from Dunbar to Moody dated 5 May 1964, the same year that Moody's public artwork *Savacou* was installed on the University of the West Indies' Mona Campus in Kingston. In his letter, Dunbar thanked Moody for providing source material for the article, hoping that the *Jamaican Daily Gleaner* would give him a 'good spread'.

Both Moody and Dunbar were members of the United Kingdom Committee for the exhibition of contemporary arts 'Trends and Confrontations' section of the First World Festival of Negro Arts,

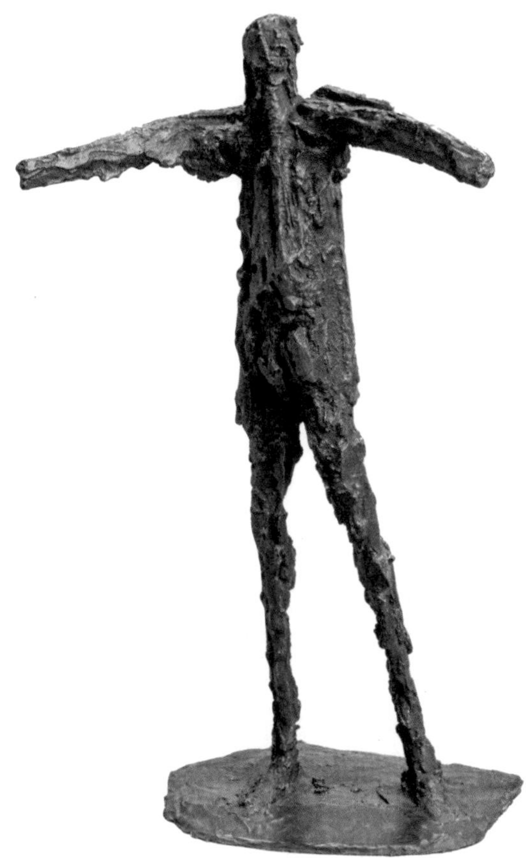

held in Dakar in 1966. Minutes of the Société Africaine de Culture United Kingdom sub-committee chart the selection process of the committee alongside the trials and tribulations of the festival that was initially supposed to take place in 1963.[26]

Sadly, little is known about Moody's portrait of Dunbar, except that it was made from concrete and fibreglass and that it was exhibited three times, the first being at the Society of Portrait Sculptors Eighth Annual Exhibition in 1960. It was then exhibited at the West Indian Prime Minister's Independence Conference in 1961, and that same year it was exhibited as part of his solo exhibition at the Woodstock Gallery alongside nineteen of his other artworks.[27] The same materials and method of casting an amalgam of concrete and fibreglass can

Elisabeth Frink, *Birdman V*, 1959,
bronze, 45 × 19 × 17.5 cm (17 3/4 × 7 1/2 × 7 in.)

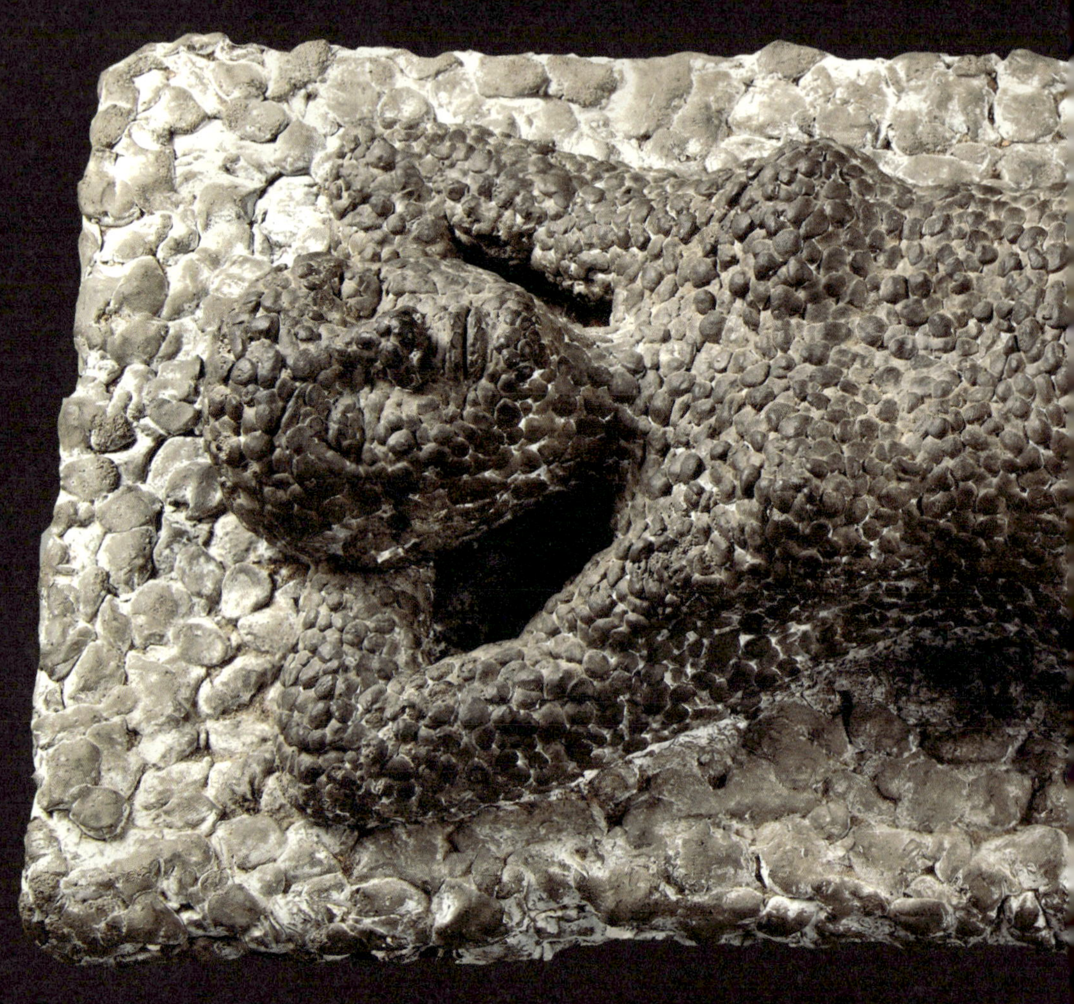

Ronald Moody, *Reclining Figure*, 1959–60, concrete and fibreglass, 16 × 64 × 30 cm (6 3/8 × 25 1/4 × 11 4/5 in.)

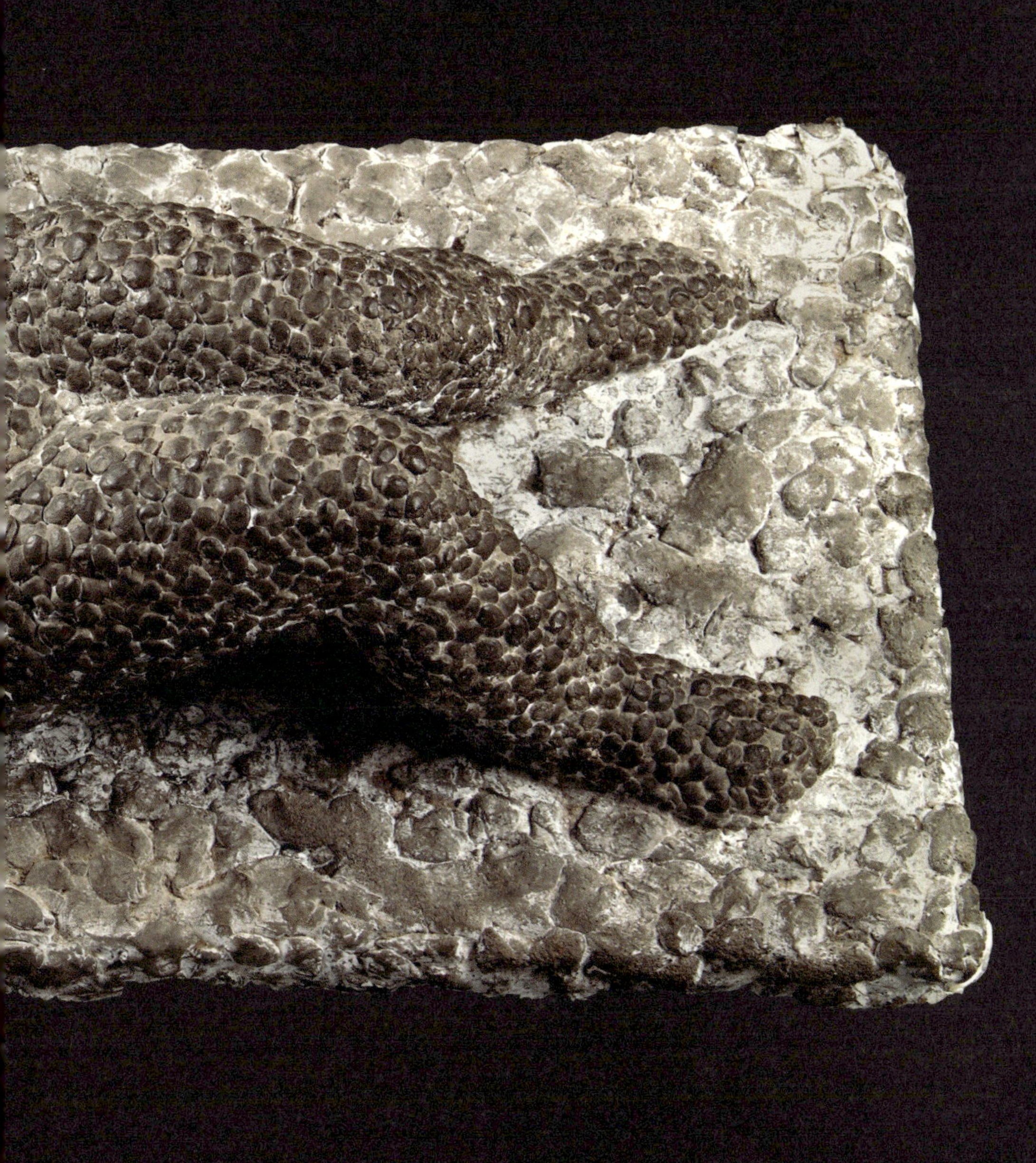

be seen in his portrait *Ahmed* (1962), as well as his portrait of Logue. The portrait of Ahmed, despite the somewhat basic material, exudes a warmth, sensitivity and intimacy; it was the last in this style of portrait. Unfortunately, nothing is known about the sitter.[28]

Much is known about Rudolph Dunbar, however. Born in Guyana, he moved to New York, aged nineteen, to enrol in the Institute of Musical Art (now the Julliard School) in 1919. He worked with leading composer William Grant Still and other Harlem Renaissance musicians.[29] He then travelled to Paris, where he studied music composition and conducting at the Sorbonne. During 1926–27, Dunbar performed on clarinet and saxophone in the Plantation Orchestra for C. B. Cochran's Blackbirds revue, which travelled to London via France and starred the enigmatic Florence Mills.[30] Dunbar and the Plantation Orchestra recorded four numbers from the revue on 1 December 1926. In the 1920s, US musicians in touring Black revues and troupes received restrictions on visas or work permits due to Britain's 'colour bar' legislation. Theoretically, the restrictions did not apply to West Indian musicians such as Dunbar as they were considered imperial subjects.[31] Dunbar continued his studies in Germany and Austria before settling in London in 1931. While in London, he wrote a weekly column for the *Melody Maker*, opened the Rudolph Dunbar School of Clarinet Playing and authored the music textbook *Treatise on Clarinet Playing*. He was the first Black man to conduct the London Philharmonic Orchestra, as well as the Liverpool Philharmonic and the National Philharmonic (Britain) in the 1940s. In the 1960s, he gained a type of notoriety throughout Europe, making him the first Black conductor to conduct the Leningrad Philharmonic, the Moscow State Symphony Orchestra and the Baku Philharmonic in Krasnodar, North Caucasus.[32]

Dunbar died in 1988, disheartened by the knowledge that he had been blacklisted by the BBC – a bitter public row that had left him humiliated and led to scarce opportunities later in his career. Dunbar cited a letter written by Maurice Johnstone, BBC Head of Music Programmes, that had come into his possession, in an affidavit. The letter disparaged him and promoted rumours that questioned

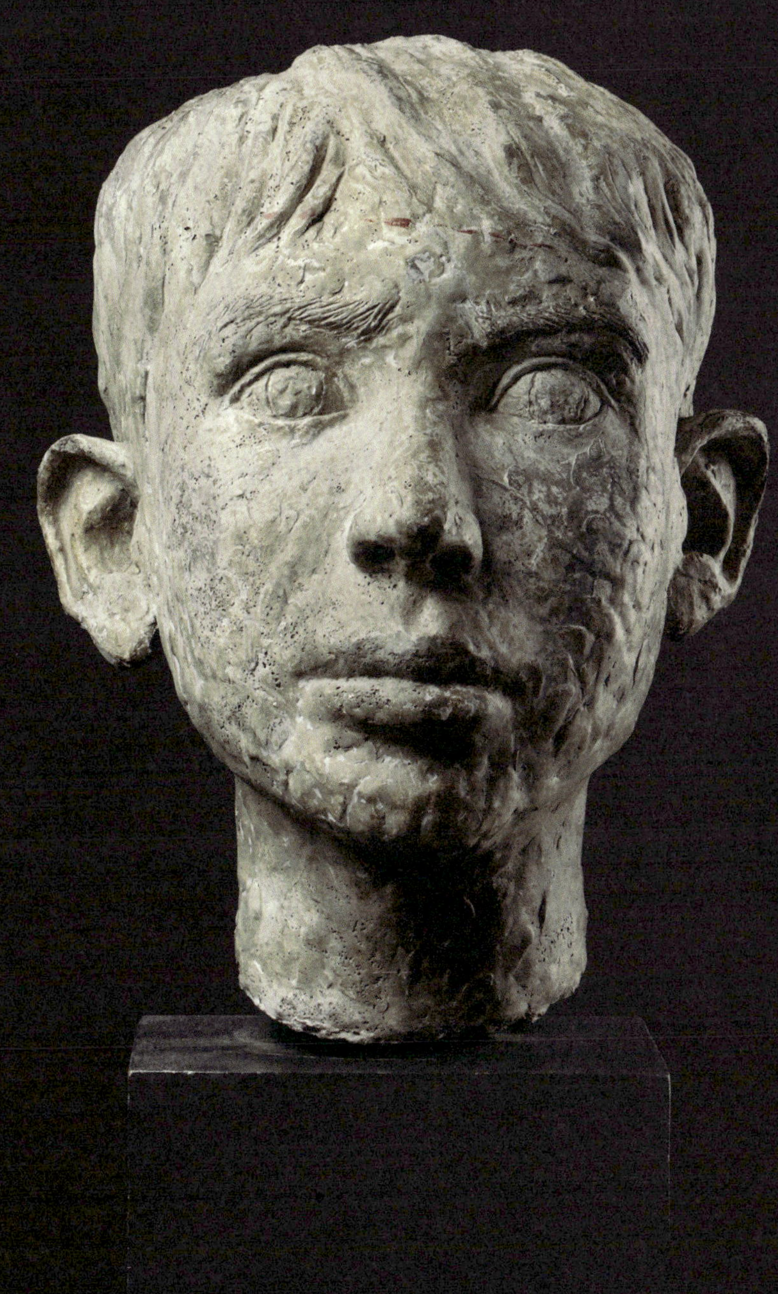

Ronald Moody, *Ahmed*, 1962, concrete and fibreglass, 32 × 23 × 23 cm (12 ⅝ × 9 ⅛ × 9 ⅛ in.)

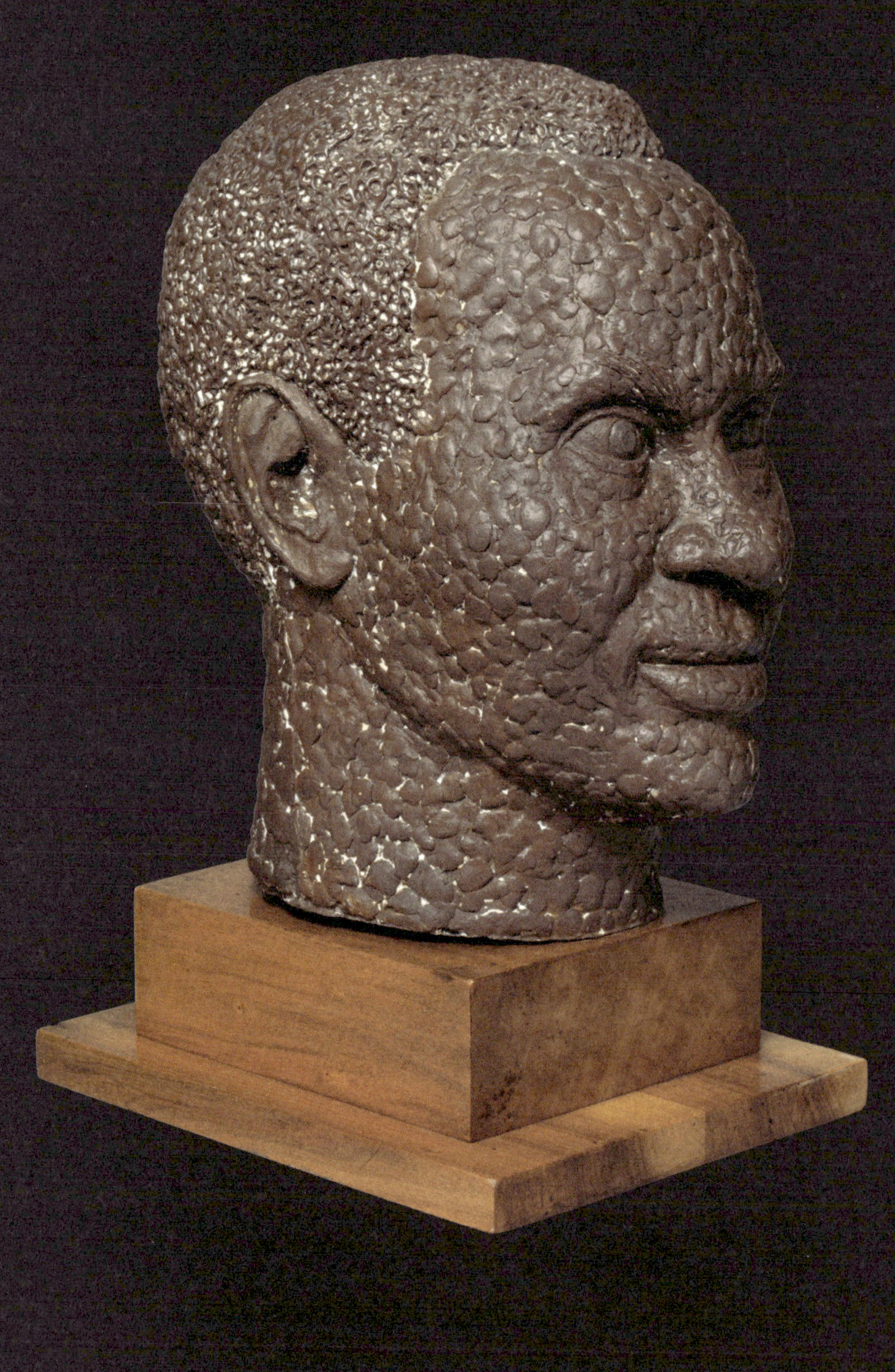

Ronald Moody, *Paul Robeson*, 1968, copper and resin, 38.7 × 22.8 × 29 cm (15 ¼ × 9 × 11 ½ in.)

his effectiveness as a conductor, mounting a racist campaign that essentially ruined his career in Britain.[33] Pioneering figures such as Dunbar demonstrate the important role of Black cultural expression in the making of British popular culture in its broadest sense in the 1920s and '30s, while equally illustrating some of the insurmountable hurdles, the inequalities of imperialism, racism and the class struggle for a Black person in Britain during this period.[34]

In 1968, Moody produced a portrait of civil rights activist, bass-baritone concert artist, stage and film actor and professional football player Paul Leroy Robeson. The portrait was originally commissioned by the Akademie der Künste, Berlin.[35] Moody's initial response was an expression of delight; he had known Robeson but hadn't seen him for a number of years. It is likely that they would have known each other through the activities of his brother Harold.[36] The Akademie housed a Paul Robeson archive and was in the process of preparing for his seventieth birthday celebration; they provided Moody with photographs of Robeson from a number of different views and angles.[37] In a letter dated 27 February 1968, Moody told the director of the archive Victor Grossman that he had begun a portrait of Robeson some years earlier, but sadly never had the chance to complete it as he was called away.[38] Robeson confirmed this in a letter to Moody expressing gratitude for contributing well wishes for his birthday, expressing hope that they would get to see each other again soon and promising he'd 'be a better sitter, than before'. The letter also included a small cut-out pasted-on figure of Moody's sculpted bird, *Savacou* (1964), almost like emblem of acknowledgment and admiration.[39] Correspondence to Moody from Lloyd L. Brown on 8 June 1971 discusses having returned from London, Berlin, Moscow and Leningrad, visiting friends of Robeson, collecting greetings from them on a portable tape recorder. Brown, a journalist and novelist, helped Robeson chronicle his career for his autobiography *Here I Stand*, which was published in 1958.[40] He describes visiting Robeson in his home in Philadelphia, where he listened to all the messages with Marian Forsythe, Paul's sister, who took great care of him until his death in 1976.[41] Brown writes:

> After dinner, we went into the living room and I turned on the tape recorder. As I sat, looking at Paul and reading the emotions on his face as he followed intently every word, I realised that here, strangely, was a Robeson concert in reverse. (Always at his concerts I used to sit so that I could see the faces of his listeners, the radiant smiles and the tears that glistened on the upturned happy faces. More than forty years ago a London newspaper critic had written of a Robeson concert: 'He broke our hearts with beauty.') Well, it seemed to me that now it was Paul listening to those audiences – that the messages of friendship and love, of old times, of children and grandchildren, that came pouring from the little box on the table before him were a return flow from the countless people in many lands whom he had enraptured.[42]

Moody was keen to complete the portrait so that it could be exhibited as part of the Society of Portrait Sculptors 'Human Rights Exhibition' to be held at St Paul's Cathedral in December 1968.[43] The exhibition included portraits of figures that included Winston Churchill, Mahatma Gandhi, Emmeline Pankhurst, Moody's bust of his brother Dr Harold Moody and Dr Martin Luther King.[44]

Of course Moody also created several portraits of his niece, Cynthia Moody, the person that went on to tenaciously secure the preservation of his life and legacy. Cynthia was the daughter of Ronald's brother Charles, also a dentist, who initially qualified at the University of Pennsylvania before moving to Britain in 1919 to work at both Guy's Hospital and Kings College Hospital, London. In 1930, Charles returned to Jamaica with his wife, Ruby (who was Welsh and Scottish), and their children, when Cynthia was six and half.[45] Cynthia, like her uncle, received a classical education, which she felt served her 'enormously in all sorts of analytical areas'. She was fluent in French and spoke Italian. Aged thirteen, she came back to England with her mother after her father died, attending school in Honor Oak until she was evacuated to Reigate when the

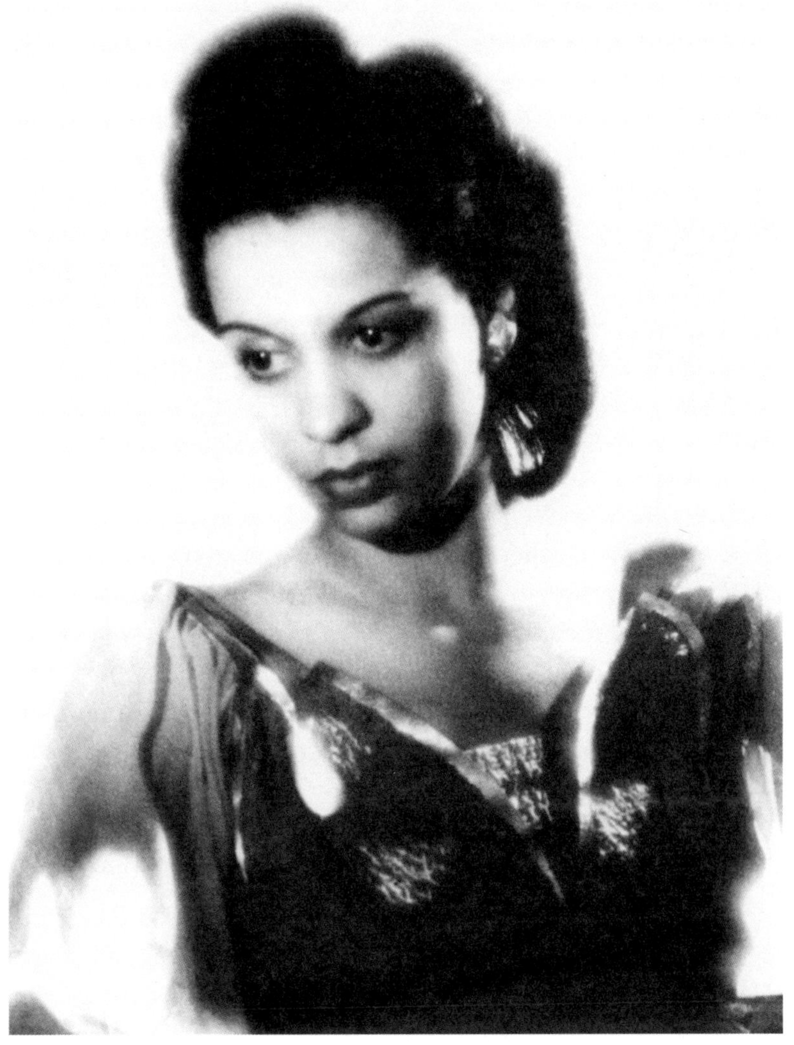

war broke out. As a teenager she was interested in art and admired the artistic path of her uncle Ronald. However, the war impeded her educational designs on fashion, her then passion, and she was attracted to the idea of documentary films as she felt it presented a freedom that she desired. An interview with Cynthia for the British Entertainment Communications and Theatre Union (BECTU) History Project, describes her experiences as a film professional:

Photograph of young Cynthia Moody, n.d.

the people, networks and being on location. It creates a picture of an embedded, networked, social figure – like her uncle – and one of the few women in the field during this period. Her love for the craft and the people is evident. She worked for the award-winning De Lane Lea picture and sound post-production company,[46] situated in the heart of Soho, which was founded in 1940 by Major William De Lane Lea as a dubbing studio for English and French films.[47] Cynthia recalls socializing in the historical pub the Highlander, which was later re-named the Nellie-Dean, on 89 Dean Street, Soho, London, where it wouldn't be unusual to bump into the likes of poets Dylan Thomas (1914–1953) and George Baker (1913–1991) and renowned theatrical director and scholar Duncan Ross (1908–1968).[48] Cynthia was known as an accomplished and respected filmmaker and editor; she worked for the Shell Film Unit and received a thorough training in all aspects of film. She set up two companies, one dedicated to documentaries and the other for advertisements.[49] Films she edited include *Final Appointment* (1954), *Alias John Preston* (1955), starring the actor Christopher Lee, *The Carringford School Mystery* (1958) and *Little Girls Never Cry* (1962), starring a young Roberta Tovey, who later becomes known for her role as Susan in Dr Who in the 1960s.[50]

Moody produced two renditions of Cynthia. The first, created in 1952, is made of terracotta and depicts a hairstyle that Cynthia never wore. Instead, Moody had reproduced the hairstyle of another terracotta portrait he had made previously, of Anne Boas (1952), the stepdaughter of one of the Moody's pre-war friends, Baroness Charlotte von Schweinitz. Anne Boas emigrated to Canada, soon after the portrait had been completed and its whereabouts is unknown. Moody was obviously taken by Boas's hairstyle, as he also introduced a heavily modified version in his artworks *Leila* (1954) and *The Mother* (1958). Moody found the warmth and pliability of terracotta appealing, alongside the possibilities of modelling, without the risk of losing subtlety in casting. He created seven small heads in this material including a *Self-Portrait 4*, which, like Helene Moody's of the same era, illustrates the impact of his experience of war.

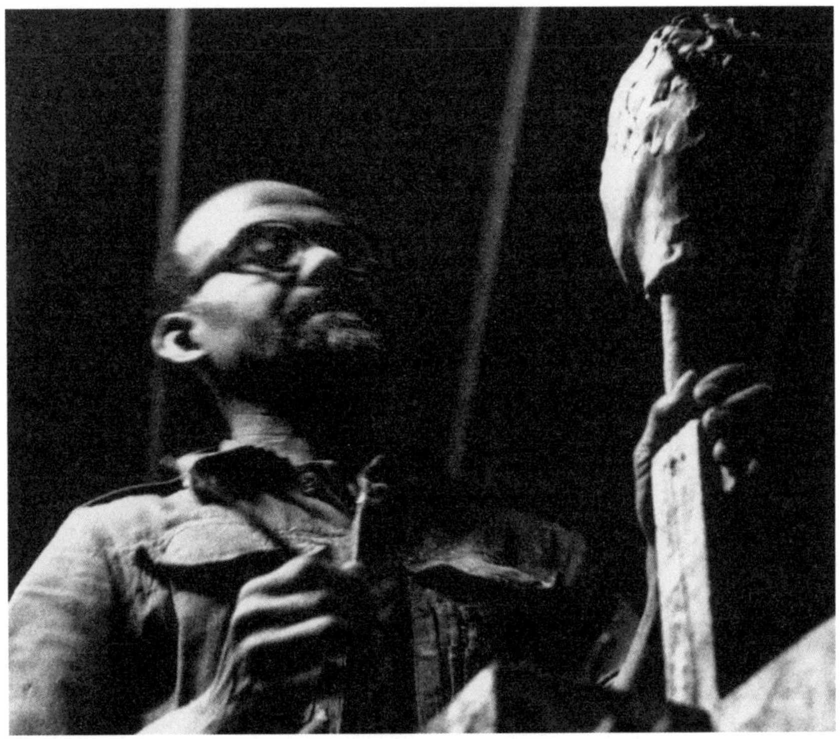

The second portrait of the artist's niece is produced in 1965, in copper resin. Moody had the year before been commissioned to sculpt the two-metre high (7 ft) bird *Savacou* (1963), cast in aluminium for the Epidemiological research unit at the University of the West Indies. This led to a turning point in the artist's use and exploration of materials, where he moved away from concrete and began experimenting with metallic resins, exploiting their potential. He used a mixture of aluminium, copper, lead and glass in his symbolic artworks but he reserved copper resin for his portraits. Moody's five portraits in this medium have a pebbly surface, developed during his experimentation with concrete, and the texture is used to provide contrast. In *Cynthia 2* (1965), the first portrait made in copper resin, the combed contours of the hair suggest a lightness, whereas a portrait of the same year, *Daphne*, also in copper resin, uses hair to imply sleekness.[51]

Ronald Moody working on the portrait of Daphne Dennison at Fleming Close Studios, Fulham, 1965

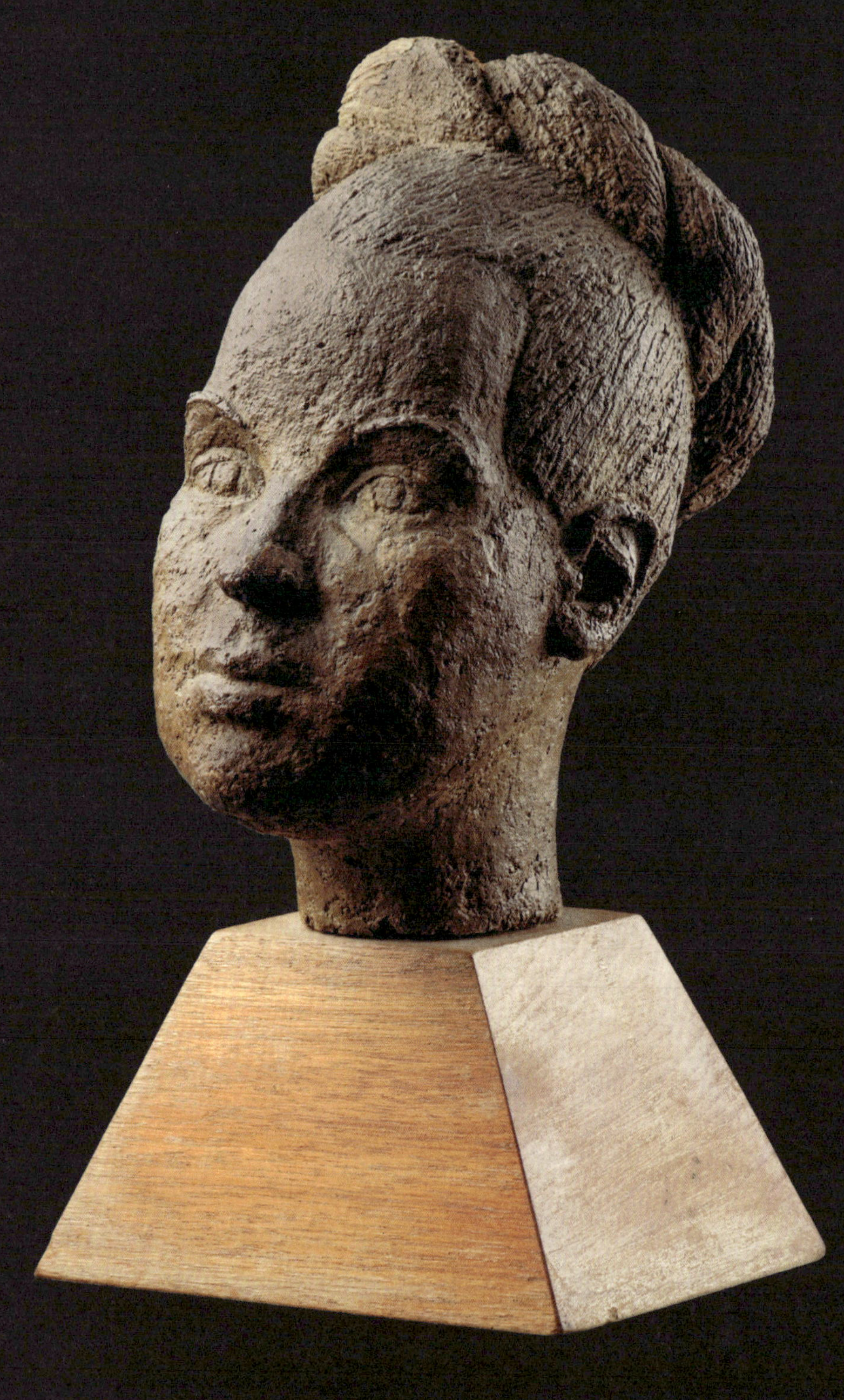

Ronald Moody, *Cynthia I*, 1965, copper resin,
34 × 27 × 31 cm (13 ½ × 10 ¾ × 12 ¼ in.)

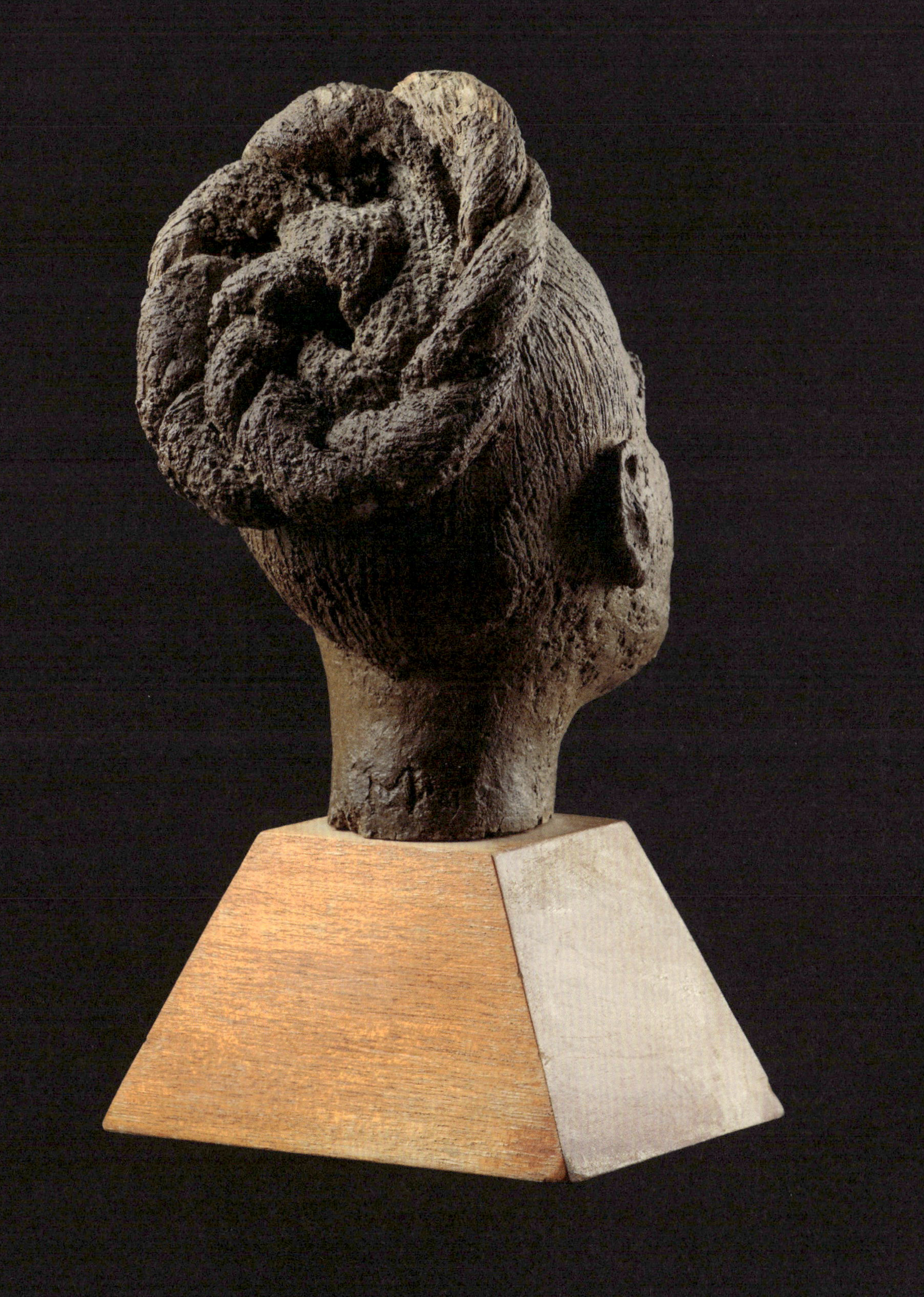

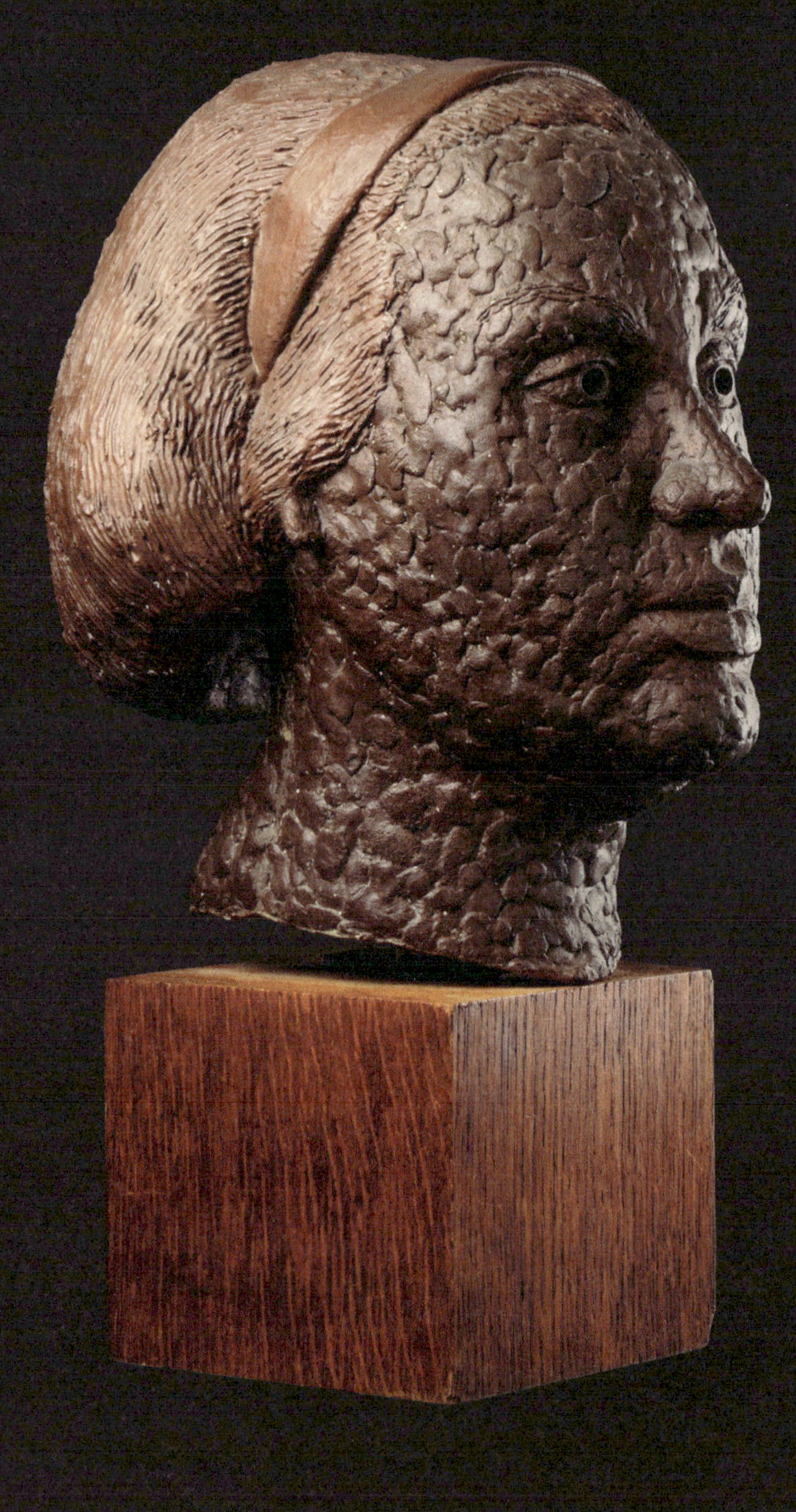

Ronald Moody, *Cynthia II*, 1965, copper resin,
34 × 27 × 31 cm (13 ½ × 10 ¾ × 12 ¼ in.)

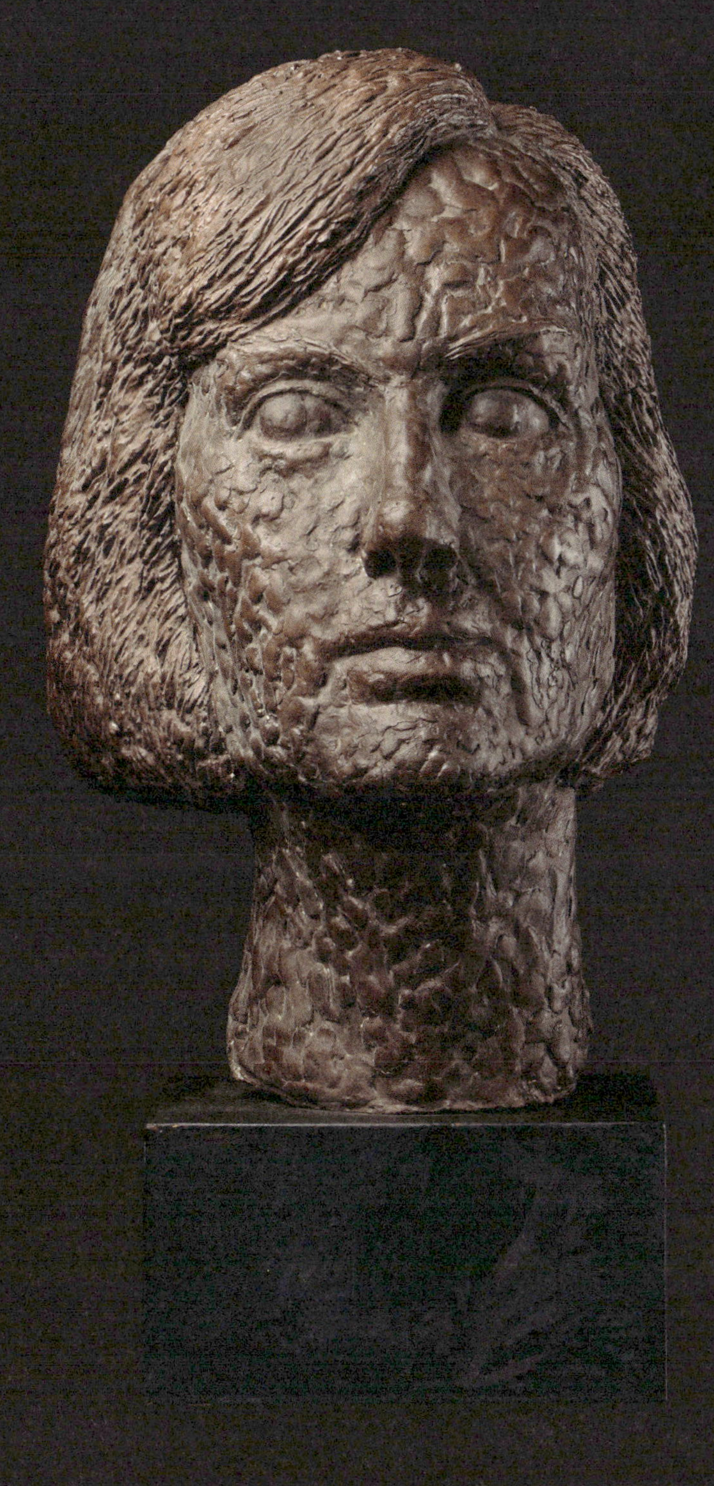

Ronald Moody, *Daphne*, 1965, copper resin,
38 × 20 × 29 cm (15 × 7 7/8 × 11 1/2 in.)

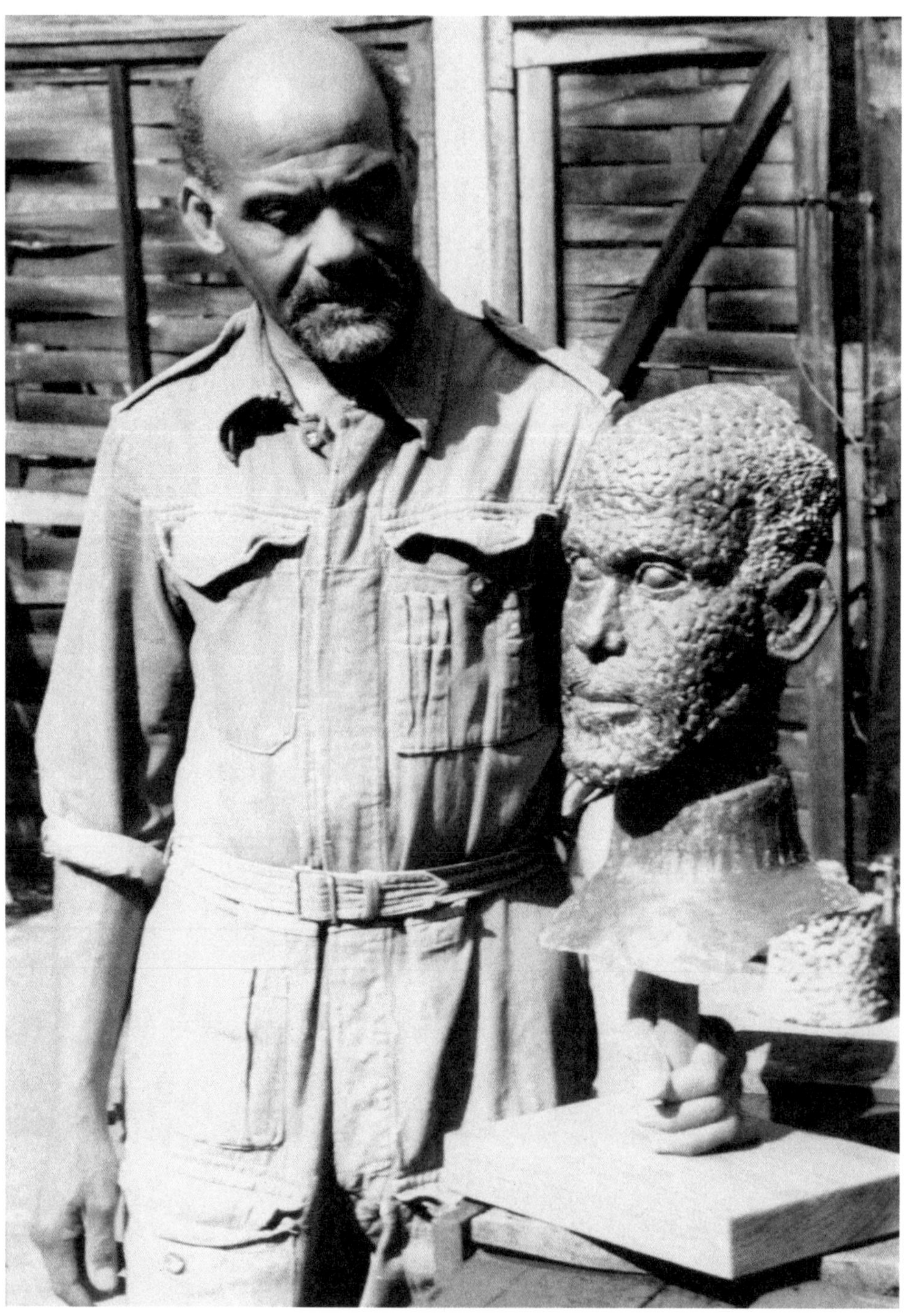

Ronald Moody with *Self-Portrait 6* in the yard at Fleming Close Studios, Fulham, *c.* 1966

Daphne Dennison (1922–1997) was born and educated in Brown's Town, Jamaica, and later became a student at the Slade School of Art, London, during its Second World War evacuation to Oxford. While at Slade, she won a prize for figure painting and a scholarship for a fourth year of study. During this period, she met John Roberts and his family in Oxford, through their mutual friend Deirdre Knewstub, youngest daughter of John Knewstub of the Chenil Galleries. Painter William Roberts portrayed her as Venus in his painting *The Birth of Venus* (1954). Dennison later taught painting and drawing at Montego Bay High School for Girls, Jamaica, before making her home in London.[52] Dennison exhibited in the 1971 show 'Caribbean Artists' at the Commonwealth Gallery alongside Althea McNish, Errol Lloyd, Keith Simon (1922–2014), Aubrey Williams and Winston Branch (b. 1947).[53] An exhibition of Dennison's paintings was held at the Commonwealth Art Gallery in July–August 1973.[54] Dennison and her husband, Roger Low, were friends of the artist and owned Moody's *Swamp Bird* (1963).[55]

In 1966, Moody created a portrait of himself, *Self-Portrait 6*, again using the copper resin technique, portraying himself with a beard and wearing a high ribbed-neck sweater. Paul Robeson's 1968 portrait is the final one of this series, the larger-than-life head expressing a man of conviction. It was around this time that Moody became fascinated by the visual effects he was able to create with coloured inks, and produced a series of over thirty 'ink paintings', which he described as 'abstracts inspired by the richness of nature and life in general.'[56]

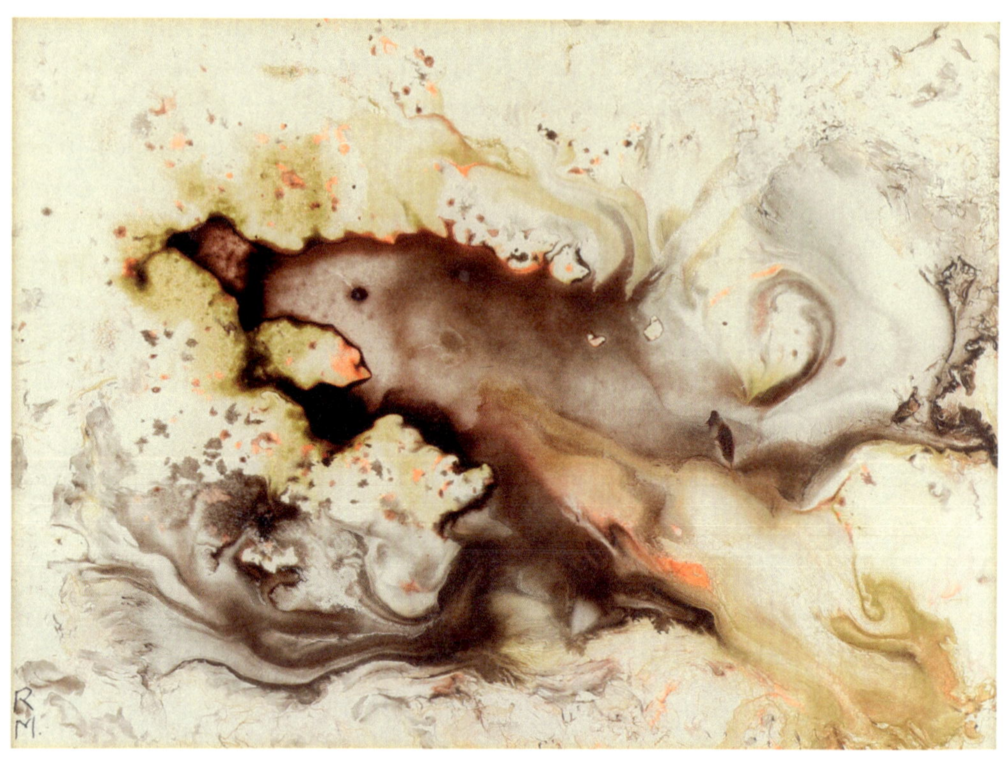

Ronald Moody, *Untitled Ink Drawing I*, *c.* 1970,
ink on paper, 31.5 × 39 cm (12 ½ × 15 ⅜ in.)

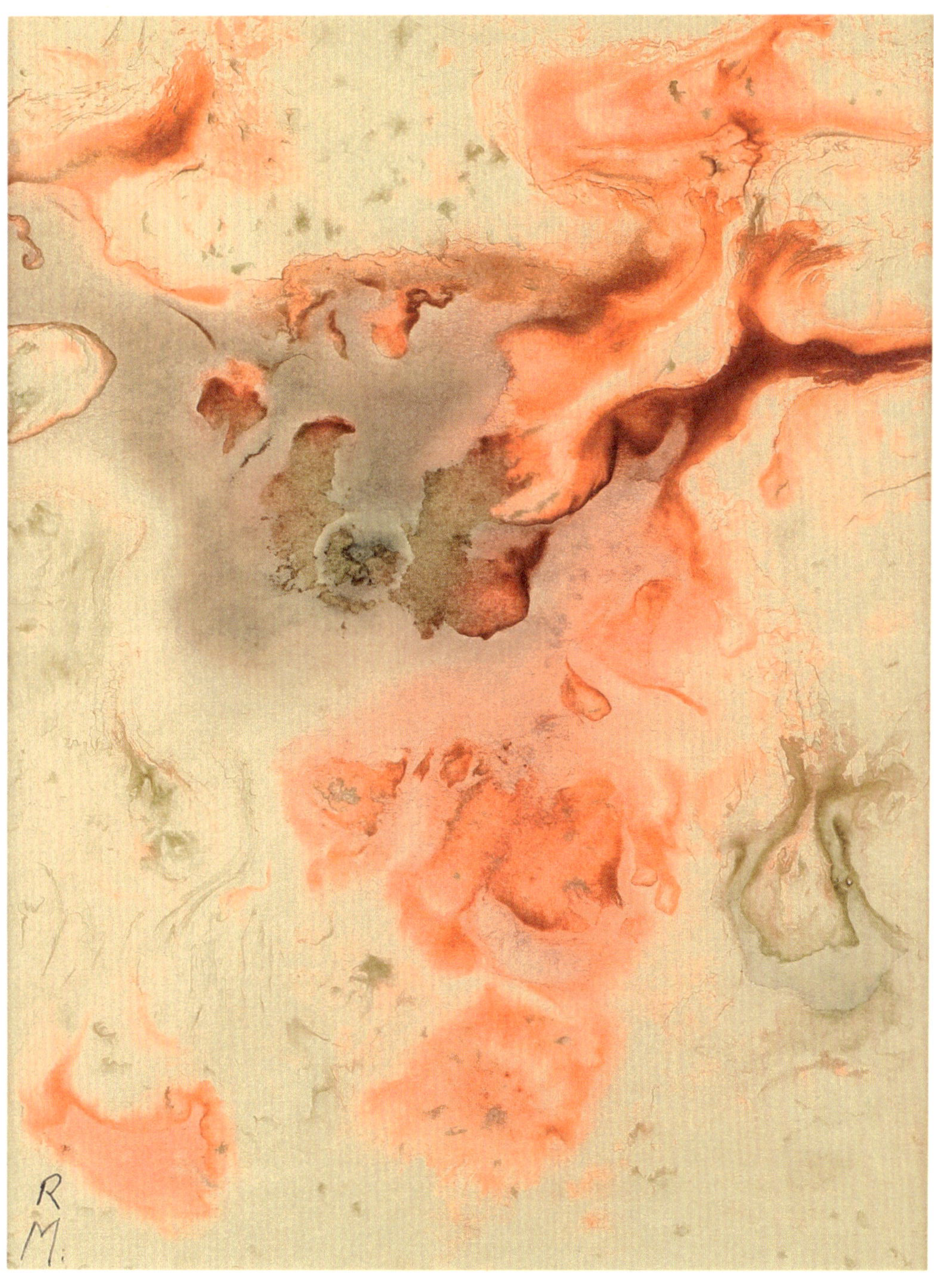

Ronald Moody, *Untitled Ink Drawing 2*, *c.* 1970,
ink on paper, 39 × 31.5 cm (15 3/8 × 12 1/2 in.)

CHAPTER 6

‘The Concrete Family’

Cynthia Moody

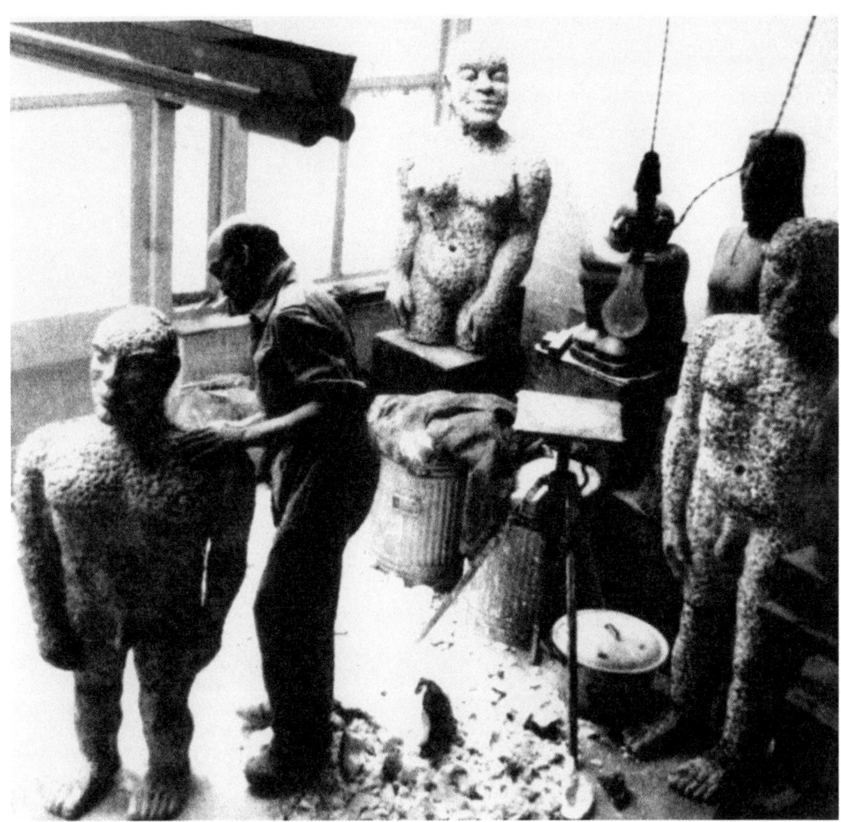

In 1957, Moody started a sculpture entitled *The Mother*, which was to be the forerunner of a number of nude torsos and full-length figures by the artist modelled in ciment fondu. These pieces mark a period of renewed strength in Moody's health that enabled him to begin sculpting on a larger scale once again. He began an experimentation into the textural effects of concrete, *The Mother* being the first large-scale figure cast in cement by the artist and an 'attempt to portray the female qualities – the Matriarch.'[1] After reading Moody's correspondence with the Brick Development Council (who had asked if he had a suitable piece of work to stand outside a specific building), a parallel can be drawn between the security of the home and the permanence of the mother figure. The grandeur of the human form is once again Moody's main preoccupation. He creates

Ronald Moody preparing *The Man*,
Fleming Close Studios, Fulham, *c.* 1958

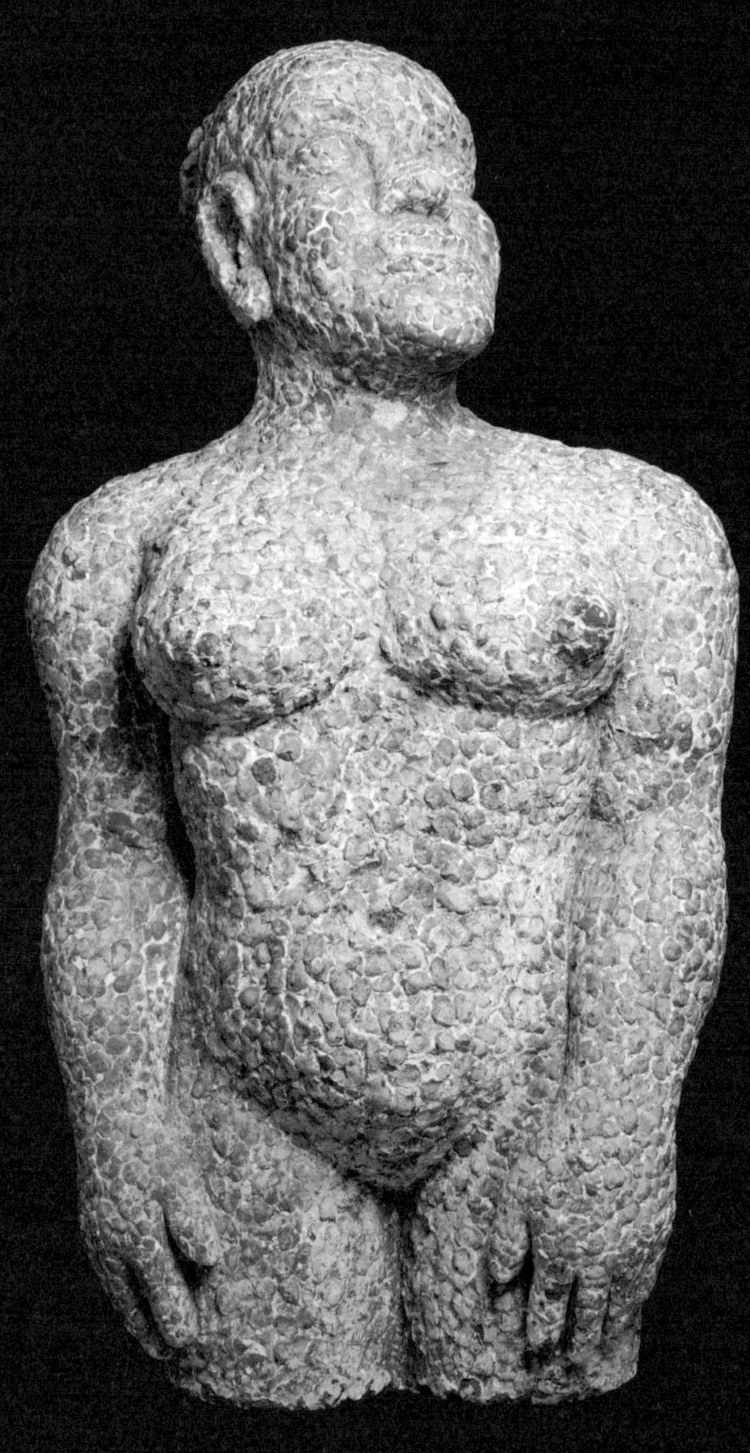

Ronald Moody, *The Mother*, 1958–59, cement,
124 × 67 × 49 cm (48 7/8 × 26 1/2 × 19 3/8 in.)

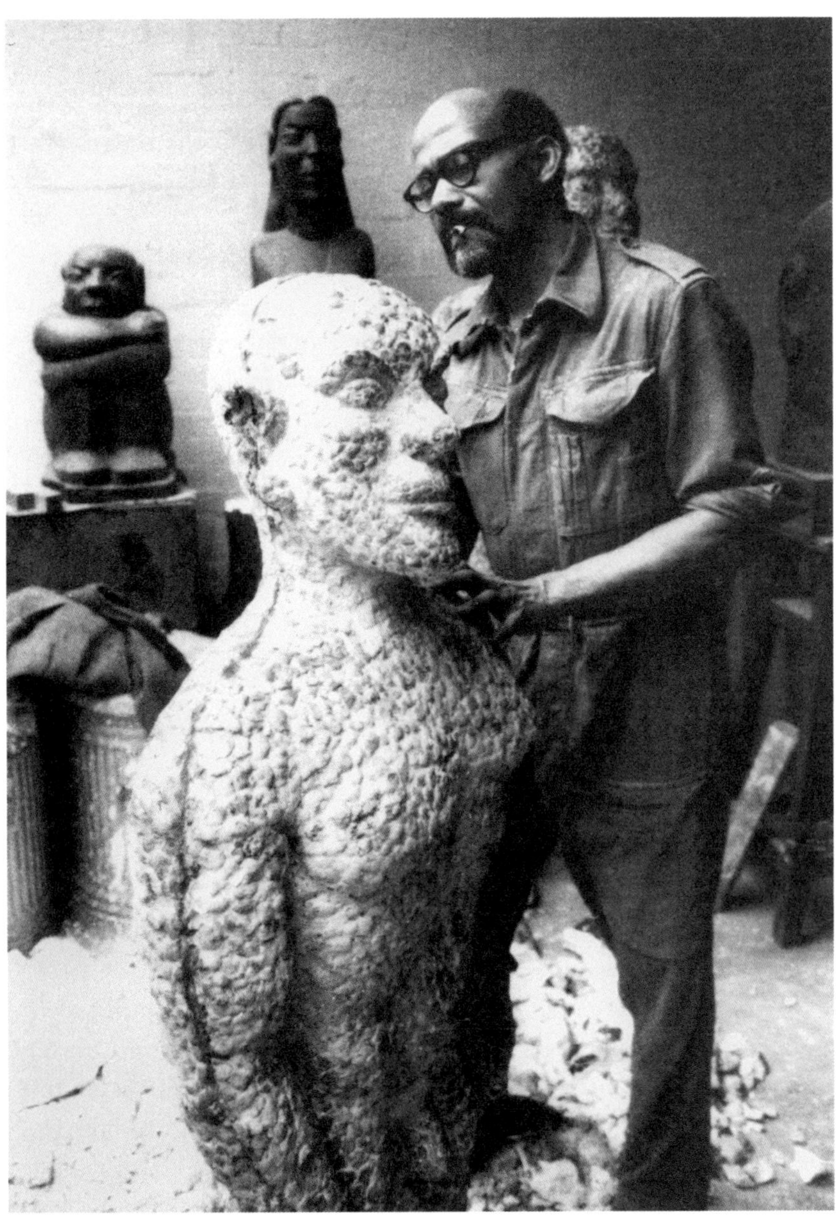

Ronald Moody working on *The Youth* at Fleming Close Studios, Fulham, 1960. Photograph by Crispin Eurich

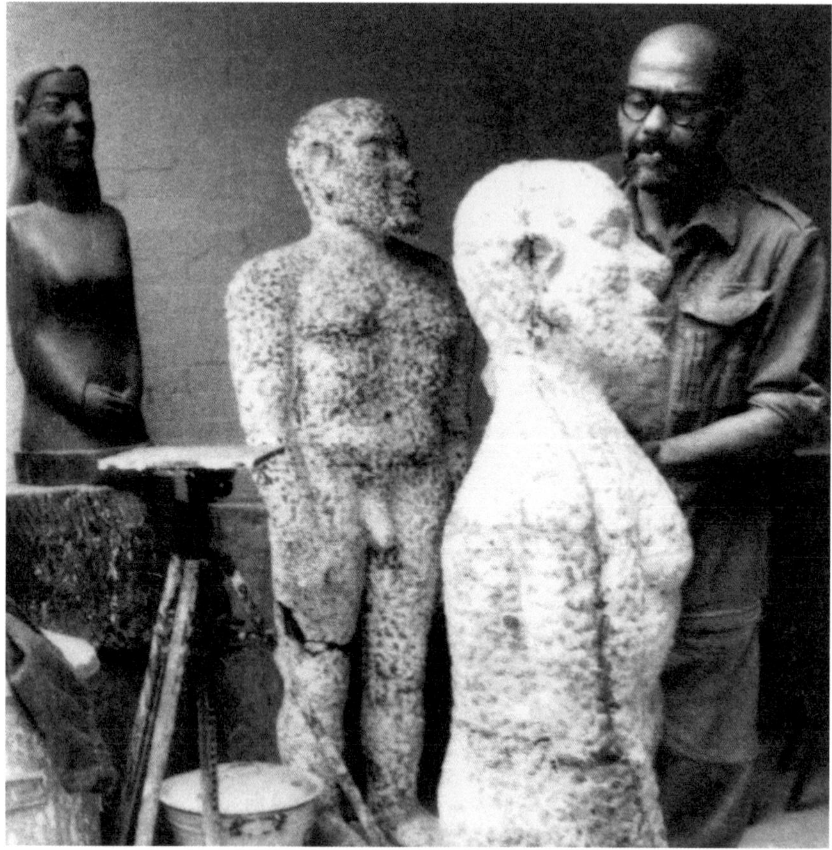

a stylised and distinct physique in his textural effects and works the concrete to construct a dominating presence.

Moody's divergence into the realms of concrete continued until 1962, when he completed the last of the series with *Little Man*. The *Concrete Family* consisted of *The Mother*, *The Man*, *The Youth* (all 1958) and *Little Man* (*c*. 1962). He used a mixture of concrete and fibreglass reinforced with steel to mould the shapes together. In all of these sculptures, a tensile strength can be seen that accommodates a sense of dignity and prevalence. The works are without movement yet propound a stillness that engages the viewer in the monolithic nudity of the pieces. These works erupted out of a period of intense creativity and brought him revived professional recognition.

Ronald Moody working on *The Youth* at Fleming Close Studios, Fulham, 1960. Photograph by Crispin Eurich

Germaine Richier (1902–1959) was a French-born sculptor who, in a similar way to Moody, heralded transformation in her works by expressing the incubus of suffering and malcontent that persecuted the world in the first half of the twentieth century. In 1947–48, Richier represented the human condition in a series of figures that are portrayed as repugnantly deformed, whose stick-like skeletons show through the mass of weight attached to these bones. When observing these figures, especially *L'Ouragane* (1948–49), it is clear to see the separate ideological conclusions that both sculptors arrive at with their separate concrete figures. Both artists model the expressive force in the stocky figures, but where Richier's *L'Ouragane* is dragged

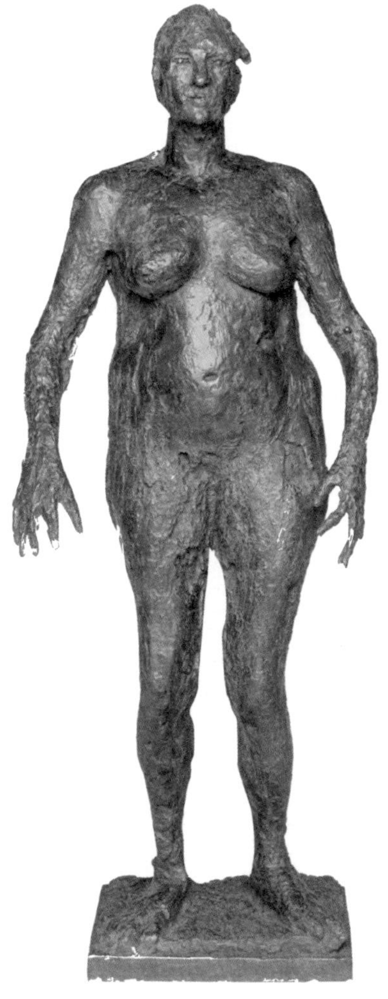

Germaine Richier, *L'Ouragane* (Hurricane Woman), 1948–49, bronze, height: 178 cm (70 in.)

down with its own weight, Moody's sculpture *Man* is well-balanced and authoritative in its pose. Italian art critic Giuseppe Marchiori (1901–1982), writing on Richier's work, interprets her figures of this period: 'And when man himself becomes the symbol of anti-natural forces, he assumes the terrifying aspect of primitive Man with his love for the horrible.'[2] I find this an interesting point to elaborate on, as Richier implies only the dramatic vulgarity of the cruel side of human beings, which in turn is immediately connected to the 'primitive'. Moody, in his declaration of the self-destructive elements that exist within humankind and the world, focuses upon a return to the ethics that were applied to earlier civilisations as a solution to universal disharmony. Richier produced *L'Ouragane* some eight or nine years before Moody began his first concrete sculpture, *The Mother*. It therefore seems plausible to suggest that Moody was influenced by Richier's choice of material and subject matter. In his group of concrete works, Moody took the statement of the monumentality of homosapiens further. And although there is a concern to magnify the threatening presence of these figures, a communicative response is evoked.

The use of concrete in these pieces may also be a reference to the way in which the medium had begun to dominate the urban environment, removing people from their connections with more fundamental elements such as earth and stone. In opposition to Richier's earlier sculptures, Moody is content to disclose both sides of the human psyche:

> My faith in Man has not been shattered.... When I speak of Man, I mean the constructive values that have sustained him through the ages. Despite his attempts at denial...in an age where the destructive side of Man has become so highly developed, it becomes of the greatest importance to find again Man, the reality, that has receded. I do not think that it is enough to expose the cruelties etc., or accept a state of impotence or, worst of all, cling grimly to dead passing truths.[3]

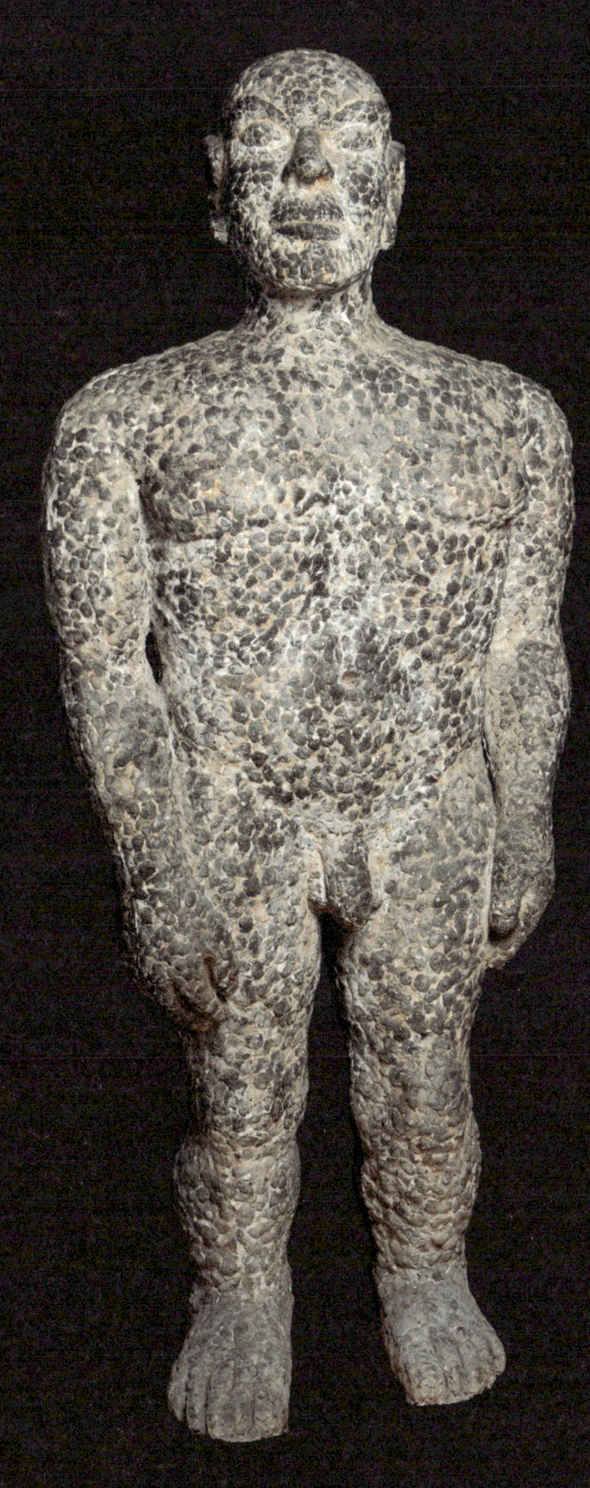

Ronald Moody, *The Youth*, 1958, cement,
154 × 68 × 26 cm (60 3/4 × 26 7/8 × 10 1/4 in.)

The *Concrete Family* has been dispersed: Leicester Museum owns *The Mother* and *Youth*; *The Man* disintegrated as soon as it was touched during an attempted removal of the piece from Moody's studio; and *Little Man*'s whereabouts is unknown. This dispersal and loss of such a unique sequence of sculptures surely reflects the discouraging attitude towards artists of such calibre that remain on the periphery of the art establishments in Britain. Moody's move towards a definite and essentially stylised figure of the human body counteracted the anatomical attention that is so heavily embodied within the traits of 'high art'. The notion of the perfect body that expresses only a mundane reference to the statuesque proportioning of the Greek ideal was regarded and disregarded by Moody, who chose to exemplify some inner sensibility in the personalities of his works.

Previously unpublished notes from Cynthia Moody's archive, courtesy of the Ronald Moody Trust.

CHAPTER 7

Looking Back

Val Wilmer

> I didn't want to write dramatic stories. I wanted to write sensitive ones and ones that recognised what people had done.
>
> *Val Wilmer*

Stepping into a Future of Photography

It's very hard to remember things from long ago. Having spent my life interviewing people, I know what it's like. People always start off by saying, 'I don't think I can remember anything!' In my case, I can't remember much about photographing Ronald Moody, but I have got some ideas about the background and context of the time and period. I always tell the story of discovering jazz as a young person, but I then amend it to say that jazz discovered me. Of course, that means that you have a responsibility, which grows more with the years, to tell the stories, alongside the opportunity to meet people and find out more about where the music came from, and that's what I did. There were one or two other women around taking photographs of musicians, but not that many. As I became interested in jazz and realised where it came from, the whole story of Black music, I became interested in other Black arts too, or, arts of the African diaspora.

I left school and went to study photography at the Regent Street Polytechnic, as it then was.[1] It was a two-year course, a technical course on how to be a professional photographer. They changed it to a three-year course when I was there. I didn't really want to stay on, I wasn't that interested in photography at the time. Also, financially it wasn't possible for me, I had to support my mother. I'd been offered a job, or so I thought, at a little jazz magazine that I wrote for. It turned out to be just one of those things that people say, and I found myself in a position where I didn't know what to do.

I bumped into one of my fellow students, who asked me what was up, and she said, 'Oh, go and see the registrar, they've always got jobs.' I said, 'Have they?' I wasn't the sort of person that hung out with the photography people, I was too busy chasing musicians and bunking off from lectures and so on. I went to see the registrar and there was

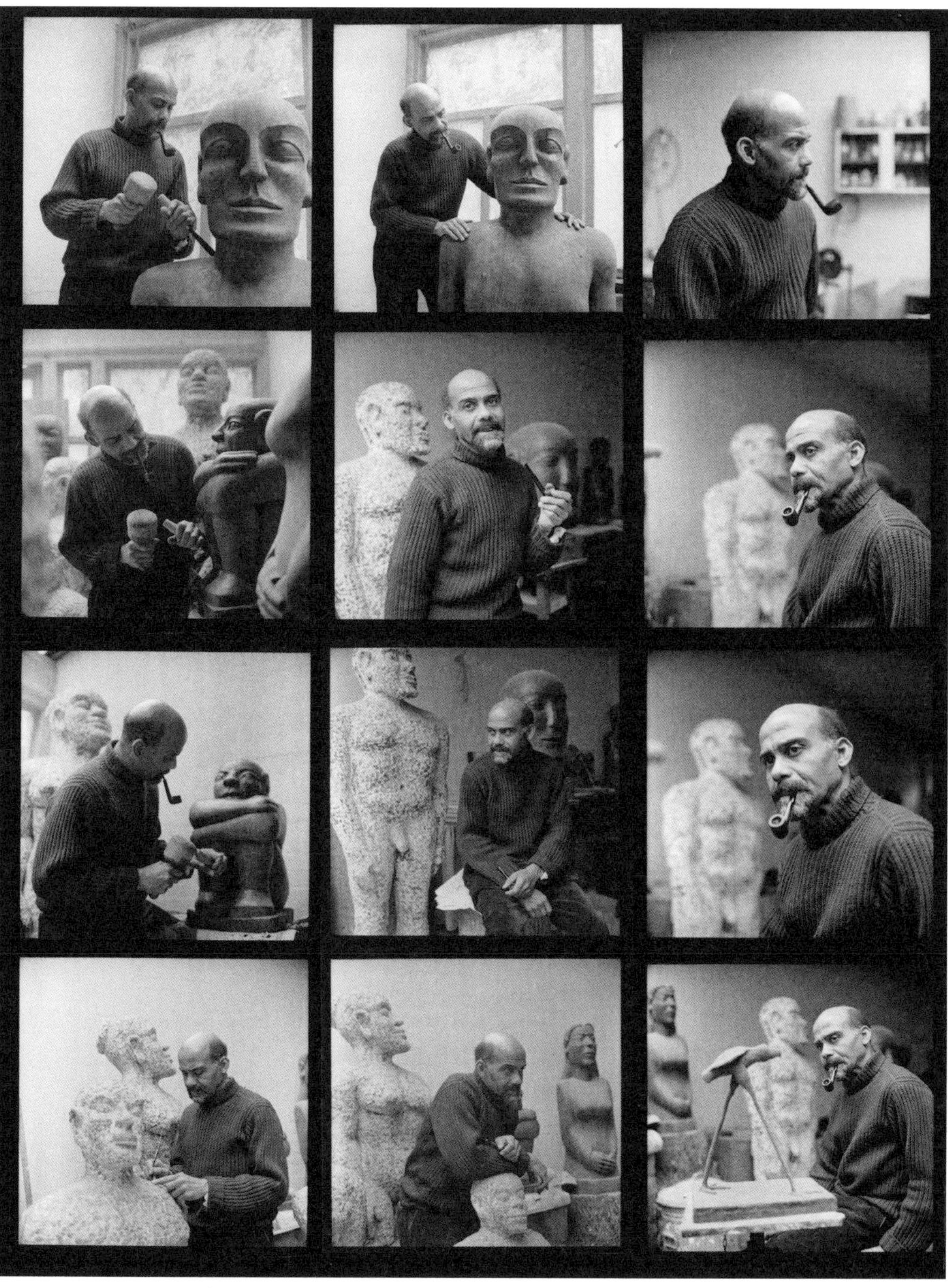

Contact sheet from Val Wilmer's shoot with Ronald Moody at Fleming Close Studios, Fulham, 1963

this job at the National Gallery. I called the National Gallery and they said, 'When can you come?' I said, 'I can come now if you like.' I went down there, this was on a Thursday, and we finished on a Friday. She said, 'When can you start?' I said, 'Monday.' She said, 'Well, it's very unusual in the civil service, but we're desperate for somebody.' There I was! That's how I got that job. It wouldn't happen today like that. There were six women printing photographs in the basement of the National Gallery behind huge steel doors that were about an inch thick, where they had kept paintings during the war – they have since been taken away. It was an amazing place to work. I didn't work there very long but I met all sorts of people there and printed a lot of things technically that I never thought I could manage. One day, I nearly smashed a whole lot of valuable glass plates by turning the light out too quickly in the darkroom and getting lost. That's how big the darkrooms were. Anyway, that was a step towards my future.

Meeting Edward Scobie:
Working for *Tropic* and *Flamingo* Magazines

One day the phone rang, and I wasn't supposed to be one of the people answering the phone, but everybody was out, so I did. There was a man on the phone, and he wanted some prints of the Hogarth drawings that showed Black people in Georgian London. I said, 'What's your name?' He said, 'Edward Scobie.' I said, 'Well, I already know you, this is Valerie.' I'd met him on the jazz scene because he was a real jazz person. He grew up as a teen in Harlem, but he was from Dominica. Anyway, he said, 'Well, why don't you come and work for us?', 'us' being a magazine called *Tropic*.

Scobie asked again, 'Why don't you come?' I said, 'Oh, I don't know, I'm just going off to Paris.' I was going to Paris; it was the first time I'd been anywhere, just for a week's holiday. When I came back, I started working in the *Tropic* office, which was my introduction to all sorts of new things in life. I mean it was a real culture shock. I was eighteen. There were other white people around sometimes, but mostly it was an all-Black situation. That was very unusual in London then, especially for me. It was on this road called Bell Street, which is either in Marylebone or Paddington depending on which way you look at it; it's off Edgware Road. There was a little Black enclave there, there was a cafe and a barber's shop, and people used to come there. Other people had various offices above the shops and in the back of these buildings. They had a gambling place, a shebeen, and everything like that, very illegal, but I didn't find out about that until afterwards. It was an extraordinary time and it was only later that I found out the relevance of many of the things that happened. *Tropic* was a monthly magazine founded in 1960 by a Jamaican called Charles I. Ross, with the help of Scobie, and lasted a year.[2] Later on, Scobie edited *Flamingo*, a magazine that ran from 1961 to 1965. The magazine described itself as 'the voice for the 350,000 West Indians and many thousands of Africans and Asians' in Britain. *Flamingo* published a wide range of news, short stories, reviews and history articles.[3]

Scobie was the only editor of *Flamingo* initially, and then he was joined by Ellis Komey, who was a Ghanaian writer. I started to work for them, and after a while Scobie left and Komey was still there. Then a man called John Harold came in, who was a white Englishman who'd worked for I think probably the *Nigerian Daily Times* in Lagos, and another man called Ken Campbell, who was Jamaican. John Harold became my go-to person. I don't know whether it was Scobie or John Harold who commissioned me to do the story on Moody, I can't remember. I had already photographed him in 1963, but the story did not come out in *Flamingo* until November 1964. That was the same time that John Harold sent me to West Africa. I spent six weeks in West Africa, which I wrote about in my autobiography *Mama Said There'd Be Days Like This* (1989).

That was how I started to know about Ronald Moody and Uzo Egonu and Andrew Salkey and George Lamming and Toussaint L'Ouverture and Edward Wilmot Blyden, people like that.[4] They were suddenly all part of my knowledge, not deeply, and they introduced things that you wouldn't normally, as a white person from the background I was from, know about or hear about. Being a woman during those times could often have its problematic side, but it was

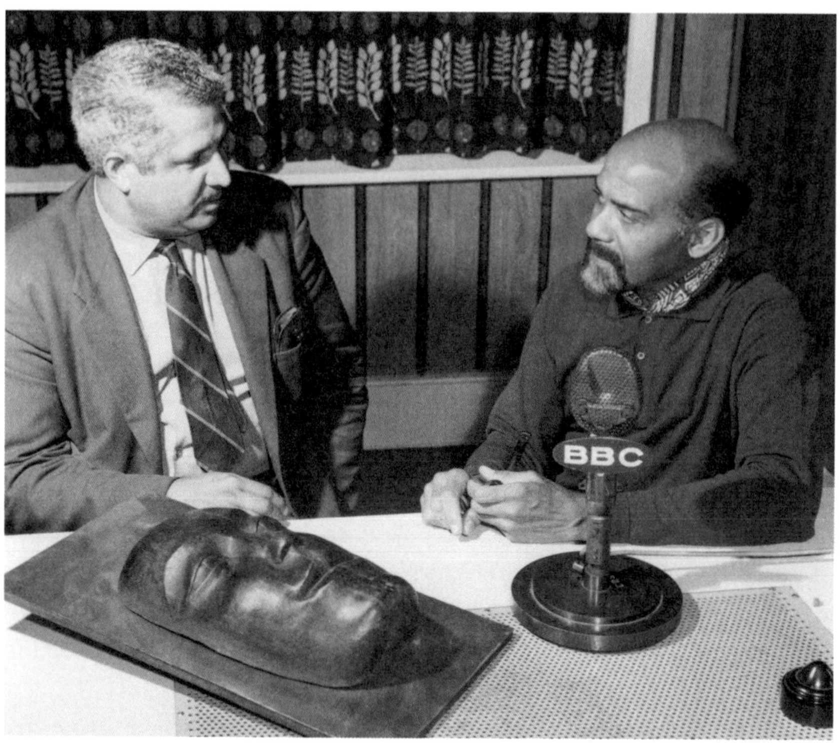

certainly a wonderful learning experience. It ended up with my pay bouncing because they ran out of funding, so the magazine had to close abruptly, and I was out on my ear. I did a couple of other odd jobs, and I worked in someone's darkroom for about a year-and-a-half, a little bit less than that. Then I went to New York. When I came back, I worked for a man I'd met at *Tropic*, a man called Alton Bowen. He had the first beer and spirit importing firm here, the first West Indian person to have that.

I worked in his shop as a receptionist. I didn't want to do this, 'I'm a journalist and a photographer.' He said, 'Please, until I get a Jamaican girl.' He gets a Jamaican girl and there I am back home again! My dear mother, very tolerant. I couldn't find a job, so I just became freelance. I don't know how I survived, but I did. Then, in the meantime, *Flamingo* started up, which was produced in many editions. First of all, there was just the British edition, which went

Ronald Moody with Edward Scobie and *Sleeper Mask*, during the BBC Caribbean Service broadcast 'The Role of the Artist in the New Society', 1962

to the Caribbean as well. Then there was an American edition, then there were editions for several African countries, all in West Africa initially, then at the end, Kenya. It was financed by the state, we discovered later. UK intelligence services MI6 were involved in financing it, as they were with many, many radical publications, both Black publications and also left-wing publications. Historian, investigative journalist and author Stephen Dorrill discovered the detail of this and gave the information to *The Observer* for an article, which was then covered by another journalist in *The Guardian.* Both articles explain how the 1960s magazine *Flamingo* was used by its founder, Peter Hornsby, an agent for MI6, to push an anti-communist agenda among Black and West Indian communities.[5] In 1989, when I wrote my autobiography,[6] I had a big party and invited everybody who had been important in my life. John Harold came along, and I said, 'Can we have lunch?' We go out and have lunch the next day and he said, 'I'm going to give you a story.' Harold sat there and started telling me about how he had discovered this whole MI6 connection. When he worked there, there was someone who didn't seem to be the right kind of person working there and he knew or felt that something was going on. He offered me the story to sell to Fleet Street, but I did not have the time. This was in 1989. Later on, I wrote a piece about Scobie for the journal *Race and Class*. I wanted to pay tribute to Edward Scobie because he really encouraged me.[7]

Sculpture is in the Air: Photographing Other Sculptors

My interest in sculpture started with the Festival of Britain in 1951. I was nine years old, but we went down to the South Bank to see the Skylon, which was one of the exhibits.[8] It was all about how wonderful the modern age is; it was a celebration of all that. To me, I became aware of sculpture, there was a lot of sculpture around. They started having sculpture exhibitions in Battersea Park, 'Sculpture in the Open Air', which went on for several years.[9] Now, I did go to a couple of those, I remember. Then, coinciding with my interest in jazz, there were a lot of concerts at the Royal Festival Hall on the South Bank. I was accustomed to going, usually to the first house, or sometimes there was something on in the afternoon. I'd go there to catch the musicians and get their autographs or to photograph them and sometimes go backstage. My brother Clive was with me sometimes, he's younger than me.[10] We were wandering around and we were aware of these sculptures. It was before that big head of Nelson Mandela by Ian Walters was installed there, that came later.[11]

One of the sculptors was called Siegfried Charoux, he was an Austrian Royal Academician.[12] His work is quite – it's not abstract, I don't know what you would call it, it's not purely figurative either, it's sort of symbolic: his *Civilisation* series, *The Judge* (1962), for example, who has his heart missing,[13] or the *Motor Cyclist* (*c.* 1957) at the Shell Centre Downstream Building off Belvedere Road, Waterloo. I was terribly impressed with all this work; I just thought it was wonderful that people could make these things, and I was fascinated with them. I'd started photographing musicians and I had this idea about photographing sculptors. I wrote to Barbara Hepworth and Anthony Caro,[14] and Siegfried Charoux, and another sculptor called Richard Bentley Claughton.[15] I did write to Elisabeth Frink and Lynn Chadwick[16] too, and other people, but they didn't reply, or they didn't want to do it. I'd done it before with actors. I did it with Alec McCowen and Tom Courtenay,[17] people like that, and they replied.

Barbara Hepworth was quite well-known by then, but even Anthony Caro wasn't particularly famous. Hepworth was very receptive. I photographed her, and she bought a lot of my photographs, which was wonderful; prints meant I made money, which was great. She was very nice. Caro was particularly kind to me and said that I was much better at photographing people than sculpture. Then he commissioned me to come back and photograph his family, which was very good of him. Charoux was amazing and he and his wife, Margarethe, became friends of mine. They lived in Hampstead, and they had a beautiful house, it's Hampstead Garden suburb I think, and I used to go round there quite often. There was a sculpture in the garden, and he wanted me to photograph it. He did it himself too, so he gave me his negatives, absolutely filthy negatives, covered all over with God knows what! I had to make prints of them for Christmas cards and stuff like that! Then after he died, Margarethe and I carried on a friendship, and she introduced me to lots of clients.

At the same time, I had a boyfriend from Nigeria who was a sculptor called Lucky Wadiri. Lucky was, well he was 'Mr Hip', you know, he was one of the jazz scene people. He wore snazzy suits and stuff. He was a friend of Ida Kar.[18] We would talk about sculpture, he would tell me about sculpture, and I wanted to meet Ida Kar because her photographs were wonderful. She was one of the people that I modelled myself on, until I started to be impressed by people like W. Eugene Smith and so on.[19] Well, actually, I had a lot of people that I admired greatly, and they were all influences really. We went to see her, but she was never in! It's a bit of a non-story! We went to her place about three times. I met people who'd say, oh yes, I knew Ida Kar very well, we always used to go around to her place. I thought, well, why was she always out when we went round there? She was never in! That's the only thing about that. Now I don't know if Lucky knew Ronald Moody, I don't remember ever having a conversation with him about Moody, but there is a connection, and I'll come to that later on. It was in my head; sculpture was in my head. I never wanted to be a sculptor, I used to like painting and drawing.

Sculpture was in the air, that's the thing. I liked art, I used to draw and paint myself, not very much, just at school really, and I did a few paintings and so on, but I didn't carry it on. There is something about sculpture that is so impressive. You just look at it and you think, how did somebody do that? I really appreciate that I've had the chance to touch Barbara Hepworth's sculptures and sit on Anthony Caro's sculptures! He let me sit on one of them! It's very funny because reading my interview with Ronald Moody he says, talking about his style of work, 'that anything is permissible in art, but it all depends on whether you think that art has anything to do with life.' Then he went on to talk about people whose constructions consist of girders and steel tubing, and of course, that is Anthony Caro!' I must admit as much as I liked Caro and I saw the power of his work, it didn't move me, and it didn't move my heart, whereas Ronald Moody's work did.

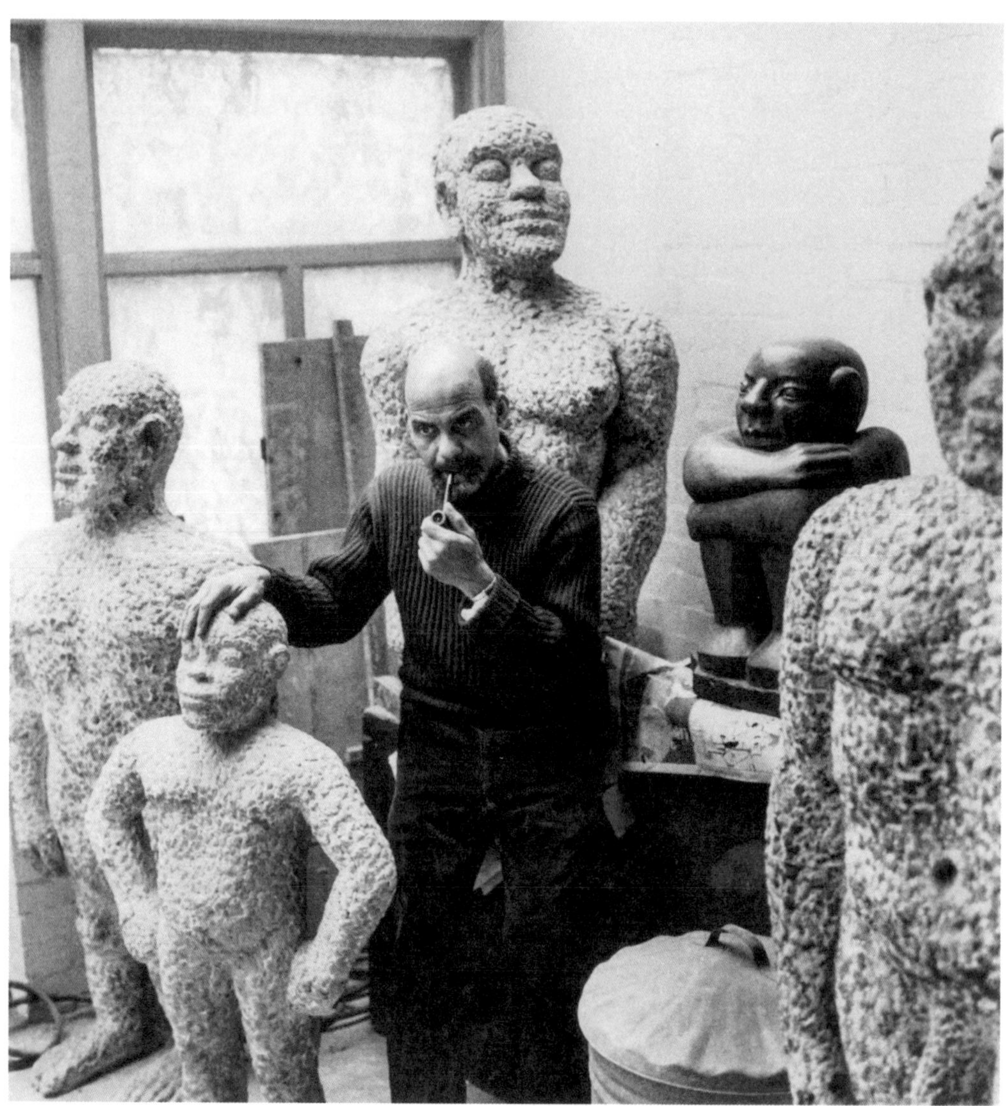

Ronald Moody with *Concrete Family* at Fleming Close Studios, Fulham, 1963. Photograph by Val Wilmer

On Cynthia Moody

I got to know Cynthia Moody in the 1990s. She wrote to me because she'd seen the photographs of Moody and liked them a lot; she thought they were the best photographs that had been taken of him. The thing is, we were very friendly for a long time. We met and were in touch all the time. I mentioned Lucky Wadiri to her. Moody and Wadiri must have been in an exhibition together, because Cynthia gave me some lead into an exhibition that he'd been in, which may have been to do with Commonwealth sculptors, and Moody was in it as well. I always wanted to write something about Lucky. He died many years ago.

In the article that Cynthia wrote about Ronald Moody's *Midonz*, she explains how she discovered the lost sculpture. She says that she 'was sifting through all Ronald's archives and sifting through forty-nine years of press clippings, and she struck gold': a 1938 item from the *New York Amsterdam News*.[20] But *I* found that article! I used to go the British Library newspaper library all the time. I used to spend Saturdays there for a couple of years. I was going through many, many publications, and often looking at the *New York Amsterdam News*. I found this news item and sent it to her. She said it was so wonderful because it had given her a clue as to where this sculpture was, and she could start from there. She was extremely pleased, and I was very pleased too. She was a very stately and rather grand woman, and I imagine that it was probably a bit of a struggle to advocate for the legacy of an 'unknown' Jamaican sculptor to mainstream art institutions in the UK. I don't mix with arts people, but recently, when I told a few people that I was going to contribute to a piece on Ronald Moody, for the best part nobody had heard of him. I still have to explain who he is. It's the same with Aubrey Williams, who I also knew quite well. They're not known particularly because Black artists aren't, unfortunately, as we know. I was interested in the Black arts scene because I was so interested in and loved jazz so much, and meeting Black musicians, some were African, some were Caribbean people, but mostly Americans, I learned so much from them in a short space of time about the history and circumstances in which that music had been created. Because of that, I had a completely different view to almost everybody I knew.

Photographing Ronald Moody

I first encountered Ronald Moody in an article in *Tropic*. That is how I first heard about Ronald Moody! At one time, I had every issue of *Tropic* (no longer), but I do remember a photograph of him, on the news page, possibly an exhibition, leaning forward and looking at a bust of one of his works. In the spring of 1963, I photographed Ronald at Fleming Close Studios in Fulham using a Rolleiflex camera, and I took twenty-four frames. I went back again in 1964 as *Flamingo* had asked me to photograph *Savacou*.[21] In the magazine, there are three photographs that come from that 1963 session. There's one in the middle, it's a bit cropped and it's a *Savacou* maquette. I have a feeling that they said to me, go and photograph this sculpture because it was being presented to the University College of the West Indies. I may have said, to John Harold probably, can we do an interview?

Ronald Moody was very accommodating to me, very friendly and nice, warm, a gentle person. My abiding feeling of him, about him, was that he was very soft physically, a soft person. Of course, at the time I was young, and I didn't understand things, but I imagine he wasn't very well because he'd been ill over the years. He had the feeling of someone who wasn't... Although he produced these powerful sculptures, he wasn't a very virile person himself. That's the only way I can express it. He was nice to be with, gentle, he was good to me. We did exchange a couple of letters. He said he liked my photographs. I then went back to see him again. That was 30 December 1976. In 1973, I had an exhibition at the V&A of my own music photographs, and I met *The Times* photography editor Norman Hall. As a result of that, I started to work for *The Times* doing shifts for about a year-and-a-half, something like that, or a year, not very often. By 1976, Michael Young was the picture editor. He phoned me up and asked me to go and photograph Ronald Moody again.

I'm sorry I can't tell you more about him from that meeting, or those meetings, I think the photographs have to speak for themselves.

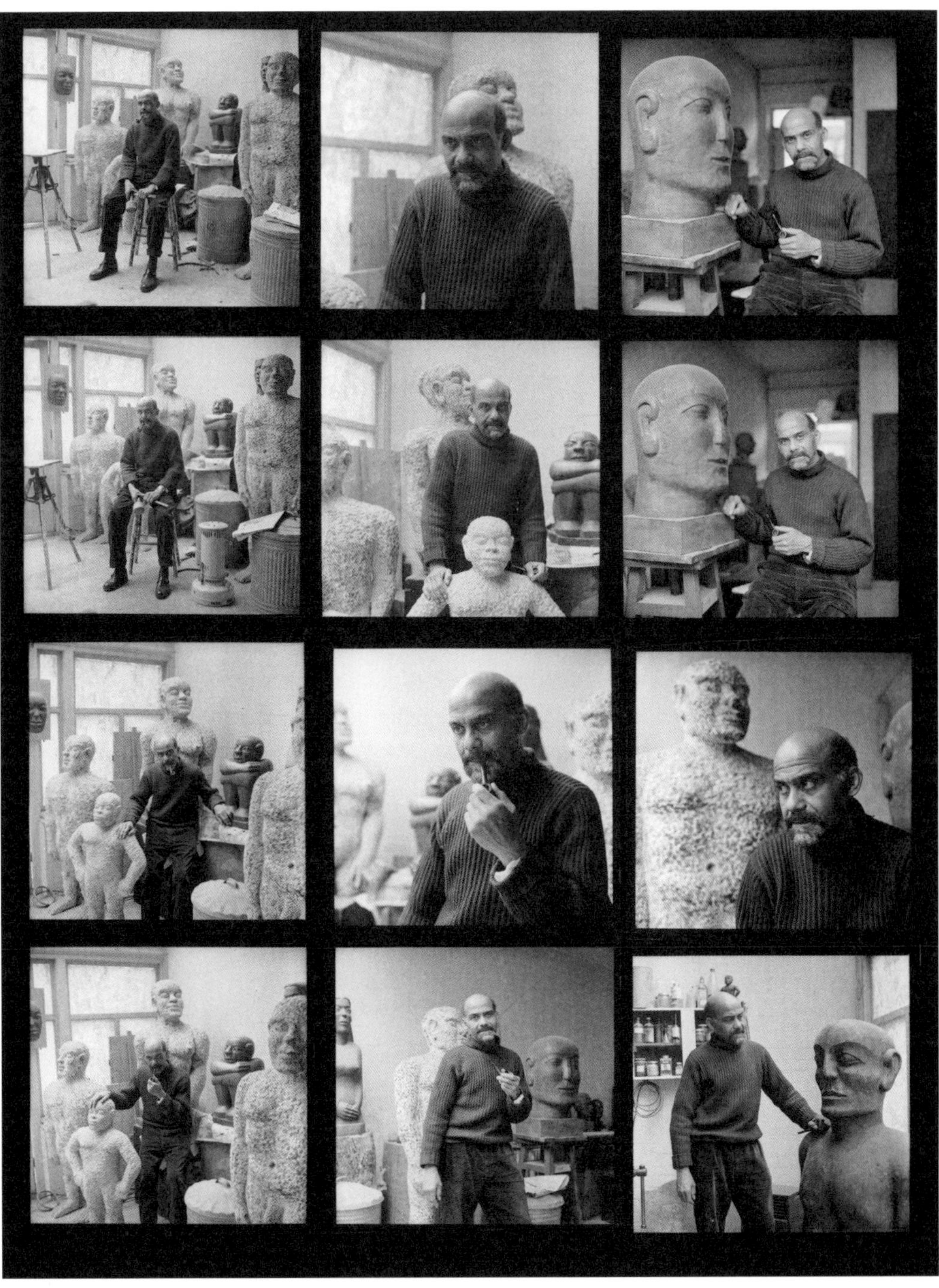

Contact sheet from Val Wilmer's shoot with Ronald Moody at Fleming Close Studios, Fulham, 1963

I don't have a story about him, what he said to me, all that's in the interview. My feeling of him was of softness and nothing abrasive. I could make a clever statement and say the only abrasive thing about him was his chisel or something, but that might be misinterpreted. He was nice, he was very nice, and that's what Cynthia saw when she found the photographs.

They do seem to be just about the only portraits of him that are known. I don't know if many others exist, but mine obviously show him in a positive light, I would say. They show somebody who's connected to their art. He looks very much like he's part of the group [of *Concrete Family*]. He's got the group of figures, the concrete figures in the studio. Ida Kar photographed different artists and also writers with their work. The thing I liked about her work was, she made them inseparable, not inseparable, but part of... They were their work. I can't really put it into words. The connection was there, and I've always tried to do that myself. I think that when you're young and you do things, it's like people who write songs, they write wonderful songs when they're nineteen, but they can't do it when they're forty. You just photograph what you see, you just go for it, you don't manipulate or try to be clever. The minute you try too hard, you can't see it. It's the same with music, it's the same with books. You can see any book that's been written, if it's been written over and over again, you can tell. It's not natural.

You want the natural thing. I hope my photographs are natural. I just walked in there, that's what I saw and that's what I photographed. They've been used quite a lot and if people like them, I think it's because I was a young person and he was a very gentle and obliging person, very warm and natural, I suppose you'd say, which is a bit of a cliché. What you see is what you get, it was that sort of thing. There was no artifice, or I hope there was no artifice, on either my part as a photographer or his as the subject. We were just ourselves. I mean, these photographs of Moody, I like them myself, and I'm not going to go around saying they're wonderful if they're not, but they are quite nice, they are quite good. The National Portrait Gallery has recently acquired one of my portraits of Moody, so it is going to be in their permanent collection. King's College also bought a photograph of Moody from me to display on their premises. It was used to accompany an article, 'Ronald Moody: Between Concrete and Wood'.[22]

I have had amazing experiences in life and I'm very grateful for that. I really am exceptionally grateful to all the people who helped me. Some of them had no need to be kind to me, but they took me into their lives and their world, and they looked after me in quite a caring way sometimes, and I really appreciate that. Of course, you learn from the bad experiences too.

I developed an affinity for creative people, well lots of people, not just artists; you develop that and mix with different people, and you become a different person. I'm a middle-class, white English woman, I'm eighty-one years old, good grief! Still here! I've had experiences that have changed me forever, and standing in a cotton field in Mississippi has been just as impactful to me as meeting Ronald Moody in a studio in Fulham and seeing the majesty of his work. These are experiences that change you forever.

This text is based on an interview between Val Wilmer and Ego Ahaiwe Sowinski that took place on 26 April 2023.

Meet Ronald Moody: Story and Pictures by Valerie Wilmer (*Flamingo*, November 1964)

I first met Ronald Moody about a year ago, when I was working on a photographic feature on sculptors. I was immediately impressed by this quiet, almost shy man whose personal gentleness is not evident in his powerful sculpture. I was also impressed by the originality of his work, for he cannot be conveniently pushed into any of the neat little pigeonholes or 'schools of thought' beloved by the critics. His figures, usually carved in wood or concrete, are basically symbolic and fall midway between out-and-out realism and abstraction. He has attempted a few abstract things but is not really interested in this approach. He says, 'I do not do non-objective art, I always do things with recognizable objects. On the other hand, it's not exactly

Royal Academy realism.' Jamaican-born Moody first came to Europe towards the end of the 1930s after studying dentistry. His sudden desire to sculpt was aroused after a visit to the British Museum. 'I simply discovered it one day by seeing some things that I liked and this got me thinking. After that I began to go to studies and friends helped me by lending me tools and so on. My parents, though, weren't too keen on my giving up dentistry.'

But parents and Jamaica were too far away to deter a man already convicted [*sic*] in a new way of life, so Moody did a professional course in London and then went to Paris. There he staged his first one-man show at the Galerie Billiet-Vorms at the end of 1937.

> The critics were very good and very helpful, so I decided to stay in Paris. I met many artists there – you know how it is, people come and go – Paris is very stimulating. It has all changed today, though; Paris has become very commercial. Now the galleries only want you to do what they think will sell and not what you really want to do. Now you even have artists quoted on the Stock Exchange. Picasso is one of the examples.

He would have stayed in France but for the outbreak of war and the Nazi persecution that caused him to flee to England in 1941. He practiced dentistry by day and sculptured at night and put on another exhibition in 1946 at London's Arcade Gallery. A period of illness followed and he was forced to spend four years in hospital, but as with most artists, the dream of exhibiting again 'offset frustration and worry. In fact that was what kept my mind intact.'

In July 1950, he was able to exhibit again and once more the critics were impressed by the latent strength lying in his sturdy figures. No particular influences are evident in his work, but as with all artists there is always some influence in the initial thought behind their work. 'At first I was very much influenced by Egyptian art,' declares Moody. 'Later I became very much interested in the art of Africa and the East, and I suppose my background lies somewhere in the middle.' Ronald Moody has been rather sweepingly described as an authority on the history of art, but he protests that 'one is a sculptor and begins to be interested in all aspects of the subject. One reads and so on but I don't set out to take a degree in the subject. Some time ago I gave a talk at Worcester College, Oxford, on the Visual Arts of the West Indies, but that's as far as it's gone.'

This year he was commissioned to sculpt a figure to stand outside the University of the West Indies in Jamaica, a gift from Professor Archibald Leman Cochran, director of the General Medical Research Council's Epidemiological Institute at Cardiff to their respective unit in Jamaica. The three-metre-tall (10 ft) figure with parrot-like head will be cast in aluminium and was a good opportunity for Moody to put into practice his interest in Caribbean mythology. It is an attempt to portray Savacou, one of the Carib gods who was in charge of thunder and the strong winds and eventually became a star in the Carib hierarchy.

The impressive figure, to be placed in front of the university, has given the sculptor his first visit to Jamaica since he left there almost thirty years ago. Ronald Moody's opinions on art are interesting and very sensible. 'I think art has to do with living things rather than theoretical attitudes, and my point of view in art is trying to emphasise that side. I am not interested in art as an end in itself but as art for life's sake. In the past art was always part of the community, it always had a function, but now it tends to be divorced from that. I do feel that someday it will be once more integrated into society.'

He has little time for the completely abstract approach but feels that out of all the experimenting some kind of synthesis will emerge. 'There is a great deal of uncertainty because of the times in which we live, the throwing overboard of things and not knowing where to go. Anything is permissible in art, but it all depends on whether you think that art has anything to do with life.' He quoted people whose constructions consist of girders and steel tubing: 'When one looks at anything as massive as a steel girder one gets some kind of reaction, but it's not necessarily enough. I feel my work has just a little more.'

And Ronald Moody's work does have just that little more. A group of his sensitively carved and moulded figures stand silently in the corner of his Chelsea studio, looking for all the world like a little family. Although they stand there silently, they are so very appealing that their creator smilingly says, 'They really look as though they are talking about us!' He has that kind of rapport with his work.

Originally published in *Flamingo*, November 1964.
Reprinted with permission of Val Wilmer.

CHAPTER 8

Savacou: An Emblem of the Caribbean Artists Movement

In 1963, a year after Jamaican Independence, Ronald Moody was commissioned by Professor Archibald Leman Cochrane (1909–1988), the director of the relatively newly established Medical Research Council's Epidemiological Research Unit in Cardiff, Wales, to produce a public sculpture for the sister Unit on the Mona Campus of the University of the West Indies (UWI). Professor Cochrane was known for the meticulous quality of his work and for his development of randomized controlled trials. His Unit had an international reputation for its surveys and studies of the natural history and causes of a wide range of common diseases. Dr William Einar Miall (1917–2004) was the director of the sister Epidemiological Research Unit, UWI, Mona Campus, Jamaica, from 1962 to 1971. He was a pioneer in research on blood pressure and hypertension trials for the Medical Research Council, which led to the establishment of the General Practice Research Framework.[1] Moody created the sculpture *Savacou* (1963) for the site, and it still stands proudly in the Mona Campus today. In a letter to Dr Miall, Moody provided his thoughts about the form of *Savacou*, alongside photographs and sketches. He explained:

> My reason for the sketches of an 'abstracted' parrot
> form is that I feel that something Caribbean in origin
> rather than a purely abstract form, seen anywhere,
> is more in keeping with the recent Independence;
> not as an aid to Nationalism but to help to foster
> the idea that the West Indies as such exist and that
> this figure is for the University of the W. I.[2]

The choice of material for this public artwork also reflected the economically buoyant years of the 1960s in Jamaica, when the mining of bauxite was becoming more and more profitable.[3] Moody researched the possibilities of how metal could be applied to attain the required outcome and advised that 'only Aluminium, stove enamelled (colourless), will successfully withstand the rain, heat and wind of Jamaica.'[4] *Savacou* is one of a group of symbolic and fantastic birds that Moody created around this time, and might

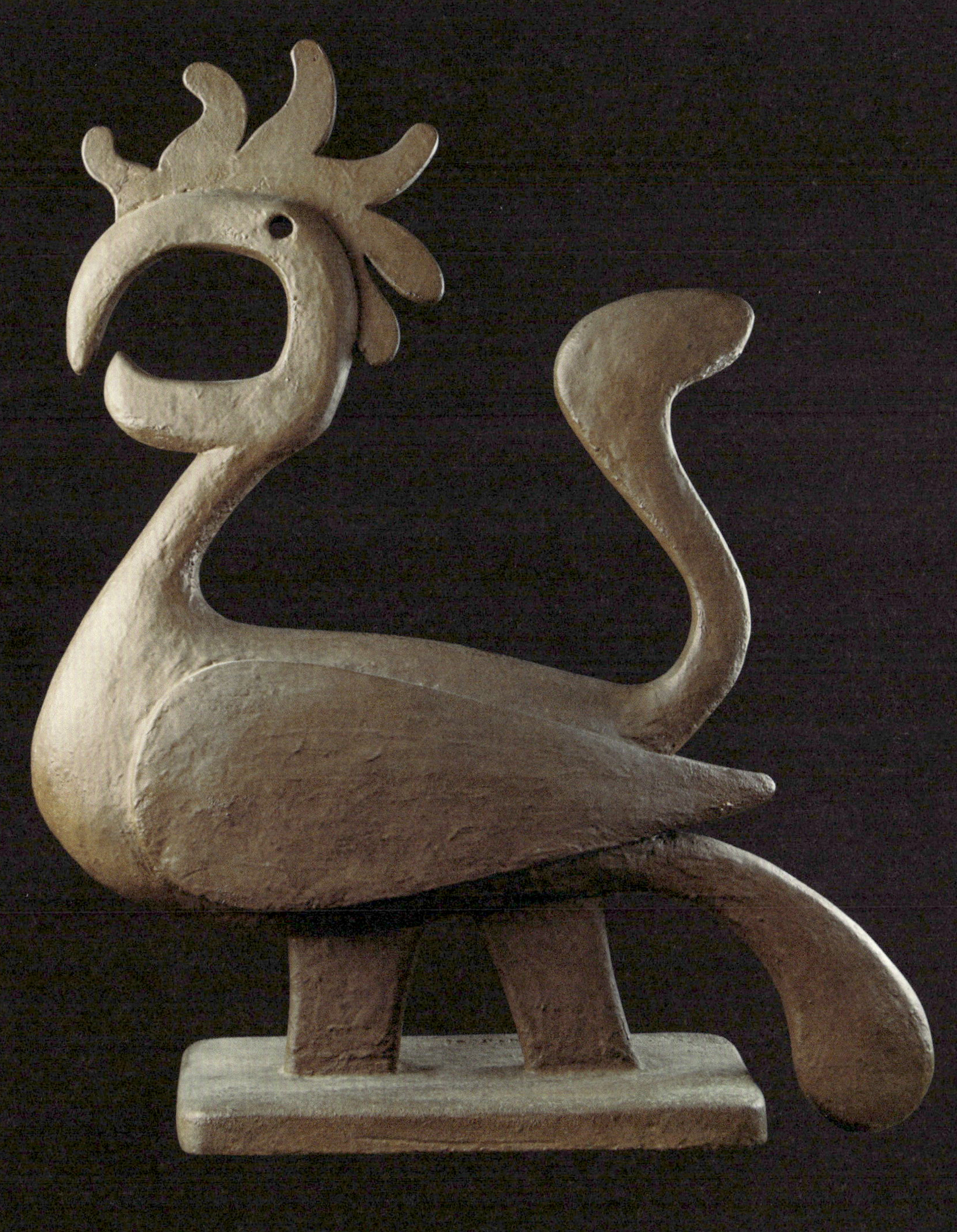

Ronald Moody, *Savacou*, 1964, plastic with copper coating, 72 × 62 × 23.2 cm (28 ⅜ × 24 ½ × 9 ⅛ in.)

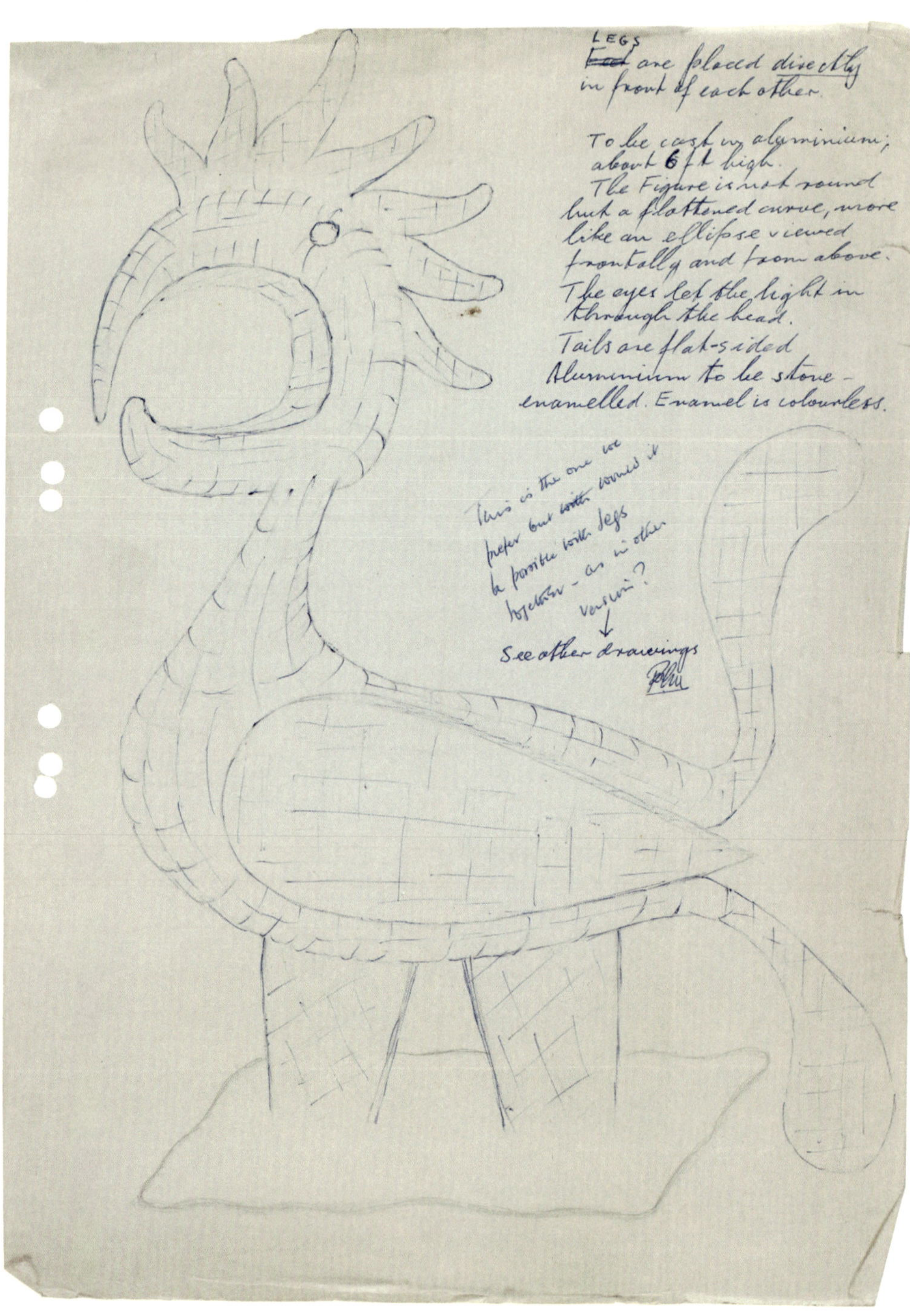

Ronald Moody, sketch of *Savacou* on one column-like leg on top of a proposed stand, 1963, ink and graphite on paper, 35.7 × 21.1 cm (14 1/8 × 8 3/8 in.)

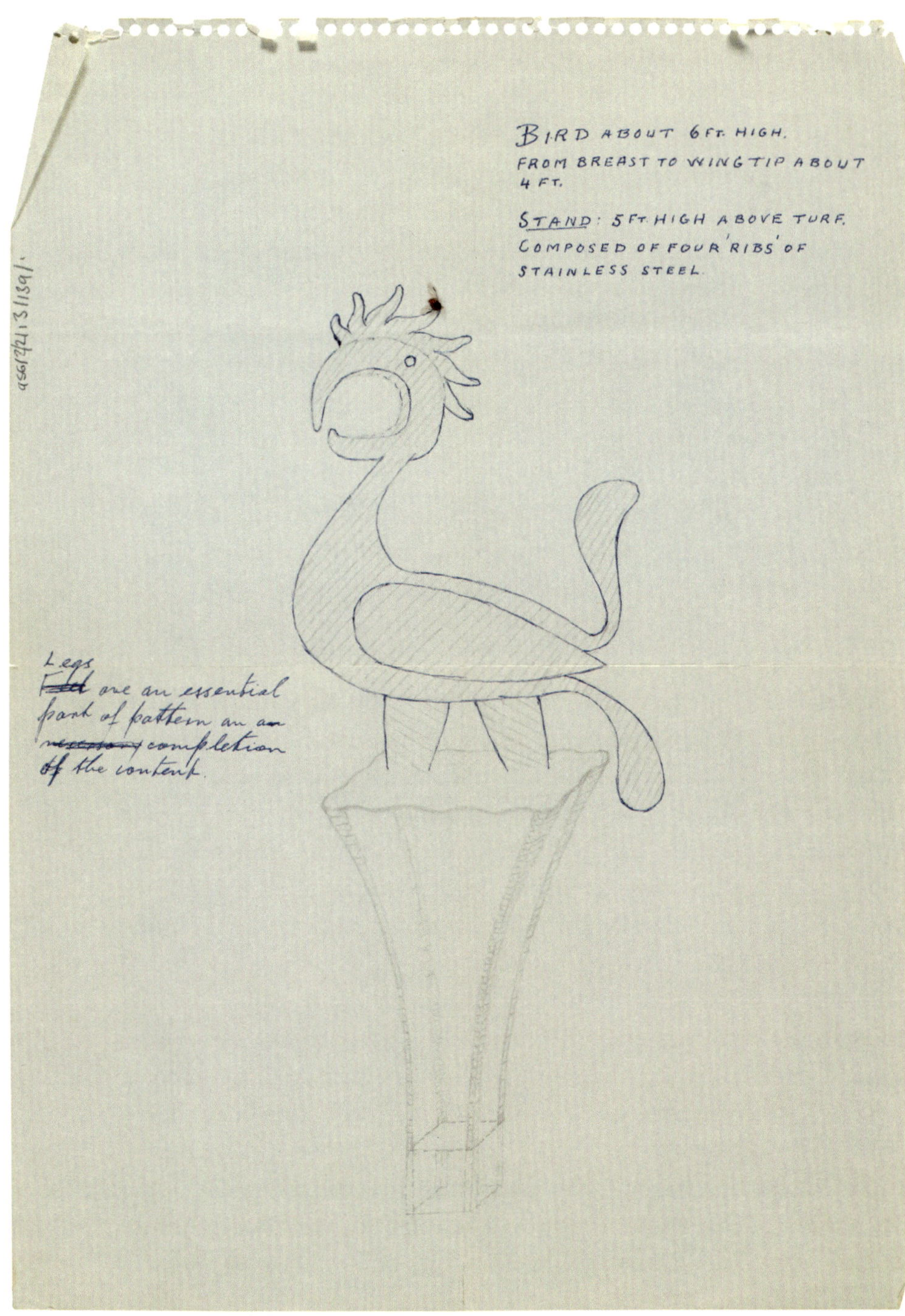

Ronald Moody, sketch of *Savacou* on two legs, 1963, ink and graphite on paper, 35.7 × 21.1 cm (14 1⁄8 × 8 3⁄8 in.)

present a visible connection back to the influence of Egyptian art. In a brief article written by Moody on *Savacou*, he states:

> The subject I chose is from Carib Cosmology. The sun, the moon and other heavenly bodies were considered to be human. In this hierarchy there is Savacou, who controlled thunder and the strong winds, became a bird and, after a sojourn on earth, changed into a star.
>
> I found Savacou a very exciting subject for a piece of sculpture. He is of West Indian origin, human and divine, and ruler over two very unruly elements. I confined myself to his stay on earth as a bird and have given him some tinge of earthly qualities; a certain arrogance expressed in his form and stance combined with a feeling of power, because of his difficult job, and perhaps a hint of things to come in the vaguely star-like shape of his comb.[5]

Moody began work on a maquette of the bird in early 1964, in plaster. While working on the maquette, he realised the proposed stand for the bird wouldn't work, so he revised his design, suggesting a pedestal. Moody was keen that the piece be able to stand up to informed criticism.[6] The *Savacou* maquette was exhibited in 'The Other Story: Afro-Asian Artists in Post-War Britain' in 1989, alongside his works *Johanaan*, *The Onlooker*, *Helene 2*, *Man... His Universe*, *Paul Robeson*, *Richard St Barbe Baker*, *Horned Bird/Orchid Bird*, *L'Homme* and *The Mother*.[7] Moody produced the first in his series of birds made in plaster in 1954, titled *Bird of Prey*, and he later produced a version carved from oak, initially giving it the same name before renaming it *Harpy* (1960). In 1962, he created a small concrete and fibreglass stilt-legged bird, *Couroumon* (1962–63), which had been the artists original visualisation of the heron incarnation of Savacou and was later cast in bronze. *Couroumon* is also the name of a star in Carib mythology, a star that controlled the tides and also caused the heavy seas that upset the canoes.[8] Before heading off to be installed in Jamaica, the aluminium bird *Savacou*, plump yet slender in equal amounts, was exhibited on the lawn of the

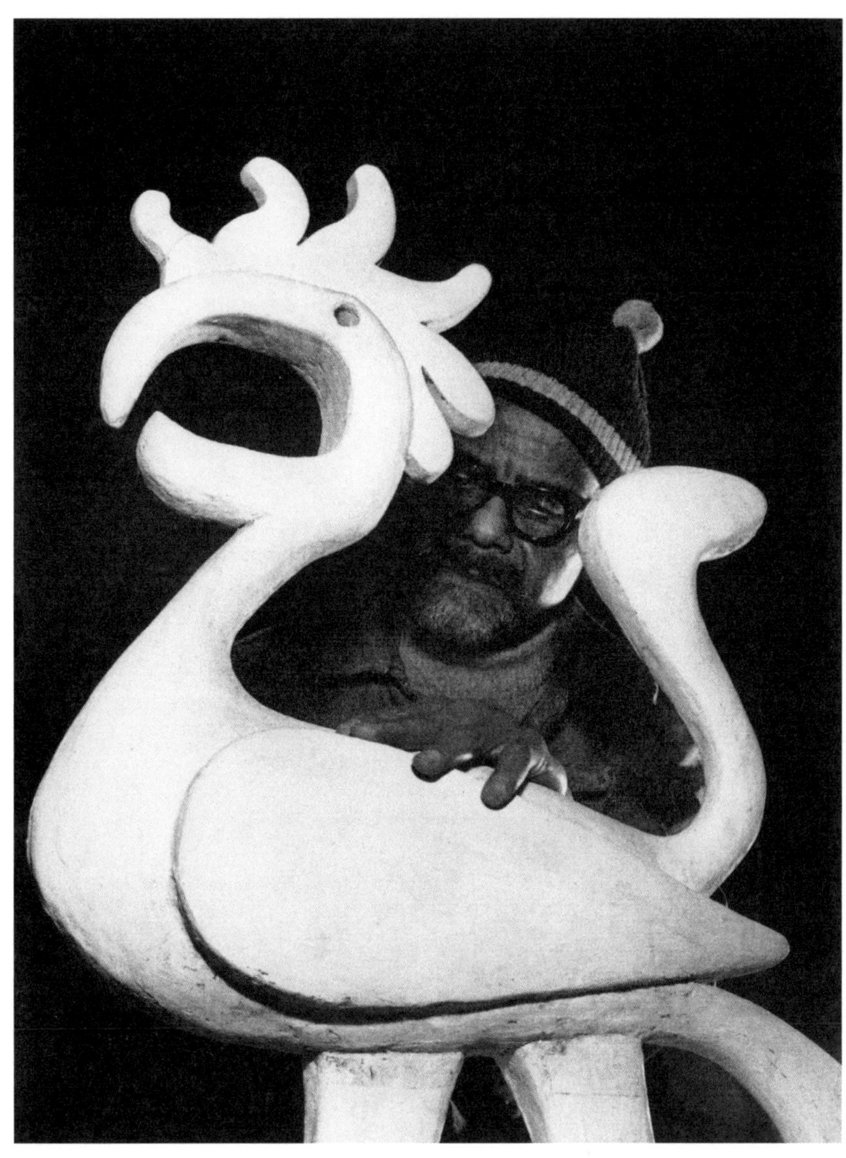

Ronald Moody working on the plaster model of *Savacou* in Fleming Close Studios, Fulham, 1963

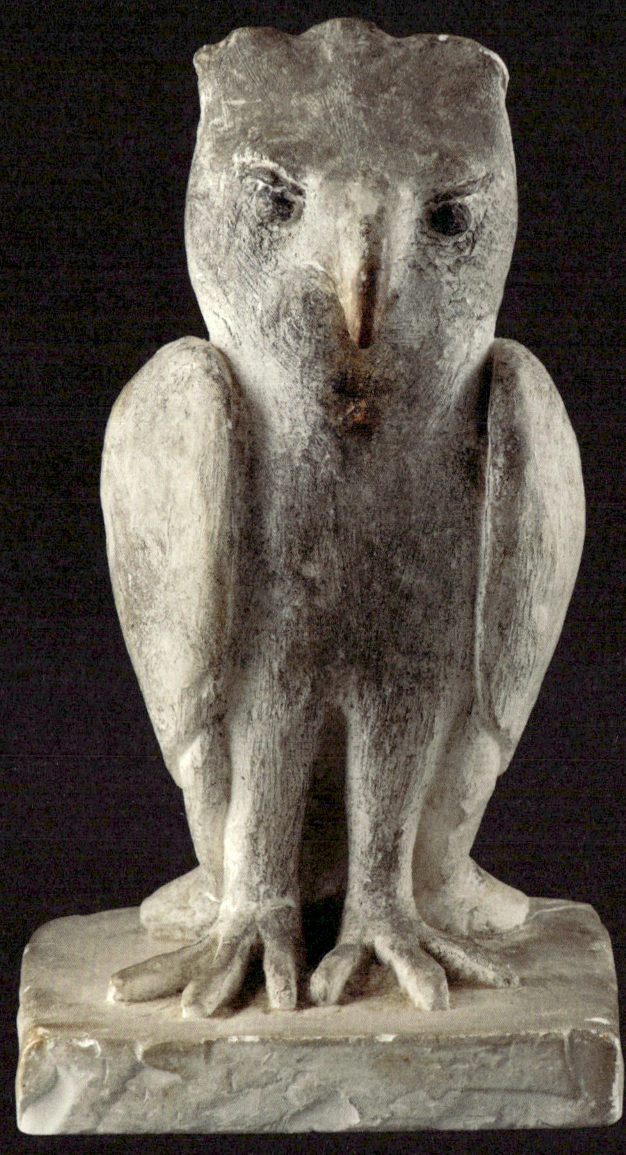

Ronald Moody, *Bird of Prey*, 1954, plaster,
22 × 12 × 19.5 cm (8 ¾ × 4 ¾ × 7 ¾ in.)

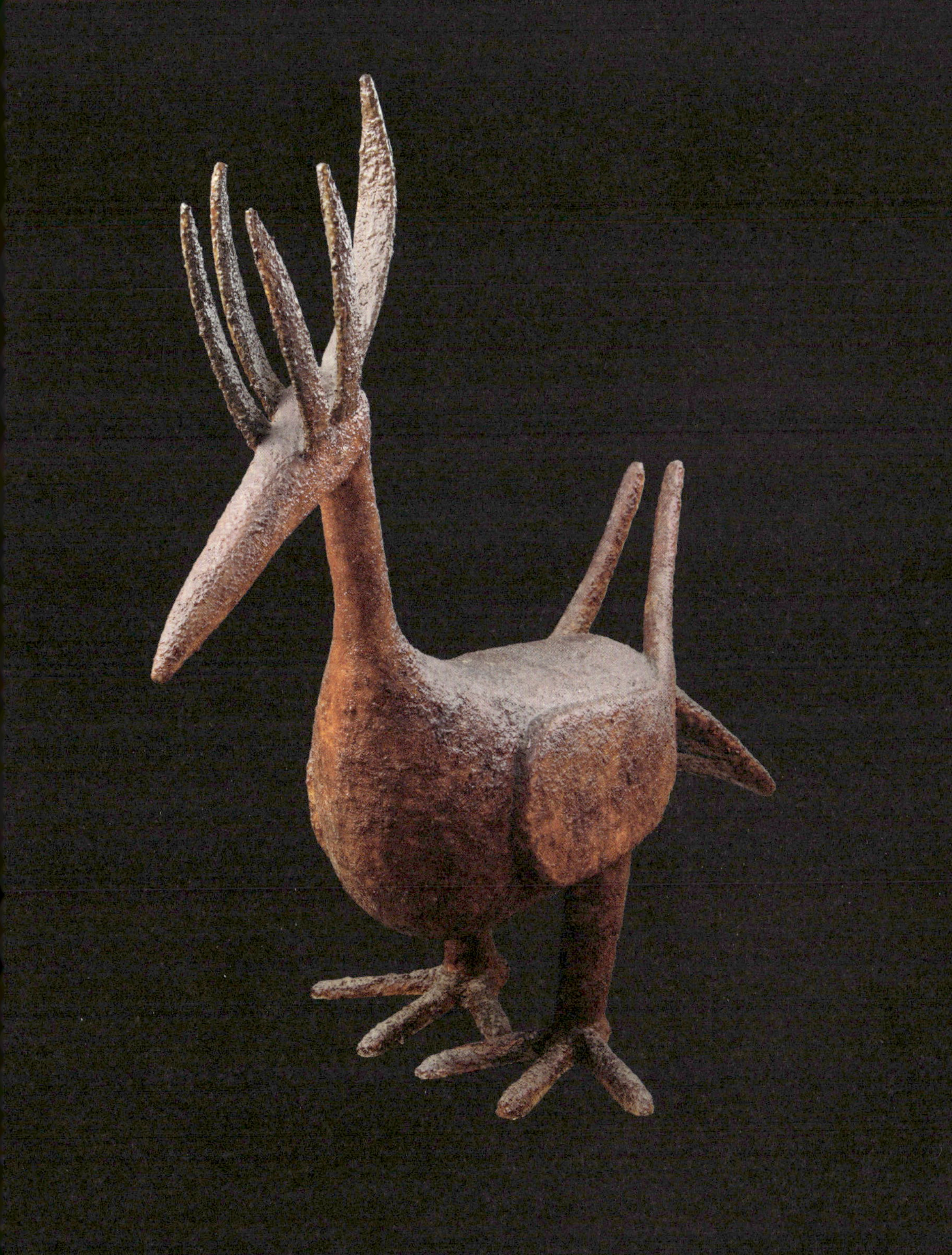

Ronald Moody, *Orchid Bird*, 1968, plaster, resin, wood chips and acrylic sheet, 114 × 95 × 29 cm (45 × 37½ × 11½ in.)

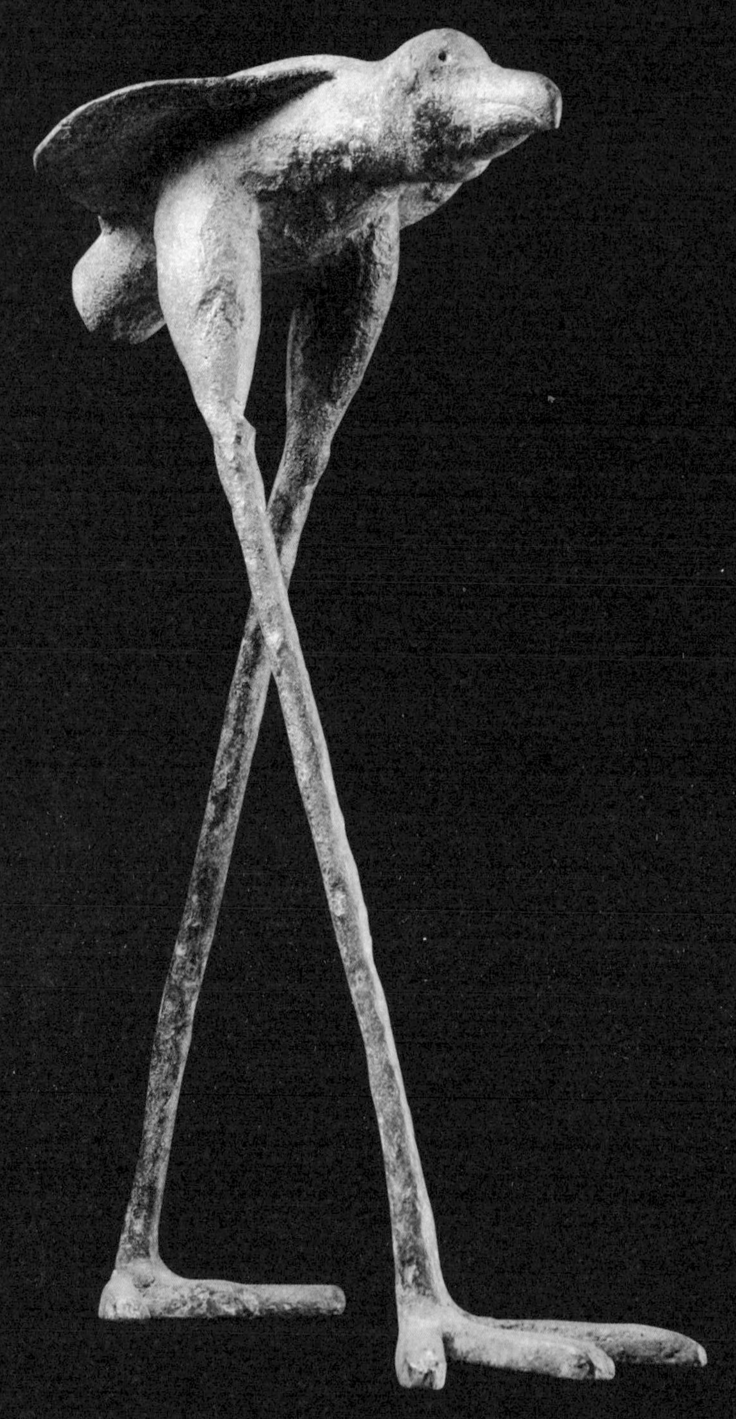

Ronald Moody, *Couroumon*, 1962–63,
bronze, 34.2 × 26.5 × 15 cm (13 ½ × 10 ½ × 6 in.)

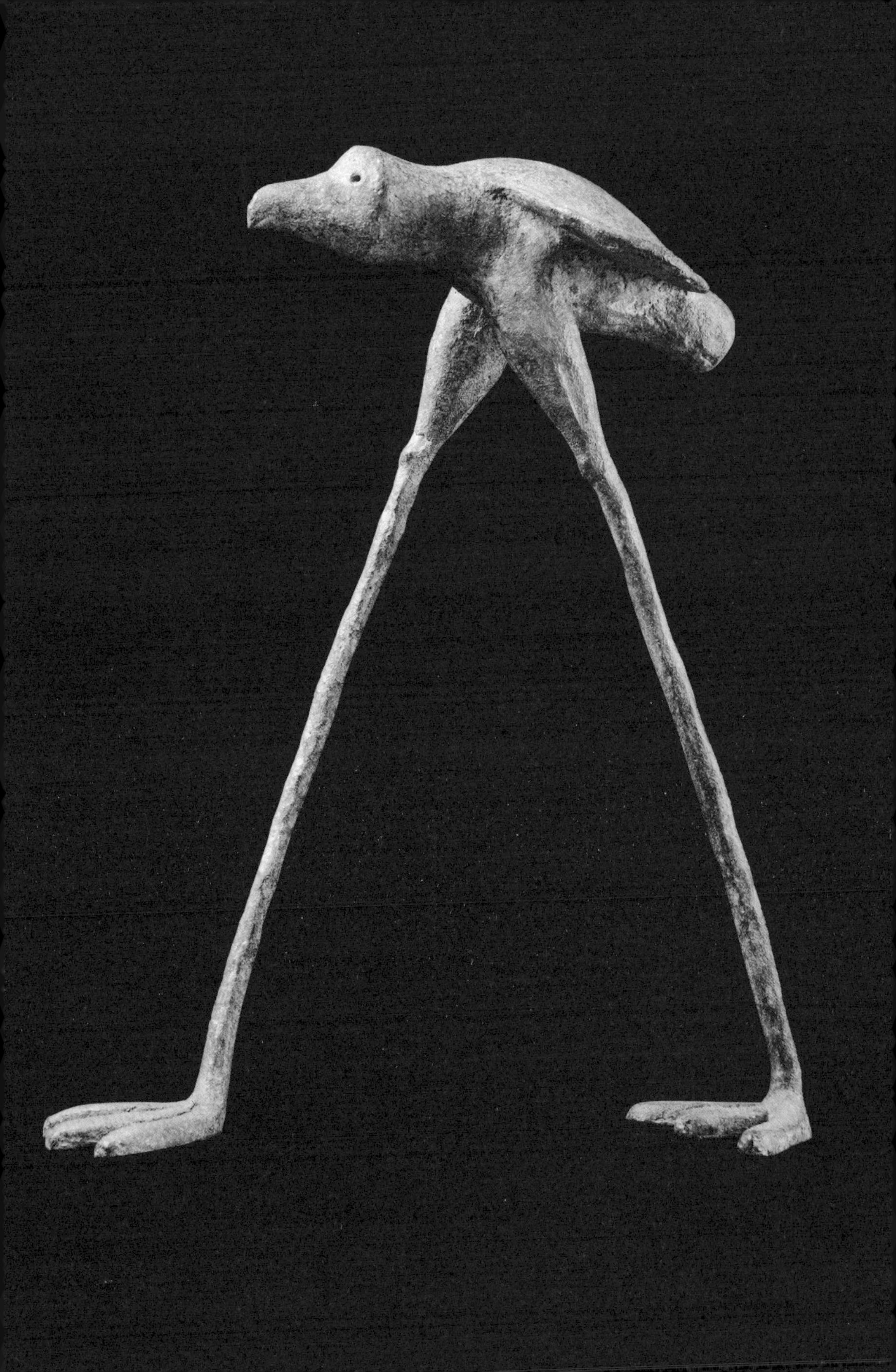

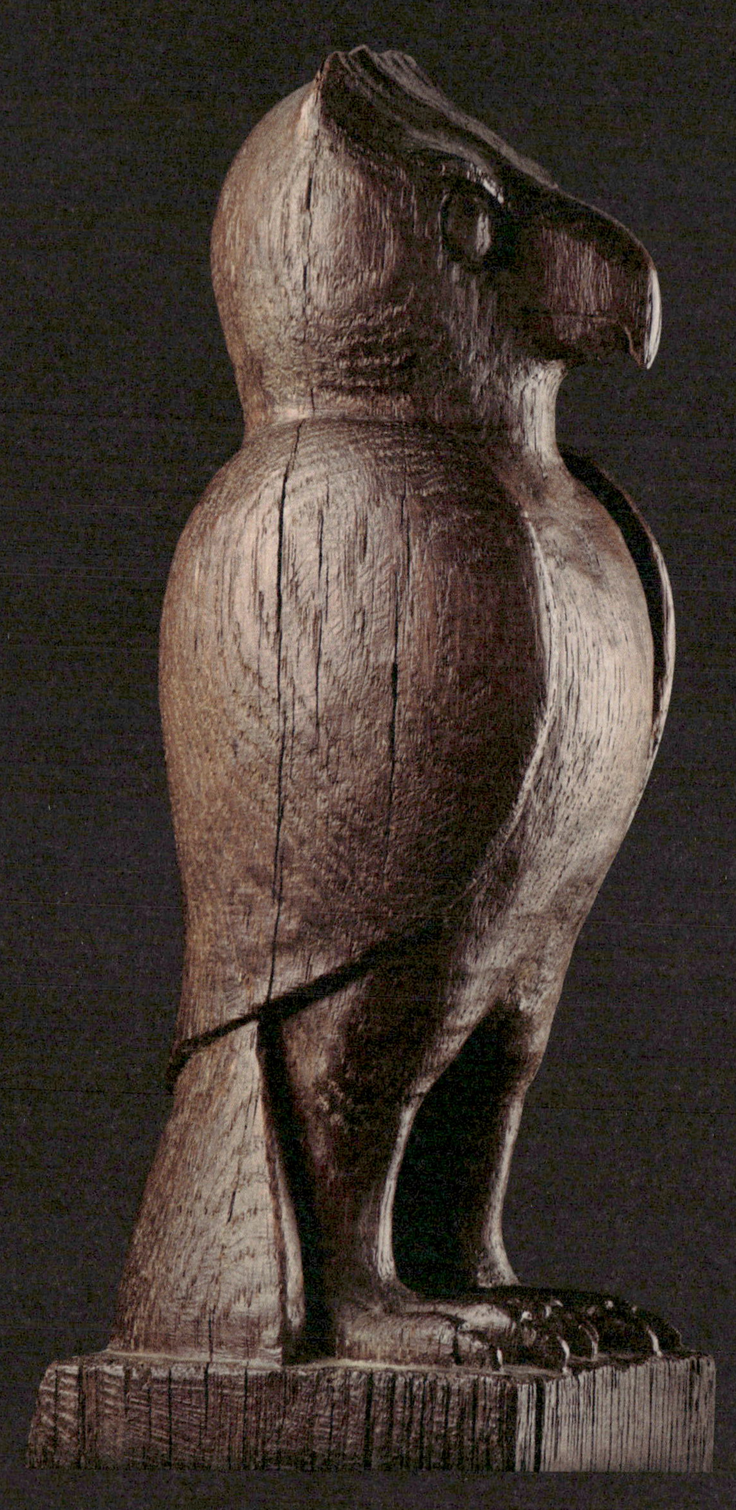

Ronald Moody, *Harpy*, 1960, oak,
46 × 11 × 11 cm (18 ⅛ × 4 ⅜ × 4 ⅜ in.)

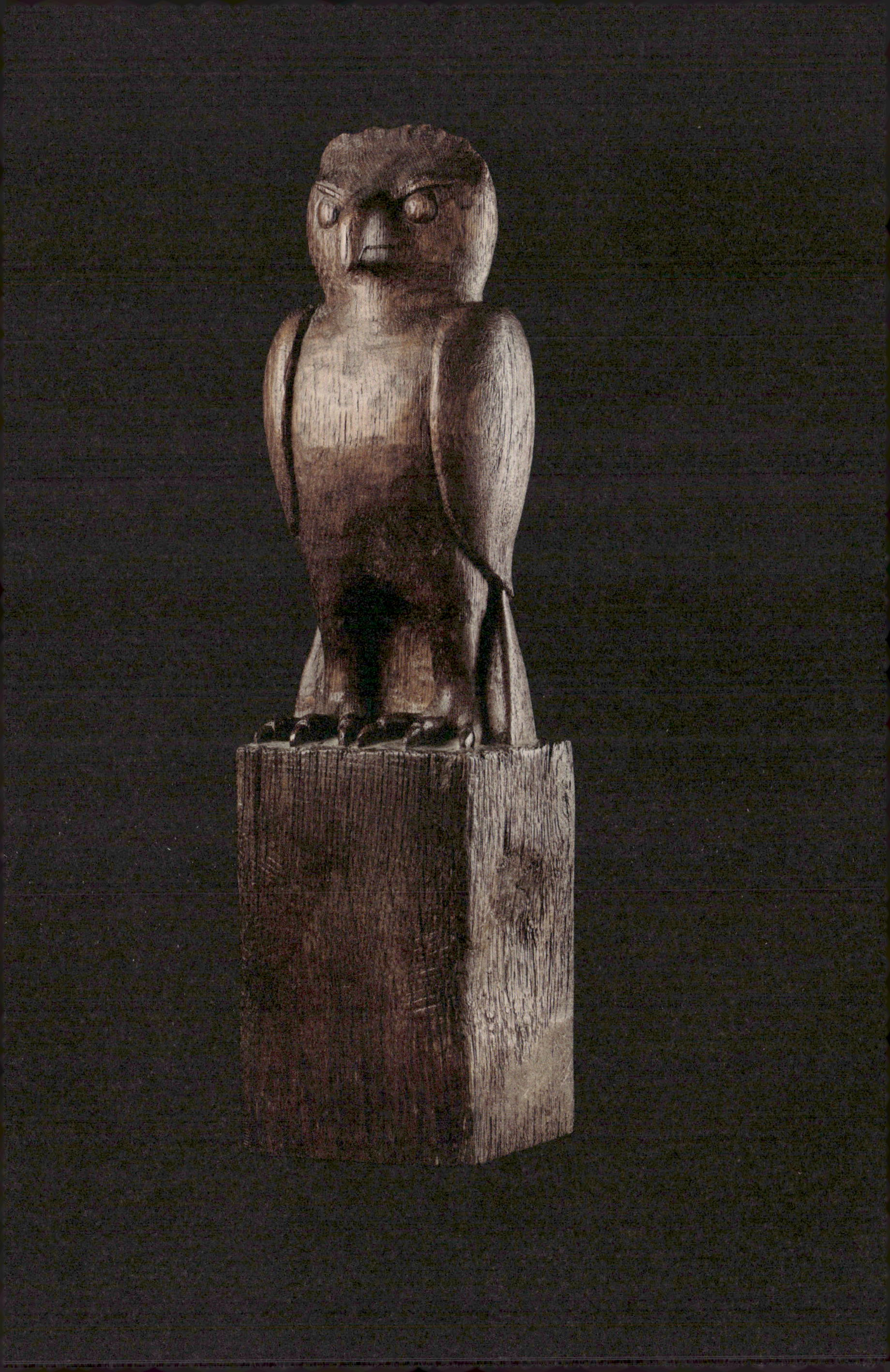

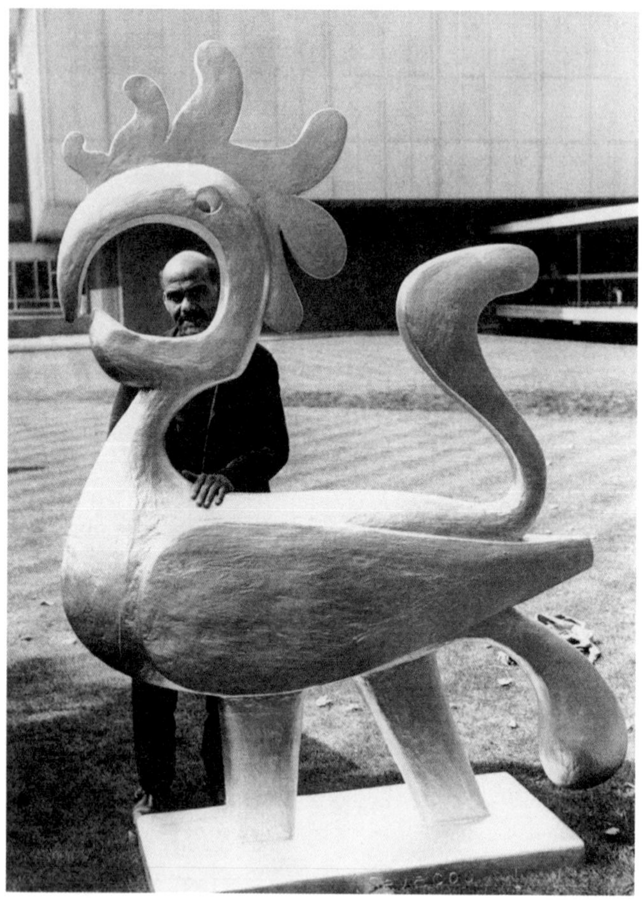

Commonwealth Institute Art Gallery, Kensington High Street, on the 24 August 1964. Moody relayed reception of its unveiling in a letter to Professor Cochrane, dated 6 September 1964:

> Savacou, covered in cellophane, arrived for his installation on the sacred lawn of the Commonwealth Institute to the clicking and mewing of innumerable cameras. (I am not sure that he approved of his new-fangled, modern covering!) It was brilliant and hot and, after he was divested of his 'alien' covering, [he] shone in all his glory, arrogant, self-confident and spurning his surroundings.[9]

Ronald Moody with *Savacou* at the Commonweath Institute, London, 1964

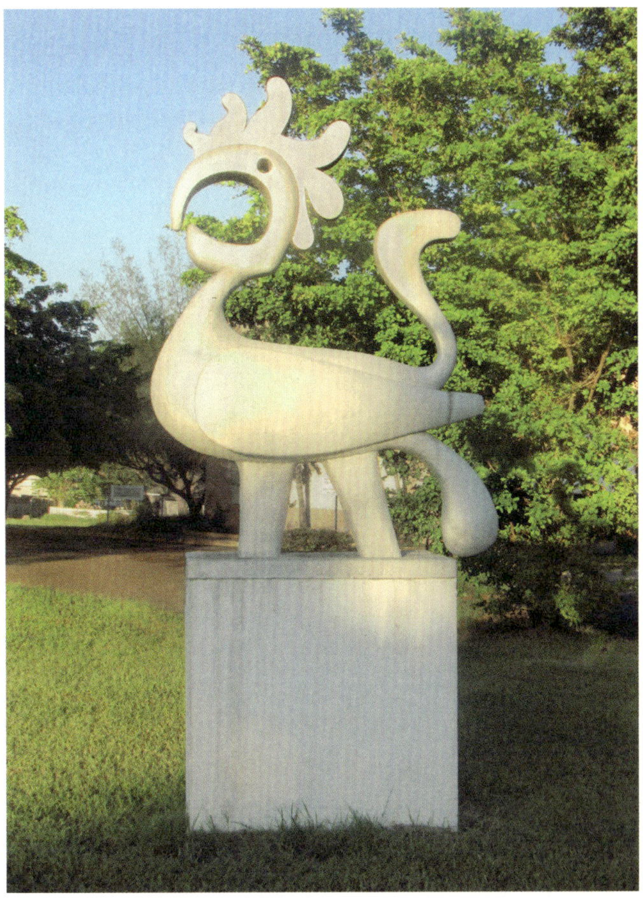

The choice to use a bird, symbolic of independence, flight, freedom and migration, is a clear statement of the importance of seeing how Moody's art could bring Carib mythology to the forefront and help make it visible. On 6 October 1964, Moody returned to Jamaica for the first time since he had left in 1923 and visited the agreed site for *Savacou* on Mona Campus, which has the backdrop of those familiar Blue Mountains. This trip renewed links with his past, and in 1967 Moody joined the Caribbean Artists Movement (CAM),[10] which began in a small, informal meeting held in a basement flat in Mecklenberg Square, London, on the evening of 19 December 1966. The origins of CAM can be traced back some years before to the University of the

Savacou at the University of the West Indies' Mona Campus, Jamaica, 2019. Photograph by Ego Ahaiwe Sowinski

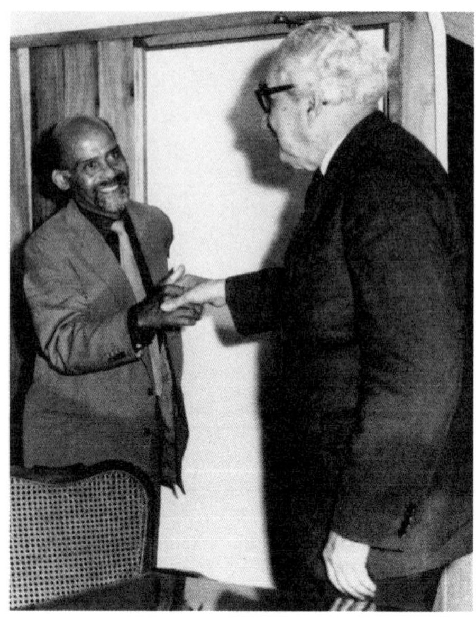

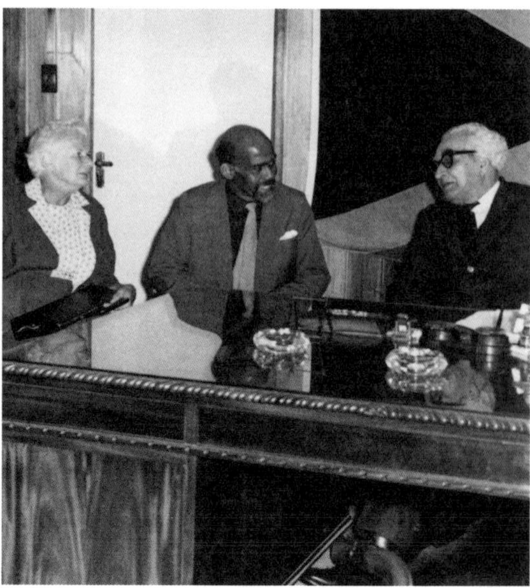

West Indies, where poet and academic Edward Kamau Brathwaite (1930–2020) had become a lecturer in the History Department in 1962, in a period that marked a new pioneering phase in Caribbean Studies. The University had opened its doors to students in 1949 and was already a creative force in the region. When CAM as an organisation ended six years later, it was noted to have a major impact on the emergence of a Caribbean cultural identity, particularly in Britain. Encouraging young members, and open to new concepts, Brathwaite was the driving spirit, insisting the movement included all arts. CAM as a movement was considered too diverse to easily be defined.[11]

CAM was founded by Brathwaite, Andrew Salkey and activist and poet John La Rose (1927–2006) and was accompanied by a magazine named *Savacou*.[12] Moody had told Brathwaite about his sculpture outside the Epidemiological Research Unit at UWI, and it was decided straight away that *Savacou* would be the journal's name. In May 1969, a typed 'Preliminary Brochure, Limited Circulation' announcing *Savacou* was issued, with Brathwaite and writer Kenneth Ramchand (b. 1939) named as general editors. The publication was created to complement the printed newsletter that documented its meetings

Moody with the Rt Hon Sir Alexander Bustamante, Prime Minister of Jamaica, during his visit to arrange the positioning of *Savacou* on the campus of the University of the West Indies, Jamaica, 1964

Ronald and Helene Moody in Jamaica with the Rt Hon Sir Alexander Bustamante, Prime Minister of Jamaica, 1964

and conferences. The magazine was published between 1970 and 1980; it was mainly literary, but in part historical and sociological. Alongside its name, the journal adopted a colophon logo based on the head of the *Savacou* sculpture, and in 1979, Moody gave permission for the Caribbean Universities' Press to use their design for the same purpose.[13] Moody participated regularly in CAM's exhibitions and debates, while maintaining his individualistic stance, contributing to activities such as the CAM Symposium on West Indian artists that took place on 2 June 1967, alongside painters Aubrey Williams and Karl 'Jerry' Craig (b. 1936), and textile designer Althea McNish.[14] Moody

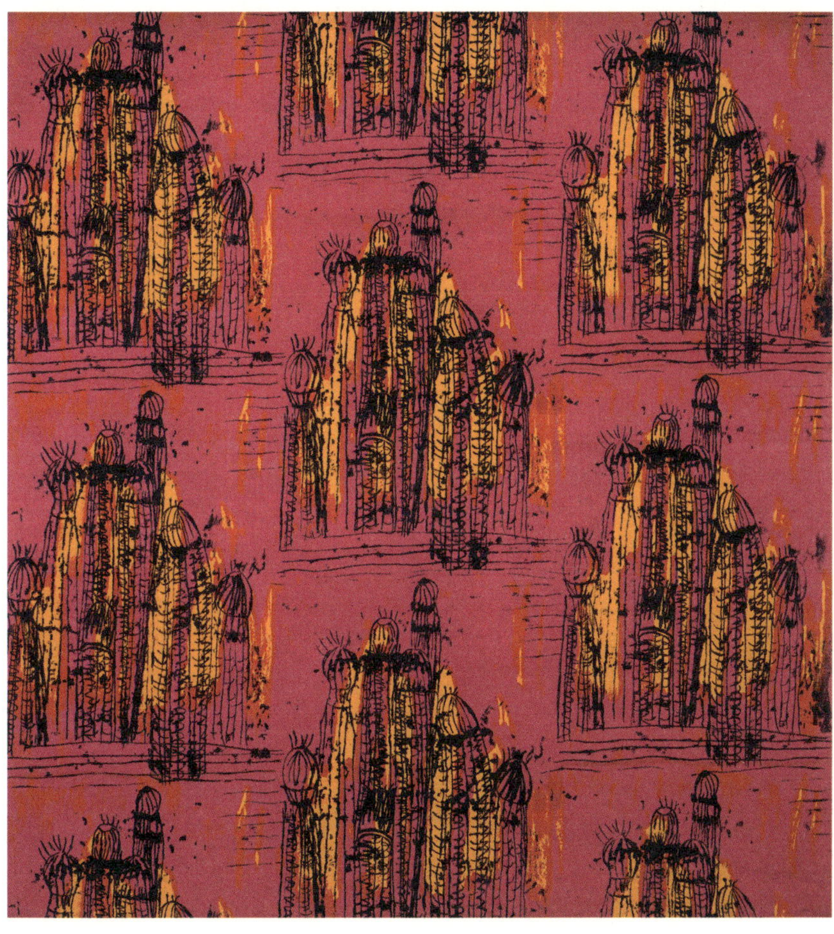

Althea McNish, *Painted Desert*, 1959, screen-printed cotton, textile design for Hull Traders Ltd

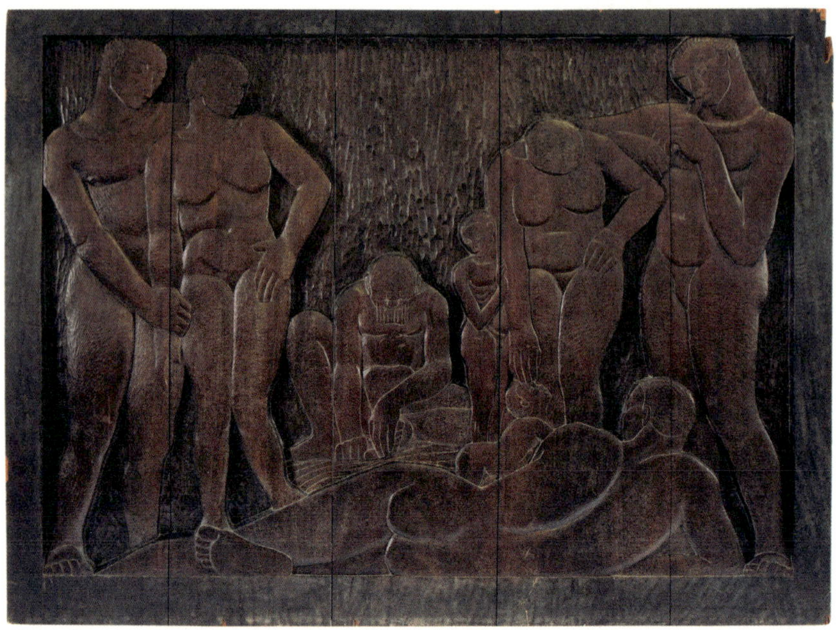

exhibited alongside Williams, McNish, Errol Lloyd, Daphne Dennison, Donald Locke (1930–2010) and Keith Simon in 1971, in an exhibition titled 'Caribbean Artists in England', held at the Commonwealth Art Gallery. The Commonwealth Institute and its galleries had opened in London in 1962, providing an important exhibiting venue for African, Asian and Caribbean artists based in the city. This exhibition, nearly a decade after opening, was deemed a venture of great importance, offering a substantial and high-profile opportunity for artists with links to the Caribbean, temporarily resident in Britain, to exhibit alongside other Caribbean artists who had made their homes in the nation's capital.[15] The long-lasting impact of CAM is evident in self-taught artist Errol Lloyd, who credits Moody, Williams and other artists of the CAM community with giving him support and practical help to fully pursue the life of an artist.[16]

The 1970s led to wider recognition of Moody's cultural contributions, and he returned to Jamaica in 1972, invited as a guest of honour by the Jamaican government to attend and participate in the Fine Arts Festival to open 'Art '72', a thirty-year review of Jamaican art

Edna Manley, *Dance for Life*, 1932, mahogany,
124.1 × 166 × 6.9 cm (48 7/8 × 65 3/8 × 2 3/4 in.)

that also marked the tenth anniversary of Independence.[17] During this visit, sculptor Edna Manley encouraged and brokered the purchase of Moody's work *Tacet* as part of what would become the National Gallery of Jamaica's permanent collection. Moody and Manley had known each other for decades: both were influenced by ancient Egypt, and both of their careers had begun in the 1930s, when Manley became known for her powerful representations of Caribbean experiences and culture as well as her political and spiritual life. They had also both exhibited in London through the interwar period, with associations such as the London Group. Manley had been elected to the London Group in 1930,[18] and Moody exhibited with them in November 1935 at the New Burlington Galleries, London. Their enduring friendship is captured in a letter from Moody to Manley dated 17 May 1957, where he asked for her thoughts and opinion on his portrait of St Barbe Baker, the 'Man of Trees', and informed her of the purchase of his artwork *Three Heads* which was destined for Delhi.[19]

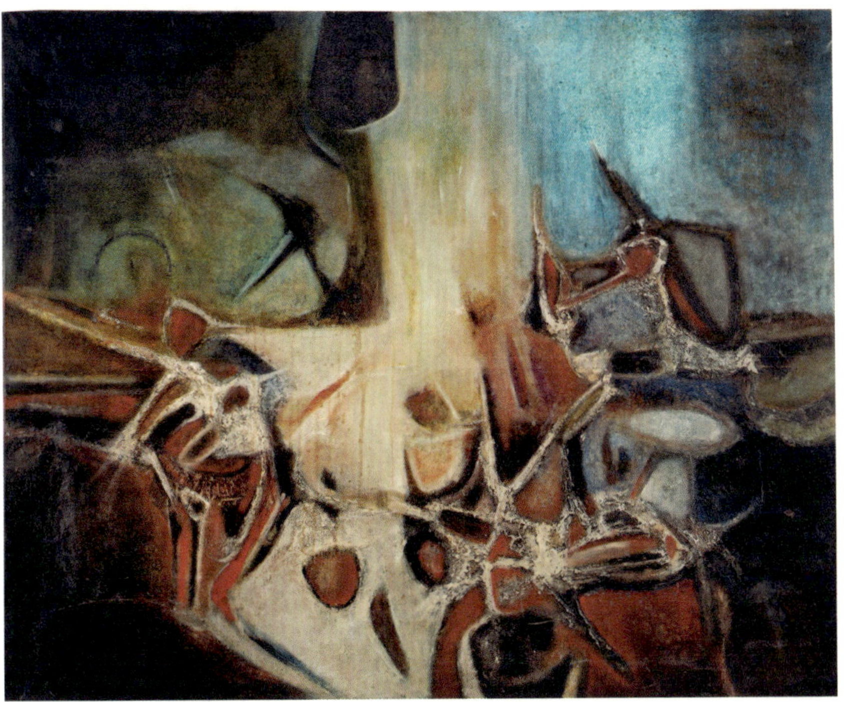

Aubrey Williams, *Heraldry at York*, 1961, oil on canvas, 151 × 182 cm (59 ½ × 71 ¾ in.)

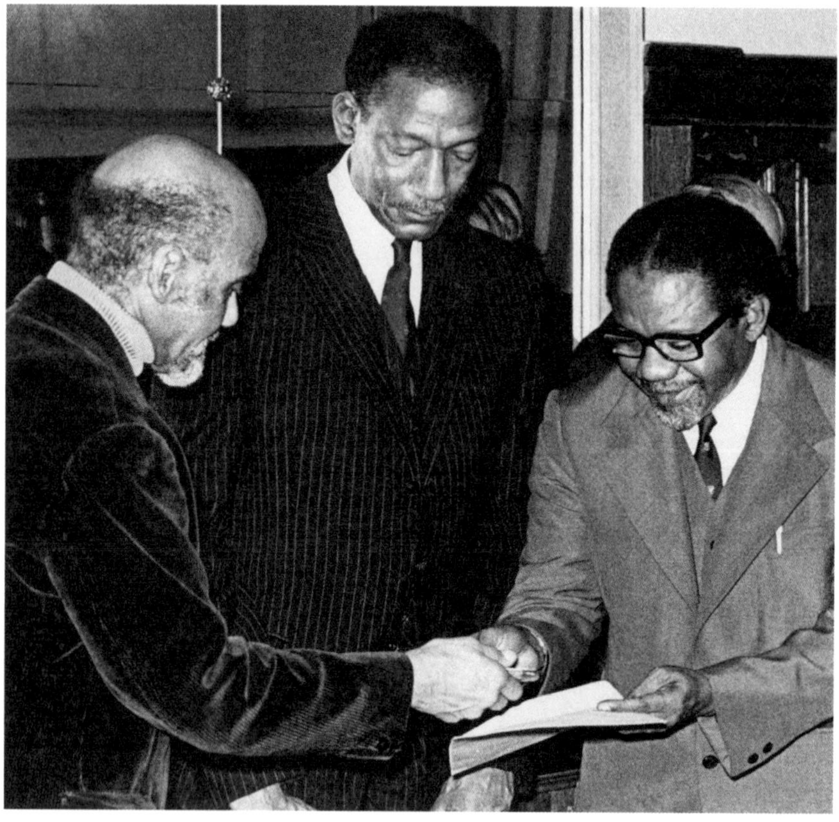

It was a busy trip filled with media interviews, and Moody also gave a series of artist talks with slides of his artworks.[20] In 1977, the Institute of Jamaica awarded him a prestigious arts award, the Gold Musgrave Medal, for his eminence as an international sculptor and for the production of a body of work of an excellence and distinctiveness that earned him the status of a Jamaican master. In 1980, the Institute awarded him a Centenary Medal for his long-standing contribution to art.[21] A Ronald Moody award was established by the Ronald Moody Estate in 1986 through an endowment of J$40,000 to the Edna Manley School for the Visual Arts (formerly the Jamaica School of Art), Kingston. The scholarship was open to final year sculpture students from the Caribbean who had completed the Diploma course at the Edna Manley.[22]

Ronald Moody being presented with the 1977 Musgrove Medal at the Jamaican High Commission, London, 1978

CHAPTER 9

Ronald Moody and the Second Festival of Arts & Culture 1977 (FESTAC '77)

'FESTAC '77', the Second Festival of Arts & Culture, took place from 15 January to 12 February 1977, and the spectacle saw more than 17,000 artists from fifty-seven countries ascend on Lagos, Nigeria, with over 500,000 spectators attending the non-stop activities and special events.[1] The festival, organised by the International Festival Committee, was designed to bring together Black and African people to create a forum for Black artists to show their works internationally, and to show their contributions to world culture, representing Black and African populations around the world.[2] The event welcomed the likes of writer Audre Lorde (1934–1992), singer-songwriters Stevie Wonder (b. 1950) and Miriam Makeba (1932–2008) and the British Afropop band Osibisa to its National Theatre, which had been specially built for the occasion.[3]

Ronald Moody was invited to serve on the UK Visual Arts Sub-Committee in January 1974, under the chairmanship of the actor Earl Cameron, to develop a programme of material. There were sub-committees for various categories: Art, Dance, Drama, Film and Documentary, Literature, and Music.[4] Other sub-committee members included photographer Neil Kenlock (b. 1950) and artist Uzo Egonu (1931–1996). They met regularly over the next few years, selecting artists to represent the UK in Nigeria and experiencing challenges in relation to coordinating and overseeing the selection process, fundraising, delays, publicity and publication, as well as an exhibition in London.[5] They put together a delegation of artists that included Winston Branch, Ossie Murray (1923–2014), Sue Smock (b. 1937), Emmanuel Jegede (b. 1943), Donald Locke (1930–2010) and Cyprian Mandala (b. 1949), as well as Moody and Uzo Egonu. The UK delegates and contributions to FESTAC '77 also included a screening of Horace Ove's 1976 film *Pressure*, a performance by Osibisa and a colloquium papers from educationalist Len Garrison (1943–2003), one of the founders of the Black Cultural Archives, London, and physician and research scientist and leader of the British Black Panther Movement of the 1960s and '70s Altheia Jones-LeCointe (b. 1945).[6]

Years earlier, in 1954, Moody had become involved with the Société Africaine de Culture (SAC) and served on the London

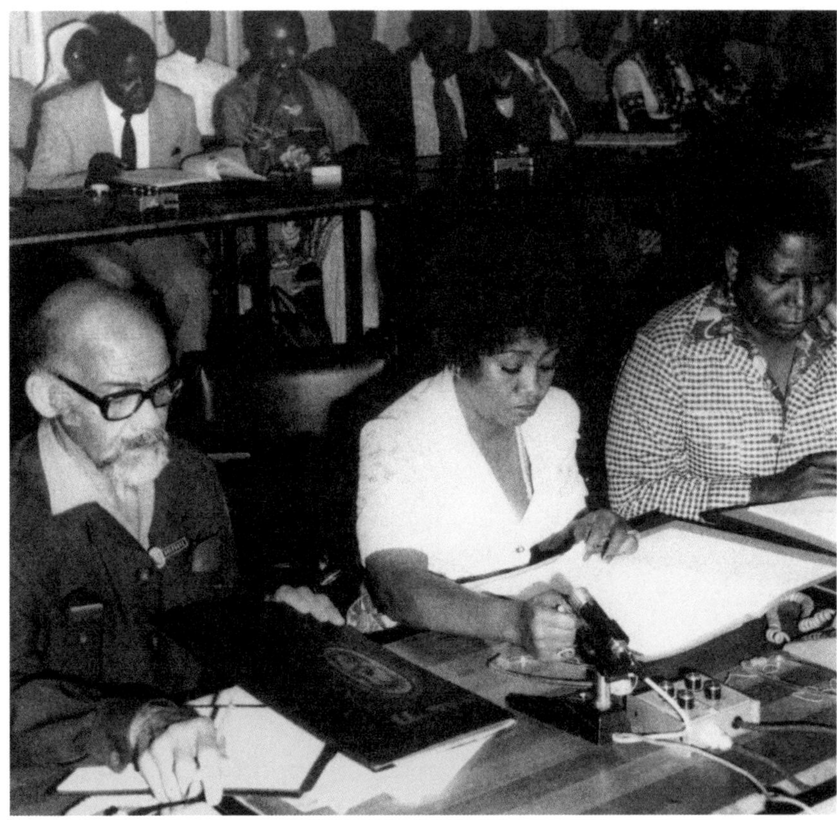

Committee for the proposed Second Conference of Negro Writers and Artists, which eventually took place in Rome in 1959. Here, Moody presented a paper titled 'The Responsibility of an Artist', and funds were secured to send and exhibit members of his *Concrete Family*, *The Mother*, *The Man* and *The Onlooker* (all 1958).[7] The SAC published Moody's essay 'Background to African Art' in 1957.[8] He also participated in the First World Festival of Negro Arts, Dakar, Senegal, in 1966, and again exhibited *The Onlooker* and *The Mother*. Both Moody and Egonu participated in the First World Festival of Negro Arts in April the following year and they also exhibited together in a group show that included Frank Bowling and Aubrey Williams at the Leicester University Arts Festival, Leicester Museum and Art Gallery.[9]

Ronald Moody as Chairman, UK Visual Arts Sub-Committee at the International Festival of Art, 'FESTAC '77', Lagos, Nigeria, 1977

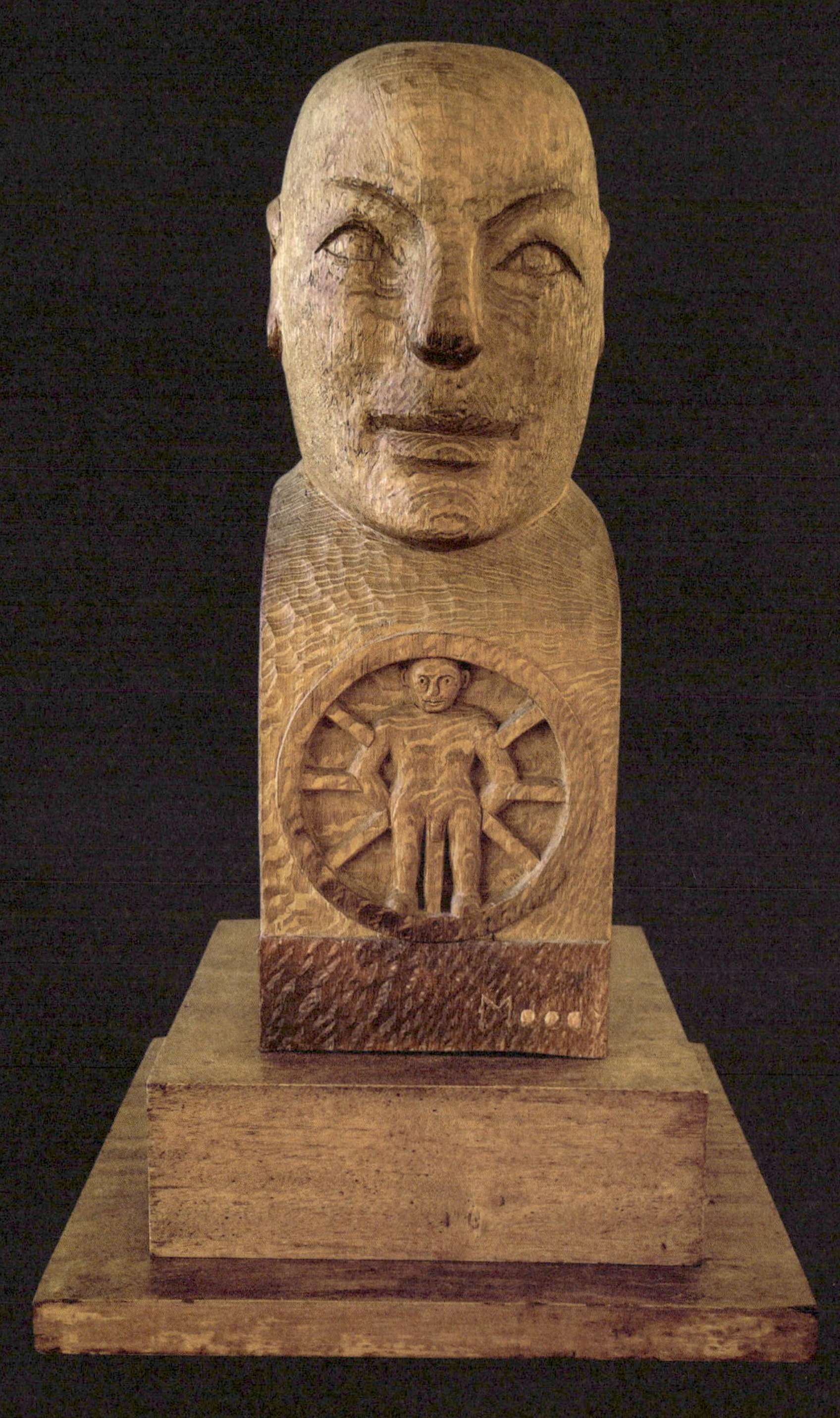

Ronald Moody, *The Wheel Within*, *1972*,
kohe-kohe, 51 × 30.5 × 25 cm (20 1/8 × 12 1/8 × 9 7/8 in.)

Friends and collaborators Moody and Egonu met in London in the 1960s and both exhibited at the Woodstock Gallery, London, in the 1950s and '60s.[10] Moody wrote an article on Egonu for *Magnet News*, which discussed his painting, education and background.[11] The piece is accompanied by an iconic black-and-white image of Egonu in his studio, surrounded by his own paintings. In 1972, they collaborated on the book *Amadu's Bundle: Fulani Tales of Love and Djinns* by Malum Amadu. The work is a collection originally from northern Cameroon/Nigeria of the Fulani people: songs, fables, tales and fairy tales about love, collected by editor Gulla Kell through dictation. Moody and Kell had collaborated in the 1950s, and Moody had produced a number of drawings to illustrate the publication, inspired by the vast collection of photographs Kell had given him. Though his drawings were not used, the experience piqued his interest in graphics. It was through Egonu's suggestion and encouragement that they approached Heinemann Educational Books to publish the story. It was translated into English by Moody, and Egonu provided the artwork for the front cover.[12] In 1970, Egonu and Moody collaborated again, converting two old-fashioned, obsolete mangles into printing presses, one for each of them. They became immersed in this process and produced several linocuts. Two of Moody's linocuts became the basis for the kohe-kohe sculpture *The Wheel Within* (1972). For Moody, the wheel represented the ceaseless repetitions of the selves and their actions, which lead to a state of self-imprisonment. During the 1970s, Moody produced other works on these existential themes, such as a piece in glass resin, *Eternal Circle* (1970), and *The Intellectual* (1970); in them we see the artist's ongoing concern for the path of humanity, but we also see him revisit the emblem of the encircling snake in *Man... His Universe* (1969) and *Technological Acrobats* (1972–73).[13] *Man... His Universe* sees Moody returns to the theme of the duality of humankind, shown as a Janus head encircled by a snake with the head of a bird and the foot of a lion. On its body are the ideograms of destruction, organic life and spiritual unity.[14] In 1973, Moody was included in the exhibition 'Contemporary Art of Africa, the Caribbean and Liverpool', which

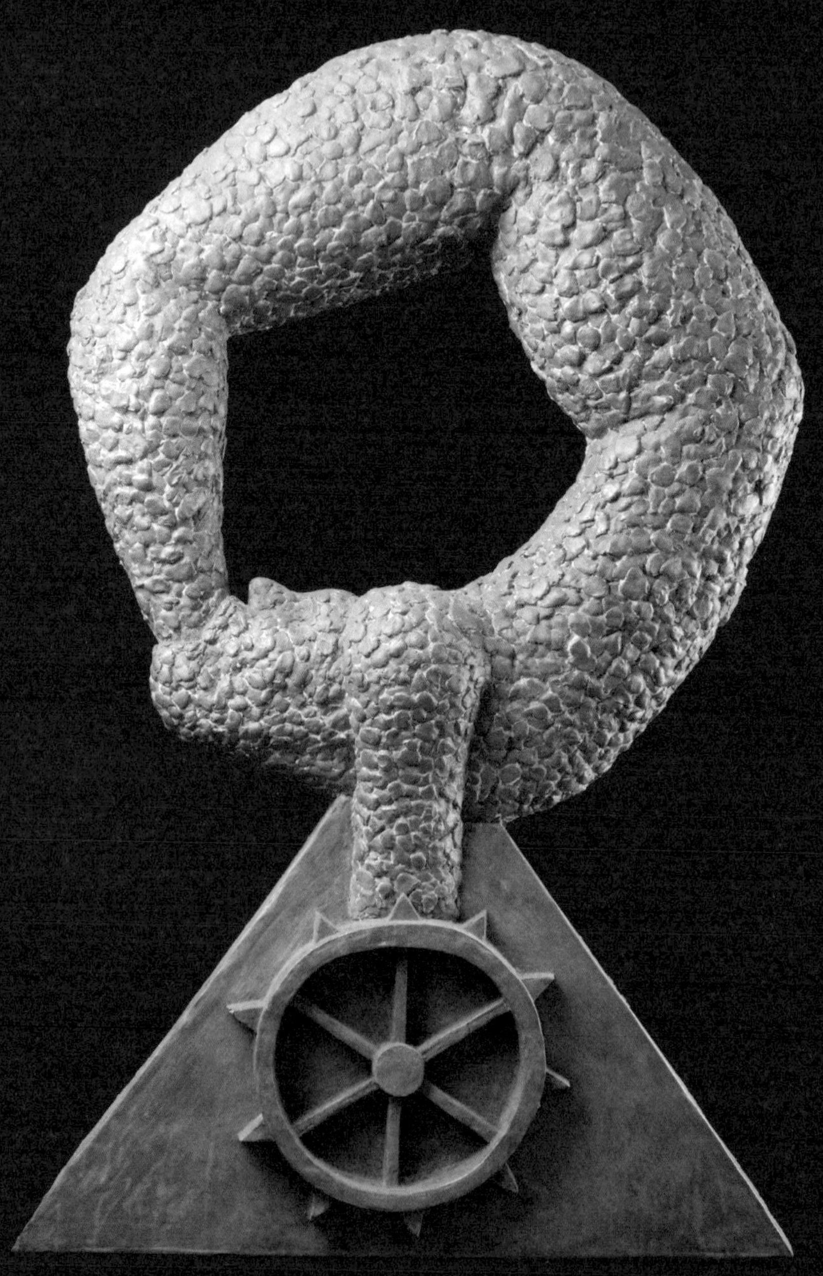

Ronald Moody, *Technological Acrobats*, 1972–73, aluminium resin, 99 × 43 × 5 cm (39 × 17 × 2 in.)

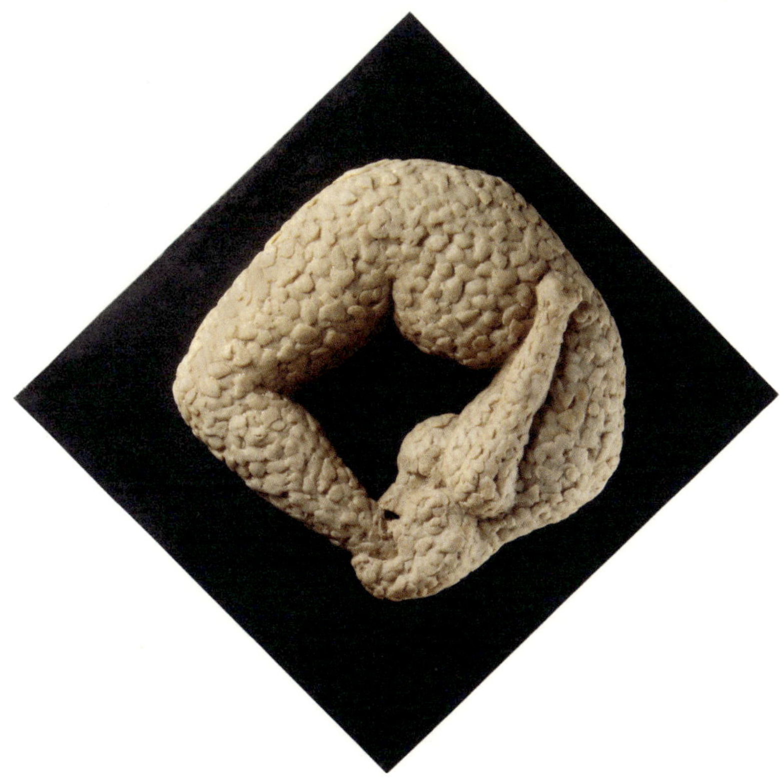

took place at the Bluecoat Gallery, Liverpool, and was organised by the UKAF Committee and supported by Merseyside Art Association.[15]

FESTAC '77's official festival emblem was the sixteenth-century Benin ivory mask depicting Queen Mother Idia. The original mask made by the carvers' guild was seized during an invasion of 1,200 British soldiers, led by British naval officer Sir Harry Rawson in response to the ambush of a previous British party under Acting Consul General James Phillips in 1897 against Benin. The masks, which are supposed to total five, and more than 3,000 other works were stolen; approximately 40 per cent of the artworks were 'accessioned' to the British Museum, while the rest became parts of private and public collections in the United States and Europe.[16] In 1977, Nigeria requested from Britain the return of the ivory hip mask of Queen Mother Idia from the British Museum for FESTAC '77. After asking for £2 million, Britain declined

Ronald Moody, *The Eternal Circle*, 1970, glass resin on black wood, 27 × 27 cm (10 ¾ × 10 ¾ in.)

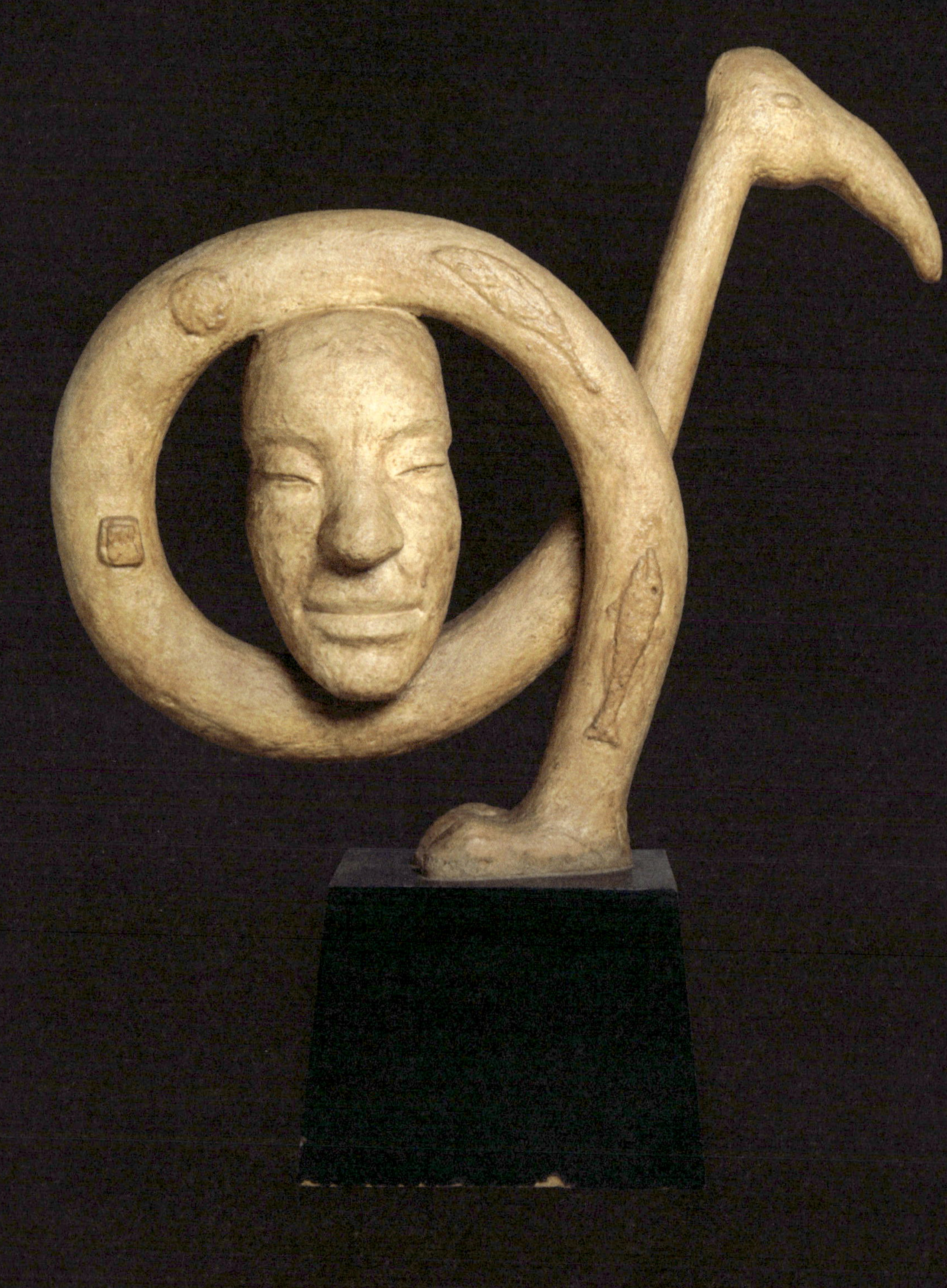

Ronald Moody, *Man... His Universe*, 1969,
glass resin, 102 × 82 × 20 cm (40 ¼ × 32 ⅜ × 7 ⅞ in.)

to lend the mask due to fragility, and possible loss or theft.[17] Moody's *Large Female Head* (1974), made of teak and resembling or evoking the artist's beloved artwork *Midonz* in both concept and form, took the artist, who had frail health at the time, over two years to complete. *Large Female Head* is one of three artworks that are part of the Centre for Black and African Arts and Civilisation (CBAAC) collection in Lagos, Nigeria, which is also where records of FESTAC are kept.[18] Moody's artworks *Vision* and *Anima* (both 1943–44), made from a dark oak beam from a cider press,[19] conclude the trinity that are part of the CBAAC collection, though have since been lost from public view.[20] *Annie II* and *Female Figure* (both 1977), made from the kohe-kohe, wood native to New Zealand, likewise revisit earlier works. The pose is virtually identical in conception to that of his 1938 work *Annie*, of friend and patron Annie van Beuningen-Eschauzier. In addition to the pose, the features – especially the eyes – are similar.[21] The kohe-kohe used in this artwork is one of two native woods of New Zealand; the other, kauri, was sent to Ronald Moody in 1966 by his nephew Harold Moody,[22] who lived there.[23] Ancient kauri is considered one of the oldest workable woods in the world, as well as one of the largest trees in the southern hemisphere, and is often used for traditional carvings and ocean-going canoe boats.[24] Moody utilised the ancient and sacred soft wood in his artworks *Hope* (1966), *The Warrior* (1974) and *Male Head* (*c.* 1978).

Suddenly, on 3 April 1978, Moody's wife Helene, whom he had shared his life with for over forty years, died from a stroke, leaving Moody in a state of profound shock. He never recovered from this blow, and his health deteriorated quite rapidly. Despite this, he continued the ritual of a daily visit to his studio and carved a small and powerful memory of Helene in *Helene 6* (1979), and completed what was to be his last sculpture, the tiny *Squatting Figure*, in 1980.[25] In 1983, to mark the twenty-first anniversary of Jamaican Independence, the Jamaican High Commission organised an exhibition on Jamaican art at the Commonwealth Institute Art Gallery. Entitled 'Remembrance', the exhibition was curated by the trade commissioner for Jamaica in Europe, Norman Rae, and was aimed to present a show of the highest quality, representative of the diverse elements and achievements

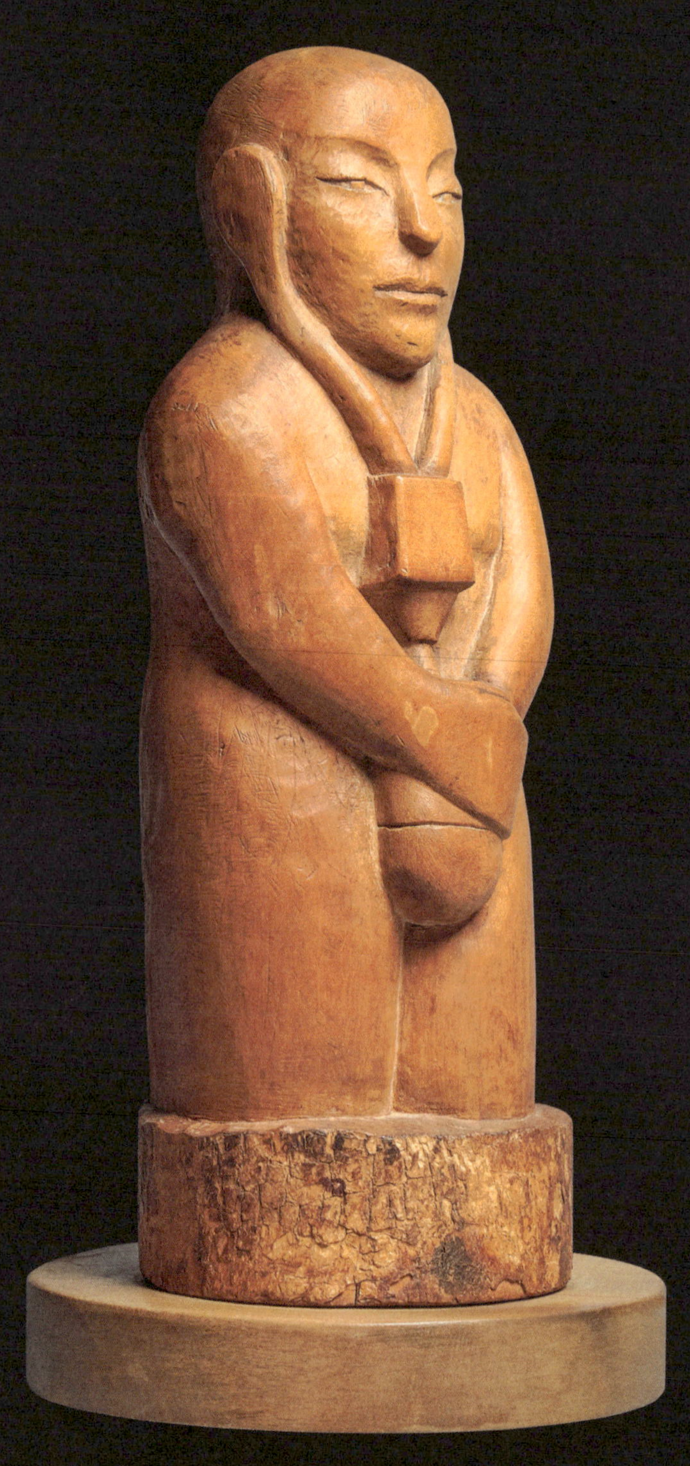

Ronald Moody, *The Warrior*, 1974, kauri, height: 46 cm (18 ⅛ in.)

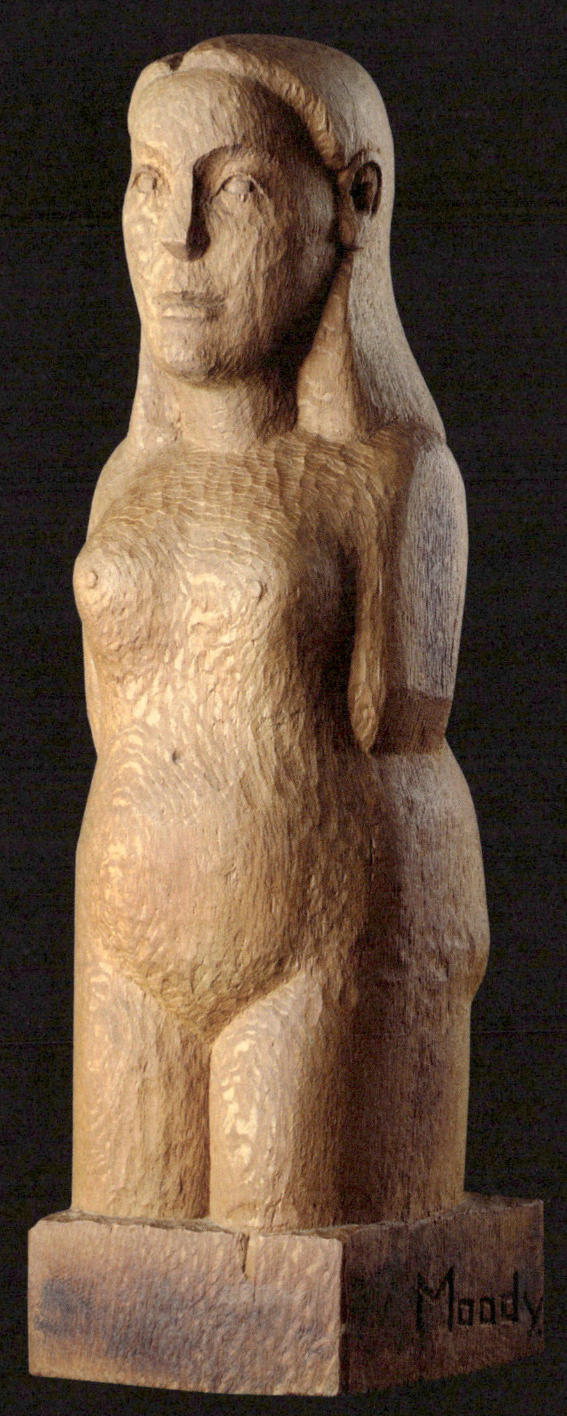

Ronald Moody, *Annie II*, 1977, kohe-kohe,
52 × 15 × 14 cm (20 ½ × 6 × 5 ⅝ in.)

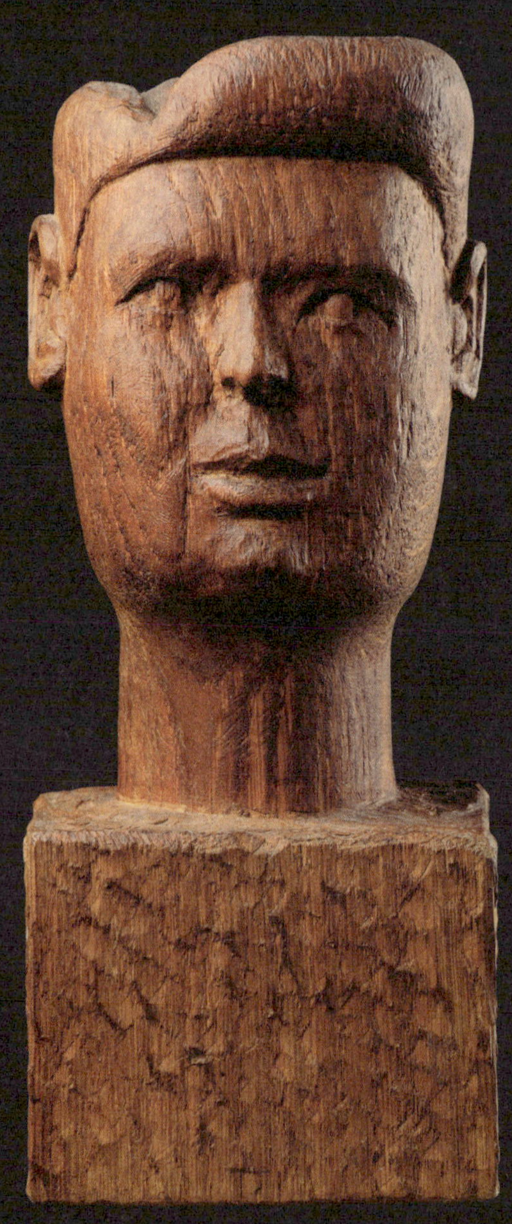

Ronald Moody, *Helene 6*, 1979,
kohe-kohe, 15 × 10 × 10 cm (6 × 4 × 4 in.)

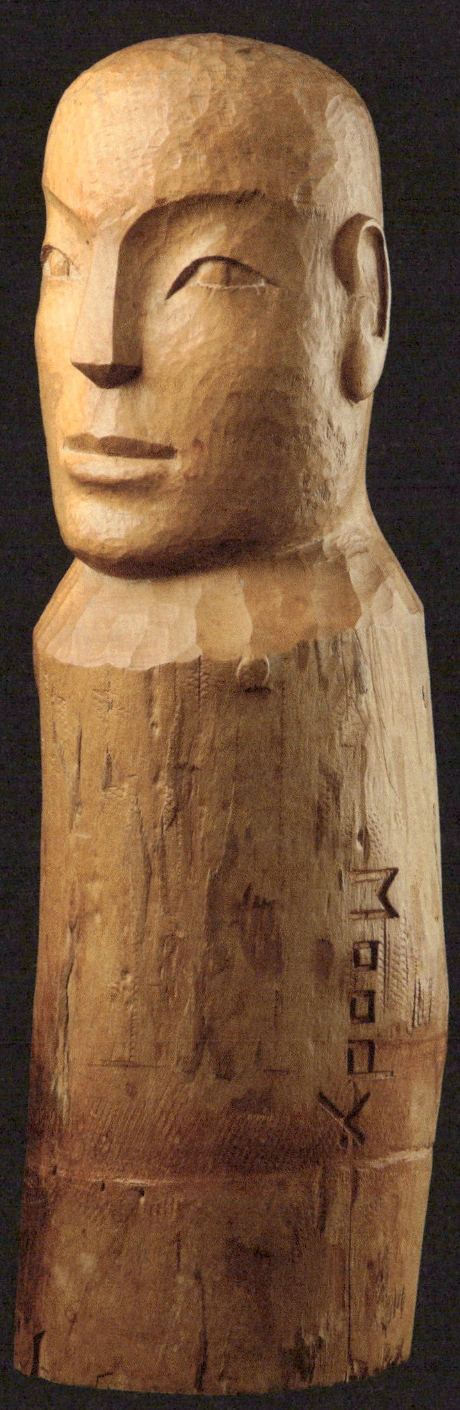

Ronald Moody, *Male Head*, *c.* 1978,
kauri, 32 × 10 × 10 cm (12⅝ × 4 × 4 in.)

of Jamaican art.[26] The exhibition celebrated and honoured pioneer Maroon artist and novelist Namba Roy (1910–1961), two decades after his death. In a show of 138 artworks, thirty-one sculptures and twenty-five paintings were Roy's.[27] Moody exhibited seven of his most important and representative sculptures, symbolic of the entire span of his career; among them were *Helene 2*, *Johanaan*, *Vision*, *Anima*, *Man... His Universe* and the *Savacou* maquette. The exhibition opened on 31 August, and Rae recalled Moody's contribution:

> For the most part, the wood pieces, except for the more intimate bust of *Helene 2*, stood quietly powerful in their archaic way. They could have been authority figures from any of several great primitive tribes – Native American, Polynesian mysteries, Ancient Mediterranean, oriental brooding silences. Clearly they were the work of a man who had studied and thought deeply about the enduring qualities of the human spirit....
>
> I know Ronald Moody was pleased by the way his pieces were shown and by the gravitas of the exhibition.
>
> He was pleased to be considered a Jamaican artist and to be included in such a gathering. He was pleased that the exhibition was opened by a first-rank art critic, Edward Lucie-Smith, well known in British journals, who had lived in Jamaica as a child.
>
> And yet, in his life, his harsh physical experience and in his aesthetics, he had moved so far from the ambience reflected in the rest of the collection that his group of sculptures stood separate – like keepers of ancient wisdom and tradition – looking benignly at the provincial development which had flourished since he left these shores and of which he, Ronald Moody, would forever be a part, biologically, and yet apart, aesthetically.[28]

Within three months of the exhibition opening, Moody was rushed to hospital after a period of increasingly frequent visits there. He then

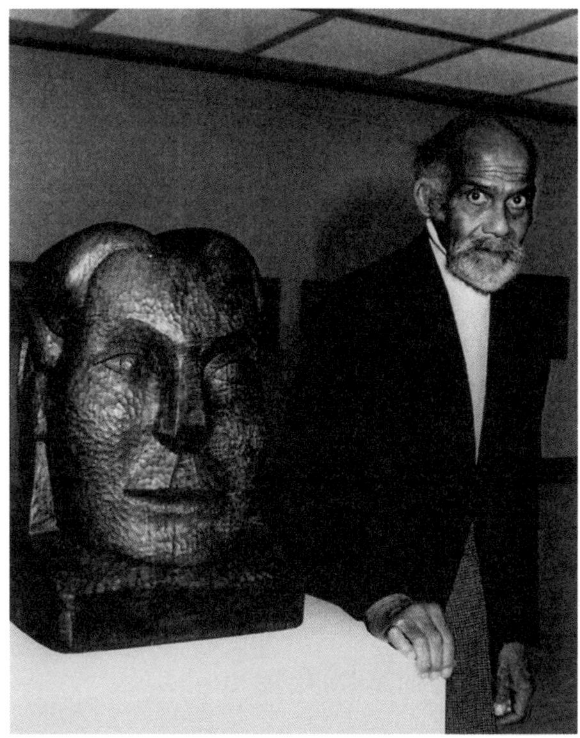

spent a period of time in Rustington Convalescent Home and was admitted to Westminster Hospital on 6 February 1984, where he died. His funeral took place at London's Golders Green Crematorium on 15 February, and the service was conducted by his nephew, Reverend Garth Moody, who shared personal reminiscences of his uncle's life and career. A wreath was sent by the prime minister of Jamaica, the Right Honorable Edward Seaga. Also in attendance were his niece Cynthia Moody, nephews Harold and Rodney, and Norman Rae. Friends from his artistic community were represented by Anne Walmsley, Errol Lloyd, Rudolph Dunbar, Rudi Patterson and Ritchie Riley.[29] Moody's great artistic achievement was to use his work to express his own inner vision of a world in which humankind achieved harmony with itself and with nature.[30] He was remembered as a quiet, modest and sensitive man, who brought to his work a great dignity, and who to the very end remained dedicated to his art and to his true vision.[31]

Ronald Moody with *Large Female Head* at the 'Remembrance' exhibition, Commonwealth Institute, London, 1983. Photograph by Robin McCarthey

CHAPTER 10

Ronald & Cynthia Moody: Evidence of a Black Visual Aesthetic

David A. Bailey

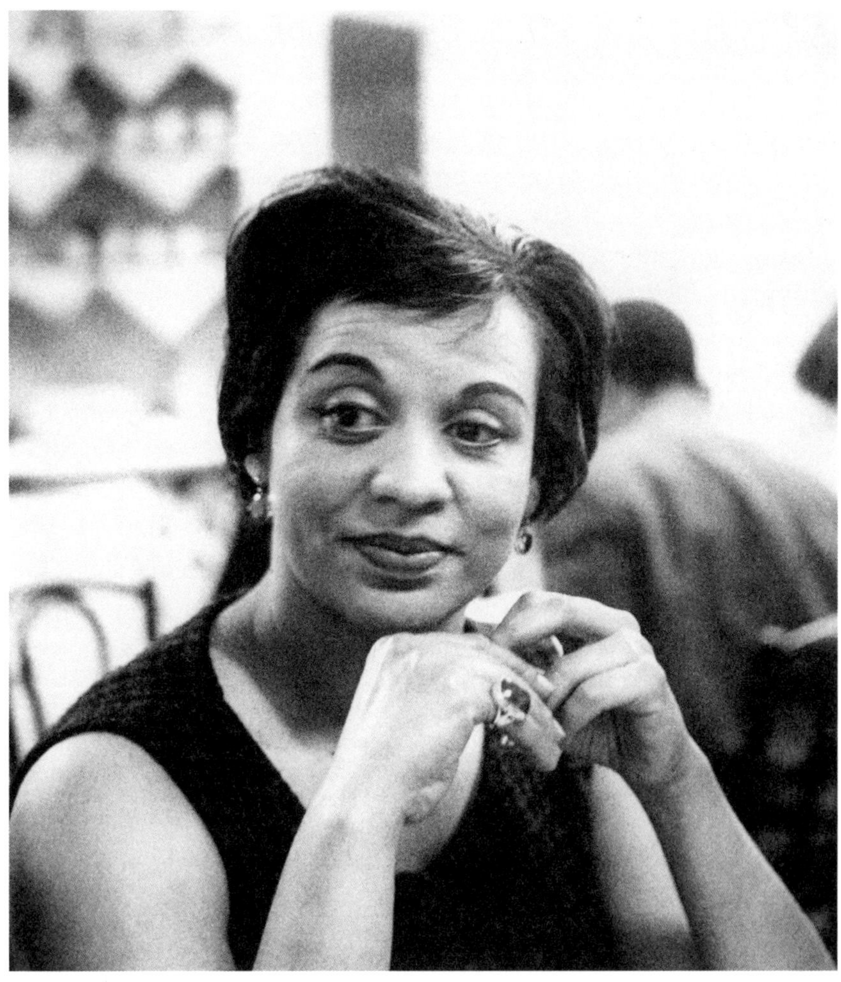

Meeting Cynthia Moody

I encountered Cynthia in a two-sided way, initially during the 1980s. There were one or two Caribbean exhibitions that featured Ronald Moody, and I think we probably met around the time of 'Remembrance' at the Commonwealth Institute, London, in 1983.[1] However, we formally met in early 1996 when I was the co-director with artist Sonia Boyce[2] of the African and Asian Visual Arts Archive (AAVAA), which was then housed at the University of East London (UEL).[3] Though based in UEL, AAVAA was a limited company, which

Portrait of Cynthia Moody, n.d.

meant it had separate auditors and accountants. One of our first tasks was to visit our accountants, who were based opposite Liverpool Street Station. One of them came up to us and said, 'you don't know this, but I am related to the Moodys', and they asked if we knew Ronald Moody and we affirmed, 'yes!' The accountant happened to be the nephew of Cynthia and provided a contact for her. We followed up and reached out to her, and ended up visiting her in Cliftonville, Bristol.

The Moodys: A Formidable Dynasty

Cynthia Moody was a very generous, fun-loving person who had an amazing style of cooking, very eclectic! Her house was full of Ronald Moody's artworks: *Midonz*, which was imposing and massive, and *Technological Acrobats*. There is *the* story about Ronald, but you can't really tell a story about him without telling the story about the Moodys – the two are intertwined. There are quite a lot of stories, from what Cynthia described, in terms of who came to Britain, what they did and who they became. It gives you an idea of the DNA of

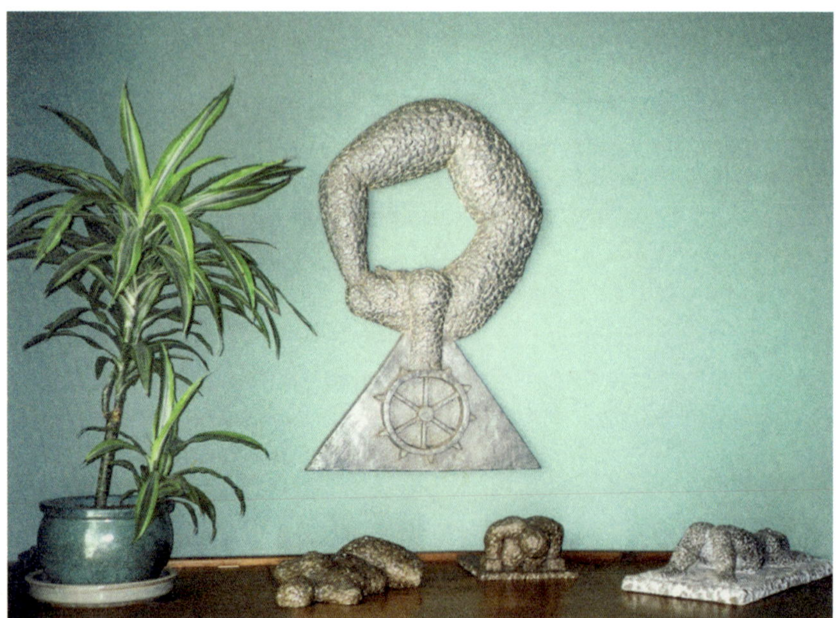

Technological Acrobats at Cynthia Moody's home, n.d.

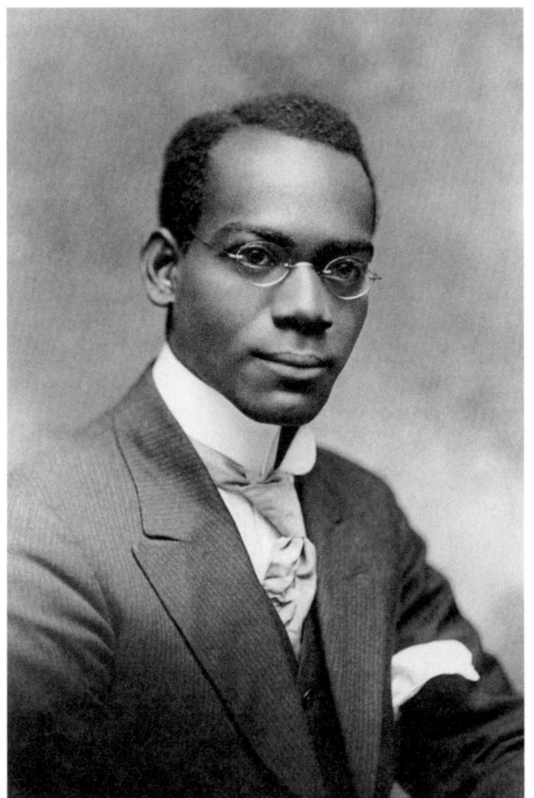

Charles Aston Moody, Ronald Moody's brother and Cynthia Moody's father, n.d.

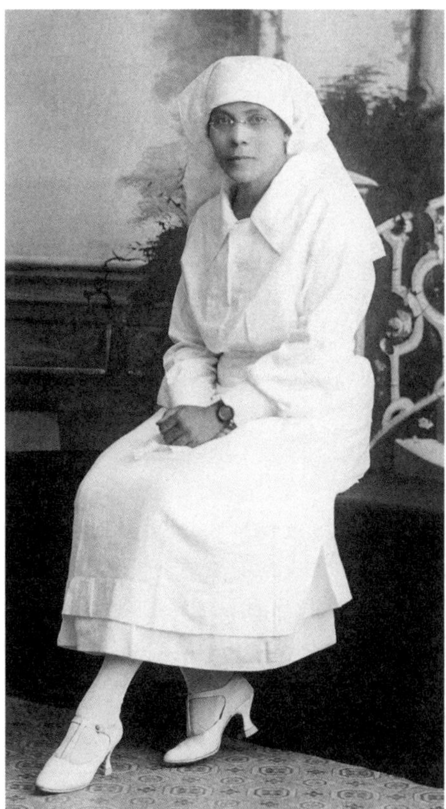

Elise Viola Moody, Ronald Moody's sister, n.d.

what it is all about: they had leadership skills and the capacity to take on any kind of intellectual challenge, whatever situation arose, which makes perfect sense when you think about Harold, or Ronald or the Moodys in that collective sense. I am under the impression that the Moodys were very upper middle class; they were also trained to be like civil servants in that Commonwealth period, which was not unusual for the pre-Windrush generation.

I always feel with Ronald that it's not only about the Moody men. Focus needs to be placed on the women within the family, who I only know a little about. Cynthia represents that grouping, in terms of her capacity and leadership. She once showed me a picture of a group of Moody women in uniform, who were all high-level military. There is so much more to be uncovered. The story of the Moodys – as one of the first family generations to really make their mark and impact on twentieth-century Britain – is one that still needs to be unpacked. A comparison would be sociologist Paul Gilroy (b. 1956), whose mother is educator and author Beryl Gilroy (1924–2001),[4] and whose sister is Darla Jane Gilroy, the futurologist and fashion designer. You could make that connection between the two generations. The uniqueness of the Moodys is the ability to make multiple intergenerational connections. When thinking and writing about Ronald, he needs to be considered in that context.

We know that Ronald was a formidable artist, ahead of his time. In parallel, there needs to be the story of Cynthia, who was a formidable figure in the film industry before the 1970s. She was not cynically critical of filmmaker Horace Ové (1936–2023),[5] but she was cynically critical of the way that he was called the 'first', as she preceded him in terms of commissioning film, directing and production, yet remains unrecognized as a pioneer. In addition to that amazing story is the story of when Ronald died. His home was overwhelmingly full of papers: there were all of these black plastic bags and all these things on the floor, which Cynthia had to assemble into an archive. The Tate noted it was in 'a perfect condition' when they acquired it in 1995.[6] It is time to really think about a Moody story, one that includes Cynthia, her sisters and other relatives. There is a need to bring together the expansive story of this dynasty that dates back to at least the nineteenth century. I imagine there is a further wealth of information in archival repositories in Jamaica and throughout the Caribbean.

Ronald Moody's Kinetic Archive

We must also think about how Cynthia had to build an archive. She learnt to be an expert in making spreadsheets and databases, and knew at least two languages, French and Dutch, in order to be able to translate material and artworks within Moody's archive. Cynthia wasn't simply collating plastic bags – she was building, translating and curating the archive. She categorised and organised Moody's writing, poetry, portraits and symbolic works. I was just lucky enough to spend time with her, assisting, to think about those things. Because of her age and mobility, I did a lot of running around for her, whether it was buying her a new computer, or connecting or reconnecting her with people who we would bring to Bristol. I was fortunate to be invited into the archive with Cynthia sitting next to me, saying, 'you need to look at this, you need to look at that, and here's a letter from Marlene Smith'.[7] She was picking and selecting material for me, knowing that these documents might be of interest. Her main ambition was for Ronald to have a show at the Tate, and for more of his works to be collected by institutions. Moody's artworks have been collected by some really interesting institutions, including the Nehru Memorial Museum, Delhi, and the Centre for Black and African Arts and Civilisation (CBAAC) in Lagos. As Cynthia would always point out to me, in terms of the archives, Ronald was always travelling around the world. Cynthia was able to confirm that Ronald and his wife Helene were escaping from Europe during the Second World War at the same time as sculptor Wifredo Lam, by either boat or by train. Who knows the kind of conversations they were having in relation to all that. Ronald was obviously somebody who was moving around, and at the same time, he documented some of his movement in his letters.

In addition to that, his archive is a kinetic sculpture in its own right. You enter it as an artwork and then you get out of it all this other stuff that has been curated and created by somebody else. For somebody to then use that material and then make artwork out of it is amazing. I have to keep coming back to this – Cynthia didn't just organise his papers, she curated, and she made an artwork out of it.

'The Living Archive of the Black Diaspora' Symposium, 1997

Cynthia was incredibly articulate in terms of talking about Ronald's work, though she was also very shy. I invited her to be on a panel to talk about his work at 'The Living Archive of the Black Diaspora' symposium, held on 14 March 1997 at the Clore Auditorium, Tate Britain. We divided the day up in terms of the keynotes of Stuart Hall (his keynote became the often-cited essay 'Constituting an Archive'),[8] Rasheed Araeen, Amina Dickerson and Els van der Plas. We then had a session with collections. I thought it would be great to think about archives and collections, and the people that represent the diversity of them. I wanted Robert Loder,[9] because he had an amazing collection. He was the founder of the Triangle Arts Trust and the person behind the 'Africa '95' season.[10] Loder was a patron of the arts, similar to the Harmon Foundation in the 1920s, but in a twentieth-century context. Cynthia represented archives and collections from a different perspective. She spoke of two things. First, she talked about how her film work gave her the background and the infrastructure to think. Second, she shared how her experiences in film informed how she was able to navigate the archive, and how it helped her to collate, research and develop Moody's narrative and make further connections. When she encountered the volume of archival material in Ronald's flat, she was able to deal with the situation as it was part of what she had to do in her job. It was something that she was used to in the sense that she organised people, and she organised stuff, administration and logistics.

Cynthia also showed a series of slides of Ronald's work, which were pretty outstanding. Another thing her film background allowed her to do was to collate visual imagery of the highest quality, and if an image wasn't good enough, she would find a way to have a work re-photographed. One of the first things she wanted me to help source was somebody to do a full-on, masterful photograph of *Midonz*. She understood that the artworks needed not only to be catalogued but also recorded visually by people who knew what they were doing. She wasn't getting her Instamatic camera out and snapping away, she was of the background of seeking excellence in any endeavour. I remember sitting next to art historian Richard 'Rick' J. Powell during her slide show,[11] and he almost fell out of his chair because the slides literally sang. Imagine seeing these high-class images while sat in the Clore Auditorium at the Tate – a lot of people were impressed by that. Cynthia's panel was chaired by Gilane Tawadros,[12] in a salon-type way: she teased out questions, which helped Cynthia relax. To this day, whenever I show people the works of Ronald, I use Cynthia's slides. I have images of the restoration of *Wohin* and works shown at the 'Caribbean Artists in England' 1971 exhibition, Guy Brett with Ronald at the Commonwealth Institute Art Gallery and Moody with *Orchid Bird*.

Rick Powell also spoke at the symposium, and it was that month that I took him to see *Midonz* with Roger Malbert, head of Hayward Gallery Touring.[13] That visit really sealed the deal for Moody's sculpture to be in the 'Rhapsodies' show. It was a key work, and I was really pleased because my role in co-curating that show was focused on the film, so I was glad that I could also contribute to the non-film element in this way. This major piece, I think, has a much bigger presence than *Johanaan* ever did. It gives you the sense of what was in Moody's head while he was making those works in the 1930s. John La Rose,[14] Guy Brett, the critic for *The Times* who wrote about Aubrey Williams,[15] and Ronald Moody also visited Bristol. Powell's is a genius that doesn't get acknowledged. He knew somehow, through his Hercule Poirot kind of instinct, that Moody's work was connected to the Harlem Renaissance, though he didn't know to what degree Moody had a relationship to other sculptors and artworks of that period. This was uncovered through the discovery of letters from the Harmon Foundation in the archive, which Cynthia brought to my attention.

'Rhapsodies in Black: Art of the Harlem Renaissance', 1997

Between 1996 and 1999/2000, at least once or maybe twice a month, I would go quite regularly to see Cynthia Moody. The most concentrated time I spent with her was in the run up to the exhibition 'Rhapsodies in Black: Art of the Harlem Renaissance', which opened in 1997 at the Hayward Gallery, then travelled to the Arnolfini in Bristol, the Mead Gallery in Warwick and then on to the United States.[16] Cynthia played a key role in the run up to the exhibition and during the tour to the US, connecting up the works and providing additional context. When Cynthia came to London, I helped to facilitate a meeting with Stephen Deuchar,[17] who was the director of Tate Britain at the time.

Moody's invitation to be part of the 1939 'Negro in Art' exhibition at Baltimore Museum of Art is a key moment of recognition of the artist as part of the Harlem Renaissance movement. He is one of the diasporic artists in Britain that we fully understand. Not only does he fit thematically within that period, he also actually exhibited with those artists. The iconic photograph of *Midonz* with the two children

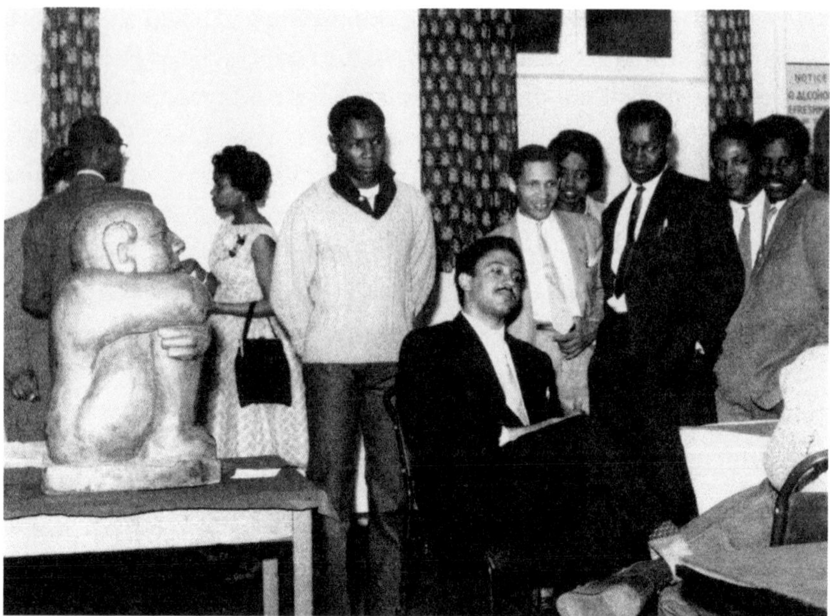

taken at that exhibition (see page 47) encapsulates that moment. You could argue that Moody's series of heads – *Johanaan*, *Midonz* and *Wohin* – was actually his response to that period. This is absolutely amazing given where we are now in the twenty-first century in terms of how we travel, how we can look at things and how we can respond to things. Somehow, obviously, he was responding to that; he was a Moody. In the same way that Harold Moody was responding to a pre-Black Lives Matter movement in London in that period. It's thanks to Cynthia that we can see the proof that there was that kind of detailed connection, in that particular way, in that moment.

Moody provides us with evidence to suggest that there is a diasporic aesthetic. He was somebody who was diasporic in that he was associated with the Harlem Renaissance. Then in the 1970s, with his whole regeneration with 'FESTAC '77', we have Africa, his background as Caribbean and as a European. Moody was already working across several diasporas. In addition to that, I think it is definitely the case with him, and with Aubrey Williams and Althea McNish, that the work itself actually questions and relates to the question of a diasporic aesthetic.

The Onlooker at the SAC First World Festival of Negro Arts, Dakar, Senegal, 1966

Midonz brings into question all of that. Is it European, is it Amerindian? At the same time, when you actually reason why he carved in wood, you notice that when you've been close up to the work, the carvings themselves and the marks he makes within them also reference other kinds of cultural diasporic references – in the nature of the making of the work as well as the physiology of it. *Midonz* is a great example, because you recognise it as a head, but it's a head that references multiple cultures, although the markings that he's made in the wood suggest that he's also annotating it and animating it with all these cultural references as well. He tries to do the same later on in concrete, which some people see as a failure, but I think it's Moody trying to use a kind of more modern aesthetic material to think through how this can translate what he'd been doing in the 1930s. The thing about Moody was that he was never static, he was always trying to transgress lots of different things. For me, he is always somebody I can reference quite happily because the work lends itself to it, in that way. It is what makes Moody unique when thinking, is there a question about the diasporic aesthetic or artist? And if there is a question, Moody comes pretty close to the answer to that question.

When the 'Rhapsodies in Black' show toured America, additional works were added. I worked with Cynthia to contact Judge Adolf Loeb in Sacramento, California, who had *Wohin* in his collection. The oak head was badly split and was in the process of being restored. We made a request for it to be loaned for the 'Rhapsodies' exhibition. None of that would have been possible unless Cynthia had built the archive and had access to the letters enabling us to see these connections. At that time, I was close to Henry Louis Gates Jr, editor of the publication *Transition*,[18] so we were able to facilitate the commission of Cynthia's essay '*Midonz*' in 1998 (reprinted in this volume, pp. 51–61).

Institutional Archival Abandonment in the 1980s and '90s: Legacies Lost and Found

It is worth noting that major British institutions such as the Tate, the British Museum and the National Portrait Gallery were really unforgivable in terms of the legacy of how they were collecting work at that time. They could have easily supported and developed a relationship, policy and strategies. The onus fell to a second generation of researchers, like myself. It was quite clear when I was speaking to Cynthia that there was a generational thing. I also felt there was a little bit of a class thing as well, because somehow she was expecting something that didn't happen. Then, like all Moodys, she decided to get on with it herself.

After 'The Other Story: Afro-Asian Artists in Post-War Britain' exhibition at the Hayward Gallery in 1989, Cynthia felt abandoned by a number of people who she'd been in conversation with during that period. She wondered why the show's curator, Rasheed Araeen, didn't follow up. But that show had had a devastating impact on Araeen's health, I don't think it was his responsibility to follow up after the exhibition and I don't think he wasn't interested; he was focused on trying to build on *Black Phoenix* and was establishing the critical journal *Third Text*.[19] It is also about the curatorial and art-historical styles that people have, and Araeen wasn't the kind of curator or historian that had that kind of engagement, or developed those relationships. However, there were people in my generation that did have that kind of engagement, people like artists Eddie Chambers (b. 1960) and Lubaina Himid (b. 1954).

While a lot of artists were emerging in the 1980s, that emergence was at the cost of another generation of artists. Uzo Egonu, Aubrey Williams and Moody were part of that cost. Somehow their work was being overtaken by something else, which was described as kind of hard-hitting and political. When you look at any of Egonu's, Williams's and Moody's works, they are in fact political and global, and the environment touches on all of those things in a radical and different way. Cynthia was very close to Egonu's wife, Katherine, and that's an archive that needs further discussion. Author Anne Walmsley was developing her own archive at the time they were having these conversations.[20] Cynthia was not alone in this feeling of abandonment, and something that needs to be discussed more widely is how mostly women during this period were left with large artist bodies of work. These include Eve Williams (Aubrey Williams), Katherine Madge Gee

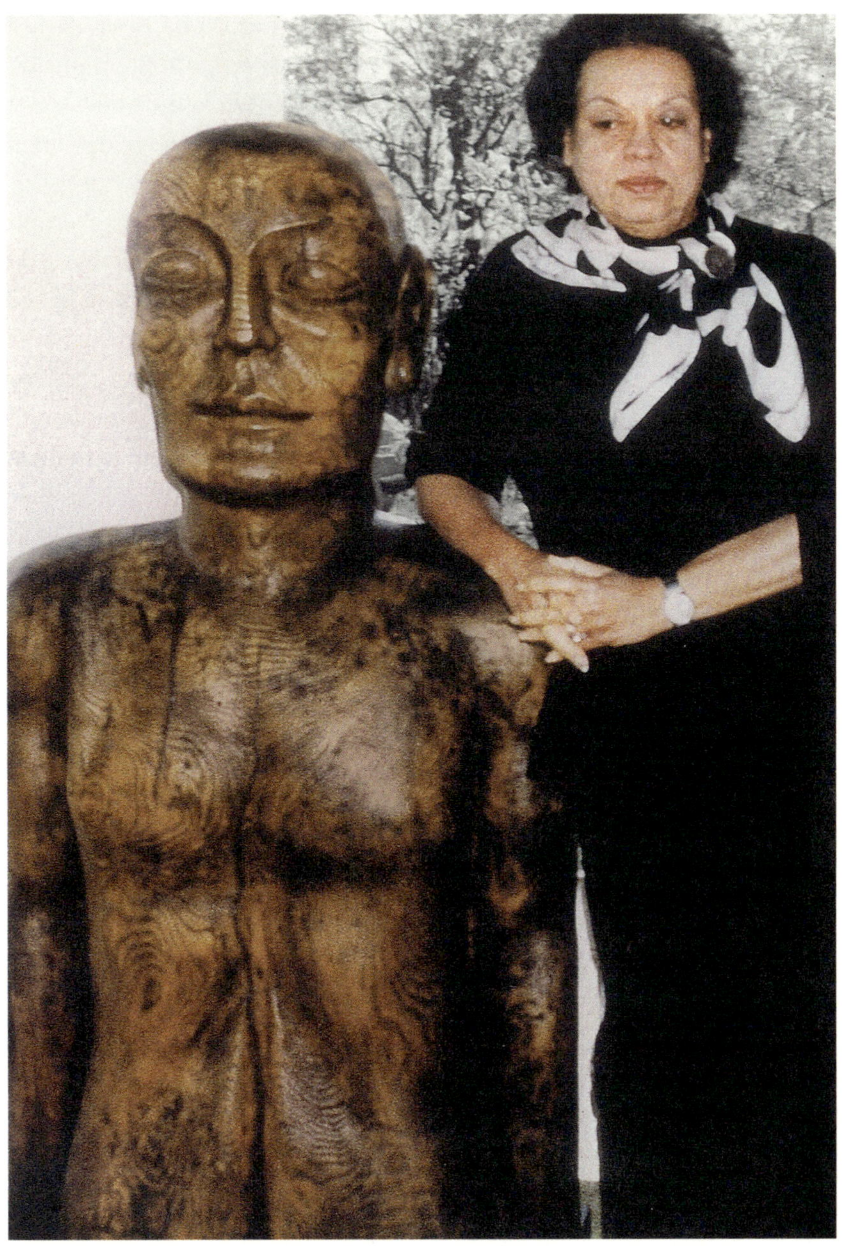

Cynthia Moody pictured with *Johanaan*, n.d.

(Uzo Egonu) and Cynthia. It was by chance that Sonia Boyce and I were able to give them another connection, to support them in that way and offer dialogue, and also to reconnect them in different ways.

When I was invited to co-curate 'Life Between Islands',[21] my main ambition was to bring the three generations within that show together, to have a dialogue. Particularly with Ronald, whose work was the first thing you saw when you came into that exhibition, and then when you came out of that first room, we deliberately put Althea McNish in the next room, and by the end everybody was coming back to what was happening in the original room. Alberta Whittle's work is very reflective of Ronald's work, in terms of how it touches on different folk and how he focuses on different elements. I was pleased to be able to have these kinds of conversations with Alex Farquharson, emphasising that we needed to make these connections, but we also needed to avoid showing this first generation as isolated, and show instead how it lays the ground for subsequent generations.

Cynthia responded to and recognised my inter-relational and multi-intergenerational collaborative practice. I do come with an agenda, but not one which means that I'm going to take this stuff away from you and we're going to put it somewhere else, without access. I come with an agenda that is more about dialogue. In the times that I met Aubrey Williams when he was alive, he recognised that as well. I have a really big passion for that earlier generation who were producing such remarkable work – they were just incredible.

Embedding Diasporic Art within the Western Canon

There is still a lot of work to be done. We are in the twenty-first century, we can make better use of technology. There isn't an excuse now. We can think about ways in which we can look at these historical figures, we can use the technology we have at the moment to bring them to a wider audience. There is a bit of territoriality, particularly around Ronald Moody's archive and where he is positioned at the Tate. It is all very precious: how you access it and how you get to borrow work from it. I would like to see institutions like Tate Britain become a bit more open. Not many people know about Moody's papers, the richness within them and all the other archives. I still say to Alex Farquharson, the director at Tate Britain, that we should have included more archival material in the 'Life Between Islands' exhibition. There are things that are already embedded in institutions, and it doesn't take much to use the technology to make it a bit more widespread. There seems to be a continuous reluctance to do that, or only a push to do that at certain times of the year, such as Black History Month, or when it connects or relates to that subject matter. The recent Tate rehang gave me the opportunity to continue to have those conversations, reframing the 1920s and '30s, illustrating London as the cosmopolitan place that it was, a hub for anti-colonial networks – one of many peaks of that period.

While I have set a tradition of focusing on certain shows that fit around a Black theme, particularly with artists like Moody, McNish and Williams, there is a need now to go beyond that categorisation. Moody wanted to be seen alongside people like Henry Moore, and with Althea McNish, who needs to be seen in a wider context than her relationship to fashion, textiles and adornment. How do you do that without breaking the canon, the essence of where the works originated, to get to a wider sense of things, so that it contributes to the wider canon, really? That's the problematic area that I am thinking about, in relation to those works and the legacy of those artists and how they speak to different constituencies within the art world and wider world, as well. This is difficult, because I am very much of the mind that Ronald Moody firmly fits into a canon that has a very particular kind of Black cultural aesthetic. It's that cultural aesthetic that needs to break into the wider Western canon, rather than be taken out of context.

This text is based on an interview between David A. Bailey and Ego Ahaiwe Sowinski that took place on 13 November 2023.

CHAPTER II

The Timeless Qualities of Ronald Moody's Art

Errol Lloyd

> One of the lessons that one can gain from looking at Ronald Moody's life is that at the end of it all, it really comes down to an expression of individuality. That is what art is all about. We're all unique individuals.
>
> *Errol Lloyd*

Meeting Ronald Moody and the Caribbean Artists Movement

I first met Ronald Moody when I joined the Caribbean Artists Movement (CAM) as a young law student in 1966. At the time I was aged twenty-three and I had done bronze busts of some well-known Caribbean people, principally C. L. R. James, the historian, political activist and writer,[1] as well as Sir Alexander Bustamante, the prime minister of Jamaica at the time,[2] and Garfield 'Gary' Sobers, the cricketer.[3] Those were my credentials for joining CAM. I hadn't yet started to paint seriously. Ronald Moody was already in his sixties when we met. I was brought up in Jamaica, where you deferred to your elders by addressing them formally, so to begin with he was always 'Mr Moody'. I wouldn't have dared to call him 'Ronald' at the time. To me he seemed a lofty, distinguished figure, whom I admired from a distance. As CAM was beginning to have exhibitions that featured his work, I was then able to make a connection between the person and the work. Also, Moody gave one or two talks at CAM symposiums, conferences and general meetings.

I eventually learnt of the visit he made to the British Museum that brought him face to face with ancient Egyptian sculpture, and this changed the course of his life – an event not so well documented at the time. Thereafter, he spent less and less time as a practising dentist, devoting more time to wood carving and later modelling in clay. This was a bold step for him, as his professional qualifications offered, on the face of it, brighter prospects than venturing into African-influenced artistic practice – particularly coming from the Caribbean, where, at the time, all things African tended to be denigrated.

Moody's outlook, however, resonated with CAM's overall perspective, as the founders – Kamau Brathwaite, John La Rose and Andrew

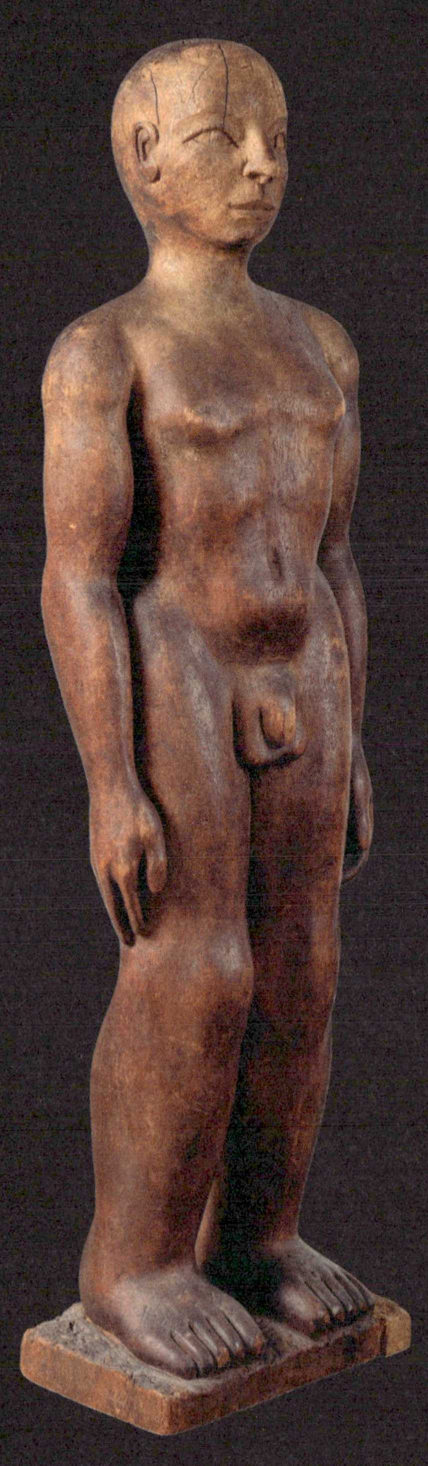

Ronald Moody, *Standing Male Figure*, 1951, cedar, height: 57.1 cm (22 ½ in.)

Salkey[4] – were quite radical in their outlook, setting the tone for CAM's general direction. This was in turn influenced by the new Independence movements in the Caribbean with an appetite for more authentic self-expression as people from the Caribbean. For instance, Aubrey Williams looked at pre-Columbian art and culture as a source of inspiration for his work.[5] Ronald Moody, too, was looking at the Caribbean region for inspiration, to express an identity that was broader than just being a member of the British Empire. Embracing a wider Caribbean identity was relatively new. When I was growing up in Jamaica, the indigenous Arawaks had already been virtually wiped out.[6] We grew up with a romanticised notion of their history and that of the Caribs, who were generally relegated to the distant past, and there were very few examples of elements of Caribbean artefacts or culture in existence. Consequently, it was innovative for Ronald Moody to tap into the dim and distant past to make geographical or cultural nexus with that region and its history, which he could incorporate in his art. Examples are his mythical Carib birds series (see Chapter 8).

The exhibitions we held at CAM were quite often ad-hoc and not formally curated; there was no budget – everything we did was from our own pockets. For instance, the prospect of getting a grant from the Arts Council of Great Britain to support our work was slim, because at the time one of their main criteria was that you had to have a national profile to qualify for support. An organisation calling itself the Caribbean Artists Movement may have suggested to disinterested parties that it was not concerned with the UK. Lack of significant funding often meant that there were no proper catalogues commemorating the exhibitions, and so recording events has come down to individual or collective memories. Unfortunately, the 1971 Commonwealth Institute Art Gallery exhibition 'Caribbean Artists in England', which indeed featured a catalogue, was not in the end the CAM exhibition initially envisioned, as in the interests of a wider Caribbean context, Anne Walmsley of CAM, in collaboration with Donald Bowen, the Commonwealth Institute curator, had decided to include non-CAM artists. Not surprisingly, however, more than half of the artists were from CAM. The exhibition catalogue numbered

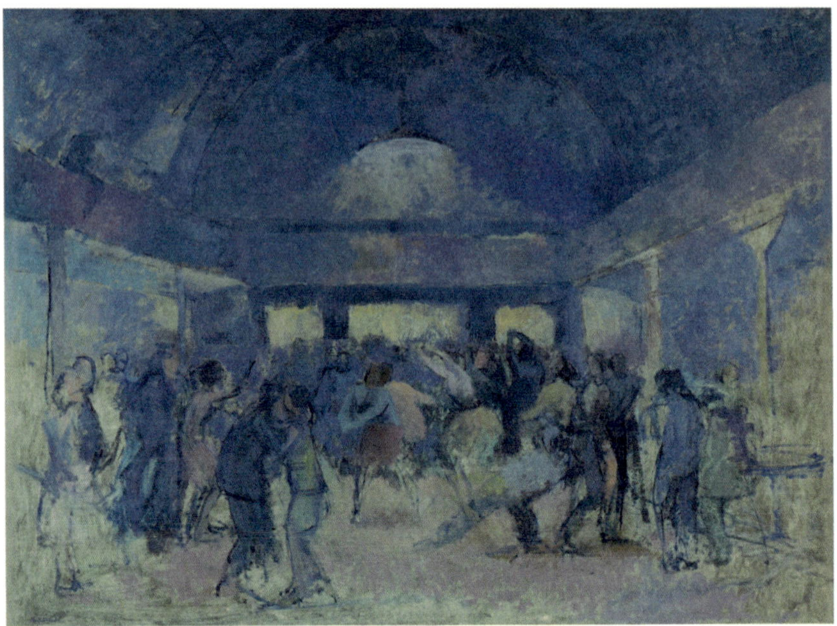

the following CAM artists: Winston Branch, Karl Craig, Art Derry, Errol Lloyd, Althea McNish, Ronald Moody and Aubrey Williams. Paul Dash was also part of the exhibition; Anne Walmsley notes in her book about the Caribbean Artists Movement that due to an oversight, his name was not included in the catalogue. The Commonwealth Institute Art Gallery was one of the few purpose-built galleries in London. Had the exhibition featured exclusively CAM artists, it may have focused attention on the movement, giving more mileage to its visual arts element at a time where its activities were coming to an end.[7]

One of the first paintings I made, titled *One Love* (1970), was included in that exhibition. The painting was an expression of something new from within me. It was a departure from the normal Western perception of Black people. The whole idea of putting forward some kind of new identity was also inspired by the Black Power and civil rights movement in the US. Many Black people started sporting afros, wearing dashikis and other distinctive clothes. We were influenced by figures such as Martin Luther King, Muhammad Ali, Dick Gregory, Stockley Carmicheal, James Baldwin and others – some of them visited

Paul Dash, *Dance at the Reading Town Hall*, 1965, oil on hardboard, 108.2 × 138.2 cm (42 5/8 × 54 1/2 in.)

Britain and a few even spoke at the Students' Centre. The situation in Britain was different, however, in that segregation rules typical of the American Southern states were enshrined in law, whereas in the UK there were no legally enforceable assaults on civil rights. What people of colour faced was termed 'colour prejudice' in those early days, suggesting somehow that it was a lesser evil. It was only later that it was recognised as systemic, deserving the more telling term, racism.

CAM was dominated, naturally, by writers, novelists and poets, largely because in those days, visual artists were at a disadvantage in publicising their work. It was costly to reproduce as art prints or posters, or in books or magazines, let alone in the rudimentary CAM newsletters. At best, artists could reproduce crude line drawings using the old-fashioned Gestetner machine duplicating process.

The visual artists within CAM were not as celebrated or as well placed as the writers, although by contrast, many of the writers had

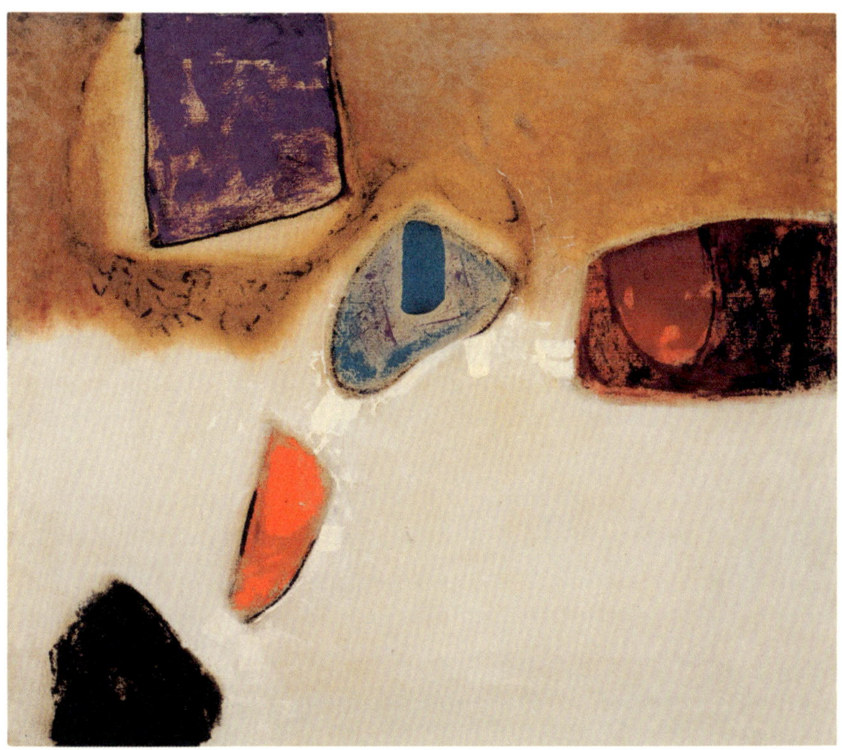

Aubrey Williams, *Warrau*, 1969,
oil on canvas, 81 × 92 cm (32 × 36¼ in.)

published books to their names that could be accessed by members. CAM art exhibitions were few and far between, and even then, only on for short periods, so, sadly, it was quite possible for people to attend CAM meetings, meet artists and not have an inkling of what their work was like. The visual arts tended to be the subject of discussion in the absence of actual observation. This was a big disadvantage, although that being said, the existence of the organisation was beneficial to artists in the sense that it did raise their profile and brought artists together. In this context, it should be borne in mind that the exhibitions that cemented the reputation of Aubrey Williams – his retrospective at the Whitechapel Art Gallery in 1998 and 'The Shostakovich' at the Commonwealth Institute in 2013 – took place long after the demise of CAM.

Ronald Moody was quite an isolated figure in the post-war years, partly through his earlier illness with tuberculosis and for that reason, I think he really welcomed the formation of CAM. Suddenly, there was a group of people from the Caribbean who were showing interest in art and artists, writers and poets, which included all the regions of the Caribbean. It is important to acknowledge in terms of legacy that he was awarded the prestigious Musgrave Medal in 1977 for his outstanding contribution to the arts, which is the highest honour given by the Jamaican government.

On reflection, one could consider CAM as essentially being as much a British phenomenon as it was a Caribbean one. Although all the artists were born in the Caribbean, all of them were actually living in the UK – some for many years – they had either trained or had started their activity as artists in Britain and were also, invariably, exposed to Modernist metropolitan influences.

One significant impact of CAM artists is their influence on future generations of Black British artists. By a kind of osmosis, I think quite a number of the artists from the generation that emerged from British art schools for the first time – Sonia Boyce, Keith Piper, Veronica Ryan, Eddie Chambers, Lubaina Himid and others – were influenced.[8] It might have occurred to them to be artists because of examples of people such as Ronald Moody and Aubrey Williams, who were at that time quite well known – not just because of CAM, for by then they had received wider exposure through involvement with universities, or Williams's retrospective at the Whitechapel Gallery, or through publications such as *Art Rage* that publicised their work.

CAM continued for about six years, and by the time it was over in the early 1970s, Moody and I still kept in touch. I had been asked to present a talk on Ronald at the Keskidee Centre in 1972, which meant doing a little research on him. This meant I was able to visit him in his studio, which allowed me to become more familiar with him and his work.[9]

Visiting Ronald Moody at his Fleming Close Artist's Studio

Moody lived in Fulham and I lived in northwest London, so it was a trek for me across London. When I had the chance to visit him, I would inevitably buy pastries from a nearby cake shop and he would make us coffee. I was always fascinated by this coffee-making, which was very ritualistic. He had an ancient hand-operated coffee grinder and seemed to take great pleasure in producing fresh, ground coffee from his store of beans. A portable camping-style burner substituted for a built-in stove, so all in all, coffee and pastries took quite a while

He had a collection of slides of his work, but you really had to press to get any information out of him as he was a bit cagey about promoting himself or talking about his own art. Once, in the early days of CAM, he gave a talk at the West Indian Students' Centre,[10] and I was quite surprised at how nervous and reticent he seemed to be. I think it was part of his personality to be retiring and self-effacing. Furthermore, he didn't talk about his major works of sculpture, but elected instead to talk about his practice with paper and inks and his experiments with a marbling technique. I recall not being particularly impressed by them, but that may have been more a reflection of my own limitations coming face to face with a technique I was encountering for the first time. After a while, on studio visits, he began to show slides of his work and press cuttings of exhibition reviews. I remember reviews relating to the artwork *Three Heads*, gifted to the Jawaharlal Nehru Museum in New Delhi, and others.[11]

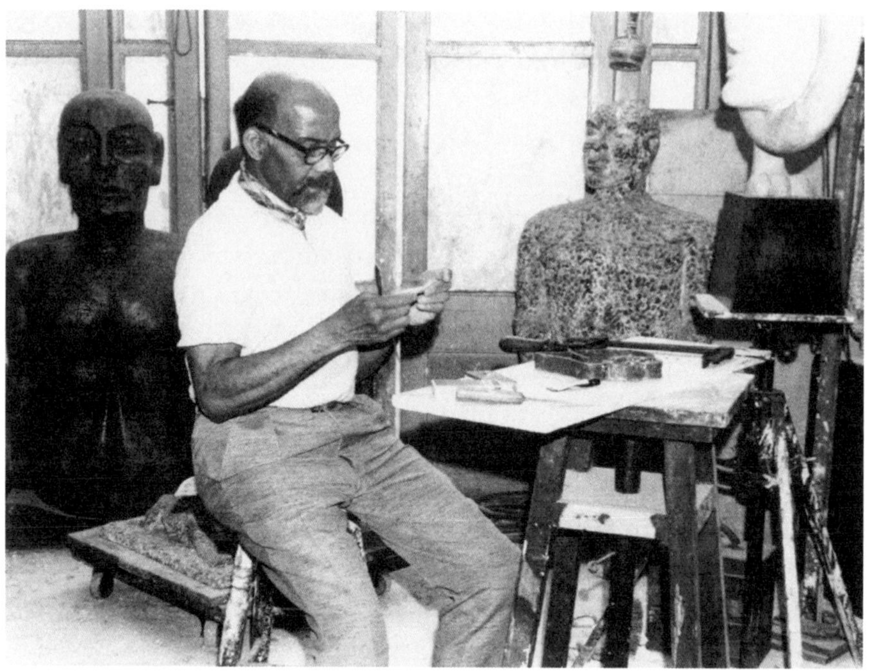

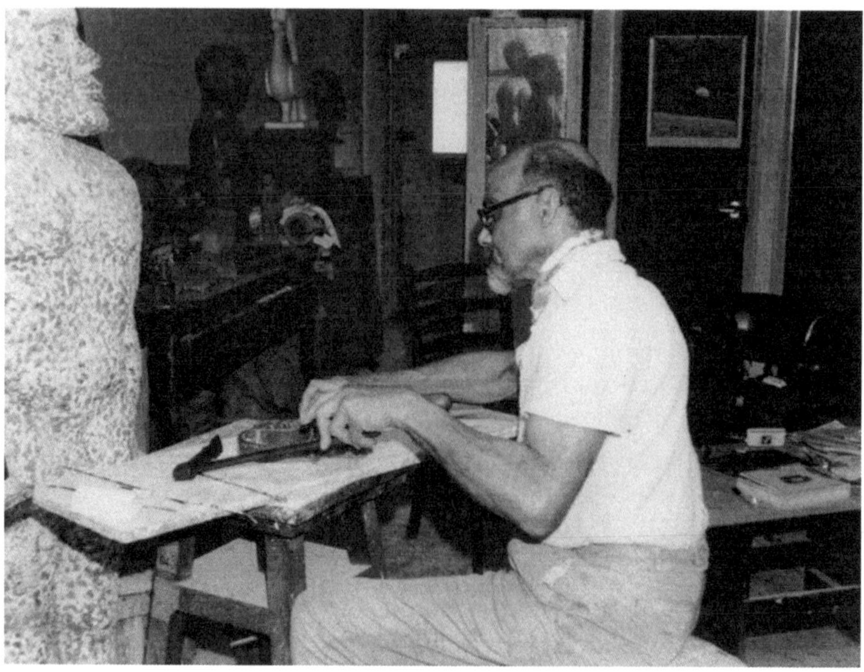

Ronald Moody at Fleming Close Studios,
Fulham, May 1970

During these visits, Moody introduced me to the technical side of casting things into bronze resin. I was very taken by the fact that he was able to do his own casting. This was critical for a sculptor because it saved the great expense of having to rely on a bronze foundry. He replicated this process using a mixture of bronze powder and resin, which was a modern possibility. Although not as valued as bronze, the result, when introduced into a plaster mould, is impressive and looks very much like the real thing. Moody taught me the rudiments of this cold casting method, and because he had been a dentist, he brought a disciplined, scientific approach to the process. Everything was meticulously weighed and apportioned so as to get the right combination of the powder resin to trigger the ideal chemical reaction. This sort of professional collaboration made for a closer friendship. On reflection, this must have been about the time he became 'Ronald' rather than 'Mr Moody', marking an important milestone in our relationship.

Alas, I have never set up a studio away from home that would facilitate the kind of messy stuff you need for sculpture and subsequent cold casting, so apart from those pure bronze pieces that were commissioned and cast in a foundry, I have not put this acquired technical skill to great practical purpose. My bust of George Lamming is an example.[12]

I saw more of Ronald Moody and as he got older. I would run the occasional errand for him, especially as his wife, Helene, had been dead for some time and he lived on his own in his spacious Redcliffe Gardens flat. I recall on one occasion, on a bank holiday weekend, he rang to say that his 'paraffin man' had let him down, which would have meant facing the weekend without heating. I picked him up and drove him to the nearest petrol station. On arrival, I simply got out of the car, leaving him in the passenger seat. I retrieved the petrol tin from the trunk, got and paid for the paraffin and came back, only to find him struggling to release himself from the seat belt, which was a novelty in those days. He was quite furious with me. I imagine he had felt like a prisoner, for, on reflection, I had deprived him of a degree of independence and robbed him of the privilege of paying for his own paraffin. We dropped the paraffin home and to cool things

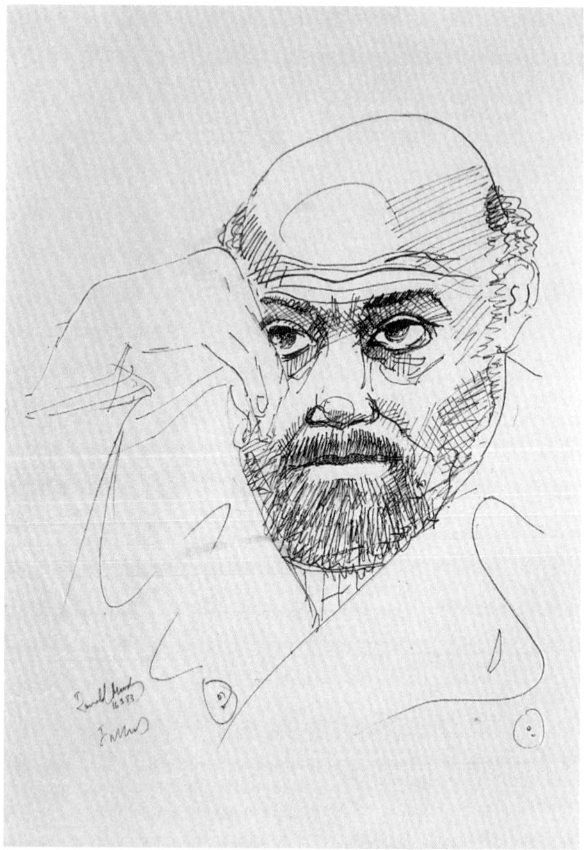

down, I suggested that we go to a nearby pub. He paid for the first round, restoring a degree of parity. I had a sketch pad to hand, and while we were chatting, I did some sketches of him. They mirrored the change in his mood from angry to being composed and reflective.

I would also visit him in hospital when his health deteriorated. Moody used to wear a hat, and I remember once, after he had been discharged from hospital, he rang me and said, 'Oh, I forgot my hat in the hospital. Could you pick it up for me?' I made my way to Westminster Hospital, asked about the hat and was given one, which I dropped off for him. A day or two later he rang and said, 'I'm sorry, but it's the wrong hat.' To my shame, I never did take the hat back to swap it for the right one. Continuing to visit him during these

Errol Lloyd, *Portrait of Ronald Moody*, c. 1983, pencil on paper, 40 × 30 cm (15 3/4 × 11 7/8 in.)

times marked another important milestone in our relationship. We kept in touch until his death. I was with him at the hospital, holding his hand as he took his last breath. I was by then older, in my forties, and that moment had a profound impact; it is something that I have never forgotten. I also wrote Moody's obituary, which was published in *Artrage*. It had been written close to the time that the magazine had to go to print. Anne Walmsley noted and was shocked that I had overlooked his relationship with CAM, but I think at the time I had felt that his other achievements had in a way trumped his membership.

Ronald Moody's Contribution to British Art, Recognised by the Minority Arts Advisory Service

In 1981, I joined the organisation MAAS, which stands for Minority Arts Advisory Service.[13] It was established by Naseem Khan, whose 1976 published report *The Arts Britain Ignores: The Arts of Ethnic Minorities in Britain* highlighted the extent to which British institutions concerned with the arts were not inclusive in attitude towards those artists who came from the Commonwealth, including white artists from places like Australia, New Zealand, South Africa and even Eastern Europe.[14] They were not really given much exposure in Britain, and places such as the Commonwealth Institute Art Gallery never really had their shows reviewed. When it came to the arts-giving foundations and those offering grants, there was very little support for non-white artists, so much so that an organisation such as CAM never got any funding during the course of its existence. Khan's report identified a certain type of insularity, and it had a big impact at the time. The following year, she received financial support from the Arts Council and other funding bodies to set up MAAS.

Any analysis of Khan's book needs to pay attention to its subtitle, *The Arts of Ethnic Minorities in Britain*. This, together with references to the 'host' community, tends to suggest that the minorities concerned were not viewed as being fully fledged British citizens with the same entitlements as members of the accommodating, so called, 'host' community. Yet at the time of the publication, it must have been clear that the vast majority of immigrants were putting down permanent roots in Britain in terms of long-term employment, housing and raising families, and of course, as taxpayers.

However, MAAS reflected the funding reality of the time and in advance of previous funded provision for non-white artists. The assumption on the part of funders, and presumedly Khan herself, was that the arts that she identified in her book as being 'ignored' would get a shot in the arm once their existence became known through research and publicity. Hence the 'Advisory Service' focus of the organisation. As it turned out, there was only limited truth to that assumption. However, there is no doubt that the report and the resultant organisation had a massive impact on the sector. Khan's book had cast the net of 'ignored' arts wide enough to include Chinese, Cypriot and Eastern European cultures, which took it out of the 'Third World' categorisation and, in all probability, made the arguments more compelling and funding more likely.

MAAS established a modest broadsheet publication called *Echo: Living Arts of Britain's Ethnic Communities* that ran from 1977 to 1980, with a wide coverage reflecting the remit of the organisation. Some people, however, objected to the term 'Ethnic Arts' or 'Minority Arts' underscored by the report, which suggested a subsidiary second division. Later, the focus narrowed around African, Caribbean and Asian (mainly Indian and Pakistani) arts, and to a lesser extent Latin American arts, which coincided with the emergence of a 'Third World' consciousness and the popularity of the term, denoting an informal political and cultural solidarity. It also coincided with MAAS's new colour publication, the quarterly magazine *Artrage*,[15] which took on the difficult challenge of appealing to such a broad range of communities through all the arts genres – music, dance, the visual arts, literature and so on. This, to a certain extent, might have also been one of its strengths. Given the challenges, it was a really good publication. It's a shame that it isn't more accessible for research, for a creative analysis of the listing could give great insight into what was happening at that time from the mid-1980s to the 1990s. Even without comments, even without reviews, just the sheer range of documentation is valuable. There was also a companion publication called *The*

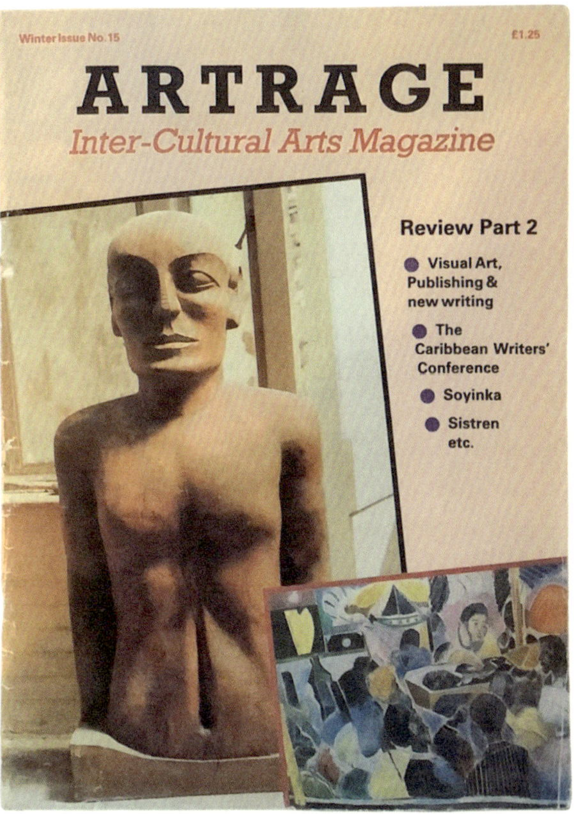

Black Arts in London that charted events in London. Unfortunately, I don't know who has a complete collection of the publications, and the organisation fizzled out around five years after I left. One my first assignments when I joined MAAS was to go to Soho to attend the Lunar New Year festival that was happening at the time. I remember it being very interesting because it was my first venture into that kind of environment. I had to review a Chinese opera, and it was a bit difficult for me, because I didn't know anything about the subject. I took the approach of reporting and providing feedback on the ambiance of the place, the atmosphere among the other people in attendance and their openness and friendliness.

When I joined the organisation, I was roped into the Minority Arts Award committee, which awarded a cash prize to outstanding

Cover of *Artrage*, no. 15, 1986, featuring *Johanaan*

artists. I took the opportunity to introduce Fay Rodrigues – a fellow member of the committee – to Ronald Moody, by taking her to his studio. His work was a revelation to her, so he was strongly recommended to the committee, not just on the basis of his sculpture but for his ongoing support of community arts events such as the 'Creation for Liberation' exhibitions of painting and sculpture in Brixton, organised by the Race Today Collective. At the time, there was very little financial support for sculptors, as sculpture had gone a bit out of fashion. Wood carving was even less fashionable in those days and, to a certain degree, still is. Ronald Moody's reputation was not as widely established as it later became when his niece Cynthia Moody acquired his estate. Cynthia really set about making sure that people knew the extent of his work and brought it to the attention of the people and institutions that Moody, through modesty or other reasons, would not have approached. I don't think Moody would have spoken to the Tate or any of those organisations. As an artist, sometimes it's better to have a third party involved. It's much easier to represent an artist and advocate on their behalf, otherwise an artist may appear too self-promoting.

Cynthia Moody: Building a Legacy – Tools of the Trade

Cynthia Moody, in her capacity as his estate executor, was able to learn a great deal more about his work.[16] Going through his letters, she had come across my name in Moody's correspondence, and that led her to me. She lived in Bristol, and the first time we met, she visited me in my home in Willesden, London. Before that, all our communications were by phone or by letter. Later on, I visited her a couple of times in Bristol. I was very impressed by how diligent her archival work was: her historical research into the background of his work, as well as collecting his work and making sense of his uncatalogued archives. It was a labour of love, really; she herself was retired at the time, which meant that she was able to devote an incredible amount of time to that activity. To be frank, without her, Moody's whole legacy would likely be lost, as nobody else had the resources or the time to look into it as thoroughly as she did.

At the time, the chance or the prospect of any kind of public grant for a third party to do that work would have been slim.

Through my association with Cynthia and her research, I learned that Moody was a member of the Theosophical Society,[17] which was quite in vogue in pre-war and immediate post-war years. People were exploring new philosophies, different lifestyles and ways of being. I remember once setting out with a friend of mine to an exhibition in Hampstead. We had got the address wrong and wandered into a building, opening an imposing door into a meeting of the Theosophical Society of Great Britain. We felt trapped – we didn't feel like we could just turn around and walk out. So we sat there. To me, it was completely esoteric stuff, I had not the slightest understanding of what the person in the pulpit was talking about. Eventually, we worked up the courage to make an awkward exit. However, it did make me realise how strange the whole thing must have seemed to a lot of people at the time, because it was definitely based on esoteric Eastern philosophical concepts. I also learned from Cynthia of Moody's interest in German culture, including German philosophers and also Goethe Lieder music, especially the song cycles of Franz Schubert. He also taught himself how to speak German – we should bear in mind that he had been living in Britain in the pre-war years, before anti-German sentiment set in.

I have some correspondence between myself and Cynthia tucked away somewhere. I don't throw stuff away, but I am not very good at collating such material. However, I do have to hand Ronald Moody's clay-modelling tools that she gifted to me at some point in the 1980s. I have no idea why she gave them to me; she knew of my interest in sculpture, but I imagine it would have been difficult for her to find a place for them to be cared for if I hadn't accepted them. What would she have done with them? At the time of Moody's death, his reputation was nowhere near what it is now. There was no museum interest, and generally people didn't know about him. Most of his contemporaries had died long ago. Although Moody's public sculpture *Savacou* (1964), installed at the University of the West Indies' Mona Campus, Kingston,[18] would have been a big deal, it was outside of England. Moody's tools would not have had any particular appeal to any British

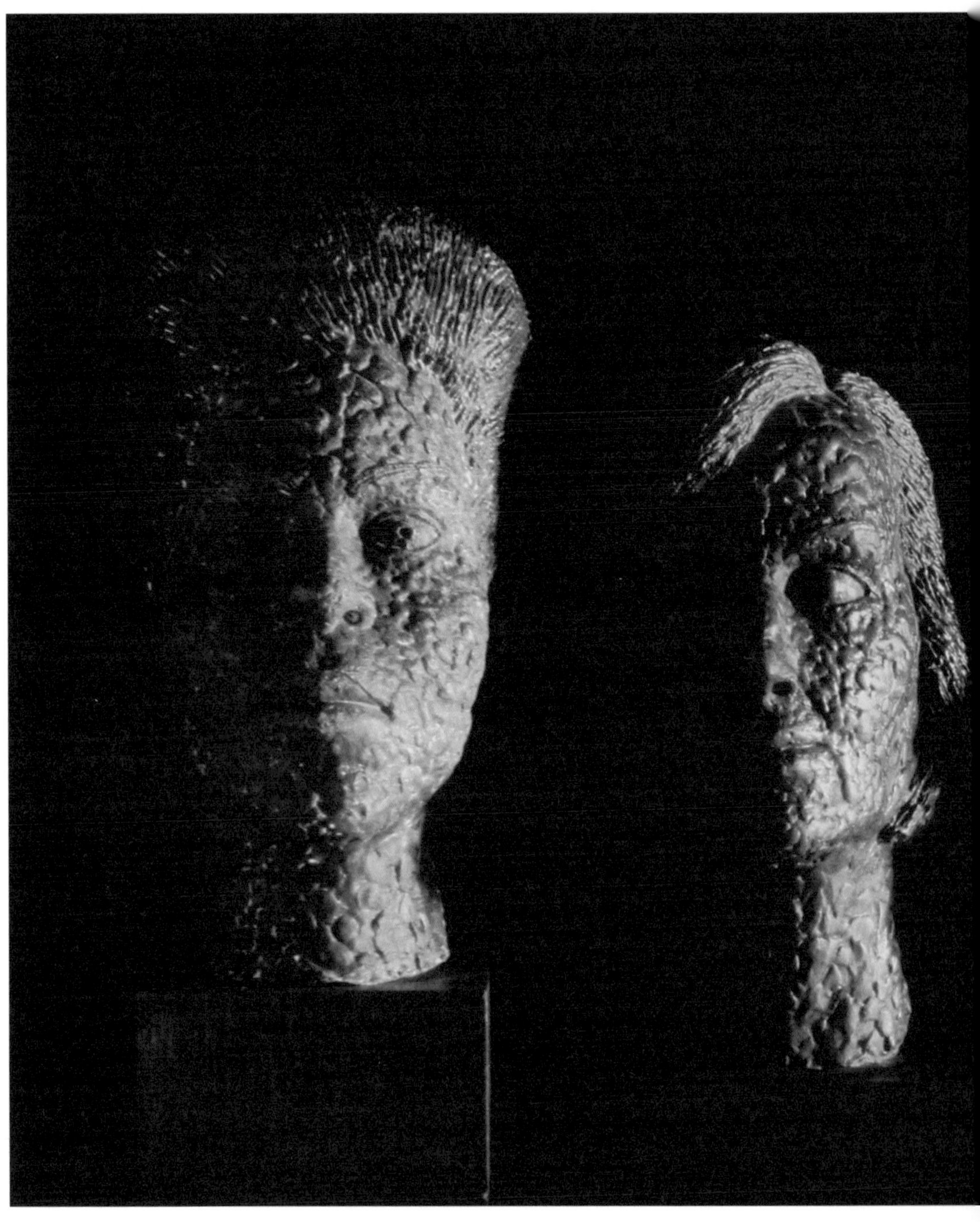

Cynthia Moody and Sculptures, n.d. Photograph by Susan Loder

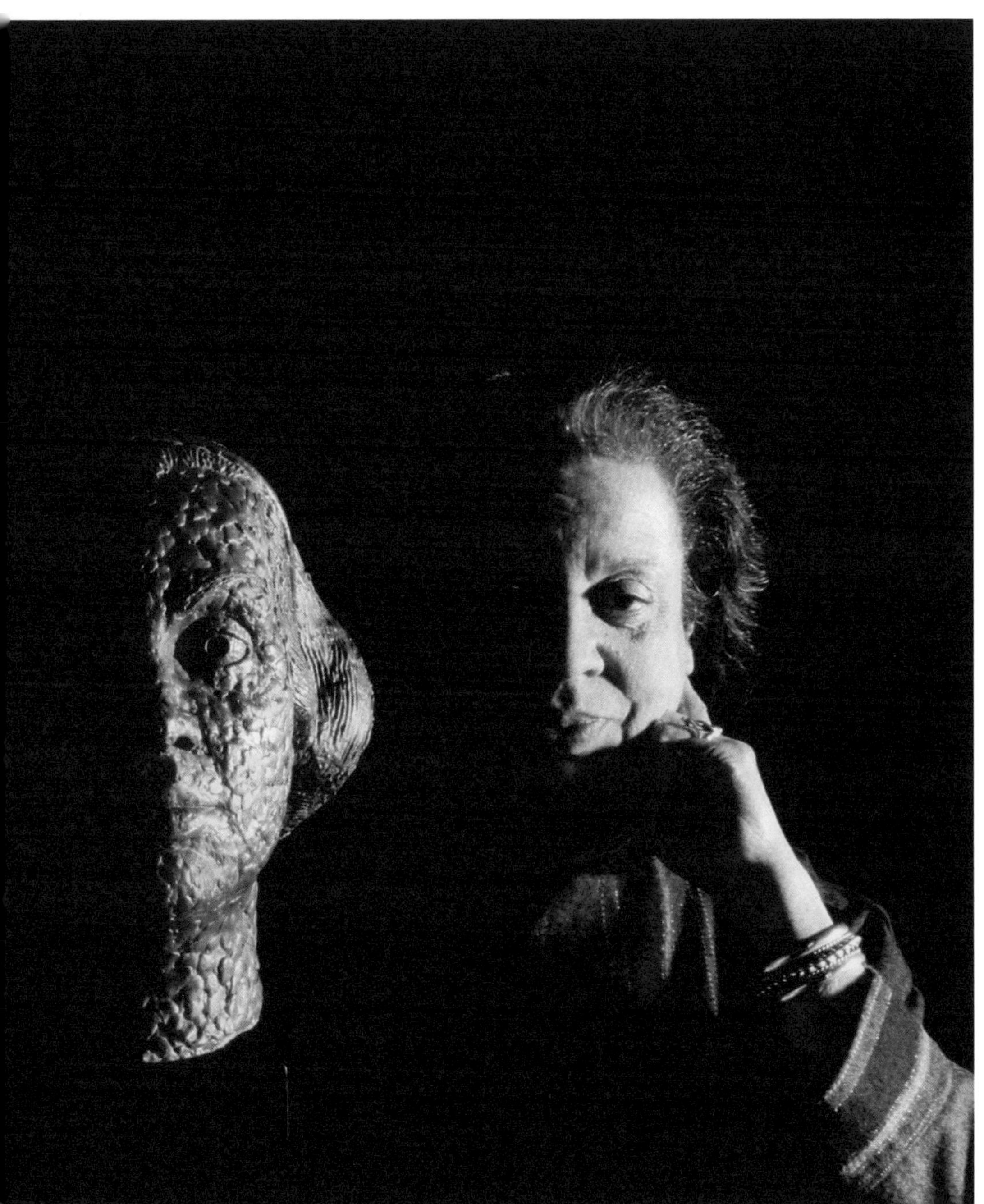

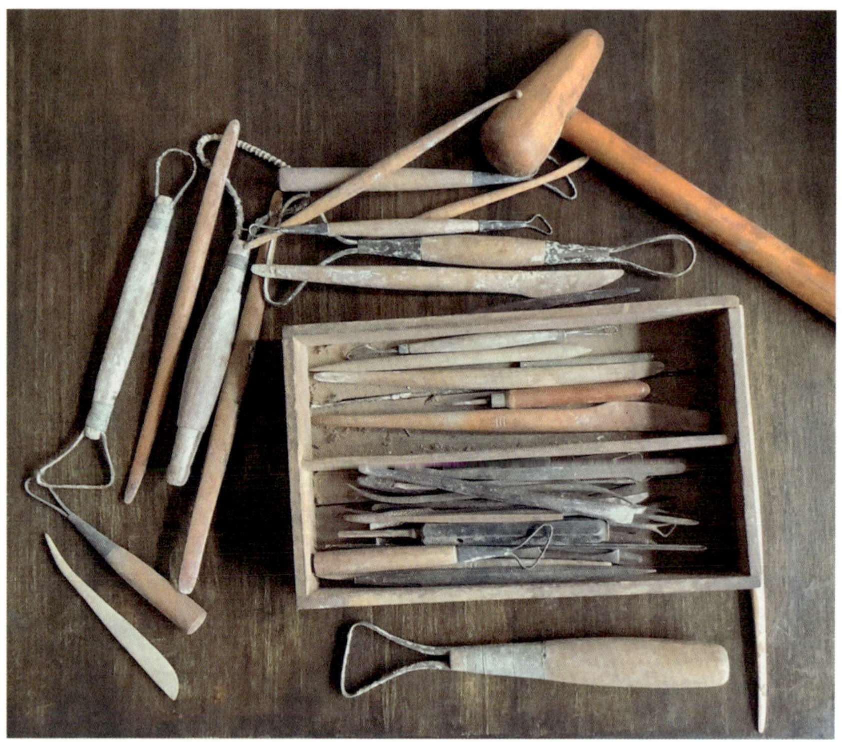

institution at the time of his passing. For his contemporaries – people like Barbara Hepworth and Henry Moore – it was usual for the paraphernalia of their trade to be kept intact. In Moody's case, the box containing his tools is itself an artefact of interest. On the outside of the box, Cynthia Moody scribed her signature, which helps to provide authenticity. The tools themselves have not been cleaned, so have retained their patina and tell-tale markings of their earlier use. Objects and styles change radically with time, and artefacts such as Moody's tools help to build narrative and context. The tools number approximately fifty, many more than I had thought. There are about thirty-five of the small ones piled on top of each other in the box. Most of the tools would have been appropriate only for modelling clay. I have no idea what has become of the chisels and hammers he used. Marvellously, one of the wooden hammers he used when wood carving remains. But I dare say he would have had more than one.

Ronald Moody's tools

Commonwealth Artists in Britain: Ronald Moody – an Artist with Conviction

I imagine it would have been impossible for Moody to achieve anywhere near the level of recognition of his contemporaries. They had so many more resources at their command, plus other advantages. Henry Moore or Barbara Hepworth, for instance, were able to create massive works for public display. When your work is commissioned, supported and then put in a public space, naturally, your reputation will be enhanced no end. The kind of sculpture Ronald Moody was involved in was very time-consuming and quite expensive, especially the works that had to be cast in bronze. Then, having done that, the question remained: who would purchase these works of art if the artist is not accepted as part of mainstream society?

Additionally, when Moody started to work as a sculptor in the 1930s, he might have been considered at that stage a Jamaican sculptor. He wouldn't have been residing long enough in England to be considered British, even if, in strict constitutional terms, he was. Being a British subject at that time did not necessarily cut much ice. Quite often, when people came to England from the colonies to study, the notion was that you would study and then return home. There would not have been the infrastructure or any support from within the Caribbean community in those days for artists. When Moody started out in the 1930s, he would have been literally one of the very first Jamaicans pursuing sculpture, or any kind of art or painting, simply because generally speaking, people did not have the leisure time to pursue art. There was no support for it either. Any kind of art would be something pursued on a fairly amateur basis and not with the intent of securing a livelihood. Somebody like Edna Manley,[19] who went to Jamaica in the 1920s after the First World War, would also have been among the earliest artists. In local Jamaican polite society, there were some people who could be referred to as expats, who would engage in some form of painting or other form of art. But they tended to be more involved with genteel landscape painting or still life. Moody and Manley would have had an uphill struggle in terms of support in the context of either the Caribbean or Britain. Moody pursuing a life of

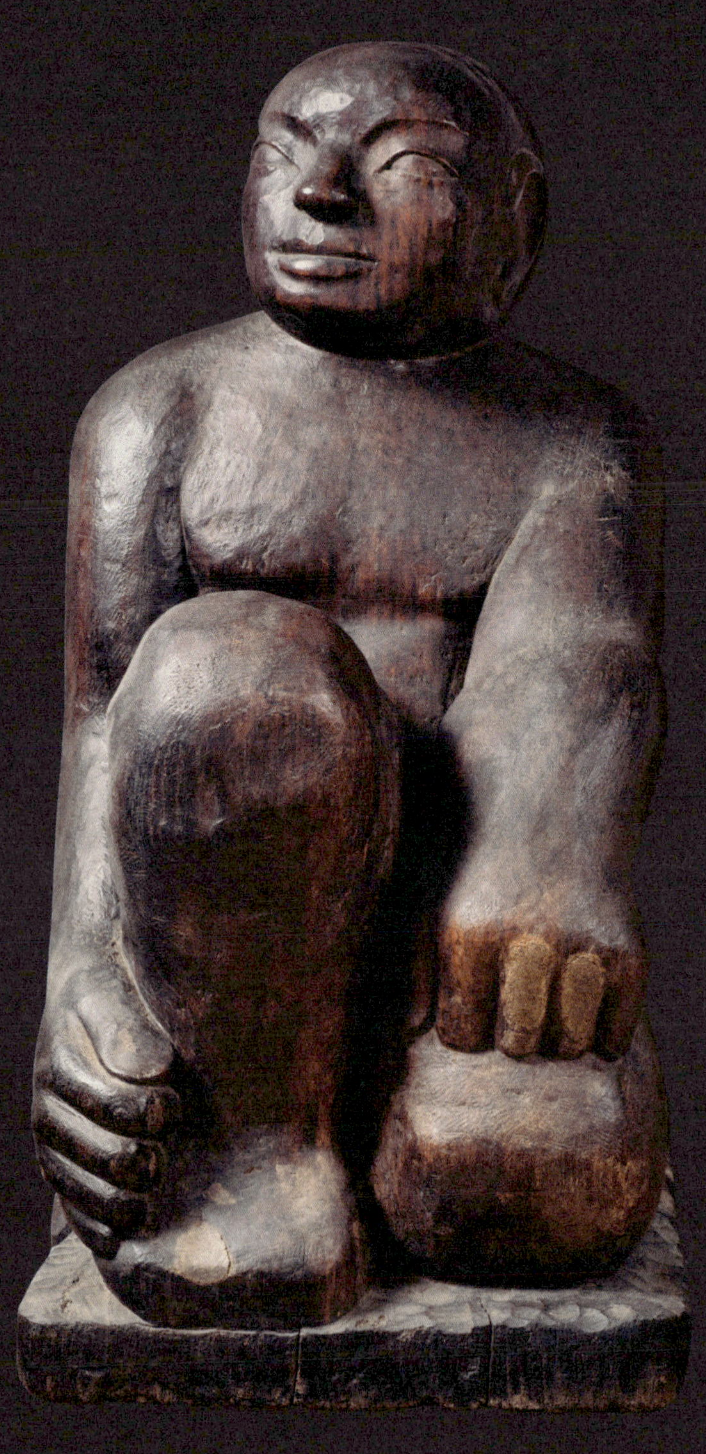

Ronald Moody, *Small Kneeling Figure*, 1960, teak, height: 58.4 cm (23 in.)

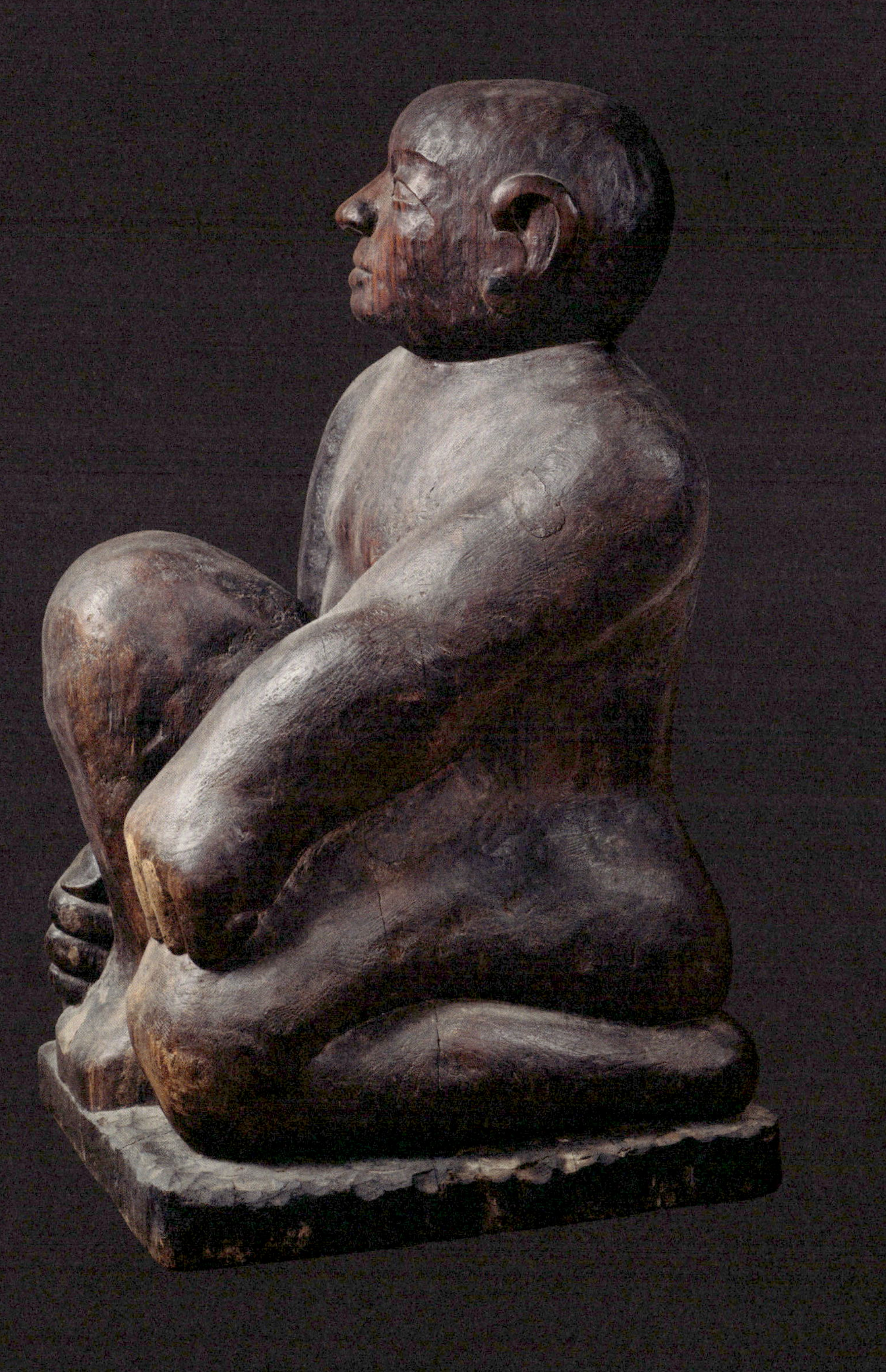

art in the 1930s would have been viewed as being quite brazen, in a way. Even in my time, it is something that you approach with nothing other than trepidation.

One of the lessons that one can gain from looking at Ronald Moody's life is that at the end of it all, it really comes down to an expression of individuality. That is what art is all about. We're all unique individuals, and Moody's output can't be mistaken for anybody else's. It is always challenging to describe to later generations the mood, spirit and general atmosphere of previous decades. This is especially so when there is a dearth of documentary evidence to hand. To a certain extent, we must rely on conjecture that when Moody set out to England from Jamaica in the 1920s to study dentistry, he would have had very good prospects and been open to any colonial professional loyal to the Empire. His decision to embrace Egyptian art was very much against the grain of the prevailing spirit and values of the times for people from the Caribbean. His was a rejection of mainstream European standards. In those days, the prevalent that standards of beauty and excellence in art were European. They remained so, even many decades later. Coming from Jamaica, with his educational background as well, makes it quite remarkable that Moody embraced Egyptian art.

When I was about thirteen or fourteen growing up in Jamaica, a teacher called Alan Hadfield from Yorkshire came to teach at my boarding school. He was a Quaker and a conscientious objector, and had been imprisoned. He was a bachelor and seemed to have travelled with all his worldly possessions, including some terracotta heads and figurines. His classroom at the time doubled up as a kind of common room where students would meet between games and supper. His sculptures were on show, and I showed such keen interest that when he embarked on a bust of one boy in clay, he invited me to join him. It was my first introduction, and surprisingly, I was good at it. This was the beginning of my developing interest in art. When I went home for my holidays that year, a lovely new library had been built in my town, called Saint Ann's Bay, with attractive cut stone and expansive glass widows, set over two acres of beautifully landscaped grounds.

The large fountain outside with goldfish in it was an attraction for young people to hang out and meet their friends. In the library, I came across a book published in 1960 titled *American Negro Art* by Cedric Dover, featuring on the cover a sculpture by Richmond Barthé.[20] I discovered to my amazement that the two bronze sculptures in the library were by that same artist! One sculpture was of a Black man with a bare torso holding a kind of spear, the other one was a bust of the Custos of the Parish. I was very curious and borrowed this book, took it home and relayed the experience to my mother. The bust of the Custos of the Parish was quite a smart move, because I think it may have been through him, an influential white man, that Barthé's sculpture and the book had been acquired for the library.

It so happened that my mother had met Richmond Barthé (who had been living in Jamaica for several years) in nearby Ocho Rios, where she worked. She was managing the local branch of an In Bond chain that specialised in bone China and high-end jewelry, catering to wealthy American and British tourists. It was in that context that she had met Barthé. (I have in my possession a handwritten postcard featuring one of his paintings that he sent her, regarding a gold watch he had bought at her store.) Anyway, he mentioned that her son had an interest in sculpture and invited her to bring me to his studio. He lived on the outskirts of Ocho Rios in a suburb called Colegate, where my mother – a progressive modern woman with her own car – drove me one day in early 1960. Barthé took us to his studio, purpose-built on a slight rise at the rear of his house, where he showed us a male nude figure in a reclining position raising himself from the ground. He explained that it represented the awakening of Africa – a period that coincided with the recent attainment of Independence in Ghana and the agitation for freedom from foreign domination by a raft of other African countries. He further explained and that the sculpture was linked to the burgeoning civil rights movement in America. Because of Cedric Dover's book, I had some idea of the Harlem Renaissance and the key role Barthé had played in it, but the civil rights movement was news to me. I was surprised that such a large, almost life-sized figure was modelled in plasticine and not clay. Barthé explained that it had to be transported to the US for casting into bronze as there was no foundry in Jamaica, so it needed to be more robust than clay. Curiously, as we were leaving the studio and drew up beside his house, a bee kept buzzing around him. He said – in all seriousness, I thought – that the bee was saying goodbye to him ahead of his departure for the US the following day.

Years later, in 1966, after I had been living in London, I related the story of visiting Richmond Barthé's studio to my flatmate at the time, Richard Small, a fellow law student. He managed to find for me a bookseller who had a copy of *American Negro Art*, which I still have. We were living near a bronze foundry where I bought some clay and, wondering what to do, I remembered my visit to Richmond Barthé's studio and decided to attempt a replica of the reclining figure. I had never been to art classes or done life drawing and had to rely entirely on my memory, but I was sufficiently pleased with the outcome to have it cast into bronze resin. The sculpture bears a brass plaque: 'The Awakening of Africa by Errol Lloyd – Homage to Richmond Barthé'. The artwork was exhibited for the first time in a solo exhibition, 'Errol Lloyd: My Life in Colour', at the 198 Contemporary Arts and Learning gallery in London in 2022.[21] I like that story because it's a connection, however convoluted, with the Harlem Renaissance, with Jamaica, with England and with Ronald Moody.

Moody's legacy, then, relates us also to being true to whatever your individual vision happens to be, because what he was doing at the time was not fashionable. He would have had very little moral or material support. It would have taken some conviction – and he has said himself that he felt a strong compulsion – to go along with his urge to sculpt. I recently visited the Egyptian Rooms at the British Museum, and I can understand that powerful impact. I was also given a tour of the Egyptian collection at the Fitzwilliam Museum in Cambridge.[22] I imagine that Moody was influenced by Egyptian art's timelessness. He was not geared towards creating contemporary art – that is the beauty of what he did, actually. It is a great achievement to have that level of detachment from what was considered to be contemporary and fashionable. It was his exposure

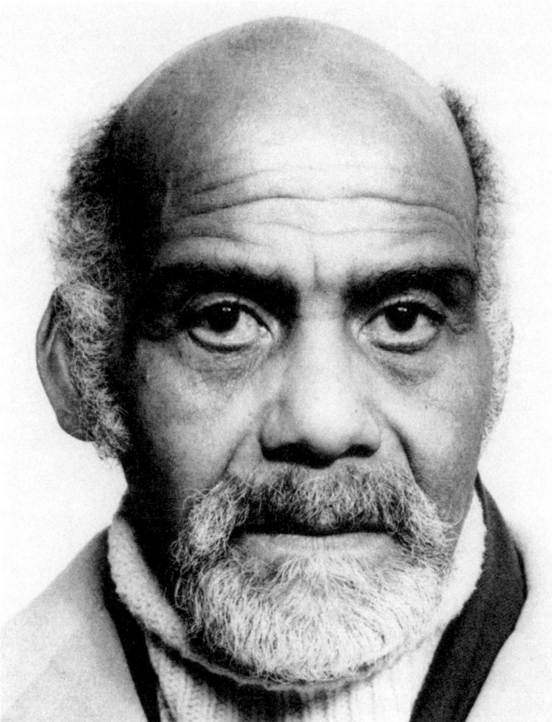

to the Egyptian Room that made him want to become an artist – the timeless quality he felt in that moment. Moody somehow, in his art, found a way to capture the energy of what he felt.

His concerns, similar to painter Aubrey Williams, were generated outside of the Western art canon and were not considered to be of particular interest, coming as they did from a non-white person. Quite likely, it would have been a different matter if a white artist had shown interest in African art or ancient Egyptian sculpture, in the way that Paul Gauguin received attention for his interest in Polynesian art and culture, or Picasso with African art. There was something about the British art scene, I think, that was not particularly inclusive or outward-looking. For instance, the average English person or British person would be very hard pressed to name one well-known artist from Australia, New Zealand, South Africa or Canada. In other words, even from the white Commonwealth, let alone people from the Black

Late portrait of Ronald Moody, 1983.
Photograph by David Sharkey

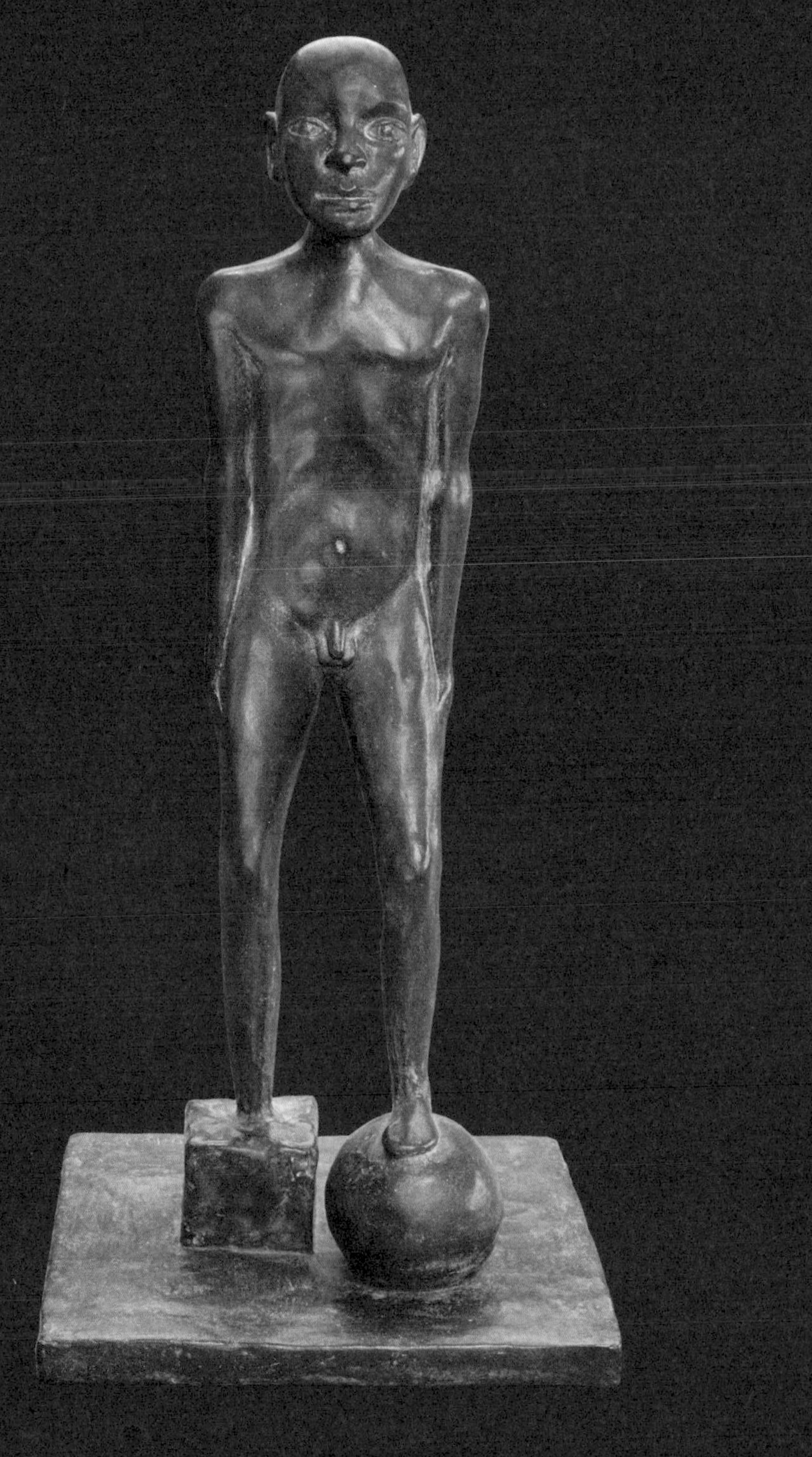

Ronald Moody, *Unknown Political Prisoner*, 1952, bronze, 53 × 14 × 12 cm (20 7/8 × 5 1/2 × 4 3/4 in.)

Commonwealth or those countries that were not considered to be in the same category. There seemed to be a lack of interest in people who were not considered British in the same sense that people who were British, and even then those that were born here, had to really agitate and mount a campaign to be taken into account. To a certain degree, there was a different attitude from some other European countries. Artist Uzo Egonu, for instance, had some good feedback and responses from Germany. Ronald Moody had success in Paris, Amsterdam and America before the Second World War. The support he would have received at this time – the connections and exposure – would have been a great source of inspiration and encouragement. The whole business of not putting the same value on things or on people that are not part of your narrative is a relic of the Empire. Post-war, with a gap of five years, Moody was plagued with health problems. Things had changed; war tends to change everything. He had more difficulty accessing wood, but he was sometimes able to get it from the wharf area during this period. Think about the lasting impact of the recent Coronavirus (Covid 19) pandemic, the levels of trauma during that period – life on pause, things cancelled, careers scuppered – just by not being around for two years.

The nature of Moody's work sufficiently dealt with a rather broad concern and interest in humankind. He was part of that post-Second World War existential moment as people tried to come to terms with a new kind of reality. Moody's symbolic sculptures, such as *Unknown Political Prisoner* (1952), *Hope* (1966–67), or *Hiroshima 1* and 2 (both 1977), in one way could be considered somewhat axiomatic, but they also illustrate his interest in much broader issues. Some of the timeless qualities of Egyptian sculpture, for instance, were not necessarily tied to contemporary things. Part of the dynamic of Western art is to be always moving on, always inventing something new. There has to be a sense of pushing the boundaries. There has been less regard for art that could be considered timeless art – art that didn't need to be considered to be at the cutting edge of current practice. However, there are some sculptors and some artists who have created work coming from similar philosophical origins to Roland Moody who have had more recognition than him. Part of it is the whole mindset that one encountered in England at that time. I remember at one stage walking into a gallery in the West End of London. I just walked in and said, 'I'm an artist. I wonder if you have any interest in exhibitions and so on, by me'. The person didn't even ask anything about me or about what I'd done. He just referred me to the ethnographic section of the British Museum without any further query. There is an assumption, in a way, that you are an ethnic person and therefore what you're doing is not going to be in any way of interest. To a certain extent, you can actually sympathise with galleries, because they're not charities and they have to operate on a commercial basis. If the general public are not interested in buying art from certain types of artists, there is going to be no incentive to promote that kind of work. I do think things are changing, now, so that the legacy of somebody like Ronald Moody will be taken more seriously into consideration. The reason for that, of course, is that you have institutions like the Tate, the National Portrait Gallery and others, who have actually purchased his work. At Tate Britain, Moody's sculpture *Johanaan* (1936) is now regularly on view. This gives a tremendous amount of status to an artist as a form of endorsement.

One thing that militates against Ronald Moody's growing reputation is that wood carving is still considered outdated. I remember that when my daughter pursued a sculpture degree at Central St Martins, she expressed an interest in wood carving and the attitude was dismissive. She was told by the dean that it was a craft that was not taught there. This was during a time when there was a lot of interest in new art expressions such as video art, performance, installations and suchlike. In a way, the carvings of Ronald Moody might have seemed passé, or certainly not sufficiently contemporary, given the time. But I think that the subject matter and the treatment should definitely overcome any reservations that may be entertained about Moody's chosen medium, for it was perfect for what he had to express.

It is very important that there are new voices and new publications allowing people to pursue novel avenues of academic study.

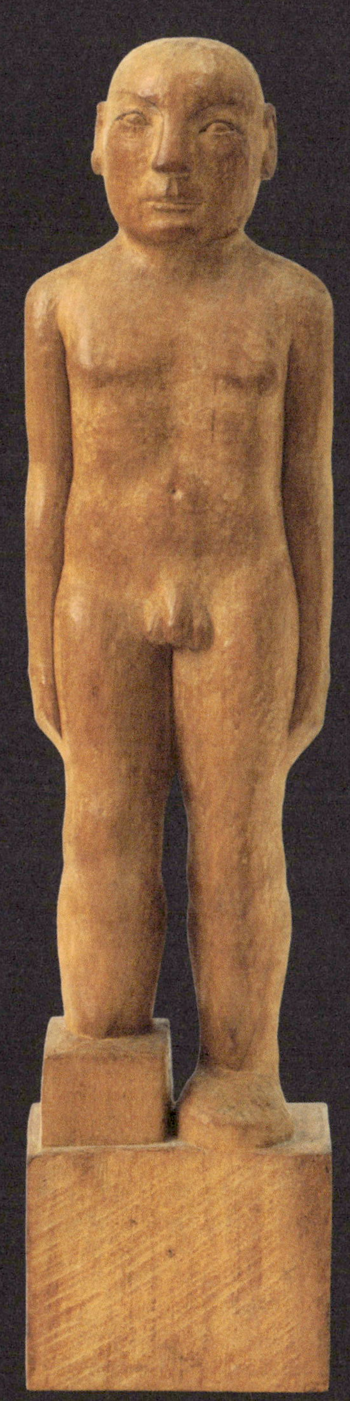

Ronald Moody, *Hope*, 1966–67, kauri,
67 × 14.7 × 10 cm (26 ½ × 5 ⅝ × 4 in.)

Someone told me they wanted to pursue an MA focused on the Caribbean Artists Movement some years ago but they were discouraged from doing so, as there weren't enough publications on the subject or the academic underpinning. However, more material published on CAM will of course bolster its reputation and legacy. Additionally, it is difficult for artists to have a reputation established retrospectively compared to when they are alive – exhibiting, actively making contacts and building networks to promote their work. It may sound cynical, but when retrospective, following the death of an artist, for instance, there may not be sufficient incentives for third parties to promote or even preserve the work, especially if there is no established market value attached to it. Ronald Moody was a retiring figure, and it is not until you do the research yourself or benefit from other people's research that you begin to realise the scope of what he achieved alongside his involvement with a wellspring of artistic and cultural movements throughout the twentieth century.

This text is based on an interview between Errol Lloyd and Ego Ahaiwe Sowinski that took place on 3 August 2023.

Notes

Introduction

1 As part of a research project focusing on seminal exhibitions by *Afterall*, the wall texts for 'The Other Story' have been helpfully archived at: https://theotherstory.afterall.org/hayward-gallery.html [accessed 1 November 2023]. *Afterall*'s research into 'The Other Story' began with a symposium on 3 April 2009, 'Exhibitions and the World at Large' (co-organised by *Afterall* and TrAIN for University of the Arts London; hosted by Tate Britain as part of Goodwin's Cross-Cultural Programme). A paper on the subject of 'The Other Story' by Jean Fisher, commissioned for this occasion, is also available online: www.tate.org.uk/research/publications/tate-papers/no-12/the-other-story-and-the-past-imperfect [accessed 1 November 2023].

Chapter 1

1 Printout of a black-and-white photograph of Christina Emmeline Ellis (*c.* 1960–1952), Ronald Moody's mother, captioned 'Mater', in the garden of their family home in Jamaica, n.d. Papers of Ronald Moody, Tate Archive, TGA 956/5/2/10.

2 Printout of a black-and-white photograph of Charles Ernest Moody (1861–1921), Ronald Moody's father, captioned 'Pater', n.d. Papers of Ronald Moody, Tate Archive, TGA 956/5/2/9.

3 Cynthia Moody, 'Ronald Moody: A Man True to His Vision', *Third Text: Third World Perspectives on Art and Culture*, vol. 3, nos 8–9, 1989, pp. 5–25.

4 Stephen Bourne, 'The Life of Dr Harold Moody', available online: www.pearson.com/uk/educators/schools/issues/diversity-and-inclusion/representation/the-life-of-dr-harold-moody.html [accessed 1 November 2023].

5 'The League of Coloured Peoples: Harold Moody', *Making Britain: Discover How South Asians Shaped the Nation, 1879–1950*, The Open University in collaboration with the University of Oxford and King's College London, available online: www5.open.ac.uk/research-projects/making-britain/taxonomy/term/616 [accessed 1 November 2023]. *Making Britain* is an inter-disciplinary research project examining the formative contributions South Asians made to Britain's literary, political and cultural life in the period 1870–1950.

6 Copies of the portrait of Harold Moody exist in both plaster and bronze. The unrealised catalogue raisonné compiled by Cynthia Moody notes that the plaster (now owned by Pallant House, Chichester) was part of the artist's collection. Bronze 1 is owned by Southwark Borough Council (purchased 2008), and bronze 2 was purchased in New Zealand at auction in 1996 by the National Portrait Gallery, London.

7 BBC transcript of the broadcast *Caribbean Survey: An Exile Looks Back,* 12 January 1953. Papers of Ronald Moody, Tate Archive, TGA 956/3/6/12.

8 *Ibid.*

9 Cynthia Moody, 'Ronald Moody: A Way of Life', *Caribbean Beat*, issue 46, November/December 2000, available online: www.caribbean-beat.com/issue-46/a-way-of-life#axzz8CNsfjfxF [accessed 1 November 2023].

10 Petrine Archer-Straw and Kim Robinson, *Jamaican Art: Then and Now* (LMH Publishing Ltd, new ed., 2011), p. 5.

11 Cynthia Moody, 'Ronald Moody: A Man True to His Vision', *op. cit.*, p. 5.

12 BBC transcript of *Caribbean Survey: An Exile Looks Back, op. cit.*, p. 5.

13 Cynthia Moody, 'Ronald Moody: A Man True to His Vision', *op. cit.*

14 Gemma Romain, 'Ronald Moody: Archival explorations of a Black Jamaican artist in interwar London', *Media Diversified*, April 2015, available online: https://mediadiversified.org/2015/04/05/ronald-moody-archival-explorations-of-a-black-jamaican-artist-in-interwar-london [accessed 1 November 2023].

15 Gemma Romain, 'Ronald Moody: Sculpture and Interwar Britain', *Equiano Centre*, University College London (UCL), available online: www.ucl.ac.uk/equiano-centre/educational-resources/fusion-worlds/artists/ronald-moody-sculpture-and-interwar-britain [accessed 1 November 2023].

16 Eight parodies written by Ronald Moody printed in the *Royal Dental Hospital Magazine*, published between February 1928 and October 1929. Papers of Ronald Moody, Tate Archive, TGA 956/3/3/1-6.

Chapter 2

1 BBC transcript of *Calling the West Indies: Close-Up*, 31 January 1943. Ronald Moody interviewed by Una Marson. Papers of Ronald Moody, Tate Archive, TGA 956/3/5/1.

2 Guy Brett, 'A Reputation Restored: The Rediscovery of Sculptor Ronald Moody', (Tate Research Publication, 2003), available online: www.tate.org.uk/art/artists/ronald-moody-2298/reputation-restored [accessed 1 November 2023].

3 Cynthia Moody, 'Ronald Clive Moody: A Summary of his Life, Work and Times', *Black British Art*, n.d. Ronald Moody Artist File, Stuart Hall Library, AR12.

4 Cynthia Moody, 'Ronald Moody: A Man True to His Vision', *op. cit.*

5 'Museum Insights: The Raid on Benin, 1897', Smithsonian, National Museum of African Art, available online: https://africa.si.edu/exhibitions/current-exhibitions/visionary-viewpoints-on-africas-arts/the-raid-on-benin-1897 [accessed 1 November 2023].

6 'Negro Art', Adams Gallery, London, 1935.

7 'The Official Organ of *The Keys*', *The Keys*, 1 April 1935. British

Newspaper Archive [accessed 26 January 2023].

8 'Henry Moore's Sculptures', available online: www.tate.org.uk/art/artists/henry-moore-om-ch-1659/henry-moores-sculptures [accessed 1 November 2023].

9 Ann Compton, 'An Essentially Different Kind of Rhythm: Rediscovering Henry Moore's Sculpture in Wood', in *Henry Moore: Sculptural Process and Public Identity*, Tate Research Publication, 1 March 2015: www.tate.org.uk/art/research-publications/henry-moore/ann-compton-an-essentially-different-kind-of-rhythm-rediscovering-henry-moores-sculpture-r1151313 [accessed 1 November 2023].

10 *Johanaan* (1936) was purchased by the Tate in 1992.

11 *Midonz* (1937) was purchased by the Tate in 2010.

12 Also known as *Naissance*, *Naissante* (1937) was one of the works hidden throughout the war in the deserted Paris studio of Moody's friend Kobus Hooykaas.

13 *Midonz* (1937) was purchased by the Tate in 2010.

14 *L'Homme* (1937–38) is part of Leeds Art Gallery, Leeds Museums and Galleries permanent collection.

15 Cynthia Moody, 'Ronald Clive Moody: A Summary of his Life, Work and Times', *op. cit.*

16 Jan van Deene, art critic reviewing the exhibition in the *Algemeen Handelsblad van Vrijdag* in 1938 (n.d.). Quoted in Cynthia Moody's notes for the Ronald Moody catalogue raisonné, Ronald Moody Trust.

17 Cynthia Moody, 'Ronald Moody: Archive Index' / Black British Art, Ronald Moody Artist File, Stuart Hall Library, INIVA Catalogue.

18 Rose-Marie Stolberg, 'Art and Politics in the 1920s', *Sociétés et Représentations*, vol. 51, no. 1, 18 June 2021, pp. 243–61.

19 Cynthia Moody, 'Ronald Moody: Portraits', 1996 / Black British Art, Ronald Moody Artist File, Stuart Hall Library, INIVA catalogue.

20 Photocopy of a certified copy of Ronald and Helene Moody's marriage certificate, 28 February 1949. Papers of Ronald Moody, Tate Archive, TGA 956/7/1/16.

21 Cynthia Moody, 'Ronald Clive Moody: A Summary of his Life, Work and Times', *op. cit.*

22 BBC transcript, 'The Artist's Environment', part of the 'Discovering Art' series. Originally broadcast as one of Moody's series of talks for the BBC Overseas Service, titled 'Calling the West Indies', on 15 July 1946. Papers of Ronald Moody, Tate Archive, TGA 956/3/6/2.

23 This large-scale survey exhibition originated at Baltimore Museum of Art (BMA) and toured to Dallas Museum of Fine Art (DMA) during 1939.

24 Aaron Douglas (1899–1979) was an African American painter, muralist, illustrator and educator regarded as a central figure in the Harlem Renaissance. He developed and served as head of the art department of Fisk University in Nashville, Tennessee, from 1937 to 1966.

25 Richmond Barthé (1901–1988), African American sculptor known for his public works and association with the Harlem Renaissance; he resided in both New York and Jamaica.

26 Sargent Johnson (1888–1967), African American sculptor, ceramicist and painter associated with the Harlem Renaissance.

27 Lois M. Jones (1905–1988), African American visual artist, educator and scholar who served as a professor of art at the Howard University College of Fine Arts from 1930 to 1977.

28 Cynthia Moody, 'Ronald Moody: The Complete Works', n.d. Record no. 15401, Stuart Hall Library, INIVA catalogue.

29 Cynthia Moody, 'Ronald Clive Moody: A Summary of his Life, Work and Times', *op. cit.*

30 The Harmon Foundation, established in 1922 in the US, was created by real-estate developer and philanthropist William E. Harmon and funded playgrounds, nursing programs and vocational guidance for students. In 1925, the Foundation began presenting awards to African American individuals in numerous fields, including art. In addition to presenting awards, the Harmon Foundation organised exhibitions for Black artists to gain further recognition for their work.

31 Bridget R. Cooks, *Exhibiting Blackness: African Americans and the American Art Museum* (University of Massachusetts Press, 2011), pp. 11–12.

32 *Contemporary Negro Art*, exh. cat. (Baltimore Museum of Art, 1939), available online: https://artbma.contentdm.oclc.org/digital/collection/p15264coll3/id/74

33 Mary Brady Beattie, 'Memorandum from Mary Beattie Brady to Evelyn S. Brown, 9 August 1938', Papers of Ronald Moody, Tate Archive, TGA 956.

34 'Opportunity: Journal of Negro Life', *Encyclopedia.com*: www.encyclopedia.com/history/encyclopedias-almanacs-transcripts-and-maps/opportunity-journal-negro-life [accessed 1 November 2023].

35 Letter from Evelyn S. Brown to James S. Watson, 18 August, 1938 (Papers of Ronald Moody, Tate Archive, TGA 956) requesting further information on Ronald Moody, on the advice of Elmer Carter, who thought he would be of help.

36 'James S. Watson Papers 1913–1991', Schomburg Center for Research in Black Culture, New York Public Library, available online: https://archives.nypl.org/scm/20938 [accessed 8 October 2022].

37 Letter from Marie Seton to Evelyn S. Brown, 18 September 1938. Papers of Ronald Moody, Tate Archive, TGA 956.

38 'Former Guggenheim Jeune Gallery, London, Mondrian Route', available online: www.mondrianroute.com/areas/londen/

guggenheim-jeune-gallery [accessed 1 November 2023].
39 'Peggy Guggenheim: A Centennial Celebration', available online: http://pastexhibitions.guggenheim.org/peggy [accessed 1 November 2023].
40 Cynthia Moody, 'Ronald Clive Moody: A Summary of his Life, Work and Times', *op. cit.*
41 Jeffrey C. Stewart, *The New Negro: The Life of Alain Locke* (Oxford University Press, 2018), p. 775.
42 Kobena Mercer, 'Afro-Modernism's Musée Imaginaire', in *Alain Locke and the Visual Arts*, Richard D. Cohen Lectures on African and African American Art (Yale University Press in association with the Hutchins Center for African & African American research, Harvard University, 2022), p. 99.
43 *American Negro Exposition 1863 1940: Chicago Coliseum Official Program and Guide Book*, exh. cat. (Exposition Authority, 1940).
44 Cynthia Moody, 'Ronald Moody: The Complete Works', n.d. Record no. 15401, Stuart Hall Library, INIVA catalogue.
45 *Ibid.*

Chapter 4

1 Cynthia Moody, 'Ronald Moody: A Man True to His Vision', *op. cit.*, p. 10.
2 Address book, n.d. Papers of Ronald Moody, Tate Archive, TGA 956/6/3/1.
3 Cynthia Moody, 'Ronald Clive Moody: A Summary of his Life, Work and Times', *op. cit.*
4 Cynthia Moody, 'Ronald Moody: A Man True to His Vision', *op. cit.*, p. 10.
5 BBC transcript of *Calling the West Indies: Close-up*, 31 January 1943. Ronald Moody interviewed by Una Marson. Papers of Ronald Moody, Tate Archive, TGA 956/3/5/1.
6 Papers of Ronald Moody, Tate Archive, TGA 956/2/1/3.
7 Papers of Ronald Moody, Tate Archive, TGA 965/2/1/3.
8 Letter from Harold Moody to Helene Moody, 6 October 1941. Papers of Ronald Moody, Tate Archive, TGA 956/2/1/3/61.
9 Cynthia Moody, 'Ronald Clive Moody: A Summary of his Life, Work and Times', *op. cit.*
10 *Ibid.*
11 Cynthia Moody's unrealised catalogue raisonné, entry on *Marseille Figure*, ref. IN/69, unpaginated. Held with Cynthia Moody's papers by the Ronald Moody Trust.
12 Cynthia Moody, 'Ronald Moody: A Man True to His Vision', *op. cit.*, p. 11.
13 Typescripts of poems entitled 'Marseilles 1940, 23 Jul 1940–24 Jan 1942'. Papers of Ronald Moody, Tate Archive, TGA 956/3/3/3.
14 Cynthia Moody, 'Ronald Moody: The Complete Works', n.d. Record no. 15401, Stuart Hall Library, INIVA catalogue.
15 The essay 'A Way of Life' by Ronald Moody, published as 'Ronald Moody Talks Sculpting' in the *West Indian Gazette*, November 1961. Personal Papers of John La Rose, George Padmore Institute, LRA/01/0274/06.
16 Cynthia Moody, 'Ronald Moody: The Complete Works', n.d. Record no. 15401, Stuart Hall Library, INIVA catalogue.
17 Ronald Moody's notes on the symbolism of *Three Heads* (1946). Papers of Ronald Moody, Tate Archive, TGA 956/2/2/14/4.
18 Cynthia Moody, 'Ronald Clive Moody: A Summary of his Life, Work and Times', *op. cit.*
19 Cynthia Moody, 'Ronald Moody: The Complete Works', n.d. Record no. 15401, Stuart Hall Library, INIVA catalogue.
20 'Talks: BBC Transcripts, 4 July 1946–25 September 1953', Papers of Ronald Moody, Tate Archive, TGA 956/3/6.
21 BBC transcript of *Calling the West Indies: Close Up*, Ronald Moody interviewed by Una Marson, 31 January 1943, Papers of Ronald Moody, Tate Archive, TGA 956/3/5/1.
22 'Una Marson: Pioneer and Activist', 21 October 2021. British Newspaper Archive Blog, British Library, available online: https://blog.britishnewspaperarchive.co.uk/2021/10/20/una-marson-a-pioneer-and-activist [accessed 1 November 2023].

Chapter 5

1 Cynthia Moody, 'Ronald Moody: Portraits', 1996 / Black British Art, Ronald Moody Artist File, Stuart Hall Library, INIVA catalogue.
2 The Ronald Moody bust of Elsie Cohen is part of the permanent collection at the National Portrait Gallery, London.
3 The Academy Cinema, Oxford Street, London. Those closely associated with the cinema included Elsie Cohen, George Hoellering, Peter Strausfeld and Ivo Jarosy: https://academy-cinema.com [accessed 1 November 2023].
4 Cynthia Moody, 'Ronald Moody: The Complete Works', n.d. Record no. 15401, Stuart Hall Library, INIVA catalogue.
5 Cynthia Moody, 'Ronald Clive Moody: A Summary of his Life, Work and Times', *op. cit.*
6 Cynthia Moody, 'Ronald Moody: Portraits', 1996 / Black British Art, Ronald Moody Artist File, Stuart Hall Library, INIVA catalogue.
7 Cynthia Moody, 'Ronald Moody: The Complete Works', n.d. Record no. 15401, Stuart Hall Library, INIVA catalogue.
8 'Sculpture Returns', *Evening News*, 12 December 1949. Additional Papers of Ronald Moody and research material compiled by Cynthia Moody, TGA 201041, Tate Archive (uncatalogued).
9 Letter from Helene Moody to Ronald Moody, 23 June 1949. Papers of Ronald Moody, Tate Archive, TGA 956/1/1/13/116.
10 Letter from Helene Moody (*née* Coppel-Cowan) to Ronald Moody, 12 August 1949. Papers of Ronald Moody, Tate Archive, TGA 956/1/1/13/149.
11 Graham McCann, *Bounder! The Biography of Terry-Thomas* (Aurum, 2009), p. 42.
12 Christmas cards, November 1955–*c.* 18 December 1980. Papers of Ronald Moody, Tate Archive, TGA 956/1/2/71.

13 Cynthia Moody, 'Ronald Moody: The Artist's Collection', n.d. Record no. 15784, Stuart Hall Library, INIVA catalogue.
14 Amanda Bidnall, *West Indian Generation: Remaking British Culture in London, 1945–1965* (Liverpool University Press, 2021), p. 15.
15 Leila Zerai, 'Dr Harold Moody is right up there with Churchill and Queen Victoria', *London News Online*, April 2021, available online: https://londonnewsonline.co.uk/dr-harold-moody-is-right-up-there-with-churchill-and-queen-victoria [accessed 1 November 2023
16 The Society of Portrait Sculptors: www.portrait-sculpture.org [accessed 1 November 2023]
17 Exhibition Catalogues, 19 January 1935–1938. Papers of Ronald Moody, Tate Archive, TGA 956/8/1.
18 Letters from the Society of Portrait Sculptors, *c.* 10 November 1953–24 March 1972. Papers of Ronald Moody, Tate Archive, TGA 956/1/3/58.
19 Letter from Ronald Moody to Louis Wulff, 10 October 1959. Papers of Ronald Moody, Tate Archive, TGA 956/2/2/10/13.
20 Christopher Logue's website: www.christopherlogue.co.uk [accessed 1 November 2023].
21 Mark Espiner, 'Christopher Logue Obituary', 3 December 2011, available online: www.theguardian.com/books/2011/dec/03/christopher-logue [accessed 1 November 2023].
22 Cynthia Moody, 'Ronald Moody: The Complete Works', n.d. Record no. 15401, Stuart Hall Library, INIVA catalogue.
23 *Ibid.*
24 Cynthia Moody, 'Ronald Clive Moody: A Summary of his Life, Work and Times', *op. cit.*
25 Cynthia Moody, 'Ronald Moody: The Complete Works', n.d. Record no. 15401, Stuart Hall Library, INIVA catalogue.
26 Subject File relating to exhibitions L–Z. 31 January 1951 –14 December 1982. Papers of Ronald Moody, Tate Archive, TGA 956/2/2/4(50/97).
27 Cynthia Moody, 'Ronald Moody: Portraits', 1996 / Black British Art, Ronald Moody Artist File, Stuart Hall Library, INIVA catalogue.
28 *Ibid.*
29 Otis Alexander, 'W. Rudolph Dunbar 1907–1988', *Blackpast.org*, 31 March 2021: www.blackpast.org/global-african-history/people-global-african-history/w-rudolph-dunbar-1907-1988 [accessed 1 November 2023].
30 Antoine T. Clarke, 'Rudolph Dunbar: A Striking Example of His Musical Period', *Clarinet.org*, International Clarinet Association, 2 June 2021, available online: https://clarinet.org/rudolph-dunbar-a-striking-example-of-his-musical-period [accessed 1 November 2023].
31 *Ibid.*
32 *Ibid.*
33 *Ibid.*
34 Caroline Bressey, 'Black Modernism, Racism and the Making of Popular British Culture in the Interwar Years', *The Conversation*, 12 November 2014, available online: http://theconversation.com/black-modernism-racism-and-the-making-of-popular-british-culture-in-the-inter-war-years [accessed 1 November 2023].
35 Paul Robeson Archive, Akademie de Künste, available online: www.archivportal-d.de [accessed 1 June 2023].
36 Letter from Ronald Moody to Victor Grossman, 7 February 1968. Papers of Ronald Moody, Tate Archive, TGA 956/2/2/12/(91/123).
37 Letter from Victor Grossman to Ronald Moody, 22 February 1968. Papers of Ronald Moody, Tate Archive, TGA 956/2/2/12(92/123).
38 Letter from Ronald Moody to Victor Grossman, 27 February 1968, *op. cit.*
39 Letters from Friends of Paul Robeson and Salute to Paul Robeson, n.d. Papers of Ronald Moody, Tate Archive, TGA 956/1/3/49/3.
40 Lloyd L. Brown and Paul Robeson, *Here I Stand* (Beacon Press, 1958/1988).
41 'The History of Paul Robeson's House', available online: www.paulrobesonhouse.org/history-of-robeson-house [accessed 1 November 2023].
42 Letters from Friends of Paul Robeson and Salute to Paul Robeson, 8 June 1971. Papers of Ronald Moody, Tate Archive, TGA 956/1/3/49/2.
43 Letter from Ronald Moody to Victor Grossman, 10 July 1968, *op. cit.*
44 Exhibition catalogue for the Society of Portrait Sculptors 'Human Rights Exhibition' at St Paul's Cathedral, London, December 1968. Papers of Ronald Moody, Tate Archive, TGA 956/8/1/26.
45 Stanley Gelbier and Helen Nield, 'Ronald Clive Moody (1900–1984), dentist and leading black sculptor, and his brothers', *Dental Historian*, vol. 66, no. 1 (2021), pp. 67–74, available online: https://bda.org/library/history/Documents/Dental-Historian-2021-67-74-ronald-moody.pdf [accessed 1 November 2023].
46 Transcript of BECTU History Project Interview with Cynthia Moody, 25 June 1990, available online: https://historyproject.org.uk/interview/cynthia-moody [accessed 1 November 2023].
47 De Lane Lea production company: www.wbsl.com/de-lane-lea [accessed 1 November 2023].
48 'Nellie Dean of Soho', *Hidden London*, available online: https://hidden-london.com/nuggets/nellie-dean [accessed 1 November 2023].
49 Anne Walmsley, 'Cynthia Moody Obituary', *The Guardian*, 15 July 2013, available online: www.theguardian.com/theguardian/2013/jul/15/cynthia-moody-obituary [accessed 1 November 2023].
50 'Cynthia Moody (1924–2013)', *IMDb*, available online: www.imdb.com/name/nm0600462 [accessed 1 November 2023].
51 Cynthia Moody, 'Ronald Moody: The Complete Works', n.d. Record no. 15401, Stuart Hall Library, INIVA catalogue.

52 *The Birth of Venus* (1954) by William Roberts, see: www.englishcubist.co.uk/venus.html [accessed 1 November 2023].
53 *Caribbean Artists in England*, exh. cat. (Commonwealth Institute of Great Britain, 1971).
54 *Portrait of Daphne* (1942–43) by William Roberts, see: www.englishcubist.co.uk/daphne.html [accessed 1 November 2023].
55 Cynthia Moody, 'Ronald Moody: The Complete Works', n.d. Record no. 15401, Stuart Hall Library, INIVA catalogue.
56 Cynthia Moody, 'Ronald Moody: A Way of Life', *op. cit.*

Chapter 6

1 Ronald Moody, notes for the BBC programme *Full House*, January 1973. TGA 956/2/2/11/4.
2 Quote from *Modern French Sculpture* (Oldbourne Press, 1964).
3 Ronald Moody, 'A Way of Life', published as 'Ronald Moody talks sculpting', *op. cit.*

Chapter 7

1 Since 1992, the University of Westminster, London.
2 Naomi Oppenheim, 'Popular History in the Black British Press: Edward Scobie's *Tropic* and *Flamingo*, 1960–64', *Immigrants and Minorities*, vol. 37, no. 3 (2019), pp. 136–62.
3 *Flamingo Magazine*, September 1961–December 1965. British Library Collection, available online: www.bl.uk/collection-items/flamingo-magazine-september-1961 [accessed 24 June 2023].
4 Uzo Egonu (1931–1996), Andrew Salkey (1928–1995), George Lamming (1927–2022), Toussaint L'Ouverture (1743–1803) and Edward Wilmot Blyden (1932–1912).
5 J. Doward, 'Sex, ska and Malcolm X: MI6's covert 1960s mission to woo West Indians', *The Guardian*, 26 January 2019, available online: www.theguardian.com/world/2019/jan/26/west-indians-flamingo-magazine-m6-anti-communist-mission [accessed 1 November 2023].
6 Val Wilmer, *Mama Said There'd Be Days Like This: My Life in the Jazz World* (Women's Press, 1989).
7 Val Wilmer, 'Inspiration's Humble Instrument: Memories of Ed Scobie, *Race and Class*, vol. 46, no. 2 (2004), pp. 49–53.
8 The Skylon was the 'vertical feature' that was an abiding symbol of the Festival of Britain. It was designed by architects Hidalgo Moya, Philip Powell and Felix Samuely.
9 'Sculpture in the Open Air', triennial exhibitions in Battersea Park, held from 1948 to 1966 between May and September in the Sub Tropical Garden, including sculptures by artists such as Jacob Epstein, Alberto Giacometti, Barbara Hepworth, Henry Moore, Auguste Rodin and Karel Vogel.
10 Clive Wilmer (b. 1945), a British poet, critic, literary journalist, broadcaster and lecturer.
11 Ian Walters (1930–2006), English sculptor.
12 Siegfried Charoux (1896–1967), figurative sculptor.
13 *Civilisation: The Judge* (1962) is in the Tate collection: www.tate.org.uk/art/artworks/charoux-civilization-the-judge-t00597 [accessed 1 November 2023].
14 Anthony Caro (1924–2013).
15 Richard Bentley Claughton (1917–1997), English sculptor.
16 Lynn Chadwick (1914–2003), English sculptor.
17 Alec McCowen (1925–2017) and Tom Courtenay (b. 1937), English actors.
18 Ida Kar (1908–1974), Russian photographer.
19 W. Eugene Smith (1918–1978), American photojournalist.
20 Cynthia Moody, 'Midonz', *Transition*, no. 77 (1998), pp. 10–18.
21 Letter from Val Wilmer to Ronald Moody, 21 April 1964. Papers of Ronald Moody, Tate Archive, TGA 956/2/2/10/(36/36).
22 Luke Roberts, 'Ronald Moody: Between Concrete and Wood', *Kings English*, 4 December 2019, available online: https://blogs.kcl.ac.uk/english/2019/12/04/ronald-moody-between-concrete-and-wood [accessed 1 November 2023].

Chapter 8

1 'Dr W. E. Miall', *The Independent*, 2 August 2004, available online: www.independent.co.uk/news/obituaries/dr-w-e-miall-550208.html [accessed 1 November 2023].
2 Letter from Ronald Moody to Dr Miall of the Epidemiological Research Unit (Jamaica), 14 June 1963. Papers of Ronald Moody, Tate Archive, TGA 956/2/2/13/16.
3 Petrine Archer-Straw and Kim Robinson, *Jamaican Art: Then and Now* (LMH Publishing Ltd, new ed., 2011), p. 57.
4 Letter from Ronald Moody to Professor A. L. Cochrane of the Epidemiological Research Unit (South Wales), 5 November 1963. Papers of Ronald Moody, Tate Archive, TGA 956/2/2/13/26.
5 Brief article titled '*Savacou* 1963–1965'. Papers of Ronald Moody, Tate Archive, TGA 956/2/2/13/135.
6 Letter from Ronald Moody to Professor A. L. Cochrane of the Epidemiological Research Unit (South Wales), 3 January 1964. Papers of Ronald Moody, Tate Archive, TGA 956/2/2/13/36.
7 Rasheed Araeen, *The Other Story: Afro-Asian Artists in Post-War Britain*, exh. cat. (South Bank Centre, 1989).
8 Brief article on Carib beliefs by Ronald Moody, n.d. Papers of Ronald Moody, Tate Archive, TGA 956/2/2/13/136.
9 Letter from Ronald Moody to Professor A. L. Cochrane of the Epidemiological Research Unit (South Wales), 6 September 1964. Papers of Ronald Moody, Tate Archive, TGA 956/2/2/13/78.
10 Cynthia Moody, 'Ronald Moody: A Way of Life', *op. cit.*
11 Louis James, 'The Caribbean Artists Movement', in *West Indian Intellectuals in Britain* (Manchester University Press, 2018).
12 For a complete history of the Caribbean Artists

Movement's activities see Anne Walmsley, *The Caribbean Artists Movement 1966–1972: A Literary and Cultural History* (New Beacon Books, 1992).
13 *Ibid.*, p. 202.
14 Kobena Mercer, 'Aubrey Williams: Abstraction in Diaspora', *British Art Studies*, no. 8 (2018), available online: https://doi.org/10.17658/issn.2058-5462/issue-08/kmercer [accessed 1 November 2023].
15 Eddie Chambers, *Black Artists in British Art: A History since the 1950s*, (I. B. Tauris & Co., 2014), p. 57.
16 'Paintings by the Acclaimed Jamaican artist Errol Lloyd', 3 February 2021, George Padmore Institute, available online: www.georgepadmoreinstitute.org/news-and-events/paintings-by-the-acclaimed-jamaican-artist-errol-lloyd-feature-on-the-george-padmore-institute-website [accessed 1 November 2023].
17 Cynthia Moody, 'Ronald Moody: A Way of Life', *op. cit.*
18 Debbie Challis and Gemma Romain, 'A Fusion of Worlds: Ancient Egypt, African Art and Identity in Modernist Britain', *Equiano Centre*, University College London (UCL), available online: www.ucl.ac.uk/equiano-centre/educational-resources/fusion-worlds [accessed 1 November 2023].
19 Photocopy of a letter from Ronald Moody to Edna Manley, 17 May 1957. Papers of Ronald Moody, Tate Archive, TGA 956/1/2/44/1.
20 Dawn Ritch, 'An Evening with Ronald Moody, September 1972', *Jamaica Journal*, vol. 6, no. 3, pp. 65–66.
21 Cynthia Moody, 'Ronald Moody: A Way of Life', *op. cit.*
22 *Kingston Gleaner*, 30 July 1990, p. 25.

Chapter 9

1 Arthur Munroe, 'FESTAC '77, The Second World Black and African Festival of Arts and Culture: Lagos, Nigeria', *The Black Scholar*, vol. 9, no. 1 (1977), pp. 34–37.
2 Summary of aims and purposes of the United Kingdom African Festival Committee, January 1974. Papers of Ronald Moody, Tate Archive, TGA 956/2/2/8/1.
3 Bradley Lloyd, 'Stevie Wonder, FESTAC 77, a Unifying Moment of Transatlantic Black Pride', *The Guardian*, 19 August 2020, available online: www.theguardian.com/music/2020/aug/19/stevie-wonder-festac-1977-a-unifying-moment-of-transatlantic-black-pride [accessed 1 November 2023].
4 Invitation to Ronald Moody to serve on the sub-committee on visual art for the United Kingdom African Festival Committee, January 1974. Papers of Ronald Moody, Tate Archive, TGA 956 2/2/8/2.
5 Minutes of a meeting of the exhibition sub-committee, 15 April 1976. Papers of Ronald Moody, Tate Archive, TGA 956/2/2/8/60.
6 List of UK entries for the Second World Black and African Festival of Arts and Culture, n.d. Papers of Ronald Moody, Tate Archive, TGA 956/2/2/8/68.
7 Cynthia Moody, 'Ronald Clive Moody: A Summary of his Life, Work and Times', n.d. *op. cit.*
8 Galley proofs for T*he Background of African Art* (*c.* 1956–58). Papers of Ronald Moody, Tate Archive, TGA 956/3/2/6.
9 Oguibe Olu, *Uzo Egonu: An African Artist in the West* (Kala Press, 1995), p. 30.
10 'Uzo Egonu, 1931–1996', *Bonhams*, 20 May 2015, available online: www.bonhams.com/auction/22350/lot/38/uzo-egonu-nigerian-1931-1996-second-poetess-or-a-poetess-stateless-people-series [accessed 1 November 2023].
11 Article on Uzo Egonu published in *Magnet News*, 23 April 1965. Papers of Ronald Moody, Tate Archive, TGA 956/3/2/16.
12 File of material relating to *Amadu's Bundle*, *c.* 1972. Papers of Ronald Moody, Tate Archive, TGA 956/3/1.
13 Cynthia Moody, 'Ronald Clive Moody: A Summary of his Life, Work and Times', n.d., *op. cit.*
14 Cynthia Moody, 'Ronald Moody: The Complete Works', n.d. Record no. 15401, Stuart Hall Library, INIVA catalogue.
15 Poster for the exhibition 'Contemporary Art of Africa, Caribbean and Liverpool' at the Bluecoat Gallery, Liverpool, in 1973.
16 Adam Lusher, 'British Museums may loan Nigeria bronzes that were stolen from Nigeria by British Imperialists', *The Independent*, 24 June 2018, available online: www.independent.co.uk/news/uk/home-news/benin-bronzes-british-museum-nigeria-stolen-imperialist-treasures-return-loan-elgin-marbles-looted-a8414661.html [accessed 1 November 2023].
17 Andrew H. Apter, *The Pan-African Nation: Oil and the Spectacle of Culture in Nigeria* (University of Chicago Press, 2005), pp. 62–63.
18 Centre for Black & African Art and Civilisation (CBAAC), Union of International Association.
19 Cynthia Moody, 'Ronald Moody: A Way of Life', *op. cit.*
20 Cynthia Moody, 'Ronald Clive Moody: A Summary of his Life, Work and Times', *op. cit.*
21 Cynthia Moody, 'Ronald Moody: The Complete Works', n.d. Record no. 15401, Stuart Hall Library, INIVA catalogue.
22 'Councillor Aids Aotearoa Connection to British Civil Rights Movement', *Our Auckland*, 21 March 2019, available online: https://ourauckland.aucklandcouncil.govt.nz/news/2019/03/councillor-aids-aotearoa-connection-to-british-civil-rights-movement [accessed 1 November 2023].
23 Letter from Harold Moody to Ronald Moody, 18 March 1966. Papers of Ronald Moody, Tate Archive, TGA 956/1/1/9.
24 Kate Evans, 'What a 1,600-year-old New Zealand Tree can tell us about climate change', *Ancient Kauri Trees New Zealand*

Climate Change, 13 April 2021, available online: www.vox.com/22372029/ancient-kauri-trees-new-zealand-climate-change [accessed 1 November 2023].

25 Cynthia Moody, 'Ronald Clive Moody: A Summary of his Life, Work and Times', n.d., *op. cit.*

26 Norman Rae, *A Tribute To Ronald Moody*, exh. cat. (National Gallery of Jamaica, 2000).

27 Petrine Archer, 'Namba Roy', *pertrinearcher.com*: https://petrinearcher.com/artist-bio/namba-roy

28 Norman Rae, *op. cit.*

29 'Jamaican sculptor dies, buried in London', *Jamaica Weekly Gleaner*, 22 February 1984. Additional Papers of Ronald Moody and research material compiled by Cynthia Moody, TGA 201041, Tate Archive (uncatalogued).

30 Errol Lloyd, 'Ronald Moody Obituary, 1901–1984', *Artrage* (1984), p. 8.

31 Cynthia Moody, 'Ronald Moody: A Man True to His Vision', *op. cit.*, p. 24.

Chapter 10

1 The 'Remembrance' exhibition took place at the Commonwealth Institute, London, on 31 August 1983 and marked the twenty-first anniversary of Jamaican Independence. Cynthia Moody, 'Ronald Moody: A Way of Life', *op. cit.*

2 Sonia Boyce (b. 1962) is an artist and educator. She is a Professor of Black Art and Design at the University of the Arts London. In 2020, Boyce represented Britain at the Venice Biennale, the first black woman to do so. In April 2022, she won the Venice Biennale's Golden Lion prize.

3 The African and Asian Visual Arts Archive (AAVAA) was founded in Bristol in 1989 by Eddie Chambers. Digital Preservation Europe: https://vads.ac.uk/digital/collection/AAVAA [accessed 13 November 2023].

4 Beryl Gilroy was a Guyanese educator, novelist, ethno-psychotherapist and poet. She emigrated to London in 1951 as part of the Windrush generation. Wikipedia entry available online: https://en.wikipedia.org/wiki/Beryl_Gilroy [accessed 14 November 2023].

5 See 'Horace Ové, RIP', *British Film Institute*, 18 September 2023, available online: www.bfi.org.uk/news/horace-ove-rip [accessed 13 November 2023].

6 Tate Gallery Archive: Accessions 1995. Accessions to Repository. The National Archives, available online: www.nationalarchives.gov.uk/accessions/1995/95returns/95ac70.htm [accessed 13 November 2023].

7 Letter from Marlene Smith to Ronald Moody, *c.* 12 January 1982. Papers of Ronald Moody, Tate Archive, TGA 956/1/3/57.

8 Stuart Hall (1932–2014) was a sociologist and cultural theorist. Stuart Hall, 'Constituting an Archive', *Third Text*, Spring 2001, pp. 89–92.

9 James Lamont, 'Robert Loder, art critic, 1937–2017', *Financial Times*, 18 August 2017, available online: www.ft.com/content/9a24ab5c-81e2-11e7-a4ce-15b2513cb3ff [accessed 13 November 2023].

10 'Africa '95' was a Britain-wide celebration of African music, art, dance and poetry that was held over several months in autumn 1995, with more than sixty arts institutions throughout the UK participating in related events.

11 Richard J. Powell, website available online: https://richardjpowell.com [accessed 13 November 2023].

12 Gilane Tawadros is a writer and curator. She was the founding director of the Institute of International Visual Arts (InIVA, founded 1994) and is now director of the Whitechapel Gallery (since 2022).

13 Hettie Judah, 'Roger Malbert: The Curator as "Humble Midwife"', *Frieze*, 13 September 2018, available online: www.frieze.com/article/roger-malbert-curator-humble-midwife [accessed 13 November 2023].

14 John La Rose (1927–2006) was an activist and a poet, and publisher and founder of New Beacon Books.

15 Aubrey Williams (1926–1990) was a Guyanese artist. He moved to Britain in 1952 and in 1966, came together with a group of London-based Caribbean artists and intellectuals to found the Caribbean Artists Movement. From 1970 onwards he worked in studios in Jamaica and Florida as well as in the UK.

16 Richard J. Powell et al. (eds), *Rhapsodies in Black: Art of the Harlem Renaissance* (Hayward Gallery, Institute of International Visual Arts and University of California Press, 1997). The exhibition was organised by the Hayward Gallery, London, in collaboration with the Corcoran Gallery of Art, Washington D.C, and the Institute of International Visual Arts, London. Touring: Hayward Gallery, London; Arnolfini, Bristol; Mead Gallery, University of Warwick in 1997; and the M. H. de Young Memorial Museum, San Francisco, and the Corcoran Gallery of Art, Washington D.C. in 1998.

17 'Tate Appoints Director of Tate Gallery British Art and Director of Collection', Tate Press Release, 31 October 1997, available online: www.tate.org.uk/press/press-releases/tate-appoints-director-tate-gallery-british-art-and-director-collections [accessed 13 November 2023].

18 *Transition* magazine was established in 1961 by Rajat Neogy and was published from 1961 to 1976 in various countries on the African continent, and since 1991, in the United States by Indiana University Press (since 2013 on behalf of the Hutchins Center for African and African American Research at Harvard University).

19 Rasheed Araeen began writing in 1975, before

publishing his own art journals: *Black Phoenix* (1978–79), *Third Text* (1987–) and *Third Text Asia* (2008–10).

20 Anne Walmsley (b. 1931) is an editor and scholar specializing in Caribbean art and literature, and author of *The Caribbean Artists Movement: A Literary and Cultural History, 1966–1971* (1992) and *Art in the Caribbean* (2010), both published by New Beacon Books.

21 'Life Between Islands: Caribbean-British Art 1950s – Now', Tate Britain, December 2021–April 2022, curated by David A. Bailey and the director of Tate Britain, Alex Farquharson.

Chapter 11

1 Christian Hogsbjerg and Project Muse, *C. L. R. James in Imperial Britain* (Duke University Press, 2014).

2 Hugh Lawson Shearer, *Alexander Bustamente: Portrait of a Hero* (Kingston Publications, 1978).

3 Garfield Sobers and Ivo Tennant, *Sobers: The Changing Face of Cricket* (Ebury Press, 1996).

4 Errol Lloyd, 'The Caribbean Artists Movement 1966–1972', *British Library* (2018), available online: www.bl.uk/windrush/articles/caribbean-artists-movement-1966-1972 [accessed 24 June 2023].

5 Aubrey Williams and Anne Walmsley, *Guyana Dreaming: The Art of Aubrey Williams* (Dangaroo Press, 1990).

6 Basil Reid, 'Arawak Archaeology in Jamaica: New Approaches, New Perspectives', *Caribbean Quarterly*, vol. 38, no. 2/3 (1992), pp. 15–20.

7 Records relating to exhibitions, including correspondence published, material and ephemera, *c.* 1960–97. Commonwealth Institute Art Gallery, TGA 20045, Tate Archive.

8 Sonia Boyce (b. 1962), Keith Piper (b. 1960), Veronica Ryan (b. 1956), Eddie Chambers (b. 1960) and Lubaina Himid (b. 1954).

9 Founded in 1971, the Keskidee Centre was Britain's first arts centre for the Black community, located in Islington, London.

10 The West Indian Students' Centre (WISC) officially opened in 1955 in Earl's Court, London, in a building bought with the support of West Indian governments.

11 Ronald Moody's notes on the symbolism of *Three Heads* (1946) was the only modern piece in Jawaharal Nehru's collection of classical Buddhist figures. Papers of Ronald Moody, Tate Archive, TGA 956/2/2/14/4.

12 George Lamming (1927–2022) was a Barbadian novelist, essayist and poet. Errol Lloyd, 'Portraits and Busts', available online: www.errollloyd.com/portraits-busts [accessed 1 November 2023].

13 Records of the Minority Arts Advisory Service (MAAS), 1977–94. The Black Cultural Archives, London.

14 Naseem Khan, *The Arts Britain Ignores: The Arts of Ethnic Minorities in Britain*, (Community Relations Commission, 1978). Naseem Khan (1939–2017) was a British journalist, cultural historian, educator and activist.

15 *Artrage* (February 1983–February 1996). MAAS official papers and magazines. Minority Art Archives CRER/MAA/MAAS/4/2, the University of Warwick.

16 Anne Walmsley, 'Cynthia Moody Obituary', *The Guardian*, 15 July 2013, available online: www.theguardian.com/theguardian/2013/jul/15/cynthia-moody-obituary [accessed 1 November 2023].

17 The Theosophical Society is a worldwide community whose primary object is the Universal Brotherhood of Humanity without distinction, based on the realisation that life and all its diverse forms, human and non-human, are indivisibly one. See: https://theosophicalsociety.org.uk/ [accessed 1 November 2023].

18 'UWI Mona to serve as Caribbean Branch of the US Cochrane Center', University of the West Indies, Mona Campus, 2013, available online: www.mona.uwi.edu/marcom/newsroom/entry/5177 [accessed 1 November 2023].

19 'Edna Manley: Jamaica and London', *Equiano Centre*, University College London (UCL), 2014, available online: www.ucl.ac.uk/equiano-centre/educational-resources/fusion-worlds/artists/edna-manley-jamaica-and-london [accessed 1 November 2023].

20 Barthé Papers 1901–1989. Amistad Research Center, Tulane University, available online: https://amistad-finding-aids.tulane.edu/repositories/2/resources/75 [accessed 1 November 2023].

21 'Errol Lloyd: My Life in Colour' 198, Contemporary Arts and Learning, London, 2022, available online: www.198.org.uk/portfolio/errol-lloyd [accessed 1 November 2023].

22 'Paint Like the Swallow Sings Calypso', exhibition at Kettle's Yard, Cambridge, in 2022, with Paul Dash, Errol Lloyd and John Lyons. A selection of their own works alongside works from the collections of Kettle's Yard and the Fitzwilliam Museum, on the history and themes of Carnival, available online: www.kettlesyard.co.uk/events/paint-like-the-swallow-sings-calypso [accessed 1 November 2023].

Exhibitions & Awards

Ronald Clive Moody
Born 1900 in Kingston, Jamaica
Died 1984 in London

Selected Solo Exhibitions

1937 *Sculptures de Ronald C. Moody*, Galerie Billiet-Vorms, Paris
1938 *Beeldhouwwerken door Ronald Moody*, Kunstzaal van Lier, Amsterdam
1946 *Sculpture by Ronald Moody*, Arcade Gallery, London
1950 *The Works of Ronald Moody*, Galerie Apollinaire, London
1960 *Ronald Moody Sculpture*, Woodstock Gallery, London
1961 *Ronald Moody*, Woodstock Gallery, London
2003 *Ronald Moody* (display), Gallery 20, Tate Britain, London
– *International Modern Art: Spotlight on Ronald Moody*, Tate Liverpool
2024 *Ronald Moody: Sculpting Life*, The Hepworth Wakefield

Selected Group Exhibitions

1935 *London Group Show*, New Burlington Galleries, London
1936 *62nd Autumn Art Exhibition*, Walker Art Gallery, Liverpool
1938 *Tropiques*, Galerie Billiet-Vorms, Paris
– Guggenheim Jeune Gallery, London
– XVème Salon des Tuileries, Paris
– Galerie L'Équipe, Paris
1939 XVIème Salon des Tuileries, Paris
– *Contemporary Negro Art*, Baltimore Museum of Art, Dallas Museum of Fine Art
1940 *Matières et Formes*, Galerie René Breteau, Paris
– Howard University Art Gallery, Washington, DC
1941 American-British Art Gallery, New York
– Boyer Gallery, London
1945 Beauchamp Galleries, London
1949 Artists International Association Gallery, London
1950 *Artists of Chelsea 2nd Annual Exhibition*, Chenil Gallery, London
1951 *Seven Dials Group*, Galerie Apollinaire, London
1953 *The Famous in Sculpture*, Society of Portrait Sculptors, London
– *Artists of Fame and Promise*, Leicester Galleries, London
1953–59 Kensington Artists 2nd–8th Annual Exhibitions, London
1954 *Personalities in Sculpture*, Society of Portrait Sculptors, Edinburgh, and Imperial Institute Art Gallery, London
1954 *Royal Institute of Oil Painters 67th Annual Exhibition*, Mall Galleries, London
1954–71 Society of Portrait Sculptors 2nd–18th Annual Exhibitions, London
1955 *New English Art Club*, Royal Society of British Artists Galleries, London
1956 *The Royal Academy of Arts 188th Summer Exhibition*, Royal Academy, London
1959 *The Second Congress of Black Writers and Artists*, Société Africaine de Culture (SAC) Conference, Rome
1962 *The National Society*, Royal Institute Galleries, London
1963 *The Royal Academy of Arts Exhibition*, Royal Academy, London
1964 *The Portrait in the Round*, Society of Portrait Sculptors, RWS Galleries, London
1965 *Thirteenth Annual Exhibition*, Society of Portrait Sculptors, RWS Galleries, London
1966 *First World Festival of Negro Arts*, Société Africaine de Culture (SAC), Dakar
1967 *Caribbean Artists Movement Exhibition*, Theatre Royal, Stratford, London
– *First Caribbean Artists Movement Conference: Art Exhibition*, University of Kent, Canterbury
– *The First Gemini Trust Exhibition*, Woodstock Gallery, London
1968 *Portrait Tributes: Society of Portrait Sculptors Human Rights Exhibition*, St Paul's Cathedral Crypt, London
– *Exhibition of West Indian Art*, West Indian Students' Centre, London
– *Second Caribbean Artists Movement Conference: Art Exhibition*, University of Kent, Canterbury
– *Caribbean Artists Movement Exhibition, in Association with the British Caribbean Association*, House of Commons, Westminster, London
1971 *Caribbean Artists in England*, Commonwealth Institute, London
– *Sculpture Out of Doors*, Commonwealth Institute, London
1973 *Contemporary Artists in England*, Commonwealth Institute, London
1977 *Commonwealth Artists of Fame 1952–1977*, Commonwealth Institute, London
– *The Second Festival of Arts and Culture*, FESTAC '77, Lagos
1983 *Remembrance*, Commonwealth Institute, London
1986–87 *Caribbean Expressions in Britain*, New Walk Art Gallery, Leicester; Central Museum and Art Gallery, Northampton; and Cartwright Hall, Bradford
1989 *The Other Story: Afro-Asian Artists in Post-War Britain*, Hayward Gallery, London; Wolverhampton Art Gallery; Manchester City Art Gallery; and Cornerhouse, Manchester
1992 *Visualising Masculinities*, Tate Gallery, London
1995–98 *Caribbean Visions: Contemporary Painting and Sculpture*, Centre for Fine Arts, Miami; Smithsonian Institution, Washington, DC; New Orleans Museum of Art; and other US venues
1997–99 *Rhapsodies in Black: Art of the Harlem Renaissance*, Fine Arts Museum San Francisco; Los Angeles County Museum of Art; Corcoran Gallery of Art, Washington, DC; Museum of Fine Arts, Houston; and Tate Gallery, London
– *Transforming the Crown: African, Asian, and Caribbean Artists in Britain, 1966–1996*, Studio Museum, Harlem; The Caribbean Cultural Center and The Bronx Museum of the Arts, New York
– *Three Moments in Jamaican Art*, Inter-American Development

Bank (IDB) Cultural Center, Washington, DC

1998 *Recent Acquisitions*, National Portrait Gallery, London

2000 *A Tribute to Ronald Moody 1900–1984*, National Gallery of Jamaica, Kingston

– *Representing Britain 1500–2000*, Tate Britain, London

2001 *Let Paul Robeson Sing*, National Museum of Wales and Theatre Museum, Cardiff

2012 *Migrations: Journeys into British Art*, Tate Britain, London

2014 *Spaces of Black Modernism: London 1919–39*, Tate Britain, London

– *Fusion of Worlds: Ancient Egypt, African Art and Identity in Modernist Britain*, Petrie Museum, London

2015 *No Colour Bar: Black British Art in Action 1960–1990*, Guildhall Art Gallery, London

2019 *Get Up, Stand Up Now: A Generations of Black Creative Pioneers*, Somerset House, London

2020 *Modern Conversations, Modern Bodies*, Tate St Ives, Cornwall

2022 *Life Between Islands*, Tate Britain, London

2024 *The Harlem Renaissance and Transatlantic Modernism*, Metropolitan Museum of Art, New York

Broadcasts: BBC Overseas Service

1943 *Calling the West Indies*, 'Close Up', interview by Una Marson

1946 *Discovering Art*, 'A Sculptor'

– *Discovering Art*, 'The Artist's Environment'

– *Discovering Art*, 'The Artist's Education'

1949 *What is Called Primitive Art*

1950 *Egyptian Art*; *Greek Art*; *Indian Art*; *Chinese Art*; *Gothic Art*; *Renaissance Art*; *Modern Art*

– 'Anything to Declare?', interview by Macdonald Hastings

1951 'The Artist in the Community No 1.', discussion with John Figueroa

– 'The Artist in the Community No 4.', discussion with John Figueroa

1952 *A Visit to Epstein's Exhibition*

1953 *The Mexican Exhibition*; *The Toy Museum*; *An Exile Looks Back*

1954 'West Indian Diary', interview by Billy Pilgrim

1959 *The Friday Programme*, 'Calling West Africa', discussion with Dennis Duerden and Aminu Abdullahi

1962 'The Role of the Artist in a New Society', discussion with Edward Scobie

Colloquia

1944 'Art at the Crossroads', paper delivered at the International Arts Centre, London

1958 'The Responsibility of the Artist', paper delivered at the Société Africaine de Culture (SAC) Conference, Rome

1962 'The Visual Arts in the West Indies', paper delivered at the Royal Commonwealth Society Summer School, Worcester College, Oxford

1968 'West Indian Artists', *The Caribbean Artists Movement Symposium: The Artist in the Caribbean*, University of Kent, Canterbury

1978 'Caribbean Study Course', The Commonwealth Institute, London

Awards and Recognition

1977 Musgrave Gold Medal: For his eminence as an international sculptor and for the production of a body of work of excellence and distinctiveness, which has earned him in Jamaica and internationally the status of a Jamaican master.

1980 Jamaica Institute Centenary Medal: For his long-standing contribution to art

1981 Minority Arts Advisory Service (MAAS) Award, London: for his outstanding contribution to sculpture in Britain

1986 The Ronald Moody Sculpture Award was established in Moody's memory to fund a postgraduate year for an outstanding student from Jamaica or the Caribbean Commonwealth who has completed the Diploma course of study at the Edna Manley College of Visual Arts.

2008 Moody Impact Crater: Ronald Moody became one of fifteen notable figures – artists, musicians and authors who have made significant cultural contributions to mankind – to be named after impact craters on Mercury by the MESSENGER Science Team and approved International Astronomical Union (IAU). Other accomplished figures honoured at that time include Salvador Dalí, Ben Enwonwu and Edvard Munch.

Memberships

1955 Member of the Society of Portrait Sculptors (elected to the Council in 1959)

– Member of the Artists' League of Great Britain

Collections

Centre for Black and African Arts and Civilization, Lagos
Government Art Collection, London
Graves Gallery, Sheffield
The Hepworth Wakefield
Leeds Museums and Galleries
Leicester Museum and Art Gallery
Museums Sheffield
National Gallery of Jamaica, Kingston
National Portrait Gallery, London
Amgueddfa Cymru (Museum Wales), National Museum of Cardiff
Nehru Memorial Museum, Delhi
Pallant House Gallery, Chichester
Tate, London
Guildhall Art Gallery, London
University of the West Indies, Kingston
Victoria and Albert Museum, London
And other private collections in the UK and overseas

Reading & Resources

John A. Aarons et al., *Archiving Caribbean Identity: Records, Community and Memory* (Routledge, 2022)

Malum Amadu, *Amadu's Bundle* (Heinemann Educational Books, 1972)

Rasheed Araeen et al., *The Other Story: Afro-Asian Artists in Post-War Britain*, exh. cat. (South Bank Centre, 1989)

Petrine Archer, 'Ronald Moody'. Available online: https://petrinearcher.com/artist-bio/ronald-moody

David A. Bailey and Allison Thompson, *Liberation Begins in the Imagination: Writings on Caribbean-British Art* (Tate Publishing, 2021)

David A. Bailey and Alex Farquharson, *Life Between Islands: Caribbean-British Art 1950s–Now*, exh. cat. (Tate Publishing, 2021)

Mora J. Beauchamp-Byrd et al., *Transforming the Crown: African Asian and Caribbean Artists in Britain, 1966–1996* (Franklin H. Williams Caribbean Cultural Center/African Diaspora Institute, 1997)

Amanda Bidnall, *The West Indian Generation: Remaking British Culture in London, 1945–1965* (Liverpool University Press, 2017)

Guy Brett, 'A Reputation Restored: The Rediscovery of Sculptor Ronald Moody' (Tate Research Publication, 2003). Available online: www.tate.org.uk/art/artists/ronald-moody-2298/reputation-restored

Eddie Chambers, *Black Artists in British Art: A History since the 1950s* (I. B. Tauris & Co., 2014)

Bridget R. Cooks, *Exhibiting Blackness: African Americans and the American Art Museum* (University of Massachusetts Press, 2011)

Ntone Edjabe and Akin Adesokan (eds), *Festac '77: 2nd World Black and African Festival of Arts and Culture* (Afterall Books, 2019)

Mary Lou Emery, *Modernism, the Visual, and Caribbean Literature* (Cambridge University Press, 2007)

Jean Fisher, *The Other Story and the Past Imperfect* (Tate Papers, no. 12, Autumn 2009). Available online: www.tate.org.uk/research/tate-papers/12/the-other-story-and-the-past-imperfect

Government Art Collection, *Artspark: Ronald Moody*, Government Art Collection Learning, n.d. Available online: https://artcollection.culture.gov.uk/learning

IDB Cultural Center, *Three Moments in Jamaican Art = Tres momentos en las artes de Jamaica*, exh. cat. (Inter-American Development Bank, 1998)

Sandy Jones, 'A Sculpture Merging Jamaican Culture with Utility', blog, Victoria and Albert Museum, 2023. Available online: www.vam.ac.uk/blog/museum-life/a-sculpture-merging-jamaican-culture-with-utility

Samella S. Lewis et al., *Caribbean Visions: Contemporary Painting and Sculpture* (Art Services International, 1995)

Errol Lloyd, 'Ronald Moody Obituary', *Artrage* (Spring 1984)

Kobena Mercer et al., *Alain Locke and the Visual Arts* (Yale University Press in association with the Hutchins Center for African & African American Research, Harvard University, 2022)

Cynthia Moody, 'Midonz', *Transition*, no. 77 (1998), pp. 10–18

Cynthia Moody, 'Ronald Moody: A Man True to His Vision', *Third Text: Third World Perspectives on Art and Culture*, nos 8–9, Autumn/Winter 1989, pp. 5–24

Martin Myrone et al., *Representing Britain, 1500–2000: 100 Works from the Tate Collections* (Tate Publishing, 2000)

Rianna Jade Parker, *A Brief History of Black British Art* (Tate Publishing, 2021)

Veerle Poupeye, *Caribbean Art* (Thames & Hudson, 1998, revised edition 2022)

Richard J. Powell et al., *Rhapsodies in Black: Art of the Harlem Renaissance* (Hayward Gallery, InIVA and University of California Press, 1997)

Richard J. Powell, *Black Art and Culture in the Twentieth Century* (Thames & Hudson, 1997, revised edition, 2022)

Thomas Riggs et al., *St. James Guide to Black Artists* (St James Press, 1997)

Luke Roberts, 'Ronald Moody: Between Concrete and Wood', Kings College London, 2019. Available online: https://blogs.kcl.ac.uk/english/2019/12/04/ronald-moody-between-concrete-and-wood

Gemma Romain, 'Ronald Moody: Archival Explorations of a Black Jamaican Artist in Interwar London', *Media Diversified* (April 2015)

Jeffrey C. Stewart, *The New Negro: The Life of Alain Locke* (Oxford University Press, 2018)

Anne Walmsley, *The Caribbean Artists Movement 1966–1972: A Literary and Cultural History* (New Beacon Books, 1992)

Authors' Biographies

Author

Ego Ahaiwe Sowinski is an academic, an artist and a Ronald Moody specialist. She is the co-editor and contributing author of *Mirror Reflecting Darkly: The Rita Keegan Archive* (Goldsmiths Press, 2021), contributing author of *Archiving Caribbean Identity: Records, Community, and Memory* (Routledge, 2022) and contributing co-author of *Communities, Archives and New Collaborative Practices* (Policy Press, 2020).

Editor

Eleanor Clayton is senior curator at The Hepworth Wakefield, and author of several books, including *Barbara Hepworth: Art & Life* (2021), also published by Thames & Hudson.

Other Contributors

David A. Bailey is a photographer, writer, curator, lecturer and cultural facilitator, and is artistic director of the International Curators Forum (ICF). He curated 'Life Between Islands' at Tate Britain (2021) and co-curated 'Rhapsodies in Black: Art of the Harlem Renaissance' at the Hayward Gallery (1997) and 'Back to Black: Art, Cinema and the Racial Imaginary' at the Whitechapel Art Gallery (2005). Bailey has written extensively about photography and film, and co-edited the publication *Curating in the Caribbean* (The Green Box, 2012).

Paul Dash is a Barbados-born artist who migrated to Britain in 1957, where he was associated with the 1960s Caribbean Artists Movement (CAM). His work has been exhibited at the Tate, the Barbados Museum, the Whitechapel Art Gallery, the Mall Galleries, the Guildhall Art Gallery, 198 Gallery Brixton and many more.

Errol Lloyd is a Jamaican-born artist, writer, art critic, editor, arts administrator and well-known book illustrator. He was involved with the Caribbean Artists Movement from 1966 and produced book jackets and other material for New Beacon Books, Bogle-L'Ouverture, and Allison and Busby. He also had a long association with the Minority Arts Advisory Service (MAAS) and was, for a time, editor of their magazine *Artrage*.

Cynthia Moody was a London-based filmmaker and editor who set up documentary and advertising companies. She was Ronald Moody's niece and inherited his estate in 1984. To preserve Moody's legacy, she devoted her retirement to documenting and promoting his work until her death in 2013.

Val Wilmer is a photographer and writer specialising in jazz, gospel, blues and British African-Caribbean music and culture. Her books include an autobiography, *Mama Said There'd Be Days Like This* (Women's Press, 1989), and the music hitories *Jazz People* (1970) and *As Serious As Your Life* (1977), both published by Allison and Busby. Photographic works by Wilmer are held by institutions such as the Arts Council of Great Britain, the National Portrait Gallery, the Victoria and Albert Museum, the Musée d'Art Moderne de la Ville de Paris and the Smithsonian Institution.

Acknowledgments

The Hepworth Wakefield

The Hepworth Wakefield is proud to present the first major retrospective of Ronald Moody, and to co-publish this book with Thames & Hudson. It is astonishing that it has taken until 2024, nearly 100 years since Moody first travelled to the UK from his native Jamaica, for his work to be recognised with such a publication. Our thanks go to Ego Ahaiwe Sowinski and all the contributing authors for providing such a compelling account of his remarkable life and work. This book is supported by a publications grant from the Paul Mellon Centre for Studies in British Art.

The project would not have been possible without the generous support of the Ronald Moody Trust, who have continued the tireless work of Cynthia Moody in promoting Ronald Moody's legacy. We are grateful to the public lenders who have supported the exhibition: Tate, the National Portrait Gallery, Pallant House, the British Museum, the Whitworth Art Gallery, the University of Manchester, Leicester Museums and Galleries, the National Museums Wales, Museums Sheffield, Leeds Museums and Art Galleries, the Government Art Collection, Guildhall Gallery, the Fitzwilliam Museum and the University of York, as well as all the private lenders who have so kindly lent precious works of art from their homes. Finally we would like to thank the Henry Moore Foundation for supporting the realisation of the exhibition at The Hepworth Wakefield.

Simon Wallis, Director

Author's Acknowledgments

This publication could not have been possible without the generous support, research, knowledge and the multitude of wisdoms. I would like to extend my deepest thanks to the following scholars, artists, friends and family: I am indebted to Anne Walmsley, Stuart Hall, David A. Bailey, Gemma Romain, Caroline Bressey, Debbie Challis, Sonia Boyce, Paul Goodwin, Elena Crippa, Aida Wilde, Denise Murrell, Gilane Tawadros, Makeda Coaston, Joan Anim-Addo, Hakim Adi, Lubaina Himid, Ingrid Pollard, Marlene Smith, Claudette Johnson, Charlie Phillips, Janet Browne, Maureen Roberts, Maxine Miller, Dominique Z. Barron, Zenzele Isoke, Paul Reid, Anne Ward, Stella Dadzie, Mavis Best, Elaine Holness, Suzy (and Pearl) Mackie, Francesca Bruno, Laurence Sessou, Ayo Clemons, Renee Mussai, Taylor Le Melle, Ajamu, Ain Bailey, Bridget R. Cook, Roshini Kempadoo, Joy Gregory, Kobena Mercer, Eddie Chambers, Petrine Archer, Ama Biney, Mia Morris, Veerle Poupeye, Shaheen Merali, Caroll Tulloch, Rita Keegan, Janice Cheddie, Althea Greenan, Mora J. Beauchamp-Byrd, Neil Kenlock, Donald Hind, Joy James, Micheal Cadette, Jheni Arbione, Nydia Swaby, Monique Barnett-Davidson, Liz Obi and the Remembering Olive Collective, Transmission 'crew dem' aka Kelly Foster, Etienne Joseph, Hannah Ishmael, Nathan E. Edwards, Abira Hussein, Nadine Chambers, Alexis Pauline Gumbs and Sangodore J. Wallace, J.J. Ghaddar, Zakiya Collier, Tonia Sutherland, Nazmia Jamal, Seitu K. Jones, Soyini V. Guyton, Alexandra (Susan and Nicholas) Nicome, Bolanlee Tajudeen, Tia-Simone Gardener, Erin Gleeson, Elena and Naca Favela, Phyllis Chatham, Amoke Kubat, Sayge Carroll and Keegan Xavi, Anne Gilliand, S. I. Martin, John A. Aarons, Jeanette A. Bastian, Stanley H. Griffin, Michael Ohajuru, Micheal McMillan, Erin Glasco and Itza Carbajal. It really does take an archival village. My sincerest gratitude to Stacy Ahaiwe Sowinski for the nourishing love, support and encouragement.

In memory of my sister Ugbo Rachel Ahaiwe (1976–1987).

Ego Ahaiwe Sowinski

Illustration Credits

Works by Ronald Moody © The Ronald Moody Trust **2** © Val Wilmer. Photograph by Val Wilmer **6** Tate: Purchased 2016. Photograph by Philip Connor **9** Portrait of Ronald Moody, 1966. Photograph by David Sharkey **10** © The Ronald Moody Trust **12** Wakefield Council Permanent Art Collection (The Hepworth Wakefield). Photograph by Anna Bridson **15** Purchased with aid from the Wakefield Permanent Art Fund (Friends of Wakefield Art Galleries and Museums), V&A Purchase Grant Fund and Wakefield Girls' High School, 1944. © Bowness. Photography by Jerry Hardman-Jones **19, 20, 21, 22, 23, 24, 27** © The Ronald Moody Trust **34** Loaned by Mr Peter D. Tucker, a cousin of Helene Moody **35** © The Ronald Moody Trust **36** VADS hosted by the University of the Creative Arts (UCA) **37** Purchased from Rev Dr Buckland, 1825. © The Trustees of the British Museum **38** Purchased from Joseph Sams, 1834. © The Trustees of the British Museum **39** Leeds Museums and Galleries. Photograph by Philip Connor **40** Private collection of Kate French. Photograph by Philip Connor **41** Purchased with aid from the V&A Purchase Grant Fund, Wakefield corporation and Wakefield Permanent Art Fund (Friends of Wakefield Art Gallery and Museums), 1942. © Reproduced with permission of The Henry Moore Foundation. Photograph by Jerry Hardman-Jones **43** Tate: Purchased 1992. Photo: © Tate **44** © The Ronald Moody Trust. Photograph © Cynthia Moody **47** National Archives (H-HNE-3-9). Harmon Foundation Sheffield Museums Trust **48** Pallant House Gallery, Chichester, UK (Purchased with support from Art Fund and Arts Council England / V&A Purchase Grant Fund 2021). Photograph by Philip Connor **52** Tate: Purchased 2010. Photo: © Tate **57** © Artist's collection / © The Ronald Moody Trust **59** Collection National Gallery of Jamaica. Image Courtesy of National Gallery of Jamaica **60** © The Ronald Moody Trust. Photographer unknown, *Daily Graphic* **64** © The Ronald Moody Trust. Photograph © Cynthia Moody **66** © Artist's collection / © The Ronald Moody Trust **67** Government Art Collection **69** Tate: Presented by The Ronald Moody Trust 2019. Photograph by Philip Connor **77** Photograph © Erich Auerbach Estate **78** Photograph by Ronnie Ziar **79** VADS hosted by the University of the Creative Arts (UCA) **80** © Artist's collection / © The Ronald Moody Trust. Photograph by Chris Ware **85** © BBC **93** Purchased from Mohammed Mohassib, 1912. © The Trustees of the British Museum **99** Given to the National Portrait Gallery by The Ronald Moody Trust, 2018. Photograph by Philip Connor **100** Private collection. Photograph by Michael Swinson **102, 103, 104** Amgueddfa Cymru – Museum Wales. Photograph by Philip Connor **105** Photograph by Philip Connor **106** Guildhall Art Gallery. Photograph by Philip Connor **107** Photograph © Everybody's, 1953 **109** Pallant House Gallery, Chichester, UK (Gift of the Ronald Moody Trust, 2021). Photograph by Philip Connor **110** Photograph by Philip Connor **113** Wakefield Council Permanent Art Collection (The Hepworth Wakefield) © The Elisabeth Frink Estate and Archive. All Rights Reserved, DACS 2024 **114–15** Photograph by Philip Connor **117** Photograph by Philip Connor **118** Amgueddfa Cymru – Museum Wales. Photograph by Philip Connor **121** © The Ronald Moody Trust **123** © Artist's collection / © The Ronald Moody Trust **124, 125, 126, 127** Photograph by Philip Connor **128** © Artist's collection / © The Ronald Moody Trust **130, 131** Photograph by Philip Connor **133** © The Ronald Moody Trust **134** Leicester Museums and Galleries. Photo: Leicester Museums and Galleries **135, 136** © Artist's collection / © The Ronald Moody Trust. Photographs by Crispin Eurich **137** Tate. © ADAGP, Paris and DACS, London 2024 **139** Leicester Museums and Galleries. Photo: Leicester Museums and Galleries **143** © Val Wilmer. Photograph by Val Wilmer **146** © BBC **150, 153** © Val Wilmer. Photograph by Val Wilmer **161** Wakefield Council Permanent Art Collection (The Hepworth Wakefield). Photograph by Anna Bridson **162, 163** Tate Archive. © Tate **165** © The Ronald Moody Trust. Photo © Cynthia Moody **166** Leicester Museums and Galleries. Photograph by Philip Connor **167** Tate: Presented by The Ronald Moody Trust 2019. Photograph by Philip Connor **168, 169** Sheffield Museums Trust. Photograph by Philip Connor **170, 171** Wakefield Council Permanent Art Collection (The Hepworth Wakefield). Photograph by Anna Bridson **172** © Artist's Collection / © The Ronald Moody Trust. Photo: Keystone Press Agency **173** © The Ronald Moody Trust. Photo: Ego Ahaiwe Sowinski **174** (left and right) © The Ronald Moody Trust **175** © The Althea McNish Trust. Photo: The Whitworth, The University of Manchester **176** Sheffield Museums Trust © Edna Manley Foundation 2013, courtesy Museums Sheffield **177** The University of York. Commissioned and donated to the people of York by Patrick Waddington Esq. of York, 1971. © Estate of Aubrey Williams. All rights reserved, DACS/ Artimage 2024 **178** © Artist's collection / © The Ronald Moody Trust **181** © The Ronald Moody Trust **182** Private collection of Philip Sharkey. Photo: Philip Sharkey **184, 185** Photograph by Philip Connor **186** Leicester Museums and Galleries. Photo: Leicester Museums and Galleries **188** Pallant House Gallery. Purchased with support of Art Fund, V&A Purchase Grant Fund and Private Donors (2021). Photo: Pallant House Gallery **189, 190** Photograph by Philip Connor **191** The Whitworth, The University of Manchester. Photograph by Philip Connor **193** © The Ronald Moody Trust. Photograph by Robin McCarthey **195** © The Ronald Moody Trust **196** © The Ronald Moody Trust. Photograph by Cynthia Moody **197** (left and right) © The Ronald Moody Trust **202** © The Ronald Moody Trust / press photograph **205** © The Ronald Moody Trust. Photograph by Cynthia Moody **210** Grosvenor Gallery, London. Photo: Grosvenor Gallery **212** The Syndics of the Fitzwilliam Museum, University of Cambridge. Bought from the artist with the Gow Fund. Photo: Fitzwilliam Museum **213** © The Estate of Aubrey Williams. Photo: October Gallery **216** (above and below) © Artist's Collection / © The Ronald Moody Trust **218** Courtesy Errol Lloyd **221** Courtesy Errol Lloyd. Copyright Minorities Arts Advisory Service, MAAS Ltd. **224–25** Private collection of Kate French. © The Ronald Moody Trust **226** Gifted to Errol Lloyd by Cynthia Moody. Courtesy Errol Lloyd **228–229** Grosvenor Gallery, London. © The Ronald Moody Trust. Photo: Grosvenor Gallery **233** © Artist's collection / © The Ronald Moody Trust. Photograph by David Sharkey **234** Private collection of Naomi Williams. © The Ronald Moody Trust. Photograph by Michael Pollard **237** Tate. Presented by Anne Walmsley 2021. Photo: © Tate

Index

In subheadings, **RM** indicates Ronald Moody, **CM** indicates Cynthia Moody. Illustrations page references are in *italics*.